Alternative Food Politics

Media interest in food has intensified in recent years, leading to a contemporary food landscape where 'alternative' food practices are increasingly visible. Concerns that were once exclusively the domain of activist movements motivated by environmental, animal rights, health and anti-corporate agendas are now central to primetime television cooking shows, mobile apps and social media.

This book is the first to explore the impact of popular media and culture on contemporary food politics. Through examination of a range of media and cultural texts, including news, digital media, advertising and food labelling, it brings together leading and emerging scholars in food studies, media and communications, sociology, law, policy studies, business, and geography. The book explores the practices of alternative food movements, the marketing techniques of conventional and alternative food producers, and the relationships between food industries, media, and the public. Covering topics ranging from agtech start-ups and social justice projects, to new ways of mediating food waste, celebrity, and 'ethical' foods, *Alternative Food Politics* reveals the importance of media as a driver of food system transformation.

This is a pivotal time for media and food industries, and this book is essential reading for scholars and students seeking to better understand the futures, possibilities and limits of food politics today.

Michelle Phillipov is a lecturer in Media at the University of Adelaide, Australia. Her work explores how media's intensified interest in the provenance of food and the ethics of food production is shaping public debate, consumer politics, and media and food industry practices.

Katherine Kirkwood is a PhD candidate at the Queensland University of Technology, Australia. Her research investigates popular culture's relationship with everyday Australian food culture and how media and cultural texts inform and shape Australians' approach to food, their culinary interests and concerns.

Critical Food Studies

Series editor: Michael K. Goodman

University of Reading, UK

The study of food has seldom been more pressing or prescient. From the intensifying globalisation of food, a worldwide food crisis and the continuing inequalities of its production and consumption, to food's exploding media presence, and its growing re-connections to places and people through 'alternative food movements', this series promotes critical explorations of contemporary food cultures and politics. Building on previous but disparate scholarship, its overall aims are to develop innovative and theoretical lenses and empirical material in order to contribute to–but also begin to more fully delineate–the confines and confluences of an agenda of critical food research and writing.

Of particular concern are original theoretical and empirical treatments of the materialisations of food politics, meanings and representations, the shifting political economies and ecologies of food production and consumption and the growing transgressions between alternative and corporatist food networks.

Digital Food Activism
Edited by Tanja Schneider, Karin Eli, Catherine Dolan and Stanley Ulijaszek

Children, Food and Nature
Organising Meals in Schools
Mara Miele and Monica Truninger

Taste, Waste and the New Materiality of Food
Bethaney Turner

Ecology, Capitalism and the New Agricultural Economy
The Second Great Transformation
Edited by Gilles Allaire and Benoit Daviron

Alternative Food Politics
From the Margins to the Mainstream
Edited by Michelle Phillipov and Katherine Kirkwood

For more information about this series, please visit: www.routledge.com/Critical-Food-Studies/book-series/CFS

Alternative Food Politics

From the Margins to the Mainstream

Edited by
Michelle Phillipov and
Katherine Kirkwood

LONDON AND NEW YORK

First published 2019
by Routledge
2 Park Square, Milton Park, Abingdon, Oxon OX14 4RN

and by Routledge
52 Vanderbilt Avenue, New York, NY 10017

First issued in paperback 2020

Routledge is an imprint of the Taylor & Francis Group, an informa business

British Library Cataloguing-in-Publication Data
A catalogue record for this book is available from the British Library.

Library of Congress Cataloging-in-Publication Data
Names: Phillipov, Michelle, editor. | Kirkwood, Catherine, editor.
Title: Alternative food politics : from the margins to the mainstream / edited by Michelle Phillipov and Katherine Kirkwood.
Description: Abingdon, Oxon ; New York, NY : Routledge, 2019. | Series: Critical food studies series | Includes bibliographical references and index.
Identifiers: LCCN 2018036850| ISBN 9781138300804 (hardback : alk. paper) | ISBN 9780203733080 (ebook) | ISBN 9781351402958 (pdf) | ISBN 9781351402941 (epub) | ISBN 9781351402934 (mobi/kindle)
Subjects: LCSH: Food in mass media. | Television cooking shows. | Food–Political aspects. | Food–Social aspects. | Natural foods.
Classification: LCC P96.F66 A57 2019 | DDC 306.4–dc23
LC record available at https://lccn.loc.gov/2018036850

ISBN 13: 978-0-367-58223-4 (pbk)
ISBN 13: 978-1-138-30080-4 (hbk)

Typeset in Times New Roman
by Integra Software Services Pvt. Ltd.

Contents

List of illustrations   vii
List of contributors   viii
Acknowledgements   xii

Introduction: Thinking with media: margins, mainstreams and the
media politics of food   1
MICHELLE PHILLIPOV

PART 1
Limits and paradoxes   21

1   The (continuing) paradox of the organic label: reflections on US
    trajectories in the era of mainstreaming   23
    JULIE GUTHMAN

2   Mainstreaming New Nordic Cuisine? Alternative food politics and the
    problems of scale jumping and scale bending   37
    ANDERS RIEL MÜLLER AND JONATAN LEER

3   When carrots become posh: untangling the relationship between
    'heritage' foods and social distinction   55
    ABIGAIL WINCOTT

PART 2
New political platforms   73

4   Promising sustainable foods: entrepreneurial visions of sustainable
    food futures   75
    TANJA SCHNEIDER

5   The Welcome Dinner Project: food hospitality activism and digital
       media   95
       RICK FLOWERS AND ELAINE SWAN

6   Food sovereignty: deep histories, digital activism and the emergence of
       a transnational public   113
       ALANA MANN

PART 3
Personal food politics and entanglements   **133**

7   It's not (just) about the f-ckin' animals: how veganism is changing, and
       why that matters   135
       STEPHEN HARRINGTON, CHRISTY COLLIS AND OZGUR DEDEHAYIR

8   Vitalities and visceralities: alternative body/food politics in digital
       media   151
       DEBORAH LUPTON

9   The ethical masquerade: (un)masking mechanisms of power behind
       'ethical' meat   169
       PAULA ARCARI

PART 4
Reframing production and consumption   **191**

10   The consumer labelling turn in farmed animal welfare politics: from
       the margins of animal advocacy to mainstream supermarket shelves   193
       CHRISTINE PARKER, RACHEL CAREY AND GYORGY SCRINIS

11   Confronting food waste in *MasterChef Australia*: media production
       and recalcitrant matter   216
       LUKE VAN RYN

12   Supermarkets, celebrity chefs and private labels: the 'alternative'
       reframing of processed foods   234
       MICHELLE PHILLIPOV AND KATHERINE KIRKWOOD

       Index   253

Illustrations

Figures

9.1   Standardised cartographies of meatified chicken, lamb, pig
      and cow   177
9.2   Market signage   178
10.1 Timeline of welfare regulation and labelling in Australia: eggs,
      pigs and chickens, 2000–2016   197
10.2 Coles in-store advertising of cage free eggs using celebrity chef
      Curtis Stone   201
10.3 Coles magazine advertisement for 'RSPCA Approved' chicken
      'at no added cost to you'   202
10.4 Mentions of 'free range', 'bred free range' and 'sow stalls' in
      articles about animal welfare and eggs, chicken meat and pork/
      ham in major Australian newspapers, 2000–2016   203
10.5a Proportion of newspaper articles mentioning different
      stakeholders: eggs, 2000 and 2013   206
10.5b Proportion of newspaper articles mentioning different
      stakeholders: pigs, 2006 and 2010   207
10.5c Proportion of newspaper articles mentioning different
      stakeholders: meat chickens, 2011 and 2013   208

Table

9.1   Excerpts from the web pages of 'ethical' meat producers   180

Contributors

Katherine Kirkwood is a PhD candidate at the Queensland University of Technology, Australia. Her research investigates popular culture's relationship with everyday Australian food culture and how media and cultural texts inform and shape Australians' approach to food, their culinary interests and concerns.

Michelle Phillipov is a lecturer in Media at the University of Adelaide, Australia. Her work explores how media's intensified interest in the provenance of food and the ethics of food production is shaping public debate, consumer politics, and media and food industry practices. She is the author of Fats: A Global History (Reakion Books, 2016) and *Media and Food Industries: The New Politics of Food (Palgrave Macmillan, 2017)*.

Paula Arcari researcher in the Centre for Urban Research (CUR) at RMIT University, Melbourne, where she also received her PhD. Her doctoral research drew on Foucault's account of knowledge/power/pleasure to explore how meat and food animals are 'made sense of'. Her primary interest is understanding how to challenge habitual ways of thinking and acting about nonhuman animals, drawing on a range of critical, environmental, sociological and cultural approaches and theories.

Rachel Carey is a Research Fellow in the Faculty of Veterinary and Agricultural Sciences at the University of Melbourne where her research focuses on sustainable food systems and food policy. She is a researcher on the ARC-funded project 'Regulating food labels: the case of free range food products in Australia' and also leads the Foodprint Melbourne project, which focuses on the resilience of Melbourne's city fringe foodbowl.

Christy Collis is Faculty Director of Research Quality, and Faculty Coordinator of Industry-Integrated Learning and Entrepreneurship in the Creative Industries Faculty at Queensland University of Technology.

Ozgur Dedehayir is a Vice-Chancellor's Research Fellow at the Queensland University of Technology (QUT), Australia. Dr Dedehayir received his PhD in

Technology Strategy from the Tampere University of Technology (TUT), Finland. His research focuses on the creation and the dynamics of change in innovation ecosystems. He has published in various journals in the technology and innovation management field, including *Technology Analysis and Strategic Management, Technological Forecasting and Social Change*, and *Technovation*.

Rick Flowers is based in the School of Education and International Studies at the University of Technology Sydney where he teaches subjects in the sociology of education. His research interests are in popular education, food pedagogies and intercultural learning. He was head of postgraduate programmes for six years and director for the centre of popular education. As a sole author, Rick has published widely on education and learning. With Elaine Swan, he has been studying food social enterprises in Sydney since 2011 and together they have published widely on their ethnographic and digital analysis of these enterprises, including five book chapters and eight peer-reviewed articles.

Julie Guthman is a geographer and a professor of social sciences at the University of California, Santa Cruz, who conducts research on the conditions of possibility for food system transformation. Her publications include multi-award winning books, including *Agrarian Dreams: the Paradox of Organic Farming in California*, and over forty articles in peer-reviewed journals. Her research has been funded by the National Science Foundation, the John Simon Guggenheim Foundation, the Radcliffe Institute for Advanced Study, and the Rockefeller Foundation Bellagio Center. She is a recipient of the Excellence in Research Award from the Agriculture, Food and Human Values Society.

Stephen Harrington is an Associate Professor in the School of Communication at the Queensland University of Technology, Australia. He has written extensively on the role of entertainment in the public sphere. He is the co-author of *Politics, Media and Democracy in Australia: Public and Producer Perceptions of the Political Public Sphere* (Routledge, 2017), and editor of *Entertainment Values* (Palgrave, 2017).

Jonatan Leer, Associate Professor and Head of Food and Tourism Research, University College Absalon, is a Danish researcher of food culture. His latest publications include 'The Rise and Fall of the New Nordic Cuisine' (*Journal of Aesthetics and Culture*), 'Monocultural and Multicultural Gastronationalism' (*European Journal of Cultural Studies*), and the book *Food and Media: Practices, Distinctions and Heterotopias* (Routledge).

Deborah Lupton is SHARP Professor in the Faculty of Arts and Social Sciences, University of New South Wales Sydn. She is a Fellow of the Academy of the Social Sciences in Australia and the co-leader of the Digital Data & Society Consortium. Her latest books are *Digital Sociology* (Routledge, 2015), *The Quantified Self* (Polity, 2016), *Digital Health* (Routledge, 2017) and *Fat* (2nd edition, Routledge, 2018), as well as the edited volumes *Digitised Health, Medicine and Risk* (Routledge, 2016), *The Digital Academic* (Routledge, 2017, with Inger Mewburn and Pat Thomson) and *Self-Tracking, Health and Medicine* (2017). Her current research interests all involve aspects of digital sociology: digital health, digital data cultures, self-tracking practices, digital food cultures, digitised academia, and the digital surveillance of children and young people.

Alana Mann is a key researcher in the Sydney Environment Institute and the Charles Perkins Centre for Obesity and Cardiovascular Disease at the University of Sydney. Her research on the engagement of citizens and non-state actors in activism and policy debates regarding food security and the right to food has led to sustained engagement with people's movements including La Vía Campesina, international NGOs including FIAN International and global governance institutions such as the UN Food and Agriculture Organisation (FAO). Her book on food sovereignty campaigns in Latin America and Europe, *Global Activism in Food Politics: Power Shift* was published in 2014 by Palgrave Macmillan.

Anders Riel Müller (PhD), University College Copenhagen and Nordic Institute of Asian Studies is a researcher of the cultural political economy of food and agriculture. His latest publications are 'Exporting the Saemaul Spirit' (*Geoforum*), 'Meyer as Appetizing Gastrocapitalist' (*Social Kritik*), and 'South Korea: Food Security, Development and the Developmental State' in *New Challenges to Food Security* (Routledge).

Christine Parker is a Professor at Melbourne Law School, the University of Melbourne where she researches and teaches business regulation and corporate social responsibility, lawyers' ethics, food law and policy, and animals and the law. She is the author of a number of books including *The Open Corporation: Business Self-Regulation and Democracy* (Cambridge University Press, 2002) and *Inside Lawyers' Ethics* (with Adrian Evans, 3rd edition, Cambridge University Press, 2018).

Tanja Schneider is Senior Lecturer in Sociology at the Institute of Sociology, University of St. Gallen, Switzerland, and Research Associate at the Institute for Science, Innovation and Society (InSIS), University of Oxford, UK. Tanja's research is situated at the intersections of science and technology studies (STS), economic sociology, and critical food studies. Recently, she has co-edited a volume on *Digital Food Activism* (Routledge, 2018) and her latest research project explores how digital media technologies are transforming food activism and consumers' engagements with food, eating, and food systems.

Gyorgy Scrinis is Senior Lecturer in Food Politics and Policy in the School of Agriculture and Food at the University of Melbourne, Australia. He is the author of *Nutritionism: The Science and Politics of Dietary Advice* (Columbia University Press, 2013).

Elaine Swan is based in the Future of Work research hub in the Business School at the University of Sussex where she teaches research methods. Her research interests are in critical diversity studies, therapeutic cultures and feminist food studies. With Rick Flowers, she has published widely on race, gender and food social enterprises, and together they have convened a conference stream on gender, race and food work at *Gender, Work and Organisation* and produced an edited book and a special issue on food pedagogies, and a special issue on food and the senses.

Luke van Ryn is a PhD candidate in the School of Culture and Communications at the University of Melbourne. His thesis addresses the impact of professional networking and justification in the production ecology of *MasterChef Australia*. He is currently working as a research assistant on an ARC-funded project on practices of digital commemoration. His writing has appeared in the *Journal of Broadcasting and Electronic Media, Ephemera*, and *Media International Australia*.

Abigail Wincott is a factual programme maker and Senior Lecturer in the School of Media at the University of Brighton, UK. She researches new forms of heritage and the ways heritage is mediated.

Acknowledgements

Michelle Phillipov acknowledges the support of Katherine Kirkwood, Michael K. Goodman and the staff at Routledge (especially Ruth Anderson, Priscilla Corbett and Faye Leerink) to produce this collection. Her contributions were funded by an Australian Research Council Discovery Early Career Researcher Award, 'The New Politics of Food and the Australian Media' (DE1401014120).

Katherine Kirkwood would like to thank Michelle Phillipov for her ongoing guidance and encouragement. She is grateful for the enthusiasm and feedback of Michael K. Goodman and the work of Faye Leerink, Ruth Anderson, Priscilla Corbett, and the team at Routledge. She is also grateful for the support from her supervisory team of Stephen Harrington, Peta Mitchell, and Jason Sternberg, as well as her QUT colleagues, while working on this project.

Paula Arcari's research drew on a broader PhD study funded by the Australian Government's Australian Postgraduate Award (APA) scheme, and located within RMIT University's Centre for Urban Research. She thanks Tania Lewis, Shae Hunter and Jane Daly for their valuable feedback on an earlier draft. She is also hugely grateful to Michelle Phillipov and Katherine Kirkwood for their detailed and insightful suggestions for improving her chapter.

Rick Flowers and **Elaine Swan** would like to thank Penny Elsley, volunteers and WDP participants for their time and comments on the project, Dr Teena Clerke for coding of screenshots, and the editors of the book for their insightful and incisive editing, which improved the quality of their argument and the presentation of the chapter.

Christine Parker, **Rachel Carey** and **Gyorgy Scrinis** are grateful to the stakeholders interviewed for their research, and to Josephine De Costa, Geordie Fung, Joe Lasco, Adaena Sinclair-Blakemore and Zoe Jackson for research assistance in the fieldwork and preparation of the manuscript for publication. Their research was funded by an Australian Research Council Discovery Project, 'Regulating Food Labels: The Case of Free Range Food Products in Australia' (DP150102168).

Tanja Schneider would like to thank the editors, Michelle Phillipov and Katherine Kirkwood, for inviting her to contribute to this volume and for their generous feedback during the review process. She also thanks Karin Eli for reading an earlier version of this chapter and for her valuable comments and suggestions. In addition, she would like to acknowledge the seed funding she received from the Basic Research Fund at the University of St. Gallen. Thanks also go out to Valentin Scherrer for research assistance as part of this project.

Introduction

Thinking with media: margins, mainstreams and the media politics of food

Michelle Phillipov

Over the past decade, intensified media interest in the provenance of food and the ethics of food production has contributed to an unprecedented 'mainstream' visibility of 'alternative' food politics in many of the world's most advanced economies. The practices and discourses typically associated with alternative food networks (AFNs) now regularly appear in mainstream media coverage, in primetime television cooking shows, in digital and social media, in social justice projects and start-ups, and in the labelling and advertising strategies of major food retailers and manufacturers. Food celebrities—from celebrity chefs and celebrity farmers, to social media influencers and #farmstagrammers—tout the value of eating locally and cooking with the seasons. Farmers' markets have experienced exponential growth (and considerable media fanfare) over the past two decades (Campbell, 2015), a shift paralleled by a similar increase in 'ethical' products, such as free range eggs and chickens (Egg Info, 2016). 'Ethical' platforms have become central to the advertising and marketing strategies of artisan food businesses, food start-ups and major supermarkets alike, while a proliferating range of mobile apps and web sites—from *Follow the Thing* to the *Good Fish Guide*—now allow consumers to trace the provenance and sustainability of their food, and, in some cases, to virtually 'meet' the farmer who produced it. New forms of digital food activism are further altering relationships between food, activists, audiences and consumers (Schneider et al., 2018).

As a result of a combination of new consumer politics, activist backlash against industrial food systems, and ongoing structural change in the media industries, media is now thoroughly imbricated in how contemporary food politics are imagined, enacted and appropriated. It is central to how dominant food systems are critiqued and legitimised, and how alternatives are made desirable and possible. Its tools are used both by those with a genuine investment in environmental, anti-corporate, health and animal rights agendas, and by those with more questionable commitments to a progressive food politics. While scholars have long sought to complicate the 'purity' of the politics of AFNs (e.g., Goodman, DuPuis and Goodman, 2012; Guthman, 2014), and to critique the actions of Big Food (e.g., Brownell and Warner, 2009; Nestle, 2013), the recent proliferation and expansion in the types of media genres, platforms and intermediaries engaged in questions of 'alternative' food have lent these issues prominence on a scale previously unforeseen. This is changing the ways that contemporary food politics are playing out.

At the intersection of food politics, media texts and everyday material practices, we are seeing media's increasing power as a key actor in food systems debates and as a motor of food system transformation. Equally, however, we are seeing in media's affordances and affective capacities opportunities for large agribusinesses and retailing corporations to 'greenwash' their practices more effectively. The increasing imbrication of media and food politics raises important theoretical and empirical questions about how to best understand food system change. How do we conceptualise the cultural work that media does in shaping contemporary food politics? Where is power located in these new assemblages of media and activist and market forces? Through which research sites can we empirically access these assemblages? What do we mean by 'media'? And, indeed, by 'food politics'? While there is much work to be done in relation to food politics in the Global South, some of which is touched upon in this collection (see, for example, Chapter 6 by Alana Mann), questions about food politics' mediation are especially urgent in the Global North, where there has been a much greater proliferation of cultural industries linked to food production and consumption than elsewhere in the world. The imbrication of media and food politics also raises practical questions for those interested in the politics of contemporary food systems. Is the increasing 'mainstream' interest in food politics evidence of the growing accessibility of real alternatives, or of a more sophisticated reframing of political concerns by dominant players in the food system? What does this mean for activist strategies and practices? What does 'good' food politics look like?

This collection seeks to understand media's role in a changing landscape of food politics. It brings together work from established and emerging food scholars from the disciplines of media and communications, cultural studies, geography, sociology, animal studies, law, business and management to pursue a shared interest in the cultural and political 'work' of media and its relationship to food. The collection takes a deliberately wide-ranging approach to questions of media and food politics, both to what practices and issues 'count' as political ones, and to media and popular cultural forms under examination. It considers topics ranging from online body politics and digital food sovereignty movements, to the politics of food labelling, and the marketing strategies of major supermarkets. In doing so, the chapters present a number of standpoints about, and assessments of, the potentialities of contemporary food politics that canvas questions of power, justice, lifestyle, gender, species, sustainability, food systems and economies—not all of them commensurate. But through the authors' different disciplinary approaches, we are afforded access to the complex ways in which media is contributing to the growing visibility of 'alternative' food, making possible new forms of political engagement and expression, generating new cultural meanings and potentialities, and providing opportunities for reworking and redefinition by large-scale media and food businesses.

This is important, we argue, because the complexity of the contemporary media/food landscape highlights how an understanding of media is now essential to an understanding of the limits and possibilities of food politics today. It is our contention that in the highly mediatised economies of the Global North, food politics is always-already a media politics. Consequently, we need to think *with* the role of media in shaping relationships between the media industry and food systems actors that are actively producing the terms and frameworks that characterise food politics in contexts of relative privilege. The collection takes as its case studies some of the most internationally prominent locations of alternative food: Australia, Scandinavia, the US, Canada, the UK and the EU. These cases offer insight into the dynamic relationships between media texts, food production and food consumption, and between activist practices and industry 'appropriations' of political discourses and projects. They also allow us to investigate what is gained and what is lost as alternative food politics moves from the margins to the mainstream, to consider the consequences of the increasing mediatisation of contemporary food politics, and to understand the 'agency' of media and cultural texts in enacting changes to food systems practices.

This Introduction works through key concepts and tensions that arise as popular media and culture become increasingly central to the practices of food politics today. It begins with a brief history of the rise of alternative food politics and of the role of media in shaping new meanings and practices with respect to food. It then introduces three concepts—*affordances, intermediaries,* and *micro- and macro-political capacities*—to provide a firmer theoretical foundation for the chapters that follow. These concepts assist us to unpack some of the implications of the increasing imbrication of media and food politics for consumers, food activists, food producers, retailers, and media industries. The Introduction concludes with a summary of the structure of the book.

Media and food politics

Media has been at the centre of a set of comprehensive changes to food's representational and affective economies, and these have been pivotal in shaping the contours of alternative food politics as it moves from the 'margins' to the 'mainstream'. Concerns about the consequences of a globalised and industrialised food system have given rise to a range of practices encapsulated under the broad banner of 'alternative food networks'. From farmers' markets, community supported agriculture (CSA) and organic box schemes to local and seasonal eating movements, AFNs are typically understood as attempts to invest in an alternative (smaller-scale, less exploitative) food economy and to enable consumers to 'reconnect' with the sources and producers of their food. Qualities of 'embeddedness', 'trust' and 'place' have become key markers of these alternative food practices (Goodman, 2003, p. 1). The material conditions giving rise to AFNs—the negative environmental, health and social impacts of conventional food systems, the emergence of new types of consumer politics—have been well-rehearsed in both the academic literature (e.g. Campbell, 2009; Goodman, DuPuis and Goodman, 2012) and in the best-selling non-fiction texts that have lent significant popular visibility to these issues (e.g. Kingsolver, 2007; Pollan, 2006, 2008).

While this literature would be familiar to most readers of this collection, and so would be unnecessary to reiterate here, it is worth noting that the AFN scholarship remains subject to ongoing debate about how to define the 'alternative' *vis-à-vis* the 'conventional', and about how the political efficacy of the 'alternative' should be assessed—especially given that many alternative food practices tend to locate consumption as a key site for political action. Scholars of a more optimistic bent point to the significant industry change brought about as a result of AFNs, seeing the profitable markets that now exist for products once considered marginal as reflecting significant changes in food industry practices in order to meet the demands of 'ethical' eaters—organics and Fair Trade being two of the most obvious examples. For scholars of ethical consumption, for example, the consumption 'choices' associated with AFNs are frequently understood as political pathways for articulating ethical, social, civic and political investments in an alternative food system, especially for those who may be otherwise disengaged from conventional politics (e.g. Barnett et al., 2005; Lewis and Potter, 2011).

Others have argued, however, that the apparent mainstream success of AFNs reflects not their capacity for genuine food system change, but rather their co-optation by Big Food. As Harriet Friedmann (2005, p. 231) has noted, the rise of 'green' capitalism in the latter part of the 20th Century attests to the immense capacity of dominant players in the food system to appropriate social movement demands in the interests of capital accumulation. This is a point picked up by scholars concerned that a politics of consumer 'choice' is inevitably a privileged, middle-class politics. For example, a politics of 'voting with your fork' is understood by many as not only offering opportunities for a more sophisticated co-optation by major retailers and food manufacturers, who now adopt the language and imagery of AFNs in their advertising and branding (Richards, Lawrence and Burch, 2011), but also as producing a range of exclusions on the basis of race, class, income and gender (Cadieux and Slocum, 2015; Goodman, DuPuis and Goodman, 2012; Guthman, 2007; Phillips, 2009; Stănescu, 2010).

The nomenclature associated with AFNs also remains unresolved. Scholars refer variously to 'alternative food networks' (Goodman, DuPuis and Goodman, 2012), 'alternative food initiatives' (Allen et al., 2003), 'alternative food practices' (Goodman, 2003) and 'alternative food politics' (Campbell, 2009), each with slightly different nuances about the nature of food systems structures and their significance. There has also been a great deal of literature debating which activities 'count' (or should count) as both 'alternative' and 'mainstream', with a number of scholars seeking to think with the permeability of the alternative–mainstream binary (for a summary of this scholarship, see Goodman and Goodman, 2009).

Many of the tensions that animate this broader literature also animate the contributions in this collection. It is not our intention to try to resolve them here—although we do hope to think *with* these tensions as a means to capture the different ways that contemporary food politics can be enacted and understood. In suggesting, as this collection does, that alternative food politics have moved from the margins to the mainstream, it is not our intention to clearly demarcate 'margins' from 'mainstreams', nor to definitively distinguish 'real' from 'co-opted' politics: what count as margins, mainstreams or political effects are inevitably shifting, and are as much discursively as materially constructed. However, the increased popularity and visibility of food practices that might be broadly classified as 'alternative' (or which otherwise adopt discourses of the alternative) have contributed both to the urgency of scholarly questions about the politics of food, and to broader struggles over meaning in contemporary food politics that have both industry- and consumer-driven dimensions.

Within food studies, many have sought to think through these issues and to conceptualise the complex relationships between consumers, the food industry and food systems, but to fully understand the current landscape of food politics and its implications, we also need to think beyond these relationships. Part of the challenge in fully canvassing the terrain in which food politics is now played out is the imbrication of media in political questions and concerns. It is no coincidence that the growing visibility of AFNs has occurred alongside a burgeoning food media industry, which has seen a proliferation and intensification of the number and types of media texts devoted to food, many of them invoking key themes and concepts from AFNs. Much lifestyle media, for instance, has adopted elements of AFNs as signifiers of desirable lifestyles for the urban middle classes. It often does this by offering an 'alternative hedonism' (Soper, 2004, p. 112) in which idyllic rural settings are offered as both a 'site of rescue and purification from the ravages of corporate, urban life', and as a place where consumers can develop more 'authentic' connections to the sources of their food (Phillipov, 2016, p. 113; see also Versteegen, 2010).

While media's intensified interest in food can be seen, in part, as a response to changing consumer politics and proclivities (i.e., as the practices of AFNs become more popular, media texts increasingly cater to these interests), it is also a response to internal factors within the media industry. In particular, food has offered profitable solutions to an industry undergoing significant structural change. Since the 1980s, deregulation of media markets, fragmentation of audiences, declining advertising revenues, and increased competition from online and user-generated media have each posed a range of challenges for 'traditional' media industries, and have necessitated the development of new media products, formats and strategies (see Flew, 2007; Hesmondhalgh, 2013; Waisbord, 2004). Food has often been central to this: food television has retained both audiences and advertisers at a time when overall television viewership is in decline (see Hindman and Wiegand, 2008); cookbooks have almost single-handedly saved a number of struggling publishing houses (Orr, 2012); and food has helped capture new forms and practices of audience engagement on digital media platforms (Lewis, 2018; Lupton, 2018).

Scholars have suggested that consumer interest in such media often reflects a 'broader sense of discontent with the instrumental culture of late modernity', with the focus on food an attempt to 're-enchant…the contemporary everyday through promoting less alienated, more engaged modes of consumption' (Lewis, 2008b, p. 232). But such texts also provide new opportunities for advertising, sponsorship, and the monetisation of audience engagement (see Spurgeon, 2013). Embedded marketing and integrated advertising are now features of most media spaces, and they appear across the spectrum of mainstream–alternative food media texts, irrespective of political position (see Phillipov, 2017).

The proliferation of media texts devoted to food has given new prominence to food-related issues, and it has given rise to new ways of engaging with food that both reflect and shape food politics' potentials and limitations. Media is now central to food's discursive and affective economies in ways that complicate not only the food/media boundary, but also how we might assess the effects and implications of food politics. Anna Lavis (2017) points to the power of media to remake the categories through which we understand the materialities and bodily processes associated with food and eating, highlighting how, in some circumstances, food can become media and media can become food. The blurring of the previously distinct categories of 'food' and 'media' is also captured by Tania Lewis's (2018) concept of 'digital food', a term she uses to capture the changing nature of our engagements with food in an increasingly digital world. Extending this work, this collection does not seek to disentangle media and food politics— that is, it does not attempt to demarcate media representations from political action that exists 'outside' the text—but rather it seeks to think through the cultural and political 'work' that this food-media imbrication does. What new questions or sites of struggle open up? What possibilities are foreclosed?

Analysing food and media

To provide a framework in which we can begin to answer these questions, this introduction provides a set of concepts for understanding and evaluating contemporary food politics and its position in relation to both 'margins' and 'mainstreams'. While the collection's chapters are often anchored in the authors' own disciplinary traditions, they are also united by shared concepts and concerns. Below we will briefly review three of these: affordances, intermediaries, and micro- and macro-political capacities. Each chapter either implicitly or explicitly engages with these concepts and their implications. Taken together, this collection helps us to understand what media and cultural texts 'do' with respect to food politics (i.e., their particular meanings and affordances), how they engage other media and food systems actors (i.e., the intermediaries they involve), and how we are to evaluate their political significances (i.e., their macro- and micro-political capacities). Each will be considered in turn.

Affordances

This collection takes the view that media and popular culture do not simply 'mediate' or 'represent' food politics but also operate as political entities in their own right. The question for chapters in this collection, then, is: if media and popular culture are placed at the *centre* of political questions and concerns, how does this both enable and delimit the ways that contemporary food politics can be enacted, imagined and defined? How does this change the way that food systems problems and solutions are posed? How does this affect the types of politics that become possible and those that do not?

In answering these questions, the chapters take as their subject matter media and cultural forms that are clearly recognisable as media texts—digital and social media images, television cooking shows, advertising campaigns, media releases —as well as other cultural formats, such as food labelling, that also work via mediation to generate cultural meanings and material affects. The chapters highlight the power of media and cultural texts in enabling specific ways of 'doing' food politics. In digital media studies, the term 'affordances' is often used to describe the ways that digital media platforms make possible certain types of expression and action, while delimiting others (e.g. boyd, 2010; Juris, 2012). Each media platform's affordances, embedded in both hardware and software, produce a specific 'platform vernacular'—the genres, styles, grammars and logics that come to predominate within specific platforms and which prioritise particular forms of social participation and generate particular types of meaning and affect (Gibbs et al., 2015, p. 257, 258). Media affordances and their platform vernaculars, then, can be used to reveal the specific kinds of cultural 'work' that media does in and for food politics.

For example, in Chapter 6, Alana Mann reveals how the affordances of digital media—their capacity to forge networks and collectivities across diverse geographical locations, and their ability to reorganise communication and information flows—enable locally embedded food activists to form broader coalitions focused on issues of food sovereignty. While more could be done to bridge digital divides and to disrupt the dominance of 'elite' voices in these coalitions, the capacity of these digital affordances to *produce* publics, Mann suggests, may be key to uniting the food justice concerns of both Global South and Global North in ways that can achieve genuinely transformative political and social change. At present, however, challenges to definition and implementation prevent food sovereignty movements from achieving structural change to food systems in the Global North.

In Chapter 5, Rick Flowers and Elaine Swan show how the platform vernaculars of digital and social media—their capacity for sharing, their focus on the visual, their tendency to adopt a 'home mode' genre of photography—are key to advancing the food hospitality activism of food-based social enterprises designed to combat racism. However, they argue, once the same digital texts are shared and re-mediated via mainstream media platforms, this can bring the texts into multi-modal assemblages that have the potential to take on an altogether different set of racialised meanings. In such cases, the 'platform vernaculars' of the mainstream media outlets come to redirect meanings with respect to race, often perpetuating hegemonic views.

While the concept of affordances tends to be applied primarily to digital media, we need not think of it as limited to such platforms. The concept has explanatory power for the way that cultural texts work more generally: all media and cultural texts possess specific affordances that enable some types of action and engagement while foreclosing others. Chapters in this collection consider how the affordances of a wide range of media and cultural texts produce particular types of meaning, enable representational strategies to 'mean' differently in different contexts, and reframe and redirect political questions. In Chapter 11, Luke van Ryn highlights the powerful effects of platform vernaculars on the production of broadcast television texts; these effects are often the result of media producers perceiving production conventions to be 'fixed' by both medium and genre. Using the example of *MasterChef Australia*, van Ryn shows how media producers' belief that production practices cannot be changed contributes to high levels of food waste in the food television industry. He shows how critique can be used as a way to reshape industry understandings of the affordances of food television, and that this may open up new possibilities for the development of television production methods with a keener view to environmental sustainability and a more thorough-going engagement with environmental concerns.

Julie Guthman (Chapter 1), and Christine Parker, Rachel Carey and Gyorgy Scrinis (Chapter 10) explore how industry labels associated with organic certification and animal welfare have their own specific affordances. Like the affordances of other media and cultural forms, labels enable and delimit particular kinds of action—in this case, by positing the consumer market and individual consumer 'choice' as the appropriate vehicles for food system change. As Guthman and Parker et al. illustrate, the affordances of food labels also operate as a mask: they conceal the realities of conventional production systems and present 'better', more 'ethical' alternatives as more widespread than they really are. In the case of organic labels, the onerousness of organic certification schemes serves to frame scrutiny as the appropriate response to organic production practices, but not to those of conventional production, the worst excesses of which continue unabated under a scheme of voluntary labelling. In the case of labelling for animal welfare, labels indicating higher levels of welfare can often mask the reality that they reflect only a small, incremental improvement for the vast majority of animals raised in these schemes, rather than anything significantly transformative for the lives of food animals. These chapters indicate that the 'solution' is not simply a matter of more, or more accurate, labelling. In fact, the very conventions, practices and structures that underpin cultural texts such as labels may, in themselves, prove a barrier to meaningful change in food production practices or to broadening the accessibility of 'better' options beyond middle-class markets.

Analysing the construction and circulation of media and cultural texts grants us access to the conditions that enable particular kinds of food politics—and particular kinds of food systems action—at the same time as they constrain others. At times, the mediation and re-mediation of cultural texts can produce a symbolic 'openness' that allows their meanings to be appropriated for non-progressive ends (see, for example, Chapter 12 in relation to supermarket branding strategies), but it can also allow media and cultural texts to open up new political questions and possibilities. As Stephen Harrington, Christy Collis and Ozgur Dedehayir show in Chapter 7, recent media reframing of veganism has profoundly changed how vegan lifestyle politics are enacted. The powerful discursive shift from the language of 'veganism' to one of 'plant-based diets' that has occurred across a range of media forms—from social media to cookbooks—is a clear example of how discourses 'systematically form the objects of which they speak' (Foucault, 1972, p. 49). Here, the 'object' of veganism has been constructed in ways that have opened up new lifestyle practices, new forms of (masculine) identity politics, and a mainstream acceptance of cruelty-free diets that would have been unthinkable even a few years ago.

Intermediaries

The second concept, intermediaries, raises two questions that are vital to understanding the role of media in shaping contemporary food politics: who are the key actors mediating the terms of food-related political action and debate? And how do we evaluate their roles and impacts? Throughout this collection, we see the continuing importance of 'traditional' cultural intermediaries, as well as the rise of a range of new actors engaged in shaping the terms in which food politics is played out. Early studies of media and food politics focused on the role of the celebrity chef as perhaps *the* key cultural intermediary mediating food, lifestyle and political concerns. With the explosion of lifestyle television in the 1990s and early 2000s, celebrity chefs emerged as lifestyle 'experts' educating audiences in the arts of self-governance and 'good' citizenship, and later, as 'moral entrepreneurs' tackling various food-related causes (Hollows and Jones, 2010; see also Lewis, 2008a; Ouellette and Hay, 2008). While the activities of celebrity chefs have been criticised for their tendency to impose middle-class values and to focus on personal responsibility at the expense of structural constraints (Bell, Hollows and Jones, 2017; Rousseau, 2012; Slocum et al., 2011), high-profile media campaigns driven by celebrity chefs—most notably the 'campaigning culinary documentaries' (Bell, Hollows and Jones, 2017) of Jamie Oliver—became powerful models of how to 'do' mediated food politics.

Indeed, the celebrity chef remains a powerful force in shaping the cultural identities associated with food and the public prominence of various food issues. Chapters throughout the collection highlight the role of the celebrity chef in bringing media and public attention to political questions and concerns, and for priming certain types of action. As Anders Riel Müller and Jonatan Leer show in Chapter 2, New Nordic Cuisine (NNC) and its close connection to celebrity chefs and other food celebrities was crucial to securing media interest and support for the movement—even if this reliance on celebrity superstars also ultimately served as a barrier to the mainstreaming of NNC beyond the culinary and restaurant elite; these intermediaries contributed to consumer perception of NNC as elitist and therefore incompatible with the everyday food practices of ordinary people.

Several chapters also show the ongoing role of campaigning culinary documentaries fronted by celebrity chefs in 'responsibilising' consumers to solve food crises (see Bell, Hollows and Jones, 2017). In Paula Arcari's Chapter 9, we see how *For the Love of Meat (FLM)*, the campaigning culinary documentary by Australian celebrity chef-farmer Matthew Evans, has served as a key cultural text contributing to the shaping of 'ethical meat' discourses in Australia and elsewhere, as well as to the continuing naturalisation of meat consumption. Such media texts form one part of a more pervasive set of naturalisations that ensure the ongoing domination of food animals (the three 'naturalisations' that Arcari identifies include the eating, commodification and killing of animals). In the case of *FLM*, this involves employing a range of visual and discursive techniques that objectify animals as pieces of edible flesh—a reliance on 'normalised cartographies of meat' that reinforces the '"natural" meatification of animals' bodies' (see p. 175).

In Chapter 12, Michelle Phillipov and Katherine Kirkwood show how celebrity chefs' political and culinary cachet, derived from their involvement in campaigning culinary documentaries and other media activities, can be effectively deployed in the marketing, branding and product development strategies of major supermarkets. Such strategies have become useful as methods of reframing the meanings associated with both 'processed' and 'supermarket' foods at a time of mounting criticism of supermarket practices. Through the chapter's examples of partnerships between international celebrity chefs Jamie Oliver and Heston Blumenthal and Australian supermarkets Woolworths and Coles, respectively, Phillipov and Kirkwood demonstrate how celebrity-branded food products can be used to reframe criticisms of supermarkets and supermarket food by variously drawing on the connotations of the 'artisan' and the 'alternative' (in the case of the Oliver–Woolworths partnership) and by attempting to positively revalue industrial methods of manufacture (in the case of the partnership between Blumenthal and Coles).

But alongside this more traditional figure of the celebrity chef, chapters in the collection also highlight a range of new intermediaries shaping the contemporary field of food politics, including new entrepreneurial figures, as well as ordinary people of varying political capacities. The rise of entrepreneurial intermediaries should come as no surprise. As Keith Negus observed nearly two decades ago, cultural intermediaries are crucial in shaping the institutional structure of markets and the circulation of commodities:

> cultural intermediaries shape both use values and exchange values, and seek to manage how these values are connected with people's lives through the various techniques of persuasion and marketing and through the construction of markets.
>
> (Negus, 2002, p. 504)

The reasons for this have been well rehearsed in food studies scholarship and elsewhere: as state services have shrunk, it has been left to 'the market' to pick up many of the essential services previously seen as a state responsibility. Throughout the Anglophone West, a convergence of discourses of neoliberalism and austerity have contributed to both an enhanced focus on individual consumer 'agency' and the untethering of market forces from state control; media and cultural intermediaries are now key forces in shaping and 'selling' these processes to consumers (see Potter and Westall, 2013), and, it might be added, to food industries.

In the context of food production, for example, this tendency for the state to leave regulation 'up to the market' has profoundly shaped a range of food provisioning systems, including standards for organic certification (Guthman, Chapter 1) and animal welfare (Parker et al., Chapter 10). It has also led to the involvement of an increasing number of entrepreneurial figures—whom Müller and Leer (Chapter 2, p. 43) call 'individual social change agents'—in contemporary food politics. For Müller and Leer, New Nordic Cuisine's reliance on social entrepreneurs, rather than on state-based regulation and legislation, is what prevented it from significantly transforming agri-food production in Scandinavia: without state support, the transition from 'industrial mass market production to highly differentiated, seasonal, small batch production' remained unattractive and unviable to all but a small number of niche producers (see p. 44).

For others, however, a focus on market-based, entrepreneurial solutions to food systems problems is seen as having significant transformative effects on contemporary food politics. Paula Arcari (Chapter 9) shows how niche food producers, many of whom have gained significantly in media savvy and public prominence in recent years (see Phillipov and Goodman, 2017), are now key cultural intermediaries in an affective economy of signs in which economic imperatives combine with invocations of idyllic rural lives to naturalise meat consumption and limit the possibilities for critique. In Chapter 4, Tanja Schneider argues that the involvement of entrepreneurial intermediaries such as start-ups have the potential to reshape and redefine political action with respect to food sustainability. She shows how food start-ups frequently adopt the sustainability discourses of alternative food networks while foregrounding technological solutions to food systems problems; this allows them to combine the corporate logic of eco-efficiency with AFNs' traditional concerns. In doing so, start-ups operate as 'promissory enterprises' (see p. 80) with the capacity to substantially reshape what types of sustainable food futures might become politically preferable (and politically possible) by redefining what sustainable food is and how this sustainability can be achieved.

In each of these cases, the power of the entrepreneurial intermediaries lies in the utopian visions they offer. In their various ways, audiences—whether consumers, media or financial backers—are invited to invest in a utopian food future: one centred on bucolic rural lifestyles, in the case of Arcari's ethical meat producers, or one anchored in the techno-utopia of eco-efficiency, in the case of Schneider's food start-ups. Such entrepreneurial visions are invested in a utopian redefinition of food systems sustainability that simultaneously masks the role of market forces and recentres the market as the primary source of desirable and attainable solutions to food systems problems. These examples highlight the ways in which the 'mainstreaming' of market solutions can also have more-than-market effects, producing products and practices that contribute to new ways of imagining and enacting contemporary food politics. These changes are playing a part in a significant reframing of what kind of practices 'count' as political, how political terms are to be defined and operationalised, and how political impacts are to be evaluated.

The complexities of intermediation are especially clear when we consider the role of ordinary people, who are no longer simply recipients of media messages about food politics, but who are now also key intermediaries for these messages. Media's affordances offer ordinary people increased opportunity for political participation and engagement (Highfield, 2016), but this access to a greater array of political repertoires comes with a range of implications: media's affordances can mobilise transnational publics around a shared commitment to food sovereignty, or they can result in echo chambers of middle-class identity politics (see Mann, Chapter 6). They can open up new spaces in which to enact a genuinely alternative politics, or they can serve more reactionary projects aimed at shoring up existing regimes of power (see Lupton, Chapter 8). Evaluating their political outcomes requires sensitivity to both the macro- and micro-political questions that will be discussed in more detail below, but also to the new digital economies of circulation and distribution, in which participants are simultaneously producers, consumers and intermediaries.

Media scholars have long recognised the hybrid roles that characterise participation in digital media. Such roles have been referred to in the literature under a range of terminology, most prominently as 'prosumers' (Toffler, 1980) and 'produsers' (Bruns, 2008). In addition to producer–consumer hybrids, participants are increasingly imbricated in sharing economies in which ordinary people also operate as 'influencers' and intermediaries. Recent scholarship on ordinary people and the digital points to the increasing 'professionalisation' of social media activity, including complex practices of self-branding, self-mediation and online influence (Khamis, Ang and Welling, 2017). In the context of food politics, we are increasingly seeing activists, micro-celebrities, ordinary users and a range of other media influencers occupying the same (digital) space, leading to different types of political mobilisation, and the creation and circulation of new media objects. For Deborah Lupton, the power of online intermediaries is in the micro-politics that they mobilise and enact. In Chapter 8, she shows how the everyday spaces of online food/body politics engage a range of digital media actors and agential capacities to incite 'intensely visceral affects' (see p. 164) that amplify the resonances associated with food, health, and pleasure, among others. Media influencers like Vani Hari, aka the 'Food Babe', employ these affects to galvanise support for healthier and more ethical food production system—while also shoring up their own brand power and cachet. Meanwhile, ordinary users draw upon the intensities and affordances of food and media to bring together affective communities around issues from fitness to fatness, meat eating to veganism, each with varying political effects. As Lupton's examples highlight, media's affordances and intermediations can engage a range of responses that cannot always be straightforwardly designated as either progressive or reactionary. This poses a number of challenges to how we might evaluate—or, indeed, identify—food politics today. Understanding the media politics of food, then, demands closer attention to media's macro- and micro-political capacities.

Macro- and micro-political capacities

Food studies scholars have long debated the relationship between individual action and structural change in the advancement of a genuinely transformative food politics. As mentioned above, consumption politics has often served as a key battleground for these debates. Many scholars have critiqued AFNs on the grounds that they put too much faith in individual consumer 'choice' as a motor of political change, rather than focusing on 'alter[ing] the structural features of the food system, so that all might come to eat better' (Guthman, 2007, p. 78). This structural change, many argue, is only possible once the normative, middle-class dimensions of food interventions—from school gardens to health education—are properly interrogated and addressed (Guthman, 2007; Hayes-Conroy and Hayes-Conroy, 2013). But, as scholars in media and cultural studies are often quick to point out, the scholarly and popular focus on consumer choice as a vehicle for food system change is also an effect of structural conditions. The neoliberal reinvention of government has placed media at the centre of an ever-sharper focus on 'life politics' (Lewis, 2012), with media texts offering 'resource[s] for achieving the changing demands of citizenship' in late capitalist societies, in which 'good' citizenship is frequently associated with both self-surveillance and 'proper' regimes of consumption (Ouellette and Hay, 2008, p. 31). As a result, the micro- and the macro-political are increasingly difficult to disentangle in contemporary mediated expressions of food politics.

This tension between the micro- and the macro-political is a central concern of many of the chapters here: some maintain that without major structural transformation or concerted policy intervention, the capacity for consumer politics to effect food systems change is either seriously circumscribed, as in the case of food labelling and certification (see Guthman, Chapter 1; Parker et al., Chapter 10), or inevitably limited to middle-class circles as a means of shoring up elite power, as in the cases of New Nordic Cuisine and heritage foods (see Müller and Leer, Chapter 2; Wincott, Chapter 3). As Abigail Wincott argues, inequality may be inherent to 'alternative' taste cultures like heritage foods. This is because these foods are frequently presented as an expression of alternative food politics—and eating them as a means to preserve and protect a food heritage that would otherwise be destroyed by industrial food production. However, promoting their consumption through discourses of rarity (i.e., we need to eat them to protect them from 'imminent extinction', see p. 56) also produces such food as *rarefied* in ways that shore up the social distinction of those with the privilege to access 'heritage taste' (see p. 65). Phillipov and Kirkwood show (see Chapter 12) that progressive politics can also be readily incorporated by large food systems players as a platform for rebranding and new product development. Others, in contrast, are more optimistic about the potential for critique to effect change in both media industries and food systems (see van Ryn, Chapter 11; Arcari, Chapter 9). Others still highlight the genuinely empowering dimensions of personal food politics (see Lupton, Chapter 8), as well as the potential for digital media to enable new political coalitions and forms of political expression (see Mann, Chapter 6; Flowers and Swan, Chapter 5).

For the most part, though, rather than a clear demarcation of the progressive and the reactionary, the imbrication of media and food politics necessitates that a range of intersectional concerns be considered. This includes questions of race (Flowers and Swan, Chapter 5; Harrington et al., Chapter 7), species (Arcari, Chapter 9) and gender (Harrington et al., Chapter 7; Lupton, Chapter 8; Arcari, Chapter 9). In Chapter 8, Lupton shows how, in the gendered practices of alternative food/body politics, the progressive and the reactionary often sit side by side. For example, in some circumstances the celebration of food excesses through digital memes can challenge cultural norms of the disciplined (and compulsorily thin) female body, while in other circumstances, these excesses can be resignified to endorse a violent masculinity that constructs both women and animals as objects for male consumption. Similarly, as Harrington, Collis and Dedehayir show in Chapter 7, 'masculine' versions of veganism—including the popular *Thug Kitchen* cookbooks and the growing media visibility of 'vegan athletes'—can help to assist in the mainstream acceptance of plant-based diets but can also involve recourse to racial stereotypes (in the case of *Thug Kitchen*) and/or leave problematic aspects of masculinity unchallenged (in the case of vegan athletes). In the latter example, vegan masculinity's focus on diet as a means to produce individual physical power and performance remains beholden to hegemonic masculinities that exclude 'feminine' attributes, such as care for animals or the environment.

The micro-political, then, can be a gateway to the macro-political, but the circumstances in which this might occur are not always evident in advance. The contemporary mediation of food politics has resulted in continually shifting 'alternatives' and 'mainstreams' that do not always lead participants to a clear political position. 'Alternative' discourses can be adopted by mainstream retailers and food producers to make their practices appear more palatable (see Parker et al., Chapter 10; Phillipov and Kirkwood, Chapter 12). Likewise, 'mainstream' discourses can also be used to make the alternative more widely accessible: the alternative can—often unwittingly—come to lean on hegemonic discourses of racism, sexism, class or species (Flowers and Swan, Chapter 5; Arcari, Chapter 9; Harrington et al., Chapter 7; Wincott, Chapter 3), or on individualised, market-based discourses (Guthman, Chapter 1; Mann, Chapter 6; Schneider, Chapter 4). As the 'alternative' becomes 'mainstream', it may inevitably start to draw upon the mainstream as a means to enrol a greater number of people in its politics.

In engaging with the macro- and micro-political capacities of media and food politics, the chapters highlight the different places in which 'alternatives' and 'mainstreams' appear, the varied forms that they take, the different ways they might be evaluated, and the myriad mediations and materialities that produce them. In taking these as their central questions, the chapters highlight the value of not just thinking *about* media's relationship *to* food politics, but of thinking *with* media as a force *of* food politics. Ideally, the chapters offer not only an understanding of the role of media in food politics today, but also a provocation about what this politics might look like in the future. That is, if we think *with* media's affordances, intermediaries and micro- and macro-political capacities, what might contemporary food politics look like? Which types of politics become possible? Which do not? It is our contention that as a political and analytical tool, thinking *with* media may be key to pushing forward the possibilities of alternative food politics in as-yet unexpected ways.

Structure of the book

In order to think through some of these questions and possibilities, the collection is structured in four parts. Part 1: Limits and Paradoxes considers key cultural, structural and economic barriers to the broader mainstreaming of alternative food politics. Through case studies of organic foods (Chapter 1), New Nordic Cuisine (Chapter 2) and heritage vegetables (Chapter 3), the chapters in this section illustrate the 'limits' of mainstreaming. Each of the chapters in this section address the various consequences of leaving it 'up to the market' to achieve food system change. They show how a reliance on the market as the key vehicle for change has hampered expansion and diversification in the US organics industry, limited the capacity of the 'scaling up' of alternative food production practices in Denmark, and restricted heritage 'taste' to a class and economic elite. In doing so, these chapters highlight the limits of consumer 'choice' and individual entrepreneurial action as motors for wider political change, and outline the ongoing barriers posed by class and economic difference to achieving structural transformation within the food system.

The chapters in Part 2: New Political Platforms investigate how the mainstreaming of alternative food politics has contributed to the emergence of new political spaces and activities. It shows how practices as diverse as food start-ups (Chapter 4), community dinners (Chapter 5) and digital food activism (Chapter 6) each work to construct food as a resource to be deployed in solutions to a range of pressing social and environmental problems, including food systems sustainability, social inclusion and food sovereignty. The chapters highlight both the affordances and limits of a mediated food politics, canvassing media's role in the techno-utopian redefinition of food sustainability, the production of racist meanings through the remediation of politically progressive media texts, and the problematic reframing of food sovereignty as a form of middle-class identity politics. It reveals how various 'alternative' practices are contributing to activist and market-based solutions that offer both challenges and opportunities for consumers and the food industry.

These challenges and opportunities are then explored further in Part 3: Personal Food Politics and Entanglements in relation to two topics that have become 'touchstone' concerns of popular food politics: animal ethics (Chapters 7 and 9) and personal production and consumption practices (Chapter 8). This includes contrasting perspectives on the growing media interest in meat politics—with Chapter 7 attributing to this a popular expansion of vegan diets, and Chapter 9 suggesting that it has led to a doubling down of human dominance over food animals. It also includes analysis of the various ways in which alternative food politics are (and are not) incorporated into the online/digital practices of food consumers. Through its focus on the highly visible (and contentious) issues of animals, health and food/body politics, the chapters in Part 3 highlight the shifting and complex relationships between the micro- and the macro-political in personal food politics, as well as the role of media in shaping its varied expressions and affects.

Part 4: Reframing Production and Consumption then examines the ways in which 'mainstream' media and food industries have attempted to engage with alternative food politics and practices. Based on case studies of free-range labelling (Chapter 10), primetime food television productions (Chapter 11) and major supermarkets' partnerships with celebrity chefs (Chapter 12), the chapters in this section reveal how alternative food politics have simultaneously necessitated shifts in mainstream practices, provided appealing marketing and brand management strategies for producers and retailers, and offered opportunities for the appropriation of activist practices and projects. The chapters reveal the immense power of mainstream media and food industry actors to not only appropriate alternative food discourses, but also to shape food politics debates in more positive ways. In doing so, Part 4 highlights the value of industry research as key to productively thinking 'with' media. It combines optimism about the food and media industries' capacity for change with criticism of their worst excesses—a combination essential for imagining an alternative food future as food politics move further from the 'margins' to the 'mainstream'.

References

Allen, P., FitzSimmons, M., Goodman, M. and Warner, K. (2003). Shifting Plates in the Agrifood Landscape: The Tectonics of Alternative Agrifood Initiatives in California. *Journal of Rural Studies*, 19 (1), 61–75.

Barnett, C., Clarke, N., Cloke, P. and Malpass, A. (2005). The Political Ethics of Consumerism. *Consumer Policy Review*, 15, 45–51.

Bell, D., Hollows, J. and Jones, S. (2017). Campaigning Culinary Documentaries and the Responsibilization of Food Crises. *Geoforum*, 84, 179–187.

boyd, d. (2010). Social Network Sites as Networked Publics: Affordances, Dynamics, and Implications. In Papacharissi, Z. (ed.), *A Networked Self: Identity, Community, and Culture on Social Network Sites* (pp. 36–50). New York: Routledge.

Brownell, K. D. and Warner, K. E. (2009). The Perils of Ignoring History: Big Tobacco Played Dirty and Millions Died. How Similar Is Big Food? *The Milbank Quarterly*, 87 (1), 259–294.

Bruns, A. (2008). *Blogs, Wikipedia, Second Life and Beyond: From Production to Produsage*. New York: Peter Lang.

Cadieux, K. V. and Slocum, R. (2015). What Does It Mean to *Do* Food Justice? *Journal of Political Ecology*, 22, 1–26.

Campbell, H. (2009). Breaking New Ground in Food Regime Theory: Corporate Environmentalism, Ecological Feedbacks and the 'Food from Somewhere' Regime? *Agriculture and Human Values*, 26, 309–319.

Campbell, H. (2015). Spurlock's Vomit and Visible Food Utopias: Enacting a Positive Politics of Food. In Stock, P. V., Carolan, M. and Rosin, C. (eds.), *Food Utopias: Reimagining Citizenship, Ethics and Community* (pp. 195–215). London: Routledge.

Egg Info. (2016). *Industry Data 2004 to 2014*. British Egg Information Service. Available at: www.egginfo.co.uk/egg-facts-and-figures/industry-information/data. Accessed 26 April 2018.

Flew, T. (2007). *Understanding Global Media*. Houndmills: Palgrave Macmillan.

Foucault, M. (1972). *The Archaeology of Knowledge*. Translated by Sheridan Smith. A. M. New York: Pantheon Books.

Friedmann, H. (2005). From Colonialism to Green Capitalism: Social Movements and the Emergence of Food Regimes. In Buttel, F. H. and McMichael, P. (eds.), *New Directions in the Sociology of Global Development* (pp. 227–264). Amsterdam: Elsevier.

Gibbs, M., Meese, J., Arnold, M., Nansen, B. and Carter, M. (2015). #Funeral and Instagram: Death, Social Media and the Platform Vernacular. *Information, Communication & Society*, 18 (3), 255–268.

Goodman, D. (2003). The Quality 'Turn' and Alternative Food Practices: Reflections and Agenda. *Journal of Rural Studies*, 19, 1–7.

Goodman, D., DuPuis, M. and Goodman, M. K. (2012). *Alternative Food Networks: Knowledge, Practice, Politics*. London: Routledge.

Goodman, D. and Goodman, M. K. (2009). Alternative Food Networks. In Kitchin, R. and Thrift, N. (eds.), *International Encyclopedia of Human Geography* (pp. 208–220). Amsterdam: Elsevier.

Guthman, J. (2007). Can't Stomach It: How Michael Pollan et al. Made Me Want to Eat Cheetos. *Gastronomica*, 7, 75–79.

Guthman, J. (2014). *Agrarian Dreams: The Paradox of Organic Farming in California*. 2nd ed. Oakland: University of California Press.

Hayes-Conroy, J. and Hayes-Conroy, A. (2013). Veggies and Visceralities: A Political Ecology of Food and Feeling. *Emotion, Space and Society*, 6, 81–90.

Hesmondhalgh, D. (2013). *The Cultural Industries*. 3rd ed. London: Sage.

Highfield, T. (2016). *Social Media and Everyday Politics*. Cambridge: Polity.

Hindman, D. B. and Wiegand, K. (2008). The Big Three's Prime-Time Decline: A Technological and Social Context. *Journal of Broadcasting & Electronic Media*, 52, 119–135.

Hollows, J. and Jones, S. (2010). 'At Least He's Doing Something': Moral Entrepreneurship and Individual Responsibility in *Jamie's Ministry of Food*. *European Journal of Cultural Studies*, 13, 307–322.

Juris, J. S. (2012). Reflections on #Occupyeverywhere: Social Media, Public Space, and Emerging Logics of Aggregation. *American Ethnologist*, 39 (2), 259–279.

Khamis, S., Ang, L. and Welling, R. (2017). Self-Branding, 'Micro-Celebrity' and the Rise of Social Media Influencers. *Celebrity Studies*, 8 (2), 191–208.

Kingsolver, B. (2007). *Animal, Vegetable, Miracle: Our Year of Seasonal Eating*. Great Britain: Faber and Faber.

Lavis, A. (2017). Food Porn, Pro-Anorexia and the Viscerality of Virtual Affect: Exploring Eating in Cyberspace. *Geoforum*, 84, 198–205.

Lewis, T. (2008a). *Smart Living: Lifestyle Media and Popular Expertise*. New York: Peter Lang.

Lewis, T. (2008b). Transforming Citizens? Green Politics and Ethical Consumption on Lifestyle Television. *Continuum: Journal of Media & Cultural Studies*, 22, 227–240.

Lewis, T. (2012). 'There Grows the Neighbourhood': Green Citizenship, Creativity and Life Politics on eco-TV. *International Journal of Cultural Studies*, 15, 315–326.

Lewis, T. (2018). Digital Food: From Paddock to Platform. *Communication Research and Practice*, 4 (3), 212–228.

Lewis, T. and Potter, E. (2011). Introducing Ethical Consumption. In Lewis, T. and Potter, E. (eds.), *Ethical Consumption: A Critical Introduction* (pp. 3–24). London: Routledge.

Lupton, D. (2018). Cooking, Eating, Uploading: Digital Food Cultures. In LeBesco, K. and Naccarato, P. (eds.), *The Handbook of Food and Popular Culture* (pp. 66–79). London: Bloomsbury.

Negus, K. (2002). The Work of Cultural Intermediaries and the Enduring Distance between Production and Consumption. *Cultural Studies*, 16, 501–515.

Nestle, M. (2013). *Food Politics: How the Food Industry Influences Nutrition and Health.* Berkeley: University of California Press.

Orr, G. (2012). Sweet Taste of Sales Success: Why Are Cookbooks Selling Better than Ever? *The Independent.* Available at: www.independent.co.uk/life-style/foodand-drink/features/sweet-taste-of-sales-success-why-are-cookbooks-sellingbetter-than-ever-8113937.html. Accessed 26 April 2018.

Ouellette, L. and Hay, J. (2008). *Better Living through Reality TV: Television and Post-Welfare Citizenship.* Malden: Blackwell.

Phillipov, M. (2016). Escaping to the Country: Media, Nostalgia, and the New Food Industries. *Popular Communication*, 14 (2), 111–122.

Phillipov, M. (2017). *Media and Food Industries: The New Politics of Food.* London: Palgrave Macmillan.

Phillipov, M. and Goodman, M. K. (2017). The Celebrification of Farmers: Celebrity and the New Politics of Farming. *Celebrity Studies*, 8 (2), 346–350.

Phillips, S. (2009). What We Talk about When We Talk about Food. *The Hudson Review*, 62, 189–209.

Pollan, M. (2006). *The Omnivore's Dilemma: A Natural History of Four Meals.* London: Penguin.

Pollan, M. (2008). *In Defence of Food.* London: Penguin Books.

Potter, L. and Westall, C. (2013). Neoliberal Britain's Austerity Foodscape: Home Economics, Veg Patch Capitalism and Culinary Temporality. *New Formations*, 80/81, 155–178.

Richards, C., Lawrence, G. and Burch, D. (2011). Supermarkets and Agro-Industrial Foods: The Strategic Manufacture of Consumer Trust. *Food, Culture & Society*, 14, 29–47.

Rousseau, S. (2012). *Food Media: Celebrity Chefs and the Politics of Everyday Interference.* London: Berg.

Schneider, T., Eli, K., Dolan, C. and Ulijaszek, S. (eds.). (2018). *Digital Food Activism.* Oxon: Routledge.

Slocum, R., Shannon, J., Cadieux, K. V. and Beckman, M. (2011). 'Properly, with Love, from Scratch': Jamie Oliver's Food Revolution. *Radical History Review*, 110, 178–191.

Soper, K. (2004). Rethinking the 'Good Life': The Consumer as Citizen. *Capitalism Nature Socialism*, 15, 111–116.

Spurgeon, C. (2013). Regulated Integrated Advertising. In McAllister, M. P. and West, E. (eds.), *The Routledge Companion to Advertising and Promotional Culture* (pp. 71–82). New York: Routledge.

Stănescu, V. (2010). 'Green' Eggs and Ham? The Myth of Sustainable Meat and the Danger of the Local. *Journal for Critical Animal Studies*, 8, 8–32.

Toffler, A. (1980). *The Third Wave.* New York: Bantam Books.

Versteegen, H. (2010). Armchair Epicures: The Proliferation of Food Programmes on British TV. In Gymnich, M. and Lennartz, N. (eds.), *The Pleasures and Horrors of Eating: The Cultural History of Eating in Anglophone Literature* (pp. 447–464). Goettingen: VandR Unipress.

Waisbord, S. (2004). McTV: Understanding the Global Popularity of Television Formats. *Television & New Media*, 5, 359–383.

Part 1
Limits and paradoxes

1 The (continuing) paradox of the organic label

Reflections on US trajectories in the era of mainstreaming

Julie Guthman

I am convinced that organic agriculture is essential to the revitalization of rural America.

(Former US Secretary of Agriculture, Tom Vilsack, speaking to the
National Organic Coalition in 2012)

After decades of disparagement, organic farming in the US now enjoys significant legitimacy among policy makers and consumers, and in the food industry itself. To be sure, Vilsack's comment is a far cry from that of a previous holder of that same post, Earl Butz, who, in 1971, equated a 'return' to organic agriculture as a recipe for widespread starvation. Institutionally, this heightened legitimacy is demonstrated in the full roll-out of a national organic food standard, increased (though still nominal) government funding for organic programs, and major changes in the rules for organic livestock that allow meat to be sold as organic. As for consumers, today no less than two-thirds of Americans buy organic products occasionally, and 28% buy them weekly (Greene et al., 2009). Virtually every major food manufacturer now carries an organic product line, and organic food can be found in big box retailers throughout the US, as well as in natural food stores in college towns and in upscale restaurants in cosmopolitan urban centres.

The so-called mainstreaming of organics has not been uncontested. On one side are those who claim that it has enabled a broader swathe of producers to employ at least *better* methods, and thus allowed more consumers access to at least safer and perhaps healthier food, which ostensibly should be (some of) the goals. On the other are those who point out that corporate and/or government involvement in organics has entailed a dilution of the values and practices of organic farming, and has brought unwanted competition within the organic market. These claims notwithstanding, few have investigated how mainstreaming has actually affected the farming sector in the US.

As it happens, much of the growth stemming from organic mainstreaming is in value-added production, rather than in a huge influx of new growers or a massive expansion of acreage. Indeed, growers who have transitioned to organics in response to mainstreaming have done so in hesitant and protracted ways. Mainstreaming has thus contributed to what has come to be known as bifurcation', referring to the existence of two sets of growers. One set is comprised primarily (though not solely) of those who were once—or still are—in part conventional growers, who grow and sell products for major distributors, processors, and national chains, often at the behest of those buyers. These are the ones who represent and drive mainstreaming. The other set is comprised of those who primarily (though not solely) sell in local and regional markets, and often, if not always solely, engage in direct marketing. Most, but not all, in this latter group have always grown organically, but are not necessarily certified as organic producers. One question is why growth trajectories are the way they are, given the expectations that a US federal standard would level the playing field and thus ease entry across the board. A second is what significance bifurcation has for the growth and character of the sector.

This chapter explores these two, interrelated questions, through research I conducted in 2013 in preparation for the second edition of my book, *Agrarian Dreams: The Paradox of Organic Farming in California* (2014). Although I saw many dynamics at work, I found that the structure and growth trajectories of the sector are still fundamentally shaped by the form of regulation that the organic sector has embraced. In the US (and elsewhere), for producers to legitimately claim they grow organically, they must abide by a set of standards devised by oversight bodies and must then be certified to that standard. Certification may be performed by non-profit organisations, for-profit businesses, or even state agencies. In the US, it was originally the certifiers themselves who set the organic standards, as did some states. Today the federal government sets and maintains the standards through the National Organic Standards Board (NOSB). The federal government also oversees the work of the certification organisations, but does no certification itself. Regard-less of the specifics of oversight, the entire system is voluntary in the sense that no one compels producers to adopt organic practices, unless, of course, they want to maintain organic certification. Instead they are incentivised to grow organically by the price premium that organic certification generally bestows.

But here's the thing: to reward producers with a price premium there must be consumers with the will and means to pay more for organically produced food. And that, I argue, has limited the growth of the sector, particularly in precarious times. Moreover, consumer precarity has proven to be more threatening to the conventionally-leaning segments of the sector. These quasi-conventional organic growers (growers who meet the minimum standards for certification but other-wise operate much like conventional growers) cater to consumers who are much more price sensitive about organic food than are more dedicated organic consumers, who tend to favour producers and outlets in local and regional markets. That the sub-sector best positioned to spread organic production and to bring organics to a wider audience is not only seen as morally suspect but is also on less-sure footing speaks to the limits of a voluntary label as a way to transform agricultural production.

Organic growth and change

One of the original arguments for having a federal system for certification of organics, comprising both uniform standards and forms of oversight, is that it would allow the sector to increase its share of the total food market. Growth rates in organics have indeed surpassed those in the food industry as a whole, yet the growth rate for organics after the federal standard was implemented has been less than expected. This is partly because most of the activity by the big players took place in anticipation of the rule (Howard, 2009). I suggest, too, that it may portend an inherent limit to the size of the organic market as a result of the nature of its regulatory schema.

In 2015, the US organic food industry experienced 43.3 billion USD in sales, an increase of nearly ten-fold since 1997. Growing at a pace much faster than the rest of the food industry, and recovering from slow growth during the economic downturn of 2009, as of 2015 organic food sales made up nearly 5% of all food sales (OTA, 2016). Growth was strongest for fruits and vegetables, which represented 42% of total organic food sales, with organic dairy as the second largest category with 19% of all organic sales (USDA NASS, 2016).

These increased sales must have had some connection to growth in actual production. To be sure, after six years of growth, averaging 13% annually, certified organic acreage in the US reached more than 5.4 million acres in 2011 (the latest data posted by the USDA Economic Research Service as of this writing (USDA ERS, 2017). Of this, 3,084,989 acres were cropland, while land devoted to organic pasture totalled 2,298,130 acres. However, this still represented only about 0.8% of all US cropland, while certified organic pasture represented only 0.5% of all US pasture. Overall, certified organic cropland and pasture accounted for just 0.64% of US total farmland! The number of livestock managed organically also grew exponentially during that period, but still only to a point that 2.8% of US dairy cows and 2% of layer hens were managed under certified organic systems (USDA ERS, 2013). How are we to explain this? That organic sales represent a much higher percentage of total sales of food relative to the acreage devoted to organic production owes somewhat to the higher prices that organic commodities receive. But it owes mainly to growth in processing and marketing activities that add value to products after farm gate sales, as well as to a sizeable import sector in crops such as coffee, temperate fruits and vegetables (especially from Mexico), and tropical fruits. Put differently, the market for organic foods has been more robust than have the changes in actual agricultural practices.

A corollary trend is that growth in organic farming appears to be driven more by expansion of existing operations than by conversion of new ones. This can roughly be seen in the increase of the average size of operations from 261 acres in 1992 to 418 acres in 2011 (calculated from data in USDA ERS, 2013). A slightly more nuanced statistical picture is available from California, which continues to be a dominant player in US organics, accounting for 40% of all organic farm sales in the country, including non-food crops. As of 2015, it also had the highest percentage of certified organic acreage of all states (790,413 acres), representing 18% of total US organic farm land, and the most certified operations (4,296) as well (CCOF, 2016). That California's share of sales is higher than its share of acres reflects that much of California's crop land continues to go to high value fruit and vegetable production. Yet, even in this most robust of organic markets, organic is only 3% of acreage, and farm size has increased faster than the number of operations. According to data collected and analysed by agricultural economists Klonsky and Richter (2005, 2007, 2011), the number of organic growers just about doubled between 1992 and 2009, from 1,157 to 2,330, while the number of acres in organic production increased more than tenfold in that same period, from 42,302 to 486,169. Although a good chunk of this growth in acreage owes to the statistical inclusion of pasture (previously not always certified) and the real growth in livestock operations, which require pasture, the pattern is much clearer for California's mainstay crops. The number of vegetable growers increased only 60% between 1992 and 2009, while the acres in vegetable crops increased 423%, from 37 to 120 acres. Discussions with growers in recent years corroborate this pattern. Many long-time growers have developed or purchased additional acreage since first beginning, and have transitioned their activities into livestock, the fastest growing segment. That expansion rather than conversion has been the primary pathway to growth in the more established sectors of organics suggests that the organic label is not inducing widespread entry. Indeed it appears that the organic label is working best for those already in the sector, reflecting and contributing to bifurcation.

Significant bifurcation

Bifurcation is a term that I and my co-authors, Daniel Buck and Christy Getz, first used in a 1997 article to refer to the distinctions between large growers specialising in one or two crops, using more industrial practices, and small growers, using a diversity of strategies and tending toward more agro-ecological methods. Our claims were based on a (very preliminary) study of the organic sector. Nevertheless, the article sparked a vociferous academic debate in response to readers' inferences of a clear distinction between economic opportunists and social movement-oriented growers, between industrial and agro-ecological, and/ or between large and small growers. Several scholars of organic agriculture have since suggested that the contrasts between the more commercially-minded growers and more 'lifestyle' growers are overdrawn (e.g., Constance, Choi and Holly 2008; Lockie and Halpin 2005; Rosin and Campbell 2009). Rosin and Campbell (2009), for example, reject the dualistic thinking of the bifurcation thesis, not least for the Manichean judgments it seems to imply. They note the many justifications under which organic growers operate in the New Zealand context. Similarly, Lockie and Halpin (2005) note that in Australia the differences in motivations between organic and conventional growers (and thus, by extension, quasi-conventional organic growers) are a matter of degree and not of kind, and that differences in farm size among organic growers mainly reflect differences in cropping mixes (in their case livestock grazing and grain crops versus horticultural crops) rather than ideology.

I do not contest these more nuanced findings, and I especially share concerns about using coarse, binary metrics to judge which growers are doing the right thing. In my research in California I have found that the lines are not clearly drawn, nor does the old guard have virtue cornered—especially to the extent that virtue is defined by a small-scale operation and a counter-cultural image. Indeed, some of the early hippy entrants went on to become major players. Earthbound Farms, for example, began as a two-acre market garden in the Carmel Valley and grew to command over 50,000 acres in the US and Mexico. At the same time, some erstwhile conventional growers became quite taken with organic growing practices, and increasingly incorporated complex agro-ecological practices into their production plans. Lakeside Organic Gardens, based in Watsonville California, was one such grower. After converting from conventional methods, the farm expanded from a 55 acre plot to grow over 1,700 acres in California, including 1,200 in the Pajaro Valley spread over 50 different parcels, and 500 near El Centro in the Imperial Valley (Reti, Rabkin and Farmer, 2011).

So, in what ways might it be legitimate to speak of 'bifurcation' at all, and what analytical purchase does it provide for understanding something about the dynamics of organic agriculture? At one level, the very existence of mixed growers—about one-third of operations within the California sector (but with a considerably higher percentage of acreage), according to statistics compiled by Klonsky and Richter (2011)—speaks to a subsector which, by definition, is not fully committed to organic agriculture. For that reason, some countries and international certifiers do not even allow mixed operations. These growers' lack of dedication is not necessarily a matter of desire or interest, however. Several have told me they would be happy to grow more organics, or would even prefer to, if they received a price that made it work for them. Nevertheless, they are not willing to reject the convenience of chemicals unless a buyer makes it worth their while. One such grower who had several organic contracts discussed how he had dabbled in organics more than twenty years earlier but had quit when 'the market wasn't ready', which for him meant he could not get the contract prices he wanted. In that light, the 'bifurcation' that I believe is of broader significance is less about the size of actual farming operations (whether measured in acres or sales), or even farmer perspectives and motivations, than it is about the distinctions between farmers who produce at the behest of the grower-shippers and processors, and those who grow independently. The vast majority of produce going through the large grower-shippers reaches a national market and ends up in major supermarkets (including Whole Foods), while that produced with more independent marketing arrangements tends to end up in local and regional markets—both direct markets (CSAs, farmers markets, and restaurants), and regional chains and independent grocery stores.

These marketing strategies reverberate throughout farmers' operations. Those who grow for buyers are more likely to grow ingredients for processing by major food manufacturers, tend to focus on one or two crops (and thus tend toward monocultures), and are more likely to have mixed conventional and organic operations. They specialise, in other words, according to buyer needs and demands. In contrast, those who grow independently tend to have greater diversity in crops and complexity in rotations (although not so much for fruit and nut production). They also tend to be exclusively organic and to focus on the fresh market. They may do value added processing, such as pickling, or preparing jams and jellies, but mainly as a sideline to stretch their selling season and to minimise crop waste. Diversity works to keep them in markets year round. Again these distinctions are not cut and dried. Some of the more commercially successful growers engage in both strategies. For example, Lakeside Gardens sells 15–20% of its product directly to regional stores, in addition to what they sell to major distributors and retailers (Reti, Rabkin and Farmer, 2011). Conversely, one grower I interviewed, who had a large CSA and significant farmers' market presence, sells tomatoes in wholesale markets. In other words, growers may bifurcate their operations themselves.

These different segments within organics, a quasi-conventional one that is directed to the national (and international) market, and a more dedicated organic one that is directed to the sizeable 'home market' in California, in turn tend to cater to different consumers, with differing access, ability to pay, and loyalty to organics. As such, they are subject to differing competitive pressures, pressures that matter in terms of how organic agriculture might spread. Further, even though there can be fierce competition within each segment—and some growers are much more successful than others, especially within the segment that caters to local and regional markets—what they have ceased to do, it appears, is compete with each other. I contend that this surprising lack of tension between these two market segments also indicates something about the growth trajectory of the sector.

Co-existing dynamics

To situate this competition, or lack thereof, it is first important to clarify something: as a rule, meeting organic production standards is not the biggest obstacle organic farmers face. According to a state-wide survey on organic production (reported on in Klonsky, 2010), 38% of California organic growers said that dealing with regulations and bureaucracy was their biggest concern, and 25% said that price or market access was the most important challenge they faced. The latter group specifically cited low premiums, inconsistent prices, difficulty finding buyers, and competition. Only 19% cited production problems. Mixed growers simply stay away from crops when they don't feel confident of their economic success if grown organically.

So, if prices, marketing, and competition are the next biggest obstacles for growers, how does that play out within and between these two market segments? For a long time there was significant fear that the entry of the big players (i.e., mainstreaming) would put the small players out of business. Speaking in an oral history project, partially reproduced in the book *Cultivating a Movement* (Reti, Rabkin and Farmer, 2011, p. 112), Dick Peixoto of Lakeside Gardens repeated a refrain I have heard many times over. He recounted that when he was a conventional grower, organic growers were encouraging him to 'get off the deal', but that when he started transitioning—often 100 acres at a time—the organic growers became 'ticked off' because they felt he would run them out of business. In that same project, Jeff Larkey of Route One Farms stated that competition in organics from the big guys converting was pretty fierce and was his 'biggest limiting factor' (Reti, Rabkin and Farmer, 2011, p. 49). It is important to note that Larkey and Peixoto both grow in probably the most competitive region in California, and could well have been referring to each other.

Still, it appears that much of this big–little competition has subsided. Another grower from that same region said that the big players did not put the small ones out of business because they fill different consumer niches, a claim that was echoed by several others with whom I spoke. The niches to which they referred have been characterised by the Hartman Group (2007) as the 'true naturals' and 'the new green mainstream'. Those from the new green mainstream are not only more occasional in their organic purchasing habits, they are also more likely to purchase organics in big box stores and conventional supermarkets, while true naturals—or those whom I would call 'diehards' (a much smaller percentage)— are more likely to buy from dedicated retailers and direct markets. As already suggested, growers tend to sort by marketing strategy to fill these different niches. 'Local food', especially, which in many ways emerged in response to the fear of mainstreaming, came to provide a niche for the smaller growers, or for those who are otherwise sceptical of working with corporate buyers.

Within those two broad market niches, there are significant competitive pressures, however. Within the wholesale market, the practice of 'open tickets' is much more prevalent. This is when a grower who over-produces ships excess product to a wholesaler and asks for whatever he or she can get, thereby under-cutting the prices of all other growers. Contract growers can always be under-priced by newer entrants, as well. Mitigating this latter process, organic buyers have come to realise the importance of having a sure supply. This need became particularly apparent in the early 2000s, when demand for organics was growing so fast that the sector saw significant input and product shortages in organic supply chains (Greene et al., 2009). Organic feed grains were in particularly short supply, since this was when the rules for organic livestock came into effect, requiring that livestock be fed organically. At the time, though, growers were slow to adopt organic feed crops. One large, mixed grower with whom I spoke reported that the prices for and long-term commitments to his organic production of processing tomatoes and feed grain had improved from that time onward.

By the same token, this quasi-conventional segment of the organic market is also more vulnerable to economic downturns or other causes of price fluctuations. According to the same study conducted by Greene et al. (2009), frequent buyers of organic products appear not to change their habits when times are tough, while occasional buyers draw back from paying premiums. As demand for organics slows, many mixed growers then curtail or cease organic production. Alternatively they may be forced to sell their organic products at a loss on the conventional market, as occurred for organic milk producers during the recession of 2007–2008 (ASFMRA, 2012). A change in demand for conventional product can also affect organic producers. Greene et al. (2009) found that following a period of high premiums for organic soybeans, an increase in conventional soybean prices precipitated a drop in the acreage devoted to organic soybeans. In keeping with these observations, amid years of continuous growth in acreage, the amount of US-certified organic farmland dropped precipitously between 2005 and 2006—which was probably related to the biofuel boom that drove up conventional food prices—and then declined again following the great recession years of 2007–2008 (USDA ERS, 2013). In short, growers in the quasi-conventional market may not grow organically if the conditions are not right, or if the profit margins are not sufficient to absorb the extra costs of growing organically. While this tenuous commitment to organic markets may be lamentable, these growers are also generally the ones that are producing the more affordable organic food, even as they may be squeezed by corporate buyers. Walmart's guarantee that organics will be no more than 10% more expensive than conventionally grown products is indeed a double-edged sword.

Competitive dynamics within the local and regional market segment are in many ways another ball of wax. Although it is easier to begin farming in this segment, with adequate access to land and credit, newer growers may also face difficulties in accessing the market, and thereby capturing higher prices. Many farmers' markets, for example, are commodity controlled, meaning market managers put limits on how many growers of a given commodity can sell there in order to protect existing growers from price competition. Some of the highest end and lucrative markets are particularly restrictive, and often have long waiting lists of farmers who wish to be vendors. Even those who have secured their spots face significant competition. The more successful growers carve out strategies to differentiate themselves, whether by beginning new product lines before they become saturated (e.g., livestock), improving quality, for example by picking fruit when it is ripe, or, in one notable case, signing a contract with the United Farm Workers and appealing to consumers concerned about working conditions. Less successful growers often lower their prices.

Nevertheless, this segment as a whole has been relatively immune to economic downturns, because dedicated organic consumers are somewhat less price sensitive. During the 2007–2009 economic recession, for example, some growers toyed with lowering their prices and found that doing so did not increase sales. Some even found that their economic situation improved with the crisis because, as one put it, 'people were looking more to fundamentals'. Another factor that has kept this segment vibrant is the expansion of farm–to–restaurant sales. Once the province of only a few high-end restaurants, these days a large number of independent restaurants in urban centres buy produce directly from farms, or through specialised wholesalers for the farm–to–restaurant market. Growers who are able to deliver a quality (i.e., tasty and attractive) product have regular relationships with restaurants.

Indeed, because of these relationships, some involved in farm–to–restaurant relationships do not even bother to certify organic, and thus are not counted in formal statistics on organics.

To be clear, dedicated organic growers that sell in direct markets may face precarious circumstances, just as quasi-conventional growers may have more stable markets. My reason for highlighting these observations is not to over-draw distinctions, but to suggest a paradox of mainstreaming. On the one hand, mainstreaming has brought organics to a much larger audience, at lower cost, and without really undercutting those dedicated organic growers who sell in local and regional markets. Although mixed growers may practise a shallower version of organic, it has still made for better farming practices—if not for perfect ones. This is a different assessment of the situation from the one I first wrote in Buck, Getz and Guthman (1997), which, probably all too flippantly, suggested a gradual evisceration of the meanings of organic and the appropriation of value by 'agribusiness'. On the other hand, mainstreaming, by and large, has not encouraged a wider swath of growers to convert to organics, in part because the margins they receive are apparently too small to compensate for the heightened regulatory and labour costs that quasi-organic conventional growers are concerned about. The fact that growth in organics, in terms of conversions, is slower than advocates expected and hoped for is something to reckon with. In the following paragraphs, I argue that this protracted growth depends on the nature of the organic label, which may well work against more widespread transformation.

A voluntary label

In the early 1970s, when the modern US organic movement was beginning to take form, it positioned itself as providing positive alternatives rather than endeavouring to derail conventional agriculture. As interest began to grow, and consumers wanted assurance that what they were purchasing was indeed produced differently, organic farmers found they needed to codify their practices and develop systems of verification that agreed standards were being met. At first this was a simple task: growers got together and shared their practices and, so the story goes, developed a list of dos and don'ts that fit on half a sheet of paper. Simultaneously, they created a handful of organisations to inspect growers and certify those who abided by these standards. But various events and conditions, from pesticide-related food scares to consumer willingness to pay sizable price premiums, encouraged new growers to seek rapid entry into the sector, sometimes by questionable means. In addition, new certifiers entered the market and did not necessarily share the same standards and certification practices. Meanwhile, companies were developing new formulations for organic inputs that were pushing the limits of acceptability for organic materials. So, in the interest of levelling the playing field and reducing consumer confusion, many in the organic sector began to push for state and federal legislation that would, as it were, standardise the standards. Twenty or so years of activity on this front culminated in a federal rule for organics, which finally went into effect in 2001. The rules not only standardised practices for organically grown produce, but also regularised certification, stepped up enforcement, and expanded the purview of organic regulations. Today, the list of allowable materials is hundreds of pages long, the number of accredited certifiers has expanded to over eighty, and certification has become a veritable business in its own right, separate from organic advocacy and policy-making.

As I showed in *Agrarian Dreams*, the organic sector opted early on to focus on production practices rather than social justice issues. Out of practical necessity, the avoidance of certain inputs, and the allowing of others, became a proxy for prescribing these production practices, encouraging an 'input substitution' approach to organics (Rosset and Altieri, 1997). As such, growers' willingness to produce organically became somewhat dependent on what crops they grew given available and allowable inputs. Over the years, much has been made of the politics of deciding what inputs and practices ought to be allowed, as virtually every practice and material has been put to debate in some venue or another. Those securely part of the sector have often wanted higher standards and greater material restrictions, while those seeking entry often wanted the standards and restrictions eased. The fights over allowable inputs have indeed been formidable, and more often than not have been decided in favour of rules that would ease entry into the sector (DuPuis and Gillon, 2009; Jaffee and Howard, 2010). The justification, of course, was to encourage adoption of organic practices. Nevertheless, as a result of this tendency towards relaxation of the rules, many growers practise a form of agriculture that might be called 'organic lite' (Guthman, 2004). Organic lite is thus both a cause and an effect of mainstreaming.

Still, I contend that the most significant aspect of organic regulation has become less about what is contained in the rules—after all, it is possible to create certification schemes with 'better' standards, as many 'beyond organic' endeavours attempt to do—but about the very vehicle by which producers are encouraged to change their practices: a set of standards, a system of verification and certification that is designed to ensure these standards are met, and the expectation that by meeting those standards (and paying for certification) they will be rewarded in the market place with the ability to charge a price premium. All this is predicated on the idea that the price premium will at the very least cover the costs of certification as well as the incremental costs (or yield losses) that abiding by organic standards might generate. At best, the price premium must be robust enough to incentivise organic production in order to draw new entrants into the sector. Herein lie the paradoxes of a voluntary label like 'organic'.

First, making the standards behind the label meaningful necessitates entry barriers, whether in the form of high standards, certification costs, or simply the hassle of compliance. Here it is important to remember that the burden of regulation remains the most important challenge facing organic farmers. Many growers have left the sector because of the burden of regulation, and others have likely not entered for similar reasons (Sierra et al., 2008). While barriers to entry ensure a medium to high bar for organics, and that is in many ways a good thing, they are antithetical to widespread adoption of organic practices. Those who want to transition more gradually, or wish to practise a less demanding form of sustainable agriculture, have no place within organics.

Second, since producers expect to receive a price premium in return for compliance with the standards behind the label, consumer willingness to pay is, in effect, the primary means by which better production practices are incentivised. Among other things, this poses some thorny issues regarding equitable access to safer and healthier food. Those who can't afford to pay more are stuck with food produced with more toxic chemicals. Moreover, since many consumers are simply not able to pay more—least of all farm and food labourers, who are also consumers!—there is an inherent limit on the expansion of the organic market. That the organic market has grown more slowly than expected following implementation of the federal rules arguably reflects this. Even after the economy picked up, beginning in 2009, income inequality has worsened, and true economic precarity has increased, so that a huge percentage of households are not in a position to pay more.

Third, the associated price premiums are not immune from competition. While high prices have often attracted new entrants, new entrants have also undermined the price premium by increasing the supply of organic crops. As we have seen, organic premiums have tended to be more volatile in the quasi-conventional segment of the sector, the very segment that seems to need the extra push to stay with organics. Sometimes prices simply are not good enough to make it worthwhile to grow organically, and sometimes markets are not developed enough to support organic prices, leading to organically produced crops being 'dumped' on the conventional market at significant losses to growers, who then exit the sector. Accordingly, growth is slowed, if not thwarted altogether, in the segment best positioned to cater to a more mainstream consumer base.

Finally, a voluntary label does not regulate production practices that are dangerous or unjust, but rather allows them to continue unabated. In fact, not regulating bad practices puts the cost burden on the good, to be paid for by either organic producers or consumers. Although there are conventional growers who try to do the right thing by incorporating at least some elements of organic production, for the most part, those who choose not to grow organically can and will use every trick in the book, and carry a lesser regulatory burden than do organic producers. In short, the voluntary nature of the label not only limits growth in the sector, it also fails to undermine the worst sorts of conventional agriculture. These points, however, seem to be lost on those who promote organics, who, I have found, tend to attribute slow growth to competition from other labels, including the non-codified 'local'. If the goal is to make organic *practices* mainstream, to change production rather than the marketing, something else must be done.

What (else) can be done?

Could organic agriculture have done more so far, and can it still do more in the future? Is it possible to forge a radically different way of producing food within the confines of existing social structures? Despite my strong criticisms, I am not willing to write off the transformative potential of organic—or, better said, agro-ecological—agriculture; I believe that the way that organic has been codified into a legally enforceable definition is the basis of the problem. To be crystal clear, I have no substantial problems with the practice of organic agriculture; it is the vehicle of regulation—a voluntary label—that is the issue.

Significantly, the unexpected complementarity between organic regulation and industrial agriculture has effectively invigorated a much broader food movement. Since I first began research on organics in 1995, I have witnessed ever-growing interest in deepening organic practices, such as with 'regenerative' agriculture, and even in making social justice a vital component of ecological agriculture. Some activists have aimed to do these things with different or enhanced labels —'beyond organic' approach. A better label, however, does not escape the paradoxes I have laid out above. Indeed, it makes products assigned such labels even more rarefied. Others have endeavoured to go beyond consumer-driven, market approaches to food system change by, for example, encouraging urban agriculture projects that do not involve commodity exchange, or even wage labour, for that matter. Although these movements understand the limits of market-based approaches, they still tend to focus on building better alternatives rather than on confronting the institutions that contribute to debilitated, industrial food. Neo-anarchist in their proclivities, they also tend to be largely sceptical of government solutions. My question is whether we ought to continue to focus on trying to make the alternatives more perfect for the few, or if we should work to make better systems for the many—even if that means that farmers practise 'organic lite'. I also wonder whether we can progress much further without fundamentally changing public policy.

It seems to me that to move to a system where the vast majority of food is produced in more sustainable and socially just ways would require major policy changes, and not simply a label endorsed and enforced by quasi-governmental agencies, nor the creation of alternatives which provide utopian models and make people who participate in them feel good but do not fundamentally challenge corporate behaviour. Unfortunately, state-oriented reforms seem hopelessly unattainable these days, given both the dysfunction and seemingly unstoppable rightward turn of the US government. Yet, if the election of Trump has taught us anything, it is that policy does indeed matter, and that nothing is inevitable (given the tremendous contingency on which his election rode). Because of its redistributive and regulatory capabilities, only the state has the ability to unlock and reverse some of the mechanisms of agricultural intensification and to encourage production practices that are kinder, more just, and less toxic. Whether through expanding technical support for sustainable transitions, environmental regulations that force ecologically sound innovations, or a complete overhaul of farm subsidy programs, there are other roads to take. Only by taking those roads will something like the practice of organic agriculture truly enter the mainstream.

References

ASFMRA. (2012). *Trends in Agricultural Land and Lease Values. California Chapter of the American Society of Farm Managers and Rural Appraisers.* Available at: www.calasfmra.com/db_trends/2012%20Trends.pdf. Accessed 14 May 2017.

Buck, D., Getz, C. and Guthman, J. (1997). From Farm to Table: The Organic Vegetable Commodity Chain of Northern California. *Sociologia Ruralis*, 37 (1), 3–20. doi:10.1111/1467-9523.00033.

CCOF. (2016). *Get the Numbers on Organic.* Available at: www.ccof.org/sites/default/files/Statistics%202016.pdf. Accessed 14 May 2017.

Constance, D. H., Choi, J. Y. and Holly, L.-H.-G. (2008). Conventionalization, Bifurcation and Quality of Life: Certified and Non-Certified Farmers in Texas. *Southern Rural Sociology*, 23 (1), 208–234.

DuPuis, E. M. and Gillon, S. (2009). Alternative Modes of Governance: Organic as Civic Engagement. *Agriculture and Human Values*, 26, 43–56. doi:10.1007/s10460-008-9180-7.

Greene, C., Dimitri, C., Lin, B.-H., McBride, W., Oberholtzer, L. and Smith, T. (2009). *Emerging Issues in the US Organic Industry.* EIB-55. US Department of Agriculture, Economic Research Service.

Guthman, J. (2004). The Trouble with 'Organic Lite' in California: A Rejoinder to the 'Conventionalization' Debate. *Sociologia Ruralis*, 44 (3), 301–316. doi:10.1111/j.1467-9523.2004.00277.

Guthman, J. (2014). *Agrarian Dreams: The Paradox of Organic Farming in California.* Berkeley, CA: University of California Press.

Hartman Group. (2007). *Sustainability: What's Green Now?* Available at: www.hartman-group.com/hartbeat/sustainability-what-green-now. Accessed 14 May 2017.

Howard, P. H. (2009). Consolidation in the North American Food Processing Sector, 1997–2007. *International Journal of the Sociology of Agriculture and Food*, 16 (1), 13–30.

Jaffee, D. and Howard, P. (2010). Corporate Cooptation of Organic and Fair Trade Standards. *Agriculture and Human Values*, 27, 387–399. doi:10.1007/s10460-009-9231-8.

Klonsky, K. (2010). A Look at California's Organic Agriculture Production. *ARE Update*, 14 (2), 8–11.

Klonsky, K. and Richter, K. (2005). *Statistical Review of California's Organic Agriculture, 1998–2003.* Davis, CA: Agricultural Issues Center, University of California at Davis.

Klonsky, K. and Richter, K. (2007). *Statistical Review of California's Organic Agriculture, 2000–2005.* Davis, CA: Agricultural Issues Center, University of California at Davis.

Klonsky, K. and Richter, K. (2011). *Statistical Review of California's Organic Agriculture, 2005–2009.* Davis, CA: Agricultural Issues Center, University of California at Davis.

Lockie, S. and Halpin, D. (2005). The 'Conventionalisation' Thesis Reconsidered: Structural and Ideological Transformation of Australian Organic Agriculture. *Sociologia Ruralis*, 45 (4), 284–307. doi:10.1111/j.1467-9523.2005.00306.x.

OTA. (2016). *US Organic: State of the Industry.* Available at: https://ota.com/sites/default/files/indexed_files/OTA_StateofIndustry_2016.pdf. Accessed 14 May 2017.

Reti, I., Rabkin, S. and Farmer, E. (2011). *Cultivating a Movement: An Oral History of Organic Farming and Sustainable Agriculture on California's Central Coast.* Santa Cruz, CA: University Library.

Rosin, C. and Campbell, H. (2009). Beyond Bifurcation: Examining the Conventions of Organic Agriculture in New Zealand. *Journal of Rural Studies*, 25 (1), 35–47. doi:10.1016/j.jrurstud.2008.05.002.

Rosset, P. M. and Altieri, M. (1997). Agroecology versus Input Substitution: A Fundamental Contradiction of Sustainable Agriculture. *Society and Natural Resources*, 10 (3), 283–295. doi:10.1080/08941929709381027.

Sierra, L., Klonsky, K., Strochlic, R., Brodt, S. and Molinar, R. (2008). *Factors Associated with Deregistration among Organic Farmers in California.* Davis, CA: California Institute for Rural Studies. Available at: www.cirsinc.org/publications/category/9-food-systems. Accessed 14 May 2017.

USDA ERS. (2013). *Table 2. US Certified Organic Farmland Acreage, Livestock Numbers, and Farm Operations.* Available at: www.ers.usda.gov/data-products/organic-production/. Accessed 14 May 2017.

USDA ERS. (2017). *Organic Market Overview.* Available at: www.ers.usda.gov/topics/ natural-resources-environment/organic-agriculture/organic-market-overview/. Accessed 5 December 2017.

USDA NASS. (2016). *2015 Certified Organic Survey.* Available at: http://usda.mannlib. cornell.edu/usda/nass/OrganicProduction//2010s/2016/OrganicProduction-09-15-2016. pdf. Accessed 14 May 2017.

2 Mainstreaming New Nordic Cuisine?

Alternative food politics and the problems of scale jumping and scale bending

Anders Riel Müller and Jonatan Leer

New Nordic Cuisine (NNC) has put Scandinavia on the culinary map. Before the 2000s, Scandinavia was a black spot on the atlas of global gastronomy, but the region has since become a site of pilgrimage for foodies from around the world keen to experience a locavore, vegetable-focused Nordic cuisine with an emphasis on place-based, sustainable production. It has also gained attention at the local political level and has sparked a renewed interest in food politics in the region. But how much has NNC really changed Nordic food practices?

If we were to believe the media coverage of NNC in the past decade, we might think that NNC is exemplary of an alternative food movement that has achieved significant 'mainstream' success in both the food production and social milieus (Goulding, 2013). Such notions have also been perpetuated by some researchers (e.g., Hermansen, 2012). This chapter investigates the extent to which it can be argued that such mainstreaming effects have indeed occurred in the Danish context. By 'mainstreaming', we mean the social processes through which alternative food practices become broadly accepted among producers and consumers through various formal and informal efforts. Signs of mainstreaming are visible in production and consumption statistics. Based on analysis of media texts, cookbooks, scientific literature, production data from Statistics Denmark, and consumer studies surveys, we argue that New Nordic Cuisine has been extremely successful in becoming mainstream in the restaurant scene, but that it has proven a more difficult task to popularise the movement's values and practices in the realms of food production and home cooking, particularly beyond the well-educated urban middle class. As such, we argue that the successful branding of NNC in national and international fine dining should not be read as a more general mainstreaming of NNC in terms of what is produced and eaten on an everyday basis in Denmark. Based on this analysis, we argue that the case of New Nordic Cuisine illustrates the challenges involved in mainstreaming alternative food movements that emerge from gastronomy, and show that food trends that are successful in the fine dining restaurant sector may be difficult to translate to everyday food production and consumption.

This chapter draws on the analytic concept of the 'politics of scale' from critical human geography and, specifically, on the ideas of scale jumping and scale bending (Purcell and Brown, 2005; Smith, 1992, 1996, 2004; Swyngedow,

2004). We are concerned with identifying the mainstreaming strategies associated with NNC and their effects across various scales of the agri-food sector. The chapter distinguishes three scales at which NNC mainstreaming initiatives have been targeted: the Danish fine dining restaurant scene (New Nordic Cuisine); agri-food production in Denmark through the New Nordic Food Project (NNF); and everyday home cooking and consumption in Danish households through the development of the New Nordic Diet (NND). On a theoretical level, we argue that a scalar perspective offers a fruitful way of articulating different levels of mainstreaming. This perspective helps us to understand how different scales are structured by different logics, power relations, ideals, and economic agendas, as well as how these different scalar strategies intersect and affect—or fail to affect—different scales.

New Nordic Cuisine

NNC is closely associated with the restaurant NOMA in Copenhagen, which opened in 2003. The owner, Danish food entrepreneur and TV chef Claus Meyer, and head chef, René Redzepi, developed a menu focused exclusively on Nordic ingredients. The year after its opening, the restaurant hosted a symposium with Scandinavian chefs which resulted in a Manifesto outlining ten principles and goals for a New Nordic Cuisine (Nordic Council of Ministers, 2013). The first goal was to create a cuisine that 'express[ed] the purity, freshness, simplicity and ethics associated with the region'. Others included the creation of a cuisine reflecting the changes in seasons and the use of ingredients 'whose character-istics are particularly excellent in a Nordic climate'. Overall, the Manifesto's aim was to (re)discover the Nordic terroir and to rethink Nordic food culture, while also living up to 'modern knowledge of health', and meeting ethical standards of animal welfare and 'sound production' (Nordic Council of Ministers, 2013).

From the beginning, Claus Meyer was a driving force behind NNC and the attempts to mainstream it. He had a two-phase vision for NNC. Phase one aimed to define and refine New Nordic Cuisine in relation to the elite restaurant kitchen and high-end gastronomy. The mission in phase two was to democratise the concept (Skårup, 2013, pp. 50–51), promoting a transformation of food production through the New Nordic Food program (NNF), and rendering NNC accessible to the broader public through the New Nordic Diet (NND). We understand these two phases as different attempts at scalar mainstreaming. In phase one, the scale is fine dining, and the goal is to gain recognition from the national and international culinary elite. In phase two, the goal was to popularise NNC ideology to the masses, and this phase operated on two distinct scales, namely production and consumption. So, the goal of phase one was connected to a relatively limited scale compared to the two broader scales of phase two. However, despite the limited size of phase one's restaurant scale, it gained significant attention in media and public debate, not least because of its close connection to food celebrities (Johnston and Goodman, 2015; Leer and Povlsen, 2016). This chapter considers whether the acceptance of NNC among the culinary elite and the media (Meyer's phase one) also reflects a broader mainstreaming of NNC at other scales, including production and consumption (Meyer's phase two).

Claus Meyer openly declared that the aim of NNC was to challenge the dominance of Mediterranean cuisine—notably French and Italian—in the Nordic countries. Products such as olive oil and basil were banned, while NOMA was declared a *foie gras*-free zone. NOMA, more than any other restaurant, closely followed the Manifesto and became the flagship of the movement, although other restaurants also followed the NNC ideology more or less explicitly (Leer, 2016). NNC was the Nordic region's first restaurant industry initiative to gain international recognition, not least due to Meyer's effective branding strategy using the positive associations of the Nordic. Nordic branding had been used successfully in architecture, design and politics, but gastronomically had been an 'empty label': 'the Danish food brand was polluted... when you say Nordic food... [it was a] brand that was free, open space [allowing us to] define what it is' (Meyer cited in Byrkjeflot, Pedersen and Svejenova, 2013, p. 45). Capitalising on the movement's momentum, the Nordic Council of Ministers responded with the New Nordic Food program (2006–), which so far has received more than 6 million USD in government funding (Nordic Council of Ministers, 2017).

With the international success of New Nordic restaurants, and in the slipstream of NOMA being named the best restaurant in 2010, 2011, 2012 and 2014 by the World's 50 Best Restaurants Academy, more funding followed from public and private actors. However, while NNC initially worked across various countries in Scandinavia, subsequent culinary projects inspired by NNC have had a more national focus (Neuman and Leer, 2017). Initiatives included the 'Sweden, the New Culinary Nation' campaign, which aimed to develop the food and restaurant sectors at the scale of the Swedish nation state (Neuman, 2017), and the Danish research and development project 'Optimal well-being, development and health for Danish children through a healthy New Nordic Diet' (OPUS), which received 15 million USD from a private foundation to develop, test and promote the benefits of the New Nordic Diet in Denmark (Mithril et al., 2012). Given NNC's Danish origins, and the national focus of most subsequent NNC-inspired culinary projects, this article will focus on activities in the Danish context.

New Nordic Cuisine and the politics of scale

To analyse the successes and the failures of the mainstreaming of NNC in Denmark, we are inspired by the concept of 'politics of scale' from human geography (McMaster and Sheppard, 2004; Purcell and Brown, 2005; Smith, 1992; Swyngedow, 2004). In human geography, the concept of scale is used to understand the production of spatial categories, such as the individual, the family, the local, the regional, the national, and the global. We draw here on the strand of scale theory that regards the formation of scales and their ordering as socially constructed. This means that scales' extent, characteristics and functions cannot be assumed *a priori*, but must be understood as produced, reproduced and contested through social and political struggles (Agnew, 1994; Purcell and Brown, 2005;

Swyngedow, 2004). Furthermore, scalar formations cannot be reduced to economic and social relations of production: struggles over ideology and meaning are important elements in understanding scale formation (Marston, 2004).

Actors at different scales engage in inter-scalar struggles for domination and hegemony. For example, within agri-food studies, research suggests variations in whether the construction of national cuisines has become dominant *vis-à-vis*, say, local or regional cuisines. South Korea represents an example of conscious government efforts to construct a national cuisine through appropriation, subordination and erosion of regional differences (Cwiertka, 2012; Kendall, 2011; Nelson, 2000). In other cases, such as Italy, regional cuisines still play a strong role in national culinary practices (Counihan, 2014, p. 63). Such outcomes are contingent upon the social struggles in which producers, consumers and politicians seek to define what constitutes a unified cuisine, as well as its ordering in relation to other cuisines.

We consider the ambition to mainstream NNC to be an attempt by a group of actors to reshape and reorder the existing scale formations and scale configurations of the Danish agri-food system by challenging dominant notions of what constitutes good food, good ingredients, how food should be produced, how it should be cooked, and how it should be consumed. Mainstreaming strategies have focused particularly on three scales across two phases: fine dining (phase one), and food production and home consumption/retail (phase two). Therefore, these are also the aspects we pay attention to in this chapter.

We examine the scalar strategies employed by proponents of NNC in their attempts to transform existing intra- and inter-scalar configurations and orders. NNC emerged, and established itself as a hegemonic force, at the fine dining scale. Actors from this scale have engaged in spatial expansion of NNC into other sub-scales through *scale jumping*. Scale jumping describes the strategies social actors use to take their concerns beyond the scale at which they normally operate in order to further their political agendas beyond this scale (Smith, 1992, 1996). The second scalar strategy that we are interested in is *scale bending*: that is, challenges to entrenched assumptions about what kinds of activities fit properly within each scale (Smith, 2004). By focusing on scalar politics, and the strategies of scale jumping and scale bending, we wish to shed light on the successes and failures of mainstreaming NNC from its conception as a Manifesto written by a small group of chefs and food entrepreneurs to gaining international culinary recognition and subsequent attempts to use this recognition to transform production and consumption of food in Denmark.

In our analysis, we have chosen to focus on a representative case for each scale jump. NOMA is the case we have chosen to represent the mainstreaming of NNC at the fine dining scale; we analyse this through newspaper articles in Danish and international media, cookbooks and overview works on the development of the Danish restaurant sector and NNC. We show how NNC successfully bent the fine dining restaurant scale's dominant understanding of 'good taste', but also how it provoked counter-reactions to NNC. The New Nordic Food program (NNF), funded by the Nordic Council of Ministers, is the case through which we examine the strategy to mainstream NNC in relation to food production. To do this, we draw on strategy papers, on reports examining the reception of NNC among food producers, and on statistical data on agri-food production in Denmark. Finally, the OPUS project and its New Nordic Diet (NND) will serve as the example of mainstreaming NNC in relation to everyday home cooking and consumption. This will be analysed using OPUS research results, media texts, market surveys of consumer behaviour, and statistical data on retail sales. Through analysis of these cases, we highlight the varied politics, logics and struggles encountered in each as they attempt to jump and bend scales.

New Nordic: from marginal to mainstream to passé on the restaurant scene

NOMA was successful in launching the NNC as a novel approach to Scandinavian food, albeit one that drew upon techniques from the molecular gastronomy of Ferran Adrià (de Solier, 2010) and capitalised on the interest in local food that was coming to predominate in the international restaurant scene at around the same time (Milne, 2013). Many Copenhagen chefs were initially sceptical about NOMA, and ridiculed the notion of a fine dining restaurant without French or Italian produce, as made clear in Redzepi's speech at the San Pellegrino Awards in 2009: 'They called us the stinking whale. They asked us if we had braised whale's penis on the menu' (cited in Rayner, 2009). After its international success, many chefs that were initially critical began to follow the NNC trend, and to adopt many of NOMA's techniques and aesthetic ideals (Leer, 2016). NNC became the new ideal for the culinary avant-garde on the Copenhagen fine dining scene (Troelsø, 2015, p. 106). From a scalar perspective, this could be understood as a kind of scale jumping, in which NOMA's success is closely related to its capacity to transcend the scale of the local restaurant scene (and its scepticism) and attract international recognition and acclaim. It was largely through this international recognition that NOMA and NNC gained legitimacy on the Danish restaurant scene.

This scale jump changed the ideals of fine dining in Copenhagen. According to Troelsø (2015) and his history of Danish restaurants in the 2000s, NNC was dominant from 2007 to 2012. 2007 marked the year of NOMA's international success, while the first 'discount' NNC restaurants opened in Copenhagen in 2012. The restaurant chain Cofoco had, since the early 2000s, operated a series of restaurants featuring 'gourmet food to the people', inspired by Mediterranean and French cuisines. In 2012, Cofoco launched a new restaurant, Höst, which offered a New Nordic menu for less than 50 USD per person for a four-course meal. In addition, Meyer, who, after disagreements with Redzepi, was no longer involved with NOMA (Troelsø, 2015, p. 120), was one of the people behind the restaurant RADIO, which served a four-course menu following NNC principles for 55 USD (Troelsø, 2015, p. 106). In comparison, the NOMA menu at that time was 240 USD for a 20-course tasting menu. This mainstreaming of NNC at the 'lower end' of the restaurant sector also led to a kind of fatigue with the phenomenon. For instance, the Danish business newspaper *BØRSEN* declared that it would celebrate the 10th anniversary of NOMA with an NNC-free period in their restaurant review section, and would instead celebrate non-NNC gastronomy for 80 days (Troelsø, 2013).

It also became 'cool' for new chefs to distance themselves from NNC (Leer, 2016). One of the most prominent examples of this new generation of chefs was Christian Puglisi who, after a couple of years as sous-chef at NOMA, started his own restaurant RELÆ. In 2014, he published his cookbook *RELÆ: A Book of Ideas*, in which he clearly disassociated his approach to cooking from NNC:

> I was born Italian, my mother is Norwegian, and I have lived in Italy, Denmark, Spain and France. I am a child of a globalised world, and anyone who draws up national borders and geographical restrictions on people—or vegetables—always provoked me.
>
> (Puglisi, 2014, p. 34)

At the same time, the case of Puglisi could also work to illustrate the ambivalence of this new generation, because although he sought to distance himself from NNC, Puglisi also reproduced many of its ideas, notably the strong focus on vegetables, locavorism, previously unappreciated cuts of meat (such as pork cheek and lamb neck), and 'sound production' of plant and animal products. As a result, Puglisi's project offers a compelling argument for the mainstreaming of NNC in the restaurant sector. It is an example of how a new generation of chefs both distanced themselves from NNC and held on to central elements of the movement.

We can also see evidence of the mainstreaming of NNC in the rise in the number of Michelin-starred restaurants in Denmark since NOMA's opening. The increase from eleven Michelin-starred restaurants in 2003 (Iwersen, 2004) to 29 in 2017 is often attributed to the so-called 'NOMA effect' (Mølbak, 2015), through which international recognition of NOMA and NNC led to a boom in the restaurant business in Denmark. The rise in the number of Michelin stars indicates that there has indeed been a NOMA effect, but in 2017 only a handful of the 24 starred restaurants describe their style as Nordic. The NOMA effect does not necessarily mean that all these new restaurants follow NNC taste or ideology.

In summary, NNC was initially ridiculed, but its bending of the traditional hegemonic taste ideals of French and Mediterranean cuisine rapidly became mainstream in the Danish restaurant sector. This was achieved primarily through the international recognition and media attention given to NOMA. Redzepi often communicated through international, rather than national, media. In 2015, for instance, it was the *New York Times* and not the Danish media that broke the news that NOMA would close in 2016 and reopen in a new form in 2018 (Mølbak, 2015). But with the mainstreaming of NNC in the restaurant sector, notably the introduction of 'discount' NNC restaurants, the dominance of the NNC was also challenged by new restaurateurs who distanced themselves from the movement. It could be argued that some of the central ideas of NNC were continued—notably the interest in local food, which has become more mainstream than NNC at this scale. However, it appears that in phase one, NNC has reshaped the scale of fine dining and has expanded the sector without mainstreaming a dogmatic NNC taste ideal. This also highlights the dynamic nature of the restaurant scale, where competition constantly challenges hegemonic ideals and new trends rapidly replace each other. NNC as a dominant factor in the Danish fine dining scene was quickly eclipsed and replaced by other concepts that borrowed from NNC, but also distanced themselves from it.

Mainstreaming production

New Nordic Cuisine's attempts at transferring its successes at the fine dining scale to the production scale are perhaps the least studied part of the NNC movement. This is surprising given that the way food is produced in Denmark has been a central point of criticism of NNC. For many proponents of NNC, a major aim of the movement has been to seek alternatives to the anonymous food products derived from industrialised agriculture and food processing (Astrup and Meyer, 2002; Nordic Council of Ministers, 2015). Thus, for NNC to establish itself as more than a culinary curiosity, a change to how food is produced was considered necessary in phase two. The aim was to transform food production by encouraging producers to embrace the values of seasonality, regionality, terroir, animal welfare, and 'sound production methods', as stated in the New Nordic Manifesto. In this section, we examine the New Nordic Food (NNF) project, developed by the Nordic Council of Ministers, in order to consider the effects of NNC on agri-food production in Denmark.

In addition to promoting the production values reflected in the Manifesto, the figure of the social entrepreneur was crucial to the NNF program's goal to 'initiate, facilitate and coordinate activities grounded in the New Nordic Food Manifesto from 2004' (Nordic Council of Ministers, 2017). This was very much in line with NNC's reliance on celebrity chefs at the fine dining scale. As the Nordic Council of Ministers (2015, p. 8) put it: 'The pop stars are the social entrepreneurs, the agents of change, and they need the limelight to succeed'. A social entrepreneur is a private individual who, through values-based indignation at the current state of affairs, seeks to change society through private, market-based initiatives (Dey, 2011; Dey and Steyaert, 2012). The role of public institutions such as the Nordic Council of Ministers was not to promote the principles of the Manifesto through regulation and legislation. Instead, they set out to support and encourage the initiatives of individual social change agents (Nordic Council of Ministers, 2015, p. 9; Sørensen and Müller, 2015).

The figure of the social entrepreneur, and the emphasis on private initiatives as catalysts for social change, is central to the scale jumping attempt of the NNF program. The Nordic Council of Ministers focused on developing innovative entrepreneurial networks in agri-food production (Nordic Council of Ministers, 2015, p. 9). This involved a two-step process in which the potential agents of social change needed to first agree to, or align themselves with, the values and principles set forth in the Manifesto, including locally-based, seasonal and 'traditional' production methods, with a focus on terroir, simplicity, freshness, purity and ethics (Strand and Grunert, 2010, p. 6). The second step was to encourage and facilitate entrepreneurs to put these values and principles into practice.

This strategy of promoting a set of values and production principles is, from our perspective, a scale bending strategy in which the social entrepreneur becomes the vehicle for transforming agri-food production from industrial mass market production to highly differentiated, seasonal, small batch production. The public sector operates as a facilitator for such scale bending to take place but avoids any direct intervention through the setting of rules, regulations or legislation. In fact, suggestions for a common Nordic label or certification for New Nordic Foods have been strongly opposed by those behind the New Nordic Manifesto, who argue that such initiatives would stifle the creativity and demo-cratic debate surrounding what constitutes New Nordic Food (Kolle, Mørk and Grunert, 2014, p. 27). Instead, the goal was to convince existing producers about the good qualities of NNF values and principles, which was expected to lead, in turn, to behavioural change and innovation.

Before further analysing NNF's scale bending strategy, it is necessary to briefly outline the extent, composition, and characteristics of the Danish agri-food sector. Agri-food production in Denmark is predominantly oriented towards exports of standardised plant and animal products. According to the Danish Agriculture and Food Council, three quarters of agri-food production is destined for export markets, and Danish agri-food exports account for approximately 25% of the total amount of Danish exports of goods (Landbrug og Fødevarer, 2016). Agri-food exports are characterised by a significant number of so-called 'high value' products, especially within the pork, poultry and dairy industries. The characteristics that make Danish-produced agri-food products high value in the world market include food safety, traceability and supply stability—characteristics that have more to do with quality control production and logistics processes than with NNC values such as diversified production or terroir. Export-focused production of high value, but relatively undifferentiated, agri-food products is a major structuring force in the Danish agri-food sector, resulting in consolidation of the industry into large-scale farms and food processing oligopolies (Landbrug og Fødevarer, 2016).

In 2010, the Nordic Council of Ministers commissioned a study to survey food producers' perceptions of NNC values. Thirty-eight large- and small-scale food producers from across the Nordic region were interviewed about the values, principles and economic potential of NNC (Strand and Grunert, 2010). Of the 19 small-scale producers, 18 expressed agreement with the values and practices promoted by the Manifesto (Strand and Grunert, 2010, p. 22). Among the large-scale food producers interviewed, which included the largest dairy producer and largest meat packing company in Denmark, there was a general sympathy with the values and principles of NNC and NNF, but producers remained sceptical as to whether such ideals were realistic to implement. For example, they did not regard a food system based on the local, seasonal and craft-based production envisioned by the Manifesto as compatible with automated large-scale production methods that ensure uniformity and consistency of quality.

Wider adoption of NNC principles would require a major restructuring of production systems, and a reorientation away from the export markets that are currently the foundation of the Danish agri-food sector. Large food producers maintained that any such restructuring would need to guarantee that new crops and raw materials would continue to be available with the same type of precision delivery the producers are used to today. Importantly, large-scale producers did not see any added economic gains that could justify the significant investments in retooling production processes and the higher prices that such changes would necessitate. Instead, many producers were convinced that domestic consumers would simply turn to cheaper imported products (Strand and Grunert, 2010, pp. 30–33). Small producers in the study also expressed concern about the economic feasibility of operating with only Nordic raw materials, given the limited supplies during winter, general supply reliability, and the lack of variety (Strand and Grunert, 2010, pp. 22–29). A follow-up study conducted in 2014 reaffirmed the perception of NNF as niche production. The report concluded that NNC was still seen as a concept from the world of gastronomy—a world removed from everyday life (Kolle, Mørk and Grunder, 2014, p. 28)—the implications of which we will discuss in further detail later in this chapter.

Despite the reluctant reception among food producers expressed in the studies above, the Nordic Council of Ministers was not afraid to boast of its achievements. For example, this quote from the NNF 10-year evaluation report left no room to question the success of NNF: 'If innovation is measured in value created, there is no doubt that New Nordic Food has been a success, but it is impossible to provide numbers' (Nordic Council of Ministers, 2015, p. 9). Statements such as these show the shaky ground on which many proponents' claims that NNC has been mainstreamed are founded. If mainstreaming of NNC outside the restaurant scale has indeed occurred, evidence should be visible in production statistics.

However, rather than evidence of diversified production, data from Statistics Denmark indicate a trend towards concentration and consolidation of agriculture and food processing. In 2016, the number of full-time farmers fell to fewer than 10,000 for the first time in history (Iversen, 2017). Between 2006 and 2016, the number of farms declined by 22% to approximately 36,600 farms, while large farms over 200 hectares increased by over 40% over the same period (Statistics Denmark, 2017). In food processing, only eight slaughterhouses are left in the pork sector, and two companies control more than 95% of all slaughtering. The poultry sector is dominated almost entirely by two companies. The beef and dairy sectors show less oligopolistic tendencies, but they too have experienced processes of consolidation rather than diversification (Landbrug og Fødevarer, 2016).

Organic agriculture experienced gradual growth in terms of farm area over the same period, but the number of organic farms declined overall since the early 2000s, with the exception of a small increase in 2015 (Statistics Denmark, 2017). However, organic agriculture is not a reliable indicator of the impact of NNF for two reasons: firstly, NNC and NNF do not specifically advocate organic agriculture, but rather 'sound production practices', a much looser term; and secondly, the increase in organic farm area is a trend that started in the mid-1990s and, as such, precedes NNC.

Statistical data presented by Kolle, Mørk and Grunert (2014) also indicated that the values and production methods proposed in the Manifesto had not been mainstreamed in food production. The continued perception of NNC among food producers as niche production is perhaps not surprising given the significant structural changes required for the agri-food system to adopt NNC values and principles. Mainstream Danish agriculture and food processing is structured largely by the logic of global competitiveness, which limits the potential for mainstreaming NNC values and practices. This aspect receives virtually no attention in the New Nordic Food program, which shies away from investigating the feasibility of conventional political interventions such as regulation and legislation in promoting an NNF agenda. While NNC is a critique of the industrialised agri-food system, in which standardisation and consistency of quality override regionality, seasonality and sustainable production methods, it has remained remarkably quiet on issues such as agri-food exports, organic production, land reform, health and safety standards, and access to affordable credit for small producers.

It is perhaps useful to compare NNC's values-based and entrepreneurial approach to reforming the agri-food system to that of the Danish peasant association Free Farmers. Many of the association's visions for the future of the agri-food system align closely with NNC values and principles, yet their proposed pathway to reach this vision is radically different from NNC. Free Farmers argues that large-scale food producers possess disproportionate political power, leading to policies that almost exclusively benefit large-scale industrial agriculture (Frie Bønder – Levende Land, 2009). To promote localised small-scale production, the association calls for political land reform measures, better access to credit for small-scale producers, relaxed health and safety requirements, and targeted research and extension services. Free Farmers thus engages in an altogether different kind of scale politics, in which social change is envisioned to emerge from national legislation and regulation.

Free Farmers' political program points to how NNF fails to address—or avoids addressing—the structural biases and constraints of the agri-food sector that hinder mainstreaming of the kind of food production that it sets out to promote. NNF does not address the structural, economic and political constraints that prevent producers interested in adopting practices in line with NNC values from entering the market at all. This is significant because it highlights the limitations of a strategy of relying almost exclusively on values-based social entrepreneurship to bend the scale of agri-food production. In the realm of production, the values of NNC are perceived as incompatible with the logics of a predominantly export-oriented agri-food sector, in which economies of scale and standardisation are central to global competitiveness. Compared to the fine dining scale, agri-food production is entirely different in terms of its economic size, characteristics and functions, and this impacts on the extent to which scale jumping and scale bending can occur at this scale.

Everyday home cooking and consumption

The third and final attempt at scale jumping to consider occurred in relation to home cooking and consumption. In this section, we discuss the development of the New Nordic Diet (NND) as an everyday, consumer-friendly version of NNC. In 2009, the OPUS research and development project based at Copenhagen University received a grant of approximately 15 million USD from philanthropic organisation Nordea-fonden. The OPUS project aimed to reform school lunches and home cooking habits among the general population by developing a New Nordic Diet (NND) based on NNC values and principles. For Claus Meyer and nutrition scientist Arne Astrup, the leaders of the OPUS project, reforming everyday diets was not uncharted territory. In 2002 they had co-authored a cookbook on low-fat cooking to reform what they argued was an unhealthily fatty Danish diet based on non-exportable by-products from the country's pork and dairy industries (Astrup and Meyer, 2002). This time they grounded their new intervention in the values and principles of the NNC Manifesto. OPUS was to be the vanguard of bending the scale of everyday cooking in order to encourage consumers to eat healthy, seasonally grown food, raised and processed in the Nordic region.

The OPUS project had a two-fold purpose: to investigate the health benefits of a diet based on NNC principles; and to generate broader acceptance of this new diet. At a 2009 symposium, OPUS scientists, chefs, industry representatives, and nutrition experts identified desirable 'Nordic and healthy' food ingredients that would be central to a New Nordic Diet (Meyer et al., 2010). The resulting list of ingredients included vegetables, tubers, fruits, pulses, grains, nuts, meats, fish and seafood that did well in the Nordic region and expressed a strong Nordic identity.[1] Recipes were developed based on this initial report. The stated intention was to create meals that were tasty, healthy and convenient. The NND meals were then tested in controlled experiments with a sample of families, and in meal programmes at nine schools.

As part of the experiment, OPUS conducted studies on the social accept-ability of the NND among the sample families. These studies' findings are central to understanding the limits of the scale bending strategy employed. The social acceptability studies revealed that although many families found the values of the New Nordic Diet appealing, there were several impediments to its widespread adoption. For example, many families felt that NND meals were too time-consuming to prepare (Micheelsen et al., 2014; Micheelsen, Holm and O'Doherty Jensen, 2013). Thus, a major impediment to the adoption of NND was the time, or willingness to prioritise time, for procuring ingredients and preparing meals. Despite claims by the designers of NND that they had considered convenience and ease, this was not the dominant perception among end users. Another factor limiting the acceptance of NND was the accessibility of NND ingredients and flavours. Most participants in the OPUS project found the meals to be tasty, especially those with meat, but, according to Micheelsen (2013), the limited availability of some ingredients in mainstream supermarkets was a major inconvenience. Having to shop at several grocery stores to find ingredients added to the time that participants were required to spend preparing daily meals (Micheelsen, 2013). Moreover, the meal format did not always correspond to participants' conceptions of a 'proper' meal, as dishes often lacked central components of a traditional Danish meal, such as meat and gravy. Consequently, some participants deviated from the meal plan and added 'missing' components to the recipe (Micheelsen, 2013). Micheelsen concluded that habit and familiarity were major structuring forces in what was served at the dining table. This echoed previous studies, which had concluded that Danish meal habits, especially the requirement of meat and gravy, are difficult to change (e.g., Groth et al., 2009; O'Doherty Jensen, 2009).

According to Lotte Holm, the sociologist who led the social acceptability study, people's unfamiliarity with NND meals was a key flaw in the OPUS project's design (Hoffmann, 2013). She argued that the attempt to completely reinvent the everyday diet was a major factor in the low acceptance of the NND. A more suitable strategy, she suggested, would have been to start out by studying the currently dominant food habits and modifying these incrementally. This was in line with other findings on limitations to the acceptance of NND, which also concluded that consumers would likely find the diet too strict because it did not allow them, for example, to indulge in 'foreign' cuisines (Micheelsen, 2013, p. 98). The rigidity of the NND was found to be a major obstacle to broader acceptance among consumers.

To spread the message of NND outside the OPUS project, a cookbook titled *New Nordic Everyday Food* was published in 2011 in a partnership between the OPUS project, Meyer's House of Food, and Denmark's largest grocery chain, COOP (Meyer and Astrup, 2011). However, despite extensive promotion of NND, especially through COOP supermarkets, NND had no significant impact on grocery shopping habits. The head of market research at COOP Denmark concluded that no evidence of the impact of NNC could be found in the supermarket's sales statistics: 'There is no overall tendency, and even if we do sell a bit more celery [one of the vegetables celebrated by NNC] during the season, we don't know how the ingredients are being used at home in the kitchen' (cited in Pedersen, 2013).[2] The head of produce procurement at another retail chain, Føtex, had a similar view: 'To me, it [NNC/NND] is something that circulates mostly in cookbooks, restaurants, and TV shows rather than something that has made an impact on our customers' purchasing habits in our stores' (cited in Kolle, Mørk and Grunder, 2014, p. 26).[3] Consumer scepticism about the NND appears to stem from the perception that NNC remains a concept from gastronomy, detached from the everyday lives of consumers (Kolle, Mørk and Grunder, 2014, p. 22; Micheelsen, 2013).

Researchers have also attributed the limited success of NND to its elitist representation of food preparation and consumption. In an interview, Lotte Holm argued that NND meals were too radical a departure from everyday food habits: 'Here comes [the OPUS project] with a full regime of rules and recommendations, and asks [the consumer] to stay within some given culinary restrictions to live healthily. It is completely unrealistic that people can, and will, follow them' (cited in Hoffmann, 2013).[4] In the case of NND, science, gastronomy and culinary celebrities have claimed authority as to what a meal should be like based on abstract ideals of health and Nordic identity, rather than seeking to gradually modify existing dietary habits. Thus, there are tensions between the proclaimed ideal of NNC as an open concept (as expressed in phase one) and the very strict rules and recommendations in the OPUS NND guidelines (in phase two).

Whether NNC, and, by extension, NND, is an elitist project by urban middle-class foodies was debated heavily in Danish media (Holm, 2012; Müller, 2012; Søndergaard, 2012; Sylvest, 2013). One study of news coverage of NNC found that the most cited sources were predominantly celebrity chefs, gastronomic entrepreneurs or food producers; no 'ordinary' people were interviewed (Søndergaard, 2013). It concluded that the media focused almost exclusively on NNC as a trend and a luxury, as well as on the gastronomic accolades given to the Michelin-starred restaurants, rather than on the relevance of NNC to 'every-day' eating habits. As a result, media coverage was oriented primarily towards trendsetters and well-off consumers (Søndergaard, 2012, p. 83). Media coverage also tended to focus on celebrities, who were presented as highly successful career people managing an effective work-life balance. For instance, Sørensen and Müller (2015) argue that media coverage of Claus Meyer has tended to celebrate his ability to manage a busy career as a highly successful gastro-entrepreneur while still managing to serve elaborate homemade meals for his family. This, the authors argue, is an example of how media celebrates a neoliberal fantasy of the resourceful gastro-entrepreneur who, despite his extremely busy career heading a successful enterprise, can strike the perfect work-life balance—an unobtainable ideal for most people.

In the attempt to scale NNC from fine dining to home cooking, the advocates of NNC and NND seem to have failed to account for the different political dynamics of the home cooking scale. Chefs can bend the fine dining scale through avant-gardist experimentation that appeals to adventurous clients. Home cooking is governed by forces such as convenience, familiarity, and socio-economic class. As pointed out by DeVault (1991), class is a major determinant of people's interest in, and willingness to alter, food habits. Allocating extra time and exploring new foods are not just personal preferences but are also representative of class aspirations. Even though the stated intention was to develop a new cuisine through bottom-up processes and dialogue, the dominance of celebrity chefs and expert regimes of knowledge in shaping the development of NND meals resulted in time-consuming food preparation, unfamiliar meal formats, and perceptions of elitist patronage. Media representations of the people behind NNC as super-humans able to run highly successful companies while still preparing elaborate home-cooked meals for their families further contributed to the perception of NNC and NND as elitist conceptualisations imposed from above.

Conclusion

This chapter set out to analyse attempts at mainstreaming NNC in Denmark as a series of scalar strategies. Scale has proven very fruitful as a theoretical and analytical tool to analyse mainstreaming of alternative food movements. The scalar perspective allows us to see how and where an alternative food initiative like NNC can (and cannot) become mainstream, and to understand the distinct social, ideological and economic barriers at distinct scales. Through three case studies, we analysed the scale jumping and scale bending strategies used by NNC proponents to mainstream the NNC concept, and its values and principles. The first scalar strategy was exemplified by NOMA's attempt to jump scales to gain recognition for NNC. By crafting a fine dining experience that appealed to an international elite standard, NOMA sought to challenge the status quo. NOMA's experimentation with ingredients and techniques gained international recognition from both the *Michelin Guide* and the World's 50 Best Restaurants Academy. Such international acclaim elevated NOMA to the peak of the Danish fine dining scale. Through this scale jump, NOMA also changed the standards of fine dining in Denmark—a process we refer to as scale bending. NNC's standards for what ingredients to use and how to prepare and serve them challenged the decades-old domination of French and Italian cuisines. The success of NOMA led to significant changes at the Danish restaurant scale, first at the level of fine dining, but soon after by restaurants at many levels. The popularity of NNC, however, ultimately led some chefs to distance themselves from NNC in order to establish their own names in an industry in which novelty is a major competitive factor.

The attempt at jumping scale from fine dining to agri-food production was exemplified by the Nordic Council of Ministers' New Nordic Food initiative. NNF attempted to utilise the international and national attention resulting from the success of restaurants such as NOMA to bend the agri-food production scale. The scale bending strategy relied on a similar strategy to one that had worked at the fine dining scale: using individual celebrity change-makers and entrepreneurs. NNF sought to facilitate and encourage social entrepreneurship as the mechanism for change, rather than seeking to change legislation and regulation. However, the results are, statistically speaking, negligible. NNC-inspired agri-food production remains a niche for small-scale agri-food producers who already subscribe to similar values and principles. Large-scale agri-food producers regarded NNF production principles as incompatible with their industrialised and predominantly export-oriented practices. Furthermore, large-scale producers continued to doubt the economic viability of NNC. As such, the NNF attempt to jump scale from fine dining to agri-food production proved ineffective in altering agri-food production in Denmark.

The third scale jumping attempt was to mainstream NNC to the scale of home-cooking through the OPUS project; to achieve this, chefs and gastro-entrepreneurs formed alliances with the supermarket retail chain COOP and nutrition scientists. The OPUS project proposed new ingredients and meals based on NNC values and principles. Recipes were developed through collaboration between nutrition scientists, consultants and chefs. However, the findings of some OPUS researchers demonstrated that a great number of people felt that the unfamiliar ingredients and meal compositions, along with the extra time needed to buy groceries and cook, were major limitations to adoption of the NND. In this attempt to bend scale, NNC came to represent elitist values and preferences far removed from the food preferences and constraints of the general population.

Based on our analysis, we find that attempts to mainstream NNC across different scales have had mixed outcomes. While NNC has managed to make Copenhagen a hotspot at the national and international fine dining scales, it has had difficulties in jumping scales into mainstream agri-food production and home cooking. The reliance on scale bending strategies that worked at the fine dining scale failed to account for the very different social relations that dominate at these other scales. The values-based and voluntary approaches based on celebrity entrepreneurs as figureheads have not been able to convince agri-food producers or consumers to embrace NNC in large numbers, and, in some cases, have even been counter-productive by perpetuating the notion of NNC as reserved for the privileged few. As such, NNC's success has largely been a phenomenon restricted to fine dining and the media. Both agri-food producers and consumers have regarded NNC as economically unviable and elitist. Our analysis questions others' claims of a broader mainstreaming of NNC (e.g., Hermansen, 2012). As we have sought to demonstrate, this is clearly not the case at all scales, and these differences highlight the varied structural, ideological and economic logics that can limit the mainstreaming of even seemingly successful food movements.

Notes

1 For a critique of the idea of a Nordic identity, see Andreassen (2015).
2 Authors' translation.
3 Authors' translation.
4 Authors' translation.

References

Agnew, J. (1994). The Territorial Trap: The Geographical Assumptions of International Relations Theory. *Review of International Political Economy*, 1 (1), 53–80.

Andreassen, R. (2015). The Search for the White Nordic: Analysis of the Contemporary New Nordic Kitchen and Former Race Science. *Social Identities*, 20 (6), 438–451.

Astrup, A. and Meyer, C. (2002). *Spis igennem*. København: Politikens Forlag.

Byrkjeflot, H., Pedersen, J. S. and Svejenova, S. (2013). From Label to Practice: The Process of Creating New Nordic Cuisine. *Journal of Culinary Science & Technology*, 11 (1), 36–55.

Counihan, C. (2014). Women, Gender and Agency in Italian Food Activism. In Counihan, C. and Siniscalchi, V. (eds.), *Food Activism: Agency, Democracy and Economy*. New York: Bloomsbury.

Cwiertka, K. (2012). *Cuisine, Colonialism and Cold War: Food in Twentieth-Century Korea*. London: Reaktion Books.

de Solier, I. (2010). Liquid Nitrogen Pistachios: Molecular Gastronomy, elBulli and Foodies. *European Journal of Cultural Studies*, 13 (2), 155–170.

DeVault, M. L. (1991). *Feeding the Family*. Chicago: University of Chicago Press.

Dey, P. (2011). Social Entrepreneurship and the 'New Spirit of the Third Sector'. In *Fourth Research Colloquium on Social Entrepreneurship*, August (pp. 1–39), Durham, NC.

Dey, P. and Steyaert, C. (2012). Social Entrepreneurship: Critique and the Radical Enactment of the Social. *Social Enterprise Journal*, 8 (2), 90–107.

Frie Bønder – Levende Land (2009). *Fremtiden På Landet Erhvervspolitisk Program*. Denmark: Frie Bønder – Levende Land.

Goulding, M. (2013). Nomanomics: How One Restaurant Is Changing Denmark's Economy. *Time Magazine*. Available at: http://world.time.com/2013/02/14/nomanomics-how-one-res taurant-is-changing-denmarks-economy/ Accessed 30 August 2017.

Groth, M. V., Sørensen, M. R., Biltoft-Jensen, A., Matthiessen, J., Kørup, K. and Fagt, S. (2009). *Danskernes måltidsvaner, holdninger, motivation og barrierer for at spise sundt 1995-2008*. Søborg: DTU Fødevareinstituttet.

Hermansen, M. E. T. (2012). Creating Terroir. An Anthropological Perspective on New Nordic Cuisine as an Expression of Nordic Identity. *Anthropology of Food*, 7, 7249.

Hoffmann, T. (2013). Nedtur for millionprojekt: Vi gider ikke lave Ny Nordisk mad. Available at: http://videnskab.dk/kultur-samfund/nedtur-millionprojekt-vi-gider-ikke-lave-ny-nor disk-mad. Accessed 23 July 2017.

Holm, U. (2012). Eliten længes efter en præmoderne fortid. Available at: www.information. dk/kultur/2012/04/eliten-laenges-praemoderne-fortid. Accessed 23 July 2017.

Iversen, A. J. (2017). *Nu er der under 10.000 heltids-landbrug tilbage*. København: Land-brugsavisen. Available at: http://landbrugsavisen.dk/nu-er-der-under-10000-heltids-land brug-tilbage. Accessed 30 August 2017.

Iwersen, M. B. (2004). Michelinmandens magt. *Politiken*, March 19.

Johnston, J. and Goodman, M. K. (2015). Spectacular Foodscapes. *Food, Culture & Society*, 18 (2), 205–222.

Kendall, L. (2011). Introduction: Material Modernity, Consumable Tradition. In Kendall, L. (ed.), *Consuming Korea Tradition in Early and Late Modernity* (pp. 1–17). Honolulu: University of Hawai'i Press.

Kolle, S., Mørk, T., and Grunder, K. G. (2014). *Ny Nordisk Mad 10 År Efter*. Århus: DCA Nationalt center for fødevarer og jordbrug.

Landbrug og Fødevarer. (2016). *Fakta om erhvervet*. Copenhagen: Landbrug og Fødevarer.

Leer, J. (2016). The Rise and Fall of the New Nordic Cuisine. *Journal of Aesthetics & Culture*, 8 (1), 1–17.

Leer, J. and Povlsen, K. K. (2016). *Food and Media: Practices, Distinctions and Heterotopias*. London: Routledge.

McMaster, R. B. and Sheppard, E. (2004). Introduction: Scale and Geographic Inquiry. In Sheppard, H. and McMaster, R.B. (eds.), *Scale and Geographic Inquiry* (pp. 1–22). Oxford: Blackwell Publishing Ltd.

Marston, S. (2004). A Long Way from Home: Domesticating the Social Production of Scale. In Sheppard, H. and McMaster, R.B. (eds.), *Scale and Geographic Inquiry* (pp. 170–191). Oxford: Blackwell Publishing Ltd.

Meyer, C. and Astrup, A. (2011). *Ny Nordisk Hverdagsmad*. Copenhagen: FDB.

Meyer, C., Holt, M. K., Blaubert, E. and Mithril, C. (2010). *Grundlag for ny nordisk hverdagsmad*. København: Institut for Human Ernæring, Københavns Universitet.

Micheelsen, A. (2013). *The New Nordic Diet: A Sociological Study of the Acceptance and Appropriation of a Dietary Regime*. Copenhagen: University of Copenhagen.

Micheelsen, A., Havn, L., Poulsen, S. K., Larsen, T. M. and Holm, L. (2014). The Acceptability of the New Nordic Diet by Participants in a Controlled Six-Month Dietary Intervention. *Food Quality and Preference*, 36, 20–26.

Micheelsen, A., Holm, L. and O'Doherty Jensen, K. (2013). Consumer Acceptance of the New Nordic Diet. An Exploratory Study. *Appetite*, 70, 14–21.

Milne, R. (2013). Local-Global. In Jackson, P. (ed.), *Food Words* (pp. 120–124). London: Bloomsbury Academic.

Mithril, C., Dragsted, L.O., Meyer, C., Blauert, E., Holt, M.K. and Astrup, A. (2012). Guidelines for the New Nordic Diet. *Public Health Nutrition*, 15, 1941–1947.

Mølbak, M. (2015). *NOMA har ramt folket*. Available at: http://politiken.dk/mad/art5589292/Noma-har-ramt-folket. Accessed 20 August 2017.

Müller, A. R. (2012). *Der er alternativer til noma og lørdagskylling*. Available at: www.information.dk/debat/2012/09/alternativer-noma-loerdagskylling. www.information.dk/debat/2012/09/alternativer-noma-loerdagskylling. Accessed 23 July 2017.

Nelson, L. C. (2000). *Measured Excess: Status, Gender, and Consumer Nationalism in South Korea*. New York: Columbia University Press.

Neuman, N. (2017). An Imagined Culinary Community: Stories of Morality and Masculinity in Sweden–The New Culinary Nation. *Scandinavian Journal of Hospitality and Tourism*, 18 (2), 149–162.

Neuman, N. and Leer, J. (2017). Nordic Cuisine, but National Identities: Nordic Cuisines and the Gastronationalist Projects of Denmark and Sweden. *Anthropology of Food*, 13.

Nordic Council of Ministers. (2013). *The New Nordic Food Manifesto*. Available at: www.norden.org/en/theme/ny-nordisk-mad/the-new-nordic-food-manifesto. Accessed 12 March 2016.

Nordic Council of Ministers. (2015). *The Emergence of a New Nordic Food Culture*. Copenhagen: Nordic Council of Ministers. Available at: http://newnordicfood.org/filead min/webmasterfiles/Billeder/_NNF-report_web(1)_02.pdf. Accessed 30 August 2017.

Nordic Council of Ministers. (2017). *New Nordic Food Programme Page*. Available at: www.norden.org/en/theme/ny-nordisk-mad. Accessed 10 August 2017.

O'Doherty Jensen, K. (2009). Sociological Aspects of Meat in Meals – Cultural Impacts and Meal Patterns. In *Proceedings of the 55th International Congress of Meat Science and Technology*. Copenhagen. Available at: www.researchgate.net/publication/272884895_Sociological_Aspects_of_Meat_in_Meals_-_Cultural_Impacts_and_Meal_Patterns. Accessed 30 August 2017.

Pedersen, M. (2013). *Vi vil vide, hvor fødevaren kommer fra*. Available at: www.foodculture.dk/tema/foedevarer/2013/10-aar-med-nordisk-mad/vi-vil-vide-mere-om-vores-fodevarer. Accessed 20 July 2017.

Puglisi, C. (2014). *Relæ*. London: Ten Speed Press.

Purcell, M. and Brown, J. C. (2005). Against the Local Trap: Scale and the Study of Environment and Development. *Progress in Development Studies*, 5 (4), 279–297.

Rayner, J. (2009). *Why It's Cooler in the North*. Available at: www.theguardian.com/lifeandstyle/2009/may/24/noma-restaurant-copenhagen-jay-rayner. Accessed 2 August 2017.

Skårup, B. (2013). The New Nordic Diet and Danish Food Culture. In Lysaght, P. (ed.), *The Return of Traditional Food* (pp. 33–42). Lund: Lund University Studies.

Smith, N. (1992). Contours of a Spatialized Politics: Homeless of Geographical Vehicles and the Production Scale. *Social Text*, 33 (33), 54–81.

Smith, N. (1996). Spaces of Vulnerability. *Critique of Anthropology*, 16 (1), 63–77.

Smith, N. (2004). Scale Bending and the Fate of the National. In Sheppard, H. and McMaster, R.B. (eds.), *Scale and Geographic Inquiry* (pp. 192–212). Oxford: Blackwell Publishing Ltd.

Søndergaard, M. (2012). *Ny nordisk mad - for alle eller eliten?* Odense: Syddansk Universitet.

Søndergaard, M. (2013). *Lokal er det nye nordisk.* Available at: www.foodculture.dk/tema/foedevarer/2013/10-aar-med-nordisk-mad/lokal-er-det-nye-nordisk. Accessed 20 July 2017.

Sørensen, B. Æ. and Müller, A. R. (2015). Meyer som appetitvækkende gastrokapitalist. *Social Kritik*, 27 (144), 52–61.

Statistics Denmark. (2017). *Statistikbanken.* Available at: www.statistikbanken.dk/stat bank5a/default.asp?w=1536. Accessed 8 July 2017.

Strand, M. and Grunert, K. G. (2010). *Vurdering Af Den Økonomiske Betydning Af Ny Nordisk Mad.* Århus: Århus School of Business.

Swyngedow, E. (2004). Scaled Geographies: Nature, Place and the Politics of Scale. In Sheppard, E. and McMaster, R. B. (eds.), *Scale and Geographic Inquiry: Nature, Society, and Method* (pp. 129–152). Oxford: Blackwell Publishing Ltd..

Sylvest, C. M. (2013). *Nyt nordisk køkken: Elitær klappebamse eller folkelig succes?* Available at: www.foodculture.dk/tema/foedevarer/2013/10-aar-med-nordisk-mad/eli taer-klappebamse-eller-folkelig-succes. Accessed 23 July 2017.

Troelsø, O. (2013). *10 år med nynordisk ekstase – og hvad så nu.* Available at: https://pleasure.borsen.dk/gourmet/artikel/1/249373/10_aar_med_nynordisk_ekstase_-_og_h vad_saa_nu.html?hl=YToxOntpOjA7czo0OiJOaW1ijt9. Accessed 7 August 2017.

Troelsø, O. (2015). *Danmarks Gastronomiske Revolution.* København: Forlaget Lucullus.

3   When carrots become posh

Untangling the relationship between 'heritage' foods and social distinction

Abigail Wincott

Tensions within heritage food politics

In February 2015 the *Independent* reported that the demand for heritage vegetables was soaring: 'the ultimate antidote to tasteless, mass-produced fruit and veg forced in a vast greenhouse complex to fill supermarket shelves and the pockets of multinational corporations' (Johnston, 2015). The article was illustrated by a picture of 'one of the most popular dishes at London's Portland Restaurant [. . .] almost entirely made of heritage carrots'. It shows a clump of small, whiskery carrot roots, poking upright out of a circle of sauce, a style of presentation sometimes called 'cheffy' and a marker of fine dining. Carrots grow easily in the British climate, and, like cabbage and cauliflower, are an old-fashioned and normally unglamorous stalwart of British cuisine. What is it about heritage that can boost this orange root to the status of gourmet delicacy? In the same article Rob Smith, just crowned winner of the BBC TV competition series *Big Allotment Challenge* and champion of heritage vegetables, voiced a common claim that such vegetables offer a chance to reclaim lost flavours our forebears enjoyed:

> 'I'm growing things my grandfather Albert used to grow. It tastes like the veg you used to have as a child,' he said. 'When you buy a carrot in a supermarket, you recognise it as a carrot but it tastes nothing like the thing you used to know. I wouldn't really say there's much comparison. Its flavour is much more powerful. It tastes 10 times stronger.'
>
> (Johnston, I., 2015)

Perhaps unsurprisingly, Smith is now endorsing a heritage vegetable range in one of the UK's popular seed catalogues, Dobies.

There is no single agreed definition of 'heritage' vegetables, but the term is, not surprisingly, applied to older varieties, and normally not to hybrids. Some heritage vegetables have been developed informally by farmers and gardeners saving seed, others are commercial varieties, long since dropped from catalogues in favour of more efficient crops. Rejected by mainstream industrial production, they are thus available for framing as heritage at risk. In response to their imminent extinction, consumers are urged to buy, grow or eat them, and thereby play a part in safeguarding them for future generations.

Existing outside mainstream agriculture also allows heritage vegetables to be cast in opposition to mainstream food production, and to agri-tech and retail corporations, as can be seen in the *Independent* article above. Popular media texts draw attention to the mass production of non-heritage vegetables, and associate heritage vegetables with grandparents and home vegetable plots. They associate non-heritage produce with profit, and heritage with care and carefulness. These different strands of heritage vegetable discourse come together to afford claims that growing and eating 'heritage' represents resistance to corporate dominance of the food system. In the words of a Reclaim the Fields poster, heritage vegetables might help us to 'beet the system'. There is therefore an uncomfortable tension between these politicised 'alternative' claims and the sight of so many heritage vegetables, not only in allotments and home gardens but also as part of supermarket luxury ranges and in upmarket restaurants, not to mention their prominence in the lifestyle sections of broadsheet newspapers, aimed squarely at a well-off, middle-class audience (Carolan, 2007; Jordan, 2007, 2015). As we say in Britain, they are a bit 'posh'.

'Posh' is a cosy, self-knowing kind of word. It's not really very posh to call things posh; it implies a slight mockery of the tastes and wealth of the upper classes. This self-consciousness finds its way into some media coverage of heritage vegetables. In a *Guardian* article 'Heritage and Heirloom Seeds: They Really do Taste Better' (Darnell, 2008), the writer calls them 'bespoke' vegetables, and writes of an inflation in what is needed these days to impress one's friends and neighbours. To grow one's own vegetables is now not enough to turn heads, but growing *heritage* vegetables allows one to boast 'some purple peas, some white carrots and some yellow beetroot!' In *The Guardian*'s sister paper, *The Observer*, an article teasingly titled 'Darling I only eat vintage' admits:

> There's a snobbery attached to it all, of course [. . .] During the cheese course, you could casually remark, paring knife in hand, that, 'This is an original variety of pear grown for Louis XIV in the Potager du Roi garden at Versailles. Do try it with the Brie. Baron de Rothschild produces it from a single herd of Flamandes in the heart of Meaux [. . .]' Someone may, of course, clock you on the head with a cardoon. But there is something serious afoot here. You can only really buy this age-old produce at farmers' markets. Or you can grow it from your own seeds, harvested via the internet. Thus, heritage and heirloom foods prove our credentials as non-supermarket shoppers. And, as any foodie will tell you, being caught in Tesco's on a Saturday morning is just marginally more embarrassing than being caught in a brothel with your pants down.
>
> (Spencer, 2006)

That gentle mockery of the way the middle classes use alternative food discourses for the purposes of social differentiation softens what remains a significant and growing problem of inequality in countries like the UK (Jackson, 2017).

What is it that makes heritage foods posh? Alternative food movements have generally been associated with economically privileged groups, yet there is no consensus as to the relationship between privilege and alternative consumption. A key question for anyone interested in heritage foods' radical potential is whether their upmarket associations are simply that—an association, made by retailers keen to make a profit from yet another food fad—or whether there is something that runs deeper, something inherently and irredeemably socially divisive about the heritage food project. To better understand this, in this chapter I analyse the discourse of heritage vegetables with a focus on the various ways that social exclusivity has been conceptualised. Heritage discourse itself has often been implicated in the reinforcement and reproduction of elite power (Hall, 2005, p. 24; Hewison, 1987; Littler and Naidoo, 2005, p. 3), and I tackle this idea first. I then turn to concerns from the literature on alternative consumption, concerns about social exclusion through cost, before exploring the ways the politics of heritage vegetables play out through the cultivation of tastes.

Nothing simply *is* heritage, despite the tendency in heritage discourses to presuppose the inevitable and timeless heritage-ness of a given heritage object. Heritage is a discursive practice, which brings certain things into being *as* heritage (Smith, 2006, p. 4). In this chapter, I use media texts as a source of evidence of how heritage food discourse constructs certain foods as heritage in particular ways. Using Bourdieu's ideas (1984, 1986) about cultural capital and the performance of social class through taste, I argue that explicit claims about the importance of heritage eating are what enable these foods to be 'posh', and at the same disguise the self-interest of heritage eaters and their strategies for social distinction. I suggest that the heritage food project is unfortunately socially divisive in ways that cannot be addressed through the framework of heritage itself. Given the prominence of heritage foods in the UK in recent years, it is surprising that in the popular media they have been taken at face value as 'a good thing'. Even in the academic literature, the assumption that food heritage is all to the good goes largely unchallenged.

'Heritage' foods as a consumer discourse

Heritage food research has focused on the instrumental uses of heritage foods, seeing them as a key driver of tourism and an important component of tourists' itineraries (Bessière and Tibère, 2013; Hodges, 2001; Sammels, 2016). Writers are not always concerned with unpicking the very concept of 'heritage' or asking questions about the power relations that heritage food discourse shapes or is shaped by. Of course some have taken more critical approaches, for example by examining the relations developed through the commodification of ethnic and regional heritage in Mexico (Littaye, 2015, 2016), or how the concept of 'heritage' is established and asserted in places as different from one another as Japan (de St Maurice, 2016) and France (Teil and Barrey, 2011). Nonetheless, researchers have tended to focus on production over consumption (Tregear, 2003,

p. 92). In much of the scholarly research on the subject, the consumer is usually only seen from the perspective of the producers and regional development boards who seek to attract them. There has been little research into the domestic consumption of heritage foods, or specifically on the work heritage does when it is enlisted in discourses of alternative consumption.

The context of food heritage in different parts of the world varies, as do definitions and requirements for official heritage status. Nonetheless, global food heritage discourse has been dominated by a particular idea of food culture, value and tradition that Tregear (2003) calls 'roman'—an idea based on the geographical specificity and long continuity of production associated with Italian food traditions. It may also contain elements of the French idea of 'terroir' (Delfosse, 2011; Hodges, 2001), which has come to suggest a deep connection between the land and human culinary achievements. There is a small number of certification or listing schemes for heritage foodstuffs. For example, Slow Food maintains a database called the Ark of Taste, listing and promoting heritage foods; it also works with chefs and others to encourage their production and consumption (Slow Food, 2015). The European Union operates the certification schemes Protected Designation of Origin and Protected Geographical Indication, with the aim of protecting traditional regional specialities and boosting European competitiveness in food production (Balogh et al., 2016; European Commission, 2017). Those seeking such an official stamp of heritage status for a foodstuff must provide evidence of a strong and exclusive connection to a place or a region (European Commission, 2017; Slow Food, 2015). Foods on UNESCO's intangible cultural heritage list are likewise all tied to a geographical place.[1]

This is a problem for the UK, which, by a 'roman' definition, has lost most of its food heritage as a result of early and thorough industrialisation and the effects of rationing during and after the Second World War (Tregear, 2003, p. 103). With a dearth of foods recognisable as 'heritage' under the roman definition, British producers and trade organisations have reinvented heritage foods from historic sources, like Cornish Yarg cheese, made according to historical production methods. They have also 'heritagised' products of the industrial age, like the soft drink Vimto and Harrogate toffee (Tregear, 2003, pp. 99–102). These may lack an ancient connection to a people or their land, but they can be claimed to be both traditional and British.

British producers, consumers and retailers have also embraced the concept of heritage fruit. Britain once had a large number of commercial orchards, mainly in England (Natural England, 2011, p. 1). Many trees survive, though the majority of these orchards ceased commercial production in the second half of the 20th Century (Robertson and Wedge, 2008). There has been a great deal of interest in protecting and reviving 'heritage' apples, and, to a lesser extent, other fruits like plums, but the apple remains significant as an iconic fruit specifically associated with Englishness (Jordan, 2015, pp. 98–101). Significantly, trees are literally rooted in a location, and their longevity means that many locally unique varieties survive, qualifying them for heritage status, even under the criteria of geographical certification schemes.

The 'heritage' vegetables I began the chapter with have also grown from a niche interest to a mainstream phenomenon in the UK during the last decade, no doubt helped by their regular promotion in the lifestyle media. They have mainly been produced by home growers, with 'heritage' seeds exchanged and sold, but heritage vegetables are also increasingly for sale in shops and restaurants. Unlike orchard heritage, British heritage vegetable discourse does not confine itself to 'native' varieties, and celebrates Italian, French, American and Japanese squash, beans, tomatoes and beetroot in a large number of seed catalogues, lifestyle articles and supermarket produce ranges. It is no coincidence that these are all parts of the world with their own already-developed heritage vegetable discourses; Slow Food is centred in Italy, and Terre de Semences and Association Kokopelli have promoted traditional varieties in France. 'Heirloom' vegetables have been conserved and shared widely in the United States (see Carolan, 2007; Jordan, 2015), while in Japan, Kyoto's heirloom vegetables have been developed as a key component of Japanese culinary tradition (de St Maurice, 2016, p. 67).

The Heritage Seed Library, which collects and distributes heritage seed to paying members in the UK, restricts its collection to British varieties (Heritage Seed Library, 2012). But these tend not to be what agronomists would term 'landraces'—bred over a long time according to informal grower selection—but commercial catalogue types, dropped in the 20th Century. Their connection to geographical place is therefore a connection to crop breeding stations or seed companies, rather than to small-scale or traditional farming communities. For example, the 2012 catalogue features Sutton Harbinger, bred by Sutton Seeds around 1901, and Avon Early beetroot, 'one of a series of innovative breeding lines from the former National Vegetable Research Station at Wellesbourne' (Heritage Seed Library, 2012, pp. 10, 13). Like Vimto, this is a food heritage that refuses to be restricted by roman criteria. What, then, are the characteristics associated with heritage foods in Britain?

In North America and Australia, the word most associated with the by now well-developed consumer discourses of traditional fruit and vegetables is 'heirloom', connoting a personal, family connection, the idea of something informally handed down from one generation to another (Heritage Seed Library, 2012). But in the UK the term most commonly used in consumer contexts remains 'heritage'. That word has a particular resonance in Britain, associated with the visiting of stately homes or the preservation of 'great works of art'—with the public reverence for elite culture, one might say (Hall, 2005; Smith, 2006, p. 11; Wright, 1985). This symbolic relationship is further nurtured by the development of heritage kitchen gardens in many historic properties, at which heritage varieties of fruit and vegetables are displayed in the grounds as an extension of the historic buildings, furniture and art works traditionally exhibited (Jordan, 2010; Wincott, 2015). Heritage industry critics have accused country house heritage tourism of selectivity in the pasts it portrays, and of airbrushing differences of interest in order to present a narrative palatable for the visitor (Weiss, 2007, p. 416). Jordan (2010, p. 8), in her analysis of heritage kitchen gardens, finds, too, that they are selective in their 'excessively pleasant landscapes that erase the difficulties of the very lives they seek to represent'.

The sites of heritage food discourse are many and varied in the British context, and the country house aesthetic is not ubiquitous. Across lifestyle media, menus and food packets, campaign posters and seed catalogues, there is a great deal of variation, but some common themes emerge. Heritage foods are generally characterised as diverse, colourful and better-flavoured. Meanwhile, non-heritage produce is described as bland, homogenised and offering little choice. The examples introduced above illustrate this, contrasting unusual colours and tastes that are 'powerful' and 'ten times stronger' with 'tasteless, mass-produced fruit and veg'. While heritage vegetables are associated with amateurs and enthusiasts—often grandparents, as in the Rob Smith interview above—non-heritage food production and retail are portrayed as over-efficient and cynically profit-motivated ('to fill supermarket shelves and the pockets of multinational corporations'). Though they are a feature of modern tourism, they play a larger and more significant role in domestic consumption in Britain, where they speak to wider responses to globalisation, and to anxieties about corporatised, intensive, anonymous and unaccountable food systems (Grasseni, 2011, para 2; Littler, 2009, p. 1). Yet the politics of these domestic consumer discourses of heritage food are not well understood.

Heritage foods have been mentioned in studies of other alternative consumption discourses. For example, Thomas (2008, p. 681) identifies 'heritage cookery' as a genre of lifestyle TV in her investigation of disaffection with consumerism in popular culture. Potter and Westall (2013, p. 164), in their critique of austerity chic in popular food culture, touch on the role of heritage labelled foods. These authors are critical of heritage as it is done—rolled up into a nostalgic vision of a utopian England that is white, upper middle class and male, and that appears inclusive and fun, but is deeply exclusionary. In other words, the problem is identified as a matter of the qualities of the heritage vision offered, rather than with heritage consumption *per se*. Similarly, Jordan (2015, pp. 127–128) notes that heirloom food texts target predominantly white and affluent audiences, and that tropical and Asian vegetables, or heirloom collards and okra, are rarely mentioned 'despite the centrality of these foods to soul food, Cajun, Gulah, and other cuisines'. This suggests that the category of heritage foods simply needs to expand, that being more inclusive can mitigate its exclusionary effects.

Jordan (2007, 2015) is the scholar who has consistently paid attention to the phenomenon of heritage vegetables in a consumer context. Her work has increased understanding of the development of the discourse, particularly in the US. Her content analysis of newspaper coverage of heirloom tomatoes reveals a steep increase in coverage from the late 1990s to 2005 that corresponded with a change in emphasis in texts, from environmental themes to restaurant reviews, and reference to heirloom vegetables as a marker of elite status (Jordan, 2007, p. 34). Once more, Jordan identifies this issue as one extrinsic to the project of heritage foods, arguing that while heirloom tomatoes (as her key example) have become 'status symbols' (2007, p. 36) and 'an explicit badge of an elite lifestyle' (2015, p. 61) in some quarters, they remain available in home gardens, where 'at least in high summer in a good year, they are plentiful and almost free'. She is right to say this means a wide constituency can not only enjoy these foods, but through their consumption can take part in collective action to preserve biodiversity and change the food system (Jordan, 2015, p. 71). However, it also means she has not yet fully developed the problematic issues she raises in her work: the selectivity of the themes in the discourse as it is presented to different audiences, the selectivity of what qualifies as heritage (neglecting foods of non-white Americans) and the selective demographics of the spaces of heritage vegetable shopping and eating. They may be available free in some people's back gardens, but still, what does it mean for them to be in upmarket restaurants? In other words, it is important to ask what work heritage vegetable discourse does to reproduce social class and race in certain sites. This is not undone simply by the parallel existence of these foods at other sites.

Heritage and elites

The term 'heritage' comes with heavy class baggage, particularly in the British context, where it remains closely connected to the country house experience. Indeed, the country house and estate are frequently alluded to in media texts about heritage products. For example, articles in the press that are ostensibly about heritage fruit and vegetables, their taste and their role in combatting industrialisation of food, are often accompanied by photographs of locations that are unmistakeably grand—high, old brick walls around a vegetable plot, perhaps a glimpse of a stately home in the background. There are often signs of the kind of meticulous and expert care that only a team of professional gardeners can provide, with espaliered fruit trees, weed-free borders and neat brick paths (Wincott, 2017, p. 9).

A *Guardian* journalist delights in a restored Victorian walled garden in Sussex which boasts over a hundred varieties of heritage apple. The writer devotes a large part of the article to noting the 'elegance' and order of the orchard, both of which imply paid labour. She writes about careful division of the garden, neatly clipped hedges around borders, and the way trees have been:

> coaxed into elegant forms, with traditional espalier, oblique cordons and fork-shaped palmette verriers against the red-brick wall, while others are trained as goblets and four-winged pyramids on free-standing metal frames.
>
> (Stares, 2016)

The aristocratic landowners and their staff seem to stand in for the English (or, in this account, for the British), defending British identity and independence. In emphasising calm, timelessness and structure, the walled private estate comes to stand as a bulwark of resistance against a careless globalised commerce:

> Commercial growers nowadays concentrate on a handful of cultivars selected for heavy cropping, bruise resistance, keeping quality and uniform shape; this garden, in contrast, celebrates our wealth of heirloom apples, whatever their peculiar traits.
>
> (Stares, 2016)

The Telegraph is similarly effusive about the heritage carrot's priceless qualities. In an article entitled 'Return to Roots: Heritage Varieties of Carrot' (Hart, 2011), supermarkets are said to like selling carrots, but for the wrong reasons: 'because they can chop half a carrot into mini batons, stick them in a plastic container and charge you loads' for them. This is cheating the consumer twice-over, because not only will they be expensive, they will be an undistinguished, mass-produced carrot:

> Chances are, though, that your chopped-up carrot will be a common or garden variety, developed for bulk sales, rather than taste. What you want to get your hands on is a heritage carrot, one that harks back to the days when carrots came in all sorts of colours and configurations and actually tasted—in that peculiarly sweet and intense way that one remembers from childhood—of carrot.
>
> (Hart, 2011)

The article introduces some food heroes striving to educate the consumer, and to introduce them to the joys of heritage carrots. Renowned 'posh' supermarket Marks and Spencer is said to be selling a new range of heritage carrots, pulled from the ground and deposited in a silver bucket by someone who is likened to P. G. Wodehouse's famous fictional butler, Jeeves. Two kinds of carrot are established in this narrative. One is 'common', grown and sold in bulk in undistinguished plastic wrapping, its colour a standard orange, produced with only a cynical regard for maximising profit. The other is the product of care—grown by small producers committed to producing the best quality vegetables, selected by chefs with their diners in mind. This carrot is classy, an idea hinted at by the silver bucket and the Jeevesian agronomist. Not churned out in bulk, it is a carrot you must try to 'get your hands on', but of course it rewards the discerning consumer with intense flavours otherwise lost to a golden age of the recent past.

Articles like these show a slight sense of unease with the 'poshness' or exclusivity of heritage produce. As discussed above, there is often a tongue in cheek, ironic undertow. Describing an agronomist as Jeevesian is both patronising and slightly ridiculous, just like the dinner party host boasting of their aristocratic pears. The affordability and accessibility of heritage produce is often stressed, with tips on how to find seed and grow them yourself, and promises that they are becoming available on supermarket shelves. This tension between distinction and popularisation is common to much lifestyle media, in which writers and those they interview for their articles take care to build a sense of the superiority of certain kinds of food, while at the same time sharing the secrets of distinction (Bell and Hollows, 2005, p. 11).

Heritage vegetable nostalgia is not all about the country house, however. It can often be far more down to earth and homely. In interviews and on his web site, Rob Smith, discussed above, traces his passion for heritage produce to working on his grandfather's vegetable plot and the tastes he remembers as a child (Garden Organic, 2015; Johnston, 2015; Smith, 2016). Celebrity chef Raymond

Blanc talks about labouring in his parents' vegetable garden as a child, and of thrifty practices of storing roots in the cellar, and bottling and preserving produce (Gumming, 2013; James, 2015). This rather homely myth of 20th Century working class families who were poorer but ate better is echoed time and again in consumer-oriented heritage discourse. The secret of the vegetables they enjoyed, and other thrifty tips for conserving and cooking them, are shared so that consumers might reclaim lost pleasures, as in this *Guardian* article about 'Pig Row', a small-holding run according to traditional methods:

> As a child I remember finding my way into the larder of my great aunt's kitchen and seeing shelf after shelf of pickled beetroot and beans; a harvest festival in a terrace. For the first time in 70 years there will be 'Fat Lazy Blondes' on our kitchen table; this lettuce variety won't be found in the supermarket. The 'Manchester Turnip' is going to be in our first Woolton pie. The seeds my great grandfather sowed and saved, seeds we all once saved and swapped over our back garden walls, aren't as readily available today. Over the last century we have lost 98% of vegetable varieties due to regulations. I would have sown 'Salford Black' runner beans but that's at death's door, and one pea variety, 'Champion of England', is extinct.
>
> (Oldham, 2013)

Reference to a terraced house, swapping seeds over the garden wall and making the wartime Woolton pie (a recipe for making do on wartime rations) all situate this nostalgia in a humble household. It's perhaps worth noting, too, that the industrial-age heritage foods Harrogate toffee and Vimto, mentioned by Tregear (2003), are also rather homely treats, associated with day trips to the seaside. Vegetable heritage certainly has a cosy relationship with country house heritage, but texts mix and match many themes and reference points. 'Poshness' or luxury are often there, but they are not the only ways in which heritage food discourse is instrumental in projects of social distinction.

The price of heritage

Heritage food production processes are valued for being smaller, slower and less efficient. This is, after all, why they were dropped by mainstream production, and thus became available for characterisation as endangered heritage, but it also inevitably raises prices. In Britain, heritage foods are found in gastro-pubs, pricey restaurants and posh cafés. They won't be found in the cheap and cheerful 'greasy spoon' cafés or fried chicken takeaways in the poorer parts of town. Though they are now found in mainstream British supermarkets, heritage products tend to be in luxury lines, like Sainsbury's Taste the Difference 'heritage jewels' and 'heritage Marmande' tomatoes, and Tesco's Finest range Narragansett heritage turkey or heritage Natoora carrots, each on sale at the time of writing. Produce marketed this way is an indulgence or treat—for those who can afford it, of course. But in heritage food discourse, the idea of indulgence (better taste, novelty, something a bit special) is justified by the idea that such purchases are for the greater good.

The heritage discourse of the Slow Food Movement's Ark of Taste is a good example of this combination. Its UK web site says the Ark is a catalogue of foods at 'either imminent or potential risk of extinction'. The project aims to:

> raise awareness and protect our food heritage, so that they may be redis-covered and returned to the market [. . .] By preserving these foods, creating a market and preserving them as part of the landscape, our long-term objective is preserving Britain's edible biodiversity, and with this, its food security.
>
> (Slow Food UK, 2015)

The Food Programme (BBC Radio 4, 1979–), is also a long-term champion of non-industrial, local and endangered foods. It has featured the Ark of Food and its products on several occasions. In a 2015 programme, presenter Dan Saladino learns about the rare perry pears, and the pear cider, or 'perry', made from them in a particular region of England (BBC, 2015). These pear varieties are said to have been close to extinction when a visionary farmer Tom Oliver rescued them and produced the traditional drink once more. Its commercial rebirth means there is now hope, says the presenter, but to survive, it needs wider recognition. The programme ends with the words of Oliver: 'It would be a real loss if perry were to disappear. It needs helping and supporting and championing'. Producers, chefs and consumers are characterised as champions and heroes in stories like this. The ethical quality of heritage conservation-through-consumption justifies the treat of heritage novelty and flavour—heritage is both heroism and its reward. Not everyone gets to play the hero, though, either because they are charged with routine and low-cost provisioning of the family meals, not statement food or hobby food (Bell and Hollows, 2005, p. 8), or because they simply lack the income to participate in this form of politics (Littler, 2011, p. 34).

If alternative foods tend to begin as expensive statement purchases, they often become mainstream over time. The mainstreaming of organic and fair trade has been remarkably successful, making them no longer straightforwardly middle-class (Barnett, Littler and Soper, 2005, p. 150). The presence of 'heritage' badged produce in British supermarkets suggests this is increasingly true for heritage foods. Where 'alternatives' find a large market and larger producers get involved, prices can come down, and retailers can no longer be accused of pandering to the privileged (Guthman, 2008a, p. 431; 2008b, p. 392; Lambert-Pennington and Hicks, 2016, p. 58, see also Chapter 1 in this collection). Of course, the kind of big business involvement that leads to mainstreaming may bring its own problems, including intensification and exploitation in the production of food—meaning that the resistance to corporations and industrialisation, assumed to go hand in hand with the protection and revival of traditional foods, may be lost along the way (see Guthman, 2004, on the case of organic foods). There is a widespread suspicion of 'co-optation', where the capitalist marketplace transforms the symbols and practices of countercultural opposition into depoliticised commodities and fashion statements (Thompson and Coskuner-Balli, 2007, p. 136), resulting in what might be called a heritage patina, akin to corporate environmental 'greenwashing' (Budinsky and Bryant, 2013). Jordan (2015, p. 61) feels this is happening in the US to some degree, and suggests that agribusiness may charge a premium for unusual tomatoes or heritage turkeys, and that the label may 'become a relatively hollow marketing tool' as a result.

These may well prove to be concerns with heritage foods as they become more commonplace, but they are, again, understood as problems of approach, rather than as intrinsic problems with heritage discourse. If you take the claims made by champions of heritage produce at face value, then mainstreaming is all to the good, bringing 'almost-extinct crops... out of the history books and back into vegetable patches, gardens and orchards' (Briggs and Bardo, 2012). Thinking about the implications of mainstreaming reveals another, deeper problem with heritage foods and social distinction, one that arises from the counter-posing of the mass-produced and the diverse that is at the heart of heritage vegetable discourse.

Heritage taste

Some scholars worry that alternative food politics are overly individualised and inward-looking at the expense of the development of collective identities and of the grand projects that socialism and the Labour movement once concerned themselves with (e.g., Samuel, 1994, pp. 162–163). Yet much of the discourse of food heritage does refer to exactly those large-scale social and economic problems —ownership of land and seed, the means to produce food, the dominance over the food system by a series of aggressive corporate giants, and the destruction of biological and cultural diversity in the service of ever greater profits. Lifestyle media claims of a large and growing movement of individuals do not rely on formal membership or turnout at political events. They mainly rely on the evidence of a willingness of increasing numbers of people to buy and grow heritage foods. This is framed as a demand for change (Briggs and Bardo, 2012; Chittock, 2008; Wyke, 2011), a revolution (Low, 2008; Vidal, 2007) or a movement (Klein, 2008), much as it is in the literature of campaign groups. For example, Slow Food describes itself as 'a global, grassroots movement with thousands of members around the world that links the pleasure of food with a commitment to community and the environment'.[2] Thus social movements and their organisations pursue an ideal of 'individualised collective action' (Sebastiani, Montagnini and Dalli, 2013, p. 476), or 'collective strategies of consumption' (Carfagna et al., 2014, p. 158). In the case of the burgeoning heritage movement, such collectivity emerged through the development of a new taste—the taste for heritage—that did not exist before discourses of heritage consumption emerged in the 1980s and 1990s (Jabs, 1984, p. v; Jordan, 2015, pp. 125–126).

Tastes are developed by individuals but are also largely shared, and relate to social class (Paddock, 2015; Potter and Westall, 2013). Taste both unites and separates

(Bourdieu, 1984, p. 56), but not as a matter of simple personal choice: it is classifying (Bourdieu, 1984, p. 6), and heritage taste classifies in a number of ways. Firstly, emerging tastes do not only engage the taste buds, they also engage cultural capital. Knowledge about what makes a food 'heritage', and of the value of that quality, as well as of how it can be cooked and served, is required to eat heritage, and that cultural capital is displayed every time a consumer buys or serves it (Johnston and Baumann, 2007, p. 188). A taste for heritage means an acceptance and appreciation of vegetables in atypical colours and shapes, such as white carrots or irregularly shaped tomatoes, creviced and fluted on a farmer's market stall (Jordan, 2015, p. 30). Heritage taste might also mean learning to incorporate completely unfamiliar items into one's repertoire, such as the perry featured in *The Food Programme* (which was a regional drink, and has long been out of favour), or squash, a vegetable fairly new to British tables.

More intense flavour is not an inevitable quality of older kinds of food, and the taste of fruit and vegetables can be affected by many factors, such as rainfall, soil and temperature, as well as genes (Kader, 2008). Nonetheless, intensity of flavour has become part of the myth of heritage foods' superiority. The revival of real ales since the 1970s has led to the phenomenon of super-bitter craft beers, particularly in the US, and to a general trend towards bitter food and drink, including bitter cocktails, kale and broccoli, and mature cheeses (Bryson, 2017; Taylor and Rohrer, 2017). Supposedly superior tastes imply a superior palate on the part of the consumer, someone who can appreciate complex and intense flavours, and who isn't satisfied with the supposedly bland and easy tastes of mass-produced foods—something claimed in the lifestyle texts mentioned above about a burgeoning heritage food movement.

Developing such tastes and knowledge may bring pleasure to the individual and serve the greater good through heritage conservation or change in the food system, but it is also an investment in personal embodied cultural capital for those who are in a position to draw on and develop these resources (Bourdieu, 1984, p. 12; 1986, p. 47). This acquired set of tastes and positions with regards to food are what Carfagna et al. (2014, p. 158) have called an 'eco-habitus' in the context of green consumption. The use of Bourdieu's term 'habitus' signals that alternative consumption movements like heritage need to be seen as more than a self-conscious and individualised strategy to effect change by supporting or boycotting particular products. They are also a collective strategy informed by, and directed at capitalising on, the resources at consumers' disposal. The eco-habitus, according to Carfagna et al. (2014), reconfigures existing high-status taste as a resource, and directs it towards ecological and other political goals.

For those who have cultural capital to draw on, heritage food discourse makes explicit the goal of changing the food system for the better. Implicitly, it is also a good way to reclassify basic foods such as carrots and beetroot, which would otherwise fail to distinguish their eater from the masses. In other words, it is part of what makes some carrots posh. Those convinced of the value of alternative consumption sometimes say that the dearth of working-class consumers in 'alternative' spaces results from a combination of financial exclusion and a disinterest in the wider politics of food (Paddock, 2016, p. 1047). Lifestyle features tackle this by pointing out how cheap heritage fruit and vegetables can be, as well as by educating readers on their importance. Heritage is a highly didactic discourse, whether concerned with old houses, works of art or carrots, or educating people in appropriate concern for chosen relics of the past (Hall, 2005, p. 24). Because of the different tastes and different knowledges among consumers, the very act of proselytising about heritage also makes apparent and reinforces a sense of class boundaries. But this class differentiation is latent, while the manifest struggle is between those who are presented as doing their bit for a better food system, and those who will not see the truth of how much better their food could be. Heritage food discourse is therefore implicated in a foodie culture that shames the working class food of the present by celebrating its supposed past.

For those not bitten by the heritage bug, heritage food discourse and heritage consumers may seem ridiculous, of course—something writers using ironic detachment are aware of. Thus, heritage vegetable taste does not simply impose class boundaries from above, but is part of a complex cultural dance in which distaste for the food of others can be one way we know our place (Bourdieu, 1984, p. 56). But while working class consumers may see the latest trends in heritage food as 'sterile and pretentious' (Bell and Hollows, 2005, p. 7), they lack the symbolic capital to displace the legitimacy of these tastes. Cultural capital, and membership of a community where novel and political food causes are accepted, enables middle-class consumers to pursue competitive strategies, both for distinction, and to position others' tastes as inadequate or illegitimate.

Heritage foods' association with domestic spaces of production—the repeated focus on amateur home growing and seed swapping, the insistence of Michelin-starred chefs on reminiscences about their childhood spent in the family vegetable patch—help to associate them with political sincerity and to distance them from cynical, commercial motives (Johnston and Baumann, 2007, p. 179). Mechanised and professionalised systems of non-heritage growing imply a lack of personal care, of expertise and of artistry. 'Common or garden' carrots are chopped up and stuck carelessly in plastic containers, while heritage carrots are linked with producers who are experts (agronomists and chefs, for example), and who also take care and time over their work. This ethic of care and precision is also evident in the celebration of pristine heritage gardens. The quality of care adds value to heritage produce and is available to consumers who can afford the added cost, or who can invest their own time and knowledge in growing and preparing heritage vegetables and fruit.

Lifestyle texts suggest that heritage vegetables are not only differentiated by care and time but by some character of their own. They are often anthropomorphised using their varietal names:

> They have shady pasts and are the stuff of local legend. They're strictly ex-directory and go by names such as 'Crimson Giant', 'Ragged Jack' and 'Purple Flowered Russian'. They may sound like bad guys from Reservoir Dogs, but they are actually heritage veg varieties.
>
> (Low, 2008)

There is a repeated contrast between 'tasteless, mass-produced fruit and veg forced in a vast greenhouse complex to fill supermarket shelves' (Johnston, 2015) and heirlooms with their 'peculiar traits' (Stares, 2016), quirky names and colours, and general 'rebellious lack of uniformity' (Low, 2008). The politicised taste for heritage is not only a taste for the diverse and characterful, it is a *distaste* for the mass-produced, the widely available and the undifferentiated. This echoes a distaste for the mass of the population, 'interchangeable and innumerable' (Bourdieu, 1984, p. 468).

The very core of the political aspirations of heritage as a kind of alternative consumer movement—fighting corporate power, supporting biological and cultural diversity, reclaiming better tasting food for consumers—are, in a socially divided society, unfortunately also mechanisms for reinforcing class boundaries. It can be difficult to see this because of the powerful rhetoric about passion, heroic championing of the consumer, and the assumed universal value of heritage. The sharp-elbowed middle-class consumer is hidden behind the mythical working-class forebear, though they can be glimpsed in mocking references to showing off at dinner parties. There is truth in the claims made about heritage food's value, and many want to get behind any popular movement to challenge the wanton destruction wrought by corporate greed. But we need to be mindful of the fact that the very politics of heritage vegetable discourse are extremely productive mechanisms by which specialist food retailers, chefs, lifestyle journalists and consumers profit from social distinction, while appearing to do the opposite (Johnston and Baumann, 2007; Johnston and Cairns, 2012), something of a problem affecting alternative foodie culture more widely.

Notes

1 The current list can be found at https://ich.unesco.org/en/lists. Accessed 7 November 17.
2 www.slowfood.org.uk/about/about/. Accessed 7 November 17.

References

Balogh, P., Békési, D., Gorton, M., Popp, J. and Lengyel, P. (2016). Consumer Willingness to Pay for Traditional Food Products. *Food Policy*, 61 (Supplement C), 176–184. doi:10.1016/j.foodpol.2016.03.005.

Barnett, C., Littler, J. and Soper, K. (2005). Consumers: Agents of Change? *Soundings*, 31, 147–160.

BBC. (2015). Ark of Taste: Three Counties Perry. *The Food Programme*. BBC, 18 May.

Bell, D. and Hollows, J. (2005). *Ordinary Lifestyles: Popular Media, Consumption and Taste*. Maidenhead: Open University Press.

Bessière, J. and Tibère, L. (2013). Traditional Food and Tourism: French Tourist Experience and Food Heritage in Rural Spaces. *Journal of the Science of Food and Agriculture*, 93 (14), 3420–3425.

Bourdieu, P. (1984). *Distinction: A Social Critique of the Judgement of Taste*. Translated by R. Nice. Cambridge, Mass.: Harvard University Press.

Bourdieu, P. (1986). The Forms of Capital. In Richardson, J. (ed.), *Handbook of Theory and Research for the Sociology of Education* (pp. 241–258). New York: Greenwood.

Briggs, H. and Bardo, M. (2012). The Return of Heritage Fruit and Veg Varieties. *BBC News Online Magazine*. Available at: www.bbc.co.uk/news/magazine-17912734. Accessed 12 April 2018.

Bryson, L. (2017). Is Craft Beer Too Hoppy to Drink? *The Daily Beast*. Available at: www. thedailybeast.com/articles/2017/02/21/is-craft-beer-too-hoppy-to-drink.Accessed 12 April 2018.

Budinsky, J. and Bryant, S. (2013). 'It's Not Easy Being Green': The Greenwashing of Environmental Discourses in Advertising. *Canadian Journal of Communication*, 38 (2), 207.

Carfagna, L. B., Dubois, E. A., Fitzmaurice, C., Ouimette, M. Y., Schor, J. B., Willis, M. and Laidley, T. (2014). An Emerging Eco-Habitus: The Reconfiguration of High Cultural Capital Practices Among Ethical Consumers. *Journal of Consumer Culture*, 14 (2), 158–178. doi:10.1177/1469540514526227.

Carolan, M. (2007). Saving Seeds, Saving Culture: A Case Study of a Heritage Seed Bank. *Society and Natural Resources*, 20 (8), 739–750.

Chittock, M. (2008). Shooting Stars. *The Guardian*. Available at: www.theguardian.com/ environment/2008/feb/07/ethicalliving.food. Accessed 12 April 2018.

Darnell, L. (2008). Heritage and Heirloom Seeds: They Really Do Taste Better. *The Guardian*, 5 April. Available at:http://www.guardian.co.uk/lifeandstyle/2008/apr/05/gro wingyourown.vegetables

de St Maurice, G. (2016). Edible Authenticities: Heirloom Vegetables and Culinary Heritage in Kyoto, Japan. In Brulotte, R. L. D. G. and Michael, A. (eds.), *Edible Identities: Food as Cultural Heritage*. London and New York: Routledge.

Delfosse, C. (2011). La patrimonialisation des produits dits de terroir Heritage-Making and the Enhancement of So-Called 'Terroir' Products: When Rural Meets Urban. *Anthropology of Food*, 8.

European Commission. (2017). EU Quality Logos.Available at: https://ec.europa.eu/agricul ture/quality/schemes_en. Accessed 12 April 2018.

Garden Organic. (2015). Heritage Seed Library Guardian, Rob Smith, Wins the BBC's Big Allotment Challenge. Available at: www.gardenorganic.org.uk/news/heritage-seed-library-guardian-rob-smith-wins-bbcs-big-allotment-challenge. Accessed 25 September 2017.

Grasseni, C. (2011). Re-Inventing Food: Alpine Cheese in the Age of Global Heritage. *Anthropology of Food*, 8 (8). Available at: https://journals.openedition.org/aof/6819. Accessed 12 April 2018.

Gumming, E. (2013). French Chef English Heritage. *The Daily Telegraph*, 20 April.

Guthman, J. (2004). Back to the Land: The Paradox of Organic Food Standards. *Environment and Planning A*, 36 (3), 511–528. doi:10.1068/a36104.

Guthman, J. (2008a). Bringing Good Food to Others: Investigating the Subjects of Alternative Food Practice. *Cultural Geographies*, 15 (4), 431–447. doi:10.1177/ 1474474008094315.

Guthman, J. (2008b). 'If They Only Knew': Color Blindness and Universalism in California Alternative Food Institutions. *The Professional Geographer*, 60 (3), 387. doi:10.1080/ 00330120802013679.

Hall, S. (2005). Whose Heritage? Un-Settling 'The Heritage', Re-Imagining the Post-Nation. In Littler, J. and Naidoo, R. (eds.), *The Politics of Heritage: The Legacies of 'Race'* (pp. 23–35). Abingdon: Routledge.

Hart, C. (2011). Return to Roots: Heritage Varieties of Carrot. *The Telegraph*, 16 November. Available at: www.telegraph.co.uk/foodanddrink/recipes/8891258/Return-to-roots-Heritage-varieties-of-carrot.html. Accessed 12 April 2018.

Heritage Seed Library. (2012). Catalogue 2012. Available at: www.gardenorganic.org.uk.

Hewison, R. (1987). *The Heritage Industry: Britain in a Climate of Decline*. London: Methuen.

Hodges, M. (2001). Food, Time, and Heritage Tourism in Languedoc, France. *History and Anthropology*, 12 (2), 179–212. doi:10.1080/02757206.2001.9960932.

Jabs, C. (1984). *The Heirloom Gardener*. San Francisco: Sierra Club Books.

Jackson, G. (2017, 1 February). How UK Incomes Are Becoming More Unequal in Six Charts. *Financial Times*. Available at: www.ft.com/content/fc4a3980-e86f-11e6-967b-c88452263daf. Accessed 12 April 2018.

James, R. (2015). Kew on a Plate – Raymond Blanc Talks About His New Book and BBC Series. *The City Planter*. Available at: www.cityplanter.co.uk/kew-on-a-plate/. Accessed 12 April 2018.

Johnston, I. (2015). The New (Old) Vegetables: The Popularity of 'Heritage' Seeds Is Growing Rapidly. *The Independent*, 8 February. Available at: www.independent.co.uk/life-style/food-and-drink/news/the-new-old-vegetables-the-popularity-of-heritage-seeds-is-growing-rapidly-10031479.html. Accessed 12 April 2018.

Johnston, J. and Baumann, S. (2007). Democracy versus Distinction: A Study of Omnivorousness in Gourmet Food Writing. *The American Journal of Sociology*, 113 (1), 165–204. doi:10.1086/518923.

Johnston, J. and Cairns, K. (2012). Eating for Change. In Banet-Weiser, S. and Mukherji, R. (eds.), *Commodity Activism: Cultural Resistance in Neoliberal Times* (pp. 219–239). New York: New York University Press.

Jordan, J. A. (2007). The Heirloom Tomato as Cultural Object: Investigating Taste and Space. *Sociologia Ruralis*, 47 (1), 20–41. doi:10.1111/j.1467-9523.2007.00424.x.

Jordan, J. A. (2010). Landscapes of European Memory: Biodiversity and Collective Remembrance. *History & Memory*, 22 (2), 28.

Jordan, J. A. (2015). *Edible Memory: The Lure of Heirloom Tomatoes and Other Forgotten Foods*. Chicago: University of Chicago Press.

Kader, A. A. (2008). Flavor Quality of Fruits and Vegetables. *Journal of the Science of Food and Agriculture.*, 88 (11), 1863–1868.

Klein, C. (2008). 2008 in Review: Gardens. *The Guardian*. Available at: www.theguardian.com/lifeandstyle/2008/dec/27/2008-in-review-gardens?INTCMP=SRCH. Accessed 12 April 2018.

Lambert-Pennington, K. and Hicks, K. (2016). Class Conscious, Color-Blind: Examining the Dynamics of Food Access and the Justice Potential of Farmers Markets. *Culture, Agriculture, Food and Environment*, 38 (1), 57–66. doi:10.1111/cuag.12066.

Littaye, A. (2015). The Role of the Ark of Taste in Promoting Pinole, a Mexican Heritage Food. *Journal of Rural Studies*, 42, 144–153. doi:10.1016/j.jrurstud.2015.10.002.

Littaye, A. (2016). The Multifunctionality of Heritage Food: The Example of Pinole, a Mexican Sweet. *Geoforum*, 76, 11–19. doi:10.1016/j.geoforum.2016.08.008.

Littler, J. (2009). *Radical Consumption: Shopping for Change in Contemporary Culture*. York: Open University Press.

Littler, J. (2011). What's Wrong with Ethical Consumption? In Lewis, T. and Potter, E. (eds.), *Ethical Consumption: A Critical Introduction* (pp. 27–39). London: Routledge.

Littler, J. and Naidoo, R. (2005). *The Politics of Heritage: The Legacies of 'Race'*. London: Routledge.

Low, S. (2008). Pssst, Want to Buy Some Seeds? *Delicious Magazine*, 23 October.

Natural England. (2011). Traditional Orchard Project in England: The Creation of an Inventory to Support the UK Habitat Action Plan (NECR077). Available at: http://publica tions.naturalengland.org.uk/publication/1289011?category=23034. Accessed 12 April 2018.

Oldham, A. (2013). Digging for Victory Again. *The Guardian*, 10 April. Available at: www. theguardian.com/lifeandstyle/gardening-blog/2013/apr/10/wartime-garden? INTCMP=SRCH. Accessed 12 April 2018.

Paddock, J. (2015). Invoking Simplicity: 'Alternative' Food and the Reinvention of Distinction. *Sociologia Ruralis*, 55 (1), 22–40. doi:10.1111/soru.12056.

Paddock, J. (2016). Positioning Food Cultures: 'Alternative' Food as Distinctive Consumer Practice. *Sociology*, 50 (6), 1039–1055. doi:10.1177/0038038515585474.

Potter, L. and Westall, C. (2013). Neoliberal Britain's Austerity Foodscape: Home Economics, Veg Patch Capitalism and Culinary Temporality. *New Formations*, 80 (80), 155–178. doi:10.3898/NEWF.80/81.09.2013.

Robertson, H. and Wedge, C. (2008). Traditional Orchards and the UK Biodiversity Action Plan. In Rotheram, I. D. (ed.), *Orchards and Groves: Their History, Ecology, Culture and Archaeology* (pp. 109–118). Sheffield: Wildtrack Publishing.

Sammels, C. A. (2016). Haute Traditional Cuisines: How UNESCO's List of Intangible Heritage Links the Cosmopolitan to the Local. In Brulotte, R. L. and Di Giovine, M. A. (eds.), *Edible Identities: Food as Cultural Heritage* (pp. 141–158). London: Routledge.

Samuel, R. (1994). *Theatres of Memory: Past and Present in Contemporary Culture*. London: Verso.

Sebastiani, R., Montagnini, F. and Dalli, D. (2013). Ethical Consumption and New Business Models in the Food Industry. Evidence from the Eataly Case. *Journal of Business Ethics*, 114 (3), 473–488. doi:10.1007/s10551-012-1343-1.

Slow Food. (2015). Criteria for Inclusion. Available at: www.fondazioneslowfood.com/en/ what-we-do/the-ark-of-taste/24632-2/. Accessed 25 September 2017.

Slow Food UK. (2015). The Slow Food in the UK Ark of Taste & Chef Alliance Programmes. Available at: www.slowfood.org.uk/ff-info/forgotten-foods/. Accessed 25 September 2017.

Smith, L. (2006). *Uses of Heritage*. London: Routledge.

Smith, R. (2016) About Me. Available at: http://robsallotment.com/about-me/. Accessed 25 September 2017.

Spencer, M. (2006). Darling, I Only Eat Vintage. *The Observer*, 29 January. Available at: www.theguardian.com/lifeandstyle/2006/jan/29/foodanddrink.features2. Accessed 12 April 2018.

Stares, C. (2016). Heritage Apples – Taking Your Pick of History. *The Guardian*, 14 October. Available at: www.theguardian.com/environment/2016/oct/14/heritage-apples-taking-your-pick-history-country-diary. Accessed 12 April 2018.

Taylor, A.-L. and Rohrer, F. (2017). Why Do Some People Prefer Bitter Drinks? *BBC News Magazine*, 25 October. Available at: www.bbc.co.uk/news/magazine-24616185. Accessed 12 April 2018.

Teil, G. and Barrey, S. (2011). Faire la preuve de l'« authenticité » du patrimoine alimentaire Giving Evidence of the Authenticity of Food Heritage: The Case of « Local Wines. *Anthropology of Food*, (8), https://journals.openedition.org/aof/6783.

Thomas, L. (2008). Alternative Realities: Downshifting Narratives in Contemporary Lifestyle Television. *Cultural Studies*, 22 (5), 680–699. doi:10.1080/09502380802245936.

Thompson, C. J. and Coskuner-Balli, G. (2007). Countervailing Market Responses to Corporate Co-Optation and the Ideological Recruitment of Consumption Communities. *Journal of Consumer Research*, 34 (2), 135–152. doi:10.1086/519143.

Tregear, A. (2003). From Stilton to Vimto: Using Food History to Re-Think Typical Products in Rural Development. *Sociologia Ruralis*, 43 (2), 91–107. doi:10.1111/1467-9523.00233.

Vidal, J. (2007). Digging In: Britain's Green Revolution on the Home Front. *The Guardian*, 9 April.Available at:www.guardian.co.uk/uk/2007/apr/09/foodanddrink.food. Accessed 12 April 2018.

Weiss, L. (2007). Heritage-Making and Political Identity. *Journal of Social Archaeology*, 7 (3), 413–432.

Wincott, A. (2015). Heritage in Danger or Mission Accomplished? Diverging Accounts of Endangerment, Conservation and 'Heritage' Vegetables in Print and Online. *Food, Culture and Society*, 18 (4), 569–588.

Wincott, A. (2017). Treasure in the Vault: The Guardianship of 'Heritage' Seeds, Fruit and Vegetables. *International Journal of Cultural Studies*, 1–16. doi:10.1177/13678779177 33541.

Wright, P. (1985). *On Living in an Old Country: The National Past in Contemporary Britain*. London: Verso.

Wyke, N. (2011). Gallery: Heritage Tomato Varieties. *The Times*, August 17. Available at: www.thetimes.co.uk/tto/life/food/realfood/article3137288.ece. Accessed 12 April 2018.

Part 2
New political platforms

4 Promising sustainable foods

Entrepreneurial visions of sustainable food futures

Tanja Schneider

Envisioned food futures

In a recent article published in *The Guardian*, former US President Barack Obama described his vision of a sustainable food future. He declared that:

> [t]he path to a sustainable food future will require unleashing the creative power of our best scientists, and engineers and entrepreneurs, backed by public and private investment, to deploy new innovations in climate-smart agriculture. Better seeds, better storage, crops that grow with less water, crops that grow in harsher climates, mobile technologies that put more agricultural data—including satellite imagery and weather forecasting and market prices—into the hands of farmers, so that they know when to plant and where to plant, what to plant and how it will sell.
>
> (Obama, 2017)

This vision conjures up a scenario of agricultural production that focuses on science, engineering and entrepreneurship as the main engines of a sustainable food future. Obama illustrates his vision with examples such as crop science and precision agriculture, both of which represent human scientific progress and technological development and require considerable amounts of public and private investment. Also noteworthy is what Obama does not mention: there is little reference to existing or anticipated efforts by state governments (except for public funding of research), international organisations, corporations, nongovernmental organisations, cooperatives, social movements or activists.[1]

Obama first presented a version of this article as a keynote speech at Seeds&Chips: The Global Food Innovation Summit, in Milan, Italy, on 9 May 2017. The event brought together a large number of so-called 'foodtech' and 'agtech' start-ups,[2] established food-related companies, investors, and representatives of accelerators and incubators, as well as representatives of alternative food movements (e.g., Slow Food), and food-related NGOs and associations. As the organisers state on their web site:

Seeds&Chips believes that technology is increasingly playing a key role in the food system and has the potential to solve the most important and vital challenges we face: ensuring healthy, safe and sufficient food for all.[3]

Comparing Obama's vision of a sustainable food future to the statement by Seeds&Chips reveals strong parallels: in both cases, technology is framed as a solution to broader environmental and societal problems.

Scholars in the multidisciplinary field of science and technology studies (STS) refer to such visions of innovation as *technologically deterministic*.[4] They argue that claims that present the development and use of technologies as a major cause of change in society are problematic because they present a reductionist perspective that construes technology as separate or external to society with the capacity to influence from the 'outside'. An STS perspective, in contrast, advances the (perhaps provocative) view that technology is social: all technologies are designed, produced and used by people.

I argue that an STS-informed perspective enables a closer analysis of the envisioned relationships between technology and society, like the ones articulated by Obama and by Seeds&Chips. To do so, I draw on a specific strand of the STS literature on the enactment of sociotechnical expectations and the making of futures in relation to new technologies. This conceptual repertoire informs my analysis of three food start-ups, which enables me to consider some of the described visions in detail. The material I present in this chapter forms part of an ongoing research project on emerging agtech and foodtech and the future of food.[5]

In this research I adopt an ethnographically inclined perspective on entrepreneurs' online and offline practices that can be described as embedded, embodied and everyday (Hine, 2015). I seek co-presence with various actors of the agtech and foodtech ecosystem on- and offline by attending industry events, following and engaging via web sites and other digital platforms, reading industry e-newsletters, and conducting formal interviews, informal conversations, and ethnographic field visits. In this chapter, I focus on three Swiss agtech and foodtech start-ups, analysing and comparing their promises and visions with those articulated by alternative food networks (AFNs). The start-ups are typical of wider trends in the start-up and investor arena, which, over the last five to ten years, has seen significant growth of agtech and foodtech start-ups in general, and of those addressing sustainable food production and consumption in particular.

In what follows, I consider how Swiss agricultural and food entrepreneurs configure and present their 'solutions in the making' as global solutions that can easily travel beyond national boundaries. Connected to this, I discuss how the technical solutions advanced by food start-ups are frequently presented as superior to other potential solutions for sustainable food futures—they are depicted as offering large-scale effects and positive environmental impacts. However, my analysis reveals that start-ups also draw on sustainability narratives deployed by AFNs. In other words, start-ups combine the promise of the efficiency of the agricultural production-oriented approach with the sustainability of the alternative food systems approach—two distinct perspectives often advanced in academic, industry and policy debates on food security. This leads me to question the extent to which we are witnessing the adoption and mainstreaming of the narratives of alternative food networks. I propose that what we are instead witnessing is an entrepreneurial redefinition of sustainability, and with this a redefinition of what 'counts' as a good solution for food security, who would be able to achieve it, and how. I conclude with a discussion of what this means for alternative food networks, food producers and consumers.

Unsustainable food present

The future of food is widely debated, including in academia, agriculture, industry, public policy, government, international organisations, media, social movements, consumer protection agencies, peasant organisations and non-governmental organisations. With continuing population and consumption growth, intensifying competition for land, water and energy, and the likely impact of climate change, these debates frequently centre on the key challenge of how to feed nine to ten billion people by 2050 (Godfray et al., 2010; Wheeler and von Braun, 2013). Most food strategy experts agree that without fundamental changes in how we produce and consume food, global food security and global health will come under threat (de Schutter, 2011; Foresight, 2011; McKeon, 2015; Stuckler and Nestle, 2012). There is, however, considerable debate about what changes are needed, what constitutes food security, and how it can be achieved.

Food policy experts Tim Lang and David Barling (2012) provide a socio-historical analysis of the shifting meaning of food security, and review current debates about how to achieve sustainable food systems. They identify two main perspectives: the agricultural production-oriented approach, which stipulates that food security can be achieved by producing more food; and the food systems approach, which emphasises the need to address a complex array of issues 'beyond' production, including social and environmental considerations. In Lang and Barling's (2012, p. 314) view, the agricultural production-oriented approach and the food systems approach will compete for dominance. However, both approaches are bounded by the 'basic truth [...] that the only food system to be secure is that which is sustainable, and the route to food security is by addressing sustainability' (2012, p. 322). They observe that debates on food security are still dominated by a productionist focus, but emphasise that 'even mainstream "official" analyses now attempt to address sustainability', which could be read as a 'modernising' or 'softening of the image of productionism' (Lang and Barling, 2012, p. 320). Following Lang and Barling's observation, I propose that agtech and foodtech start-ups (which tend to have a production-oriented approach) increasingly define their visions and products in relation to sustainability. However, I also suggest that it is important to ask what exactly these start-ups mean when they refer to sustainability.

Proponents of the production-oriented approach frequently present increasing production as a solution to the problem of feeding a growing global population, a problem that will have reached a critical stage by 2050. Isobel Tomlinson (2013) problematises this imperative and argues that such 'statistics are a key discursive device being used by institutions and individuals with prior ideological commitment to a particular framing of the food security issue' (Tomlinson, 2013, p. 82). This narrow framing of food security is problematic because it exclusively focuses on increasing food production, which is likely to exacerbate existing environmental challenges; it also excludes important issues from the definition of food security (Tomlinson, 2013, p. 84). Going beyond food production, the food systems approach encompasses the whole food chain, from farm to fork. This approach highlights the interconnectedness of food production, distribution and consumption, and considers resulting environmental or public health effects. A range of social movements, such as La Vía Campesina ('The Peasant Way'), are proponents of a food systems approach (see Chapter 6 in this collection). Their and other movements' efforts have given rise to an 'alternative set of discourses around concepts of ecological food provision, food sovereignty, and agroecology' (Tomlinson, 2013, p. 88).

Alternative food movements, including the Slow Food, organic and fair trade movements, aim to create new economic and cultural spaces for trading, producing and consuming food (Counihan and Siniscalchi, 2014; Goodman, DuPuis and Goodman, 2014). However, in the last decade, organic, fair trade, slow, and local foods have become increasingly available and sold beyond alternative economies or specialised fair trade and organic food shops (e.g., Sassatelli and Davolio, 2010). As chapters in this collection have already alluded to, researchers of alternative food networks and food activism tend to problematise this development. Goodman, DuPuis and Goodman (2014, p. 5), for instance, note that:

> commoditised ethical and esthetic values or 'qualities' are open to mainstream capture that threatens to neutralise the social projects and critical ambition of the alternative food and fair trade movements. [...] [T]he interface between 'alternative' and 'conventional' is becoming highly permeable and confusing as actors compete to control these new income streams.

Alkon and Guthman (2017) locate the problem in food activists' tendency to employ market-based strategies that cater to consumers who can afford to make a difference by 'shopping for change'. They argue that this 'focus on a politics of consumption [...] has limited even the most sustainability-minded among [foodies and food activists] to relatively apolitical strategies such as patronising and creating alternative food businesses' (Alkon and Guthman, 2017, p. 1).

I argue that, beyond alternative food movements, this focus on markets facilitates the development of products that can be marketed as potential solutions to current food system challenges (such as climate change or limited resources). Returning to Lang and Barling's (2012) observation that sustainability is a central characteristic of any envisioned food future, it is not surprising, then, to see the emergence of a new set of scientific and technological food innovations that might be classified as production-oriented, but which claim to contribute to the sustainability of the food system as a whole. Examples include: new farm management technologies, including drones, sensors and software; novel farming systems, such as vertical farming using robotics and new irrigation systems; and innovative foods, such as sustainable protein alternatives based on plant proteins or laboratory meat.

These novel food and agricultural innovations are developed by a vanguard of entrepreneurs who never tire of pointing out how their tools, ingredients or products require less use of natural resources (such as water or soil), and are, as a result, more sustainable than products of conventional methods. They present this 'efficiency'—as I will soon explore in more detail—as an important contribution to sustainable food systems, were their methods or products to be adopted. First, however, I will briefly introduce the conceptual framework that informs my study of entrepreneurial visions of sustainable food.

Sociotechnical expectations and futures

STS scholars have developed methods to analyse technology 'to move the debate from questions like "does technology drive history?" to arguments about a mutual relationship between technological and social change' (Kline, 2001, p. 15495). STS scholars' criticism of various versions of technological determinism, however, does not imply a general dismissal of the effects that technologies have had historically, or are having now on our everyday lives (Wajcman, 2015, p. 28). Instead, the goal is to consider technology 'as a sociotechnical product, patterned by the conditions of its creation and use' (Wajcman, 2015, p. 29).

I attend to the conditions of technologies' creation by drawing on one strand of STS: the enactment of sociotechnical expectations and their performative effects. I suggest that a focus on the creation of particular expectations from food and agricultural technologies by a range of different organisations (agtech and foodtech startups and beyond) shows how particular food futures are mobilised. The enactment of specific food futures, in turn, is pivotal in the creation of a relatively new form of agtech and foodtech entrepreneurship, one that seeks to 'disrupt' the current food system with the proclaimed aim of making food more sustainable.

Expectations, as Borup, Brown, Konrad and van Lente (2006) observe, quite literally mean a state of looking forward, and 'technological expectations can more specifically be described as real-time representations of future technological situations and capabilities' (Kline, 2001, p 15495). Technological promises and visions are often seen as interchangeable (Borup et al., 2006, p. 286). However, Borup et al., (2006, p. 286) point out that technological visions emphasise 'their enacting and subjectively normative character'. This performative understanding of expectations, as 'wishful enactments of a desired future' is a central tenet of the STS literature on sociotechnical expectations. In studies of biotechnology (e.g., Brown, 2003), neuroscience and neurotechnology (Martin, 2015; Schneider and Woolgar, 2015), and genetics (Caulfield and Condit, 2012), STS researchers and others show how expectations perform certain futures by foregrounding three dimensions of the sociotechnical: they are *generative* as they 'guide activities, provide structure and legitimation, attract interest and foster investment'; they can *mobilise resources*; and they *bridge or mediate* across different boundaries and otherwise distinct dimensions (Borup et al., 2006, pp. 285–286).

In recent years, researchers interested in sociotechnical expectations have increasingly paid attention to the role expectations play in market-making (Martin, 2015), or to what Pollock and Williams (2010) call the 'business of expectations'. These researchers discuss the role of promissory organisations, often intermediaries such as market research companies and consultancies, in mobilising hopes for new technologies. Additionally, they show how these organisations classify and assess expectations, thereby contributing to the making, but also to the on-going (e)valuation, of particular industries (cf. Pollock and Williams, 2016). For instance, Martin's (2015, p. 440) research on the neurotechnology industry shows 'how expectations play multiple performative roles in helping construct new industries, commodities and markets through the work of promissory enterprises that create forms of value that rest on expectations of the future'. Expectations in this and related research are seen as central to co-producing sociotechnical market assemblages.

Expectations, by definition, are future-oriented, and so is discussion of innovation that emphasises not only the novelty of the innovation but also its future capacities. To study innovation, researchers attend to 'future-oriented abstractions', such as 'imaginings, expectations and visions' (Borup et al., 2006, p. 285), voiced in interviews, but also expressed in company reports, press releases, industry conference presentations, and coverage in the media and trade press, and on social media platforms.

In relation to food innovation, Stephens and Ruivenkamp (2016) and Lupton (2017) have considered the prominent role that sociotechnical promises and imaginaries can play. Stephens and Ruivenkamp (2016) focus their analysis on media images of 'cultured' or 'in vitro' meat (IVM). They suggest that:

> IVM images do different promissory work from the textual narratives that often accompany them. These textual forms [...] assert the environmental, health, and innovation benefits of IVM technology. In contrast, the promise most easily afforded in the images is that IVM can be produced with the suggestion that it will resemble familiar forms of meat known today.
>
> (Stephens and Ruivenkamp, 2016, p. 347)

Lupton (2017) examines how the online news media introduces and reports 3D-printed food technologies to publics. She identifies five major promissory themes associated with 3D-printed foods in the global reportage: futuristic, creative, healthy, efficient, and sustainable (Lupton, 2017, pp. 6–13). Drawing on Stephens and Ruivenkamp's study, she argues that 'promissory themes play an integral part in contributing to broader sociotechnical imaginaries, working to specifically outline and define the potentials of new technologies' (Lupton, 2017, p. 3). These 'sociotechnical imaginaries' are 'publicly performed visions of desirable futures' (Jasanoff, 2015, p. 4 as cited in Lupton, 2017, p. 2) that are central to shaping collective ideas of 'ideal' food futures. Thus, what both Stephens and Ruivenkamp and Lupton show is the constitutive effects of visual and textual promises, and how these contribute to sociotechnical imaginaries of desirable and technology-enabled food futures.

Entrepreneurial visions of sustainable food futures

The three Swiss agtech and foodtech start-ups I analyse in this chapter—UrbanFarmers, CombaGroup and Essento—each offer novel ways of producing or consuming foods. Similar to prominent Silicon Valley agtech and foodtech start-ups, they seek to 'disrupt' conventional food production, distribution and consumption (O'Riordan et al., 2017; Sexton, 2016). UrbanFarmers and CombaGroup both develop new systems to grow vegetables (and, in the case of UrbanFarmers, fish), while Essento's focus is on developing insect-based foods for human consumption. My selection of these three start-ups is based on three rationales: each of the chosen start-ups develops new processes of food production and/or products for consumption; each has engaged investors to develop their business idea; and each has developed a prototype or system/product/platform that is already available or very close to being available on the market. This rationale is informed by my larger research project's aim of studying the role of venture capital in performing new food futures (see endnote 5). Additionally, I have chosen to study the three start-ups because they present themselves and their food production systems and products as contributing to more sustainable food futures. The research questions guiding my analysis are: How are agtech or foodtech innovation and its products described and visually illustrated on the start-ups' web sites and beyond? Which qualities of the foods are emphasised? And which expectations and sociotechnical imaginaries are present? These questions enabled me to explore how sociotechnical expectations and imaginaries contribute to enacting new food products and markets, as well as the role start-ups, as so-called 'promissory enterprises', play in creating forms of value that rest on expectations of the future.

Urbanfarmers

UrbanFarmers[6] (UF) is an urban agriculture company, founded in Zurich in 2011, that builds rooftop farms for commercial growers in the city. These rooftop farms are based on aquaponics (AP) technology, which enables growing both fish and vegetables in 'closed-loop systems'. As UrbanFarmers describes the technology on its web site: 'In AP, the recirculating aquaculture (fish farming) system discharges wastewater (effluent) that is used as organic fertiliser for plants (hydroponics)'.[7] In other words, the greenhouse contains, and is built around, two sub-systems, hydroponics and aquaculture, that are interconnected and support the growth of vegetables and fish. This technology was developed at a Swiss university of applied sciences (ZHAW Wädenswil), and commercialised by UrbanFarmers.

During my attendance at the 'grand opening' of the start-up's pilot farm in Basel in May 2013, I participated in a guided tour of the rooftop farm located in the Dreispitz area, an industrial part of town, to see the closed-loop system in practice. A 250 m^2 rooftop greenhouse built on top of an existing industrial building occupies most of the space.[8] In the greenhouse, lettuces and tomatoes grow without soil; the plants' roots are suspended in a water-nutrient solution. A smaller, windowless room in the corner of the greenhouse contains a tank in which fish, in this case Tilapia, are grown. The tour guide explained the intricate connections between the different subsystems of greenhouse, hydroponics and aquaculture. These explanations often included direct references to the technical equipment required to set up and maintain the farm, including explanations of the computerised control boards and displays.

I was astonished by the highly technically mediated and automated character that much of the infrastructure affords. While I had envisioned food, that is, plants and fish, to be the main focus of the entrepreneurs' attention, and the main interactions in the greenhouse to be between plants/fish and staff tending them, the tour left me with the impression that the key point of interaction is between humans and machines. It struck me that only after consulting the various measurements and settings on the control boards would there be an interaction between growers and plants/fish—all the while there was a measured and controlled interaction taking place between fish and plants, which sustained each other interdependently.

Of course, any greenhouse is just that: a technical, measured and fully controlled environment in which plants are grown, irrigated and stored until ready for harvest or sale. This field visit was, in fact, more revealing about my ideas about urban farming than about UrbanFarmers. I had previously encountered urban farming and gardening as a collective, civic, social movement springing up in various cities in the Global North, and aiming to re-localise food production and reconnect with nature by bringing farming back into the city. In the back of my mind were media images and reports of communities of concerned citizens and eaters self-organising and using vacant urban spaces to grow food (see also Lyson, 2014; McClintock, 2010; Müller, 2011). How did I conflate civic urban farming efforts with UrbanFarmers' activities as a start-up? Apart from my general research interest in alternative food networks and food activism (Schneider et al., 2018), which may have led to my preconceptions, I suggest that this confusion is in part related to UrbanFarmers' self-presentation in its marketing, communication and public relations efforts.

The home page of UrbanFarmers' web site welcomes visitors by inviting them to choose the English or German language version of the site. After choosing, the visitor encounters an approximately three-minute video featuring a montage of images, including landmarks of the city of Basel, shipping containers, vegetables displayed at a farmers' market, the UrbanFarmers' greenhouse, various members, helpers and visitors of the start-up, lettuces, tomato plants and tomatoes, fish swimming in a fish tank, a man riding a bicycle with an attached trolley to transport food to a well-known Swiss retailer, a supermarket's vegetable aisle and fish counter, shoppers, and young people enjoying a barbeque on a rooftop terrace. This sequence of summer images conveys youthfulness, naturalness, freshness and urbanness. In addition to the visual encounter, some ambient but fast-paced music forms the background to the video, and a youngish man with an American accent shares UrbanFarmers' mission. He starts by asking:

> What if the food you eat every day is grown right in your neighbourhood? Wouldn't vegetables grown across the street taste better than those from across the ocean? And what farmer in his right mind would ever choose to stick his produce in a shipping container for a month?

If we pause here and consider what we are *not* seeing or hearing, it becomes apparent that no technical equipment and infrastructure is displayed other than parts of the greenhouse. We see some trucks (belonging to the retailer), a container crane and shipping containers, but learn by way of the question posed in the beginning of the video that this last image is to be connoted negatively, since no farmer 'in his right mind' would 'choose to stick his produce in a shipping container for a month'. This contrasting portrayal of globalised food production and supply (in the form of shipping containers) versus local food production assists UrbanFarmers in creating an image of the company as one that is dedicated to producing local foods that are fresher due to reduced travel time. Additionally, the absence of any portrayal of technical devices in the video emphasises the naturalness of the food produced, and contrasts with my experience of the tour described above.

Once the film ends with the company's slogan 'UrbanFarmers: The fresh revolution',[9] visitors see the home page of the web site:

> We all want fresh food.
> Fresher food is better food. For too long, urban agriculture has been a hobby amongst a few dedicated enthusiasts. Introducing UrbanFarmers: we provide systems and solutions that enable enterprises to grow the freshest vegetables and fish in your city reliably, and on a large scale.

This statement describes the efforts of civic urban farmers as a 'hobby' that UrbanFarmers has professionalised and upscaled, thereby enabling entrepreneurs and established businesses to draw on the core ideal of producing food locally but in an organised, systematic, reliable and large-scale manner that goes beyond community efforts of growing food together. But what is transformed in this translation from community-based to entrepreneurial urban farming? The company's entrepreneurial vision involves a small-scale re-industrialisation of urban farming. However, this re-industrialisation is not made immediately visible to web site visitors—although it is visible to visitors to the actual site of production. This is notable, because the promotional discourses associated with the start-up foreground the image of fresh, local, and large-scale, but not industrial, food production. However, if web site visitors search for more information on how the start-up operates and how its technology 'works', they can easily find pages of the Urban-Farmers web site that detail the company's technical 'core capabilities' (such as aquaponics, system design, UF controller, UF node, UF brand) and infrastructural 'solutions' (UF bolt-on system, rooftop farms, UF box). These 'technical' sections of the web site describe urban farming as a process that, with the help of proprietary technologies such as the UF controller, can be monitored, recorded, controlled and automated, and, by extension, require less human monitoring and controlling.

How is sustainability presented in this kind of urban farming? The word 'sustainable' features prominently in UrbanFarmers' self-description of one of its core capabilities, the aquaponics technology, which is introduced on the web site as 'A Truly Sustainable Solution for Growing Fish and Vegetables in closed-loop Systems' (caps in original).[10] An analysis of the 245-word explanation of this statement reveals that what renders this technology and its use sustainable, in UrbanFarmers' view, is: significant water savings; no use of arable land; less use of fossil fuel-based fertilisers; no use of pesticides or herbicides; and no use of antibiotics (for fish farming) due to lower stocking densities and 'great water quality'. UrbanFarmers, then, emphasises how aquaponics requires fewer natural resources, presenting this 'efficiency' as an important contribution to creating a sustainable food system.

UrbanFarmers presents itself and the urban agriculture systems it sells not only as sustainable and reliable, but also as cost effective. According to the UrbanFarmers web site, this cost-effectiveness is achieved through the start-up's technical core capabilities. For instance, the UF Node, a 'proprietary operator dashboard and cloud-based operations data solution', is described as 'a "mini-ERP [Enterprise Resource Planning] system" for our farm operators enabling them to reduce cost in administration and overhead as well as streamline operations'.[11]

Summarising the benefits of its technology, UrbanFarmers concludes: 'Overall, the combination of aquaculture and hydroponics in Aquaponic technology is seen as a highly sustainable and resource-efficient production method compared to stand-alone aquaculture or hydroponics' (emphasis removed). This presentation of aquaponics considers sustainability primarily in terms of ecological and economic efficiencies. In the corporate context, the combination of ecological and economic efficiencies as an ideal pairing to achieve sustainable development is generally discussed in terms of 'eco-efficiency' (World Business Council for Sustainable Development (WBCSD), 2000). Eco-efficiency is defined as:

> [T]he delivery of competitively-priced goods and services that satisfy human needs and bring quality of life, while progressively reducing ecological impacts and resource intensity throughout the life-cycle to a level at least in line with the earth's estimated carrying capacity. In short, it is concerned with creating more value with less impact.
>
> (World Business Council for Sustainable Development (WBCSD), 2000, p. 4)

UrbanFarmers' depiction of aquaponics resonates with this definition, the significance of which I will consider in more detail in the discussion. However, I will first consider the food futures presented by the other two start-ups.

Combagroup

CombaGroup, founded in 2013, is a start-up based in Molondin in the French-speaking part of Switzerland. The start-up describes itself as 'a Swiss agro-tech company, offering innovative solutions and aeroponics production systems for the food-service and processed-salad industry'.[12] The aeroponic production method is a way to grow lettuce in greenhouses, with the plants' roots suspended in the air and regularly sprayed by an irrigation robot with the necessary water, oxygen and nutrients. This, in entrepreneurial terms, is the company's 'core capability'. When I visited the start-up in March 2017, I had the opportunity to see its prototype greenhouse, ask questions, and learn more about the workings of CombaGroup's patented mobile aeroponics technology, as well as the company's patented system to optimise spacing of the lettuce during growth.

The similarities to UrbanFarmers are apparent in terms of the set-up (such as the greenhouse), the technology-enabled production method for vegetables (aquaponics versus aeroponics), and the revolutionary ambitions (a 'fresh revolution' and 'aeroponics revolution', respectively) that target food production and distribution systems with the suggestion—in CombaGroup's words—'to relocate all their production assets next to the consumption centers'. However, the companies differ in aspects of their self-presentation. UrbanFarmers connects its entrepreneurial activities to civic urban farming initiatives that may appeal to young urbanite food consumers—so-called 'political' or 'ethical' consumers (Lewis and Potter, 2011). In contrast, CombaGroup's self-presentation speaks primarily to the businesses it seeks to win as its customers and/or potential investors. Nonetheless, CombaGroup addresses consumers' potential food concerns when highlighting that, with the help of its technology, the bagged lettuce is 'healthier' because it contains 'no pesticides', 'no fungicides' and is not affected by 'chlorinated washing'.

In my interview with one of the start-up's members, he described CombaGroup's aims in terms of sustainable food production and distribution:

> We have to stop having food that travels thousands of kilometres—it takes days before reaching the consumer. It claims to be healthy, but it's full of pesticides, it requires a lot of transportation. So, really what we want with the technology is to simplify the value-chain and make it more sustainable, for the planet and for the consumer.
>
> (Interview, 8 March 2017)

Additionally, the sustainability of CombaGroup's food production and distribution methods is highlighted on its web site, which presents the bagged lettuce produced with the company's proprietary technology as 'eco-friendly' due to 'reduced water consumption' and the fact that it involves 'no waste'. These advantages were also described in the interview, and during my visit to the prototype greenhouse. Similar to my visit to UrbanFarmers, my visit to CombaGroup conveyed the start-up's focus on its proprietary technology and infrastructural set-up, rather than food. This impression was intensified by the fact that I was visiting a prototype greenhouse that was not yet fully operating. Furthermore, this high-tech set-up, devoid of food at the time of my visit, posed a stark contrast to the surrounding Swiss countryside, which is predominantly farmland.

In CombaGroup's presentation of the benefits of its agtech innovation to producers and consumers,[13] the company states that its technology results in cheaper, fresher, healthier and eco-friendly food, as well as in improved logistics. Presumably, the end product (lettuce) will not be cheaper for consumers, but it will be cheaper to produce and hence cheaper for the producer or grower adopting this method. As summarised by CombaGroup on its web site: 'for producers, this means increased ROI [return on investment], differentiated products & marketing edge'. Or, as the company describes its business purpose on the Crunchbase data platform:

> CombaGroup [...] is developing a cost-effective and environmentally-friendly solution for growing high-quality lettuce with a longer shelf-life. CombaGroup combines technological advancements in logistics, agronomy, climate control and automation to yield up to 70x productivity gains and deliver a revolution in the supply of lettuce to packagers.[14]

Similarly to UrbanFarmers, CombaGroup emphasises both ecological and economic efficiencies.

It is useful to consider UrbanFarmers' and CombaGroup's descriptions of, and claims about, their systems' and technologies' sustainability as sociotechnical promises. These promises describe the potential of these new technologies, and play an important role in fostering sociotechnical imaginaries around novel foods and their production (Martin, 2015). At the same time, these promises are not exclusively connected to the future, but draw on existing frames of sustainable food production/consumption as advanced by AFNs, and as taken up and discussed in the food policy arena. However, while drawing on existing frames, these frames are then re-evaluated and re-defined by the start-ups. In my analysis of the two start-ups above, I have identified three re-evaluations and re-definitions: what *local* food is and how it is evaluated; what *fresh* food is and how it is evaluated; and what *sustainably produced* food is and how the companies evaluate sustainability. I will return to the redefined frames in the discussion section of this chapter. First, however, I will discuss one additional start-up, the promotional strategies of which focus on sustainable food consumption, rather than on production or distribution.

Essento

I was first introduced to Essento, another Swiss start-up, in Spring 2015 by students attending my Masters-level seminar at the University of St. Gallen, 'Food Politics and the Limits of Markets'. As part of the seminar, I asked the students to study an organisation or initiative that politicises food. While I had envisioned that students would research mainly non-profit activist organisations, such as Slow Food or alternative food networks, one student group chose to focus on the start-up Essento, which develops insect-based foods. The students were familiar with the start-up because the two founders of Essento had studied at St. Gallen.

In some ways, Essento is similar in its activities and ambitions to food activist organisations. One of the start-up's main initial efforts was to popularise locally the idea of eating insects, a culinary practice common in African and Asian countries, and to lobby for a change in Swiss food safety regulations that restricted insect-based foods to the pet food market. On 1 May 2017, food safety regulations underwent a revision, and now insect-derived food products containing three types of insect (crickets, grasshoppers and mealworms) are permitted in Switzerland. In August 2017, Essento launched its first line of mealworm-based foods—insect burgers and insect balls—which are sold (at the time of writing) in selected branches of the Swiss retailer Coop. Essento also plans to sell whole insects through its web-shop (delicious-insects.ch).

Essento's web site (available in German only)[15] is divided into four pages: 'insect facts', 'sustainability', 'FAQ' and 'Essento education'. Clicking on 'insect facts', visitors read: 'The food revolution is here! The alternative protein source of the future is now available as a food product (*Lebensmittel*) in Switzerland. Here is a list of advantages of edible insects'. Scrolling down, visitors learn about three claimed benefits of eating insects, that it is: good for the planet, great for health, and tasty for the palate. Each benefit is described with the help of infographics and supported by references to academic studies or to a report by the United Nations Food and Agricultural Organisation (FAO). This visual rendering of information enables a quick understanding of the 'facts'. For instance, a graphic in the section 'good for the planet' compares the potential impact of different animal protein sources on global warming. Insects (in this graphic, mealworms) are depicted as good for the planet because of their relatively low production of greenhouse gases compared to those emitted in the production of cow's milk, beef, pork and poultry. A second graphic in the same section shows that insects, compared to beef, are far less resource-intensive with respect to water and feed. Additionally, a higher percentage of the whole animal is edible; in the case of insects 80%, compared to 40% in the case of beef. In sum, the start-up emphasises that insects require less use of natural resources for a higher edible yield.

Essento's definition of sustainability in terms of ecological efficiency resembles that of the two previously discussed Swiss food-start-ups. However, Essento's focus on ecological efficiency is not linked with economic efficiency. In other words, Essento does not mention or discuss any potential (long-term) cost savings that a shift from raising cattle to breeding insects could entail for food production. In that respect Essento is not foregrounding the potential 'eco-efficiency' of insect-based food production. This silence about economic efficiency and its relationship to ecological efficiency is likely related to Essento's values-oriented business practices. This orientation is clearly expressed in the start-up's mission, which lists five core principles: more than profit, species-appropriate animal husbandry, global/local, sustainable quality, and awareness.[16] The first principle, in particular, indicates that the generation of revenue and profit is balanced against the other principles listed. In an interview, one of the company's core members compared Essento to other insect-based food start-ups, problematising profit-driven entrepreneurship:

> There are companies in this area stating: 'insects are a billion dollar market!' Upon hearing that I ask myself, did they not fully understand the issue? This is about so much more (see the FAO report)! This is about inducing profound change [in the food system], and not about finding other ways to earn money. This is the challenge. Or the moral question that I also ask myself repeatedly: Am I doing the right thing? What can I do differently to contribute more towards systemic change?
>
> (Interview, 20 March 2017)

Two additional factors are likely to have contributed to Essento's focus on ecological over economic efficiency: the legal context at the time, and the forms of investment that the start-up accepted. As outlined earlier, the start-up's initial task consisted of advocacy for future insect consumption, which required lobbying for changes in the Swiss food safety regulations. Initially, then, advocacy, rather than food production, played a central role in the organisation's daily activities. Thus, Essento was not in a position, at first, to produce and sell insect-based foods in Switzerland, which may have hampered investors' interest in the company and its innovative products. In the interview, it also became clear that the founders were actively looking for an investor or group of investors who share their core values and long-term goals focused on sustainable food production and consumption rather than on financial gain.

What is 'sustainable' in sustainable agtech and foodtech innovation?

My analysis of three Swiss start-ups' promises to produce and sell sustainable foods shows that in all three cases sustainability is defined in terms of ecological resource efficiency. Reduced use of water, soil and transport or the reduction of food waste are variously presented as contributing to a sustainable food system. In the case of UrbanFarmers and CombaGroup, ecological efficiency is also presented as a means for companies to save food production costs via use of new technologies in the production of food. These technologies are framed not only as reducing the use and depletion of natural resources, but also as economically optimising food production. In other words, using less soil, water, transport and intermediaries present a potential for saving costs that conventional food production does not offer. These savings have to be considered by producers, however, in relation to the initial cost of adopting and implementing the new means of production and distribution.

Whereas Lupton's (2017) study of how 3D-printed foods are depicted in online news sources found efficiency and sustainability to be two separate promissory themes, my analysis shows that, in the three selected Swiss agtech and foodtech start-ups, the promise of sustainable food is closely connected with promises of ecological and/or economic efficiencies. I suggest that the entanglement of these promises can be explained by the different audiences addressed in the media reportage Lupton studied and the promissory self-presentations of start-ups that I examined. While the former is often focused on an audience of interested publics, the latter is largely geared at conveying the start-ups' visions and products to investors and publics (and potentially media) simultaneously. I suggest that examining these self-presentations on start-ups' web sites, complemented with additional ethnographic material and interviews, enables an analysis of 'techno-economic assumptions' (Birch, 2017) that underpin the sustainable agtech and foodtech technologies discussed in this chapter. Such an analysis can unpack how economic imperatives structure start-ups' self-presentation and the values they build into their agricultural and food innovation.

Conclusion: entrepreneurial activism and the redefinition of sustainable food

What does this mean for alternative food networks? Goodman, DuPuis and Goodman (2014, p. 6) state that '[o]nce food politics is caught in the maze of competing definitions of the "real", or the "local" the game is already lost'. My exploratory analysis of entrepreneurial visions of sustainable food futures complicates this picture. Competing definitions of sustainable food might not necessarily mean that the game is lost, but rather that the rules of the game are adapting. Further research would be required to more systematically explore the different practices and situations in which sustainable foods are negotiated.[17] Ideally, such studies would attend to the network infrastructures—digital or non-digital—and to the technological, economic, scientific, and environmental assumptions underpinning these infrastructures and the relations they enable and constrain.

My initial findings lead me to suggest that promises by agtech and foodtech entrepreneurs resemble those of food activists. Start-ups often adopt communication strategies similar to those of alternative food networks and NGOs, particularly in relation to (the scale of) current environmental issues and how particular forms and materials of food production, distribution and consumption are posed as responses to environmental problems. To the extent that these communication strategies resemble those employed by food activists, the commitment with which some food start-ups seek to change the way we produce, distribute and consume food leads me to frame their promissory and promotional efforts as a form of entrepreneurial activism.

However, the solutions proposed by food activists and entrepreneurial activists differ. In the case of start-ups, they tend to be focused on technological solutions to environmental problems (Sexton, 2016; Stephens and Ruivenkamp, 2016; Yates-Doerr, 2015). Additionally, entrepreneurial efforts are limited by their dependency, in the majority of cases, on financial investments to pursue further research and development. Procuring these investments requires start-ups to show their financial viability to potential investors. In this context, they may opt to present their environmental ambitions as a business opportunity by pointing to economic efficiencies, as discussed in this chapter: good for the planet, good for health and good for the company's development. Essento presents an interesting case of entrepreneurial activism, because the start-up's founders carefully negotiate the organisation's investment, impact and growth trajectory guided by their core values. Ultimately, however, the level and type of financial investment start-ups require to realise their business ideas limit their ability to ignore financial imperatives tied to particular forms of investments, such as venture capital.

It is here, at the nexus of the financing of start-ups and the realising of envisioned food futures, that sociotechnical promises play their key roles of attracting investors' (and others') interest, mobilising resources (in this case, investments), and bridging otherwise distinct dimensions (cf. Borup et al., 2006, pp. 285–286). This is nicely illustrated in Stephens and Ruivenkamp's (2016, p. 349) study, in which, using the example of cultured meat, they argue that:

> When successful, the affordances of the promise and ontological status of IVM as meat in these images have social and material impacts. They make IVM reputable and attract money, which in turn shapes innovation practices, which in turn will reshape the imagescape once again.

My ongoing research project investigates this shaping of innovation practices and how, in turn, these practices will reshape what sustainable food is, how it will be produced, and what will be consumed under this banner. In this chapter, my exploratory analysis suggests that food innovation, fostered in particular settings, and underpinned by strong techno-economic assumptions, is not focused on mainstreaming alternative food networks' goals, but rather redefines what constitutes 'sustainable food' and how it can be achieved.[18]

This redefinition of sustainable food by entrepreneurial activists is structured by a productionist ethos, favouring technological solutions that achieve economies of scale. If, due to its potential scaling effects, such an understanding comes to dominate food policy discussions as the most viable way to achieve food security, it has the potential to become politically preferable to food systems approaches to sustainable futures. This is especially the case when the productionist ethos is presented as solving a key concern in contemporary food policy debates (and beyond): that is, sustainability. Ultimately, I argue that it is important to study the process of redefining what is sustainable food production and consumption, the situated practices and tools of redefining, and their potential implications, because these have the potential to shape collective ideas of how best to achieve food security. Based on my explorative research, I suggest that entrepreneurs privilege the use of novel technologies over other potential ways to achieve food security by presenting them as both desirable and attainable. Understanding these entrepreneurial visions is vital, as they have the potential to significantly shape the framing of collective ideas of how to achieve food security and sustainable food futures.

Notes

1 Obama briefly refers to activists in a later part of his article, when he states that activists often forget that 'once you've got the attention of the people in power, then you have to engage them', and proposes several ways to achieve this: by presenting facts, being willing to compromise, and 'propos[ing] concrete solutions'.

2 Agtech and foodtech are two abbreviations commonly used in entrepreneurial and venture capital settings for agricultural and food technology respectively. The terms are also used in (social) media reportage. A start-up is a business or company that has recently been founded on the basis of an innovative product, service or business model. To support the development of the company, start-ups seek public and/or private investments in the form of crowd funding, angel investment, venture philanthropy or venture capital.

3 www.seedsandchips.com/4-8-17news-growth-train. Accessed 14 August 2017.

4 Beyond STS, these claims have been criticised by a number of other scholars from a variety of disciplines, including, but not limited to, media and communication studies, sociology, philosophy and literary studies.

5 This exploratory research project, 'Venture Food: A Sociological Study of Venture Capital, #foodtech and the Future of Food', was financially supported by the Basic Research Fund at the University of St. Gallen, Switzerland.

6 This section is based on information available on UrbanFarmers' web site (https:// urbanfarmers.com/) at the time of writing in autumn 2017, as well as on a field visit to the company's first site in Basel in 2014, which included a guided tour of the rooftop farm and informal conversations with one of the founders during the visit. Since that time, UrbanFarmers is defunct and its web site no longer available. Versions of the web site can be accessed through digital archives (e.g. Wayback machine) of the world wide web.

7 Available at: https://urbanfarmers.com/technology/aquaponics/. Accessed 2 September 2017.

8 For a photo of the site, see https://urbanfarmers.com/projects/basel/. Accessed 2 September 2017.

9 On another page, the visitor reads the slogan 'Real freshness means food is grown where it's eaten'. This focus on the freshness of the produce, as conveyed by the various visual and textual descriptions on the web site, is nothing new to scholars of novel food and food technologies (Freidberg, 2010). However, previous research on fresh food has emphasised the shifting notions of what fresh has meant at different points in time. I explore this question in relation to UrbanFarmers in the discussion section.

10 Available at https://urbanfarmers.com/technology/aquaponics/. Accessed 3 September 2017.

11 This quote is taken from UrbanFarmers' web site, https://urbanfarmers.com/technol ogy/uf-node/. Accessed 10 December 2017.

12 https://docs.wixstatic.com/ugd/4d8b84_be8da7bb948c43e7b6e5d39b444fe768.pdf, as linked from the main web site. Accessed 4 September 2017.

13 Presentation available for download from the CombaGroup web site, https://docs. wixstatic.com/ugd/4d8b84_be8da7bb948c43e7b6e5d39b444fe768.pdf. See slide 4, 'Product—Key Benefits for Producers & Consumers'. Accessed 4 September 2017.

14 See https://www.crunchbase.com/organization/combagroup. Accessed 22 December 2017.

15 Passages cited from Essento's web site, http://www.essento.ch./ (accessed 7 September 2017), are my translations from German.

16 See www.essento.ch/unsere-mission/. Accessed 5 January 2017.

17 In the case of ethical foods this has been explored for various settings, including retailers (Lewis and Huber, 2015; Sexton, 2016; Stephens and Ruivenkamp, 2016; Yates-Doerr, 2015) and media and food industries (Phillipov, 2017).
18 The case of Essento highlights that other trajectories are possible but require careful negotiation of an organisation's development, or may even involve deviation from the standard trajectory developing a business idea into a profitable company.

References

Alkon, A. H. and Guthman, J. (2017). Introduction. In A. H. Alkon and J. Guthman (eds.), *The New Food Activism: Opposition, Cooperation, and Collective Action*. Oakland, CA: The University of California Press.

Birch, K. (2017). Techno-Economic Assumptions. *Science as Culture* 26 (4), 433–444.

Borup, M., Brown, N., Konrad, K. and van Lente, H. (2006). The Sociology of Expectations in Science and Technology. *Technology Analysis & Strategic Management*, 18 (3/4), 285–298.

Brown, N. (2003). Hope against Hype—Accountability in Biopasts, Presents and Futures. *Science Studies*, 16 (2), 3–21.

Caulfield, T. and Condit, C. (2012). Science and the Sources of Hype. *Public Health Genomics*, 15 (3–4), 209–217.

Counihan, C. and Siniscalchi, V. (eds.). (2014). *Food Activism: Agency, Democracy and Economy*. London: Bloomsbury.

de Schutter, O. (2011). *Human Rights Council. Nineteenth Session. Agenda Item 3: Promotion and Protection of All Human Rights, Civil, Political, Economic, Social and Cultural Rights, Including the Right to Development. Report Submitted by the Special Rapporteur on the Right to Food*. New York: United Nations.

Foresight. (2011). *The Future of Food and Farming*. Final Project Report. London: The Government Office for Science. Available at: www.gov.uk/government/uploads/system/uploads/attachment_data/file/288329/11-546-future-of-food-and-farming-report.pdf. Accessed 20 January 2016.

Freidberg, S. (2010). *Fresh: A Perishable History*. Boston, MA: Harvard University Press.

Godfray, H. C. J., Beddington, J. R., Crute, I. R., Haddad, L., Lawrence, D., Muir, J. F., Pretty, J., Robinson, S., Thomas, S. M. and Toulmin, C. (2010). Food Security: The Challenge of Feeding 9 Billion People. *Science*, 327 (5967), 812–818.

Goodman, D., DuPuis, M. E. and Goodman, M. K. (eds.). (2014). *Alternative Food Networks: Knowledge, Practice, and Politics*. London: Routledge.

Hine, C. (2015). *Ethnography for the Internet: Embedded, Embodied and Everyday*. London: Bloomsbury.

Jasanoff, S. (2015). Future Imperfect: Science, Technology, and the Imaginations of Modernity. In S. Jasanoff and S.-H. Kim (eds.). *Dreamscapes of Modernity: Socio-technical Imaginaries and the Fabrication of Power* (pp. 1–33). Chicago: University of Chicago Press.

Kline, R. R. (2001). Technological Determinism. In N. J. Smelser and P. B. Baltes (eds.), *International Encyclopedia of the Social & Behavioral Sciences* (pp. 15495–15498). Oxford: Elsevier.

Lang, T. and Barling, D. (2012). Food Security and Food Sustainability: Reformulating the Debate. *The Geographical Journal*, 178 (4), 313–326.

Lewis, T. and Huber, A. (2015). A Revolution in an Eggcup? Supermarket Wars, Celebrity Chefs, and Ethical Consumption. *Food, Culture and Society*, 18 (2), 289–307.

Lewis, T. and Potter, E. (2011). *Ethical Consumption: A Critical Introduction*. London: Routledge.

Lupton, D. (2017). Download to Delicious: Promissory Themes and Sociotechnical Imaginaries in Coverage of 3D Printed Food in Online News Sources. *Futures*, 93, 44–53.

Lyson, H. C. (2014). Social Structural Location and Vocabularies of Participation: Fostering a Collective Identity in Urban Agriculture Activism. *Rural Sociology*, 79 (3), 310–335.

Martin, P. (2015). Commercialising Neurofutures: Promissory Economies, Value Creation and the Making of a New Industry. *BioSocieties*, 10 (4), 422–443.

McClintock, N. (2010). Why Farm the City? Theorizing Urban Agriculture through a Lens of Metabolic Rift. *Cambridge Journal of Regions, Economy and Society*, 3 (2), 191–207.

McKeon, N. (2015). *Food Security Governance: Empowering Communities, Regulating Corporations*. London: Sage.

Müller, C. (ed.). (2011). *Urban Gardening. Über die Rückkehr der Gärten in die Stadt*. München: Oekom Verlag.

Obama, B. (2017). Barack Obama on Food and Climate Change: 'We Can Still Act and It Won't Be Too Late'. *The Guardian*, 26 May. Available at: https://www.theguardian.com/global-development/2017/may/26/barack-obama-food-climate-change. Accessed 19 October 2018.

O'Riordan, K., Fotopoulou, A. and Stephens, N. (2017). The First Bite: Imaginaries, Promotional Publics and the Laboratory Grown Burger. *Public Understanding of Science*, 26 (2), 148–163.

Phillipov, M. (2017). *Media and Food Industries: The New Politics of Food*. Basingstoke: Palgrave Macmillan.

Pollock, N. and Williams, R. (2010). The Business of Expectations: How Promissory Organizations Shape Technology and Innovation. *Social Studies of Science*, 40 (4), 525–548.

Pollock, N. and Williams, R. (2016). *How Industry Analysts Shape the Digital Future*. Oxford: Oxford University Press.

Sassatelli, R. and Davolio, F. (2010). Consumption, Pleasure and Politcs: Slow Food and the Politico-Aesthethic Problematization of Food. *Journal of Consumer Culture*, 10 (2), 202–232.

Schneider, T., Eli, K., Dolan, C. and Ulijaszek, S. (eds.). (2018). *Digital Food Activism*. London: Routledge.

Schneider, T. and Woolgar, S. (2015). Neuroscience Beyond the Laboratory: Neuro Knowledges, Technologies and Markets. *BioSocieties*, 10 (4), 389–399.

Sexton, A. (2016). Alternative Proteins and the (Non)Stuff of 'Meat'. *Gastronomica: The Journal of Critical Food Studies*, 16 (3), 66–78.

Stephens, N. and Ruivenkamp, M. (2016). Promise and Ontological Ambiguity in the in Vitro Meat Imagescape: From Laboratory Myotubes to the Cultured Burger. *Science as Culture*, 25 (3), 327–355.

Stuckler, D. and Nestle, M. (2012). Big Food: Food Systems and Global Health. *PLoS Medicine*, 9 (6), e1001242.

Tomlinson, I. (2013). Doubling Food Production to Feed the 9 Billion: A Critical Perspective on A Key Discourse of Food Security in the UK. *Journal of Rural Studies*, 29, 81–90.

Wajcman, J. (2015). *Pressed for Time: The Acceleration of Life in Digital Capitalism*. Chicago/London: Chicago University Press.

Wheeler, T. and von Braun, J. (2013). Climate Change Impacts on Global Food Security. *Science*, 341 (6145), 508–513.

World Business Council for Sustainable Development (WBCSD). (2000). *Eco-Efficiency: Creating More Value with Less Impact*. Geneva: World Business Council for Sustainable Development.

Yates-Doerr, E. (2015). The World in a Box? Food Security, Edible Insects, and 'One World, One Health' Collaboration. *Social Science and Medicine*, 129, 106–122.

5 The Welcome Dinner Project
Food hospitality activism and digital media

Rick Flowers and Elaine Swan

Introduction

In 2014, one of the authors attended a Welcome Dinner event with 200 guests in Sydney's central business district. The Welcome Dinner Project (WDP) is a food social enterprise that, in its own description, brings together 'established Australians' with 'newly arrived Australians' through potluck dinners. The WDP organises two types of 'hospitable encounter': dinners in people's homes, and dinners in community spaces. Elaine learnt about the event through social media, having become aware of the WDP via the public relations magazine of the University of Technology Sydney. Elaine sat at a table with an Iraqi family, a Malaysian Australian, and two Japanese international students, and noticed that the event was being photographed and filmed. She later joined the Facebook group. This was WDP's first major public event. At that stage, few home dinners had taken place. Four years later, the WDP has grown rapidly, and now operates in all Australian states and territories, emerging in a context of racist government policies and media reporting on refugees and asylum seekers, and alongside a resurgence of white supremacist anti-immigration politics in Australia.

Since the WDP's founding in 2014, we have studied it ethnographically and through digital media analysis. In this chapter, we examine how what we call the 'food hospitality activism' of the WDP is made visible through its online media practices, and how these meanings change in racist ways through the re-mediation of WDP images via mainstream news and entertainment media. By food hospitality activism, we mean attempts by NGOs and social enterprises to facilitate connections between people of different racial backgrounds through food and hospitality, as a way to address social injustice and racism.

To date, writing on digital food media spans various disciplines, media, genres, digital artefacts and food themes, for instance: hashtags, food and health (Rich, Haddadi and Hospedales, 2016); food blogs (Adami, 2014; Koh, 2014/2015); pro-anorexia ('pro-ana') blogs (Lavis, 2017); digital food porn (Dejmanee, 2016; Ibrahim, 2015); digital food cultures (Lupton, 2018); food web sites (Adami, 2014, 2015a; Flowers and Swan, 2017); Black hashtag activism (Vats, 2015); and fish activism and digital transmedia (Gambarato and Medvedev, 2015). But little attention has been given to the digital media associated with food hospitality activist social enterprises and their political effects, despite their proliferation internationally, from Germany, Sweden and the US to Australia (Flowers and Swan, 2017, 2018).

The WDP relies on its own web pages, plus accounts on platforms such as Facebook, Instagram, YouTube and Twitter for marketing and public communications, all of which are managed by volunteers. The WDP produces, distributes and cross-posts a range of its own, and other media-generated, multimodal texts across these platforms. In this chapter, we focus on photographs of food commensality drawn from the online presence of the WDP, and consider how the meanings of the WDP shift as the visual and verbal texts are re-mediated elsewhere. We use the terms 'visual' and 'verbal' texts in line with multimodality studies, in which visual text refers to visual elements, such as graphics, typeface, colour, and digital photographs, and verbal text to written words. In this chapter, we focus on the digital photographs and accompanying verbal texts associated with home (as opposed to community) events, as the WDP sees these home dinners as their 'ur' food hospitality events.

The WDP takes photographs and posts a selection of them on its web site, and uploads, shares, forwards, reposts and re-contextualises, and 're-genres' these images across its social media (Adami, 2014). Online magazines and newspapers published by large media companies, including News Corp and Fairfax, re-purpose WDP images and verbal texts. Media companies also generate their own images, and re-purpose those published elsewhere for their coverage of the WDP. The WDP then curates this coverage in the form of hyperlinks on its web pages. In this way, visual and verbal texts by and about the WDP move around the Internet by means of its circulation economy and audiences. Thus, cross-posting and re-mediation—re-using texts created for other purposes in other contexts—is central to the WDP and to the ways in which ideas about race are depicted and mobilised (Adami, 2014).

The various social media, online newspaper and magazine platforms have different multimodal and technological affordances, genres, conventions, audience profiles and relations with audiences. Elisabetta Adami (2014) points out that genre, meaning and form can change as texts are cross-posted on platforms with different modes of meaning-making. Thus, re-mediation and re-contextualisation, while not unique to online media, are fundamental to thinking about digital representations of the WDP, its aims, politics and visibility. On that point, this chapter examines how the WDP's representation of hospitality activism change visually, racially and politically through re-mediation by different media outlets. Our analysis shows that persistent racism occurs in online news and entertainment media reporting on the WDP. In particular, we analyse how the WDP's images of welcoming are re-mediated in ways that fit racist scripts about whiteness and acceptable images of cultural and racial diversity.

Our contribution to the scholarship on alternative food and media is threefold. First, we follow a food social enterprise's social media images as they are re-mediated and re-contextualised across various digital platforms. Second, we provide a racialised analysis of these forms of mediation by showing how the re-mediated images change the WDP's images of welcoming to consolidate racist meanings. Third, we show how seemingly 'innocent' images of food racialise. To begin, we provide a brief introduction to the project and its history. This is followed by a discussion about Australian multiculturalism, a summary of our method, and a detailed discussion of our sample of digital media texts.

The Welcome Dinner

The WDP is an example of Australian food hospitality activism. Its purpose is to bring together 'newly arrived people and established Australians to meet over dinner conversation in the comfort of their own home' (The Welcome Dinner Project, n.d., p. 1). The WDP's publicity materials explain that 'people come together across cultures over a shared meal' (Attend a Home Dinner, n.d.), and that this is a means by which 'strangers [...] become friends' (Bishara, 2015, p. 1). The project aims to:

> create a platform for meaningful connection, sparking friendships between people of diverse cultures who are living in close proximity to one another in communities throughout Australia.
>
> (The Welcome Dinner Project, n.d., p. 1)

The project's purpose is to facilitate connections between people through food, as the *Guide for Welcome Dinner Participants* explains: 'the mix of food, conversation and the opportunity to try something new, creates a perfect recipe for connection and rediscovery of our common humanity' (The Welcome Dinner Project, n.d., p. 3). It is hoped that diners will 'exchange contacts and stay in touch afterwards' (The Welcome Dinner Project, n.d., p. 2). A central part of the WDP's philosophy is that the dinners benefit established Australians as much as they do those newly arrived, because they, too, suffer social isolation.

Since 2013, the WDP has hosted over 200 dinners in homes and community spaces across Australia. Over 300 WDP facilitators have been trained, and over 5,000 people have attended a dinner. The WDP is run largely by volunteers. Funding is sporadic, with small amounts raised through crowd funding, and to date only two state governments have given grants; local councils have provided in-kind support.

The events

The WDP convenes dinner events in 'local homes'. Hosts and participants register online. A local co-ordinator selects and formally invites a mixture of about eight established Australians and eight new arrivals, ideally residing in the same area. The dinners are hosted either by an established or newly arrived person, and run for two hours: this timing is strictly adhered to by the facilitators, who are trained volunteers. The host's home and motivation are vetted by WDP facilitators, who visit the host at home before the event. The agenda includes a formal welcome, an acknowledgement of the Indigenous owners of the land, a welcome and introduction to their home by the host, and then an icebreaker. After this, guests gather around the food they have brought, and each person explains their dish. The guests then eat, share their feelings about the event, exchange contact information, and pose for a group photo.

For the WDP, the term 'established Australians' refers to anyone who has lived in Australia for over ten years, and the term 'newly arrived Australians' covers all other Australian residents. At the dinners we attended, there was a mixture of people, including international students from the Philippines, Germany and China, established Anglo- and Asian Australians, and refugees from Iraq, Iran, and Afghanistan.

The politics of welcoming

From the name 'Welcome Dinner Project' it can be understood that welcoming new arrivals into homes and to Australia through food is the organisation's central political and cultural aim. The significance of the WDP's practices of welcoming through commensality are repeated in media coverage of the WDP, in its hand-books and training courses, and at the dinners themselves. The rationale presented for the food hospitality activism of the Welcome Dinners is three-fold. First, the founder, Penny Elsley, states that many new arrivals have never been invited to an established Australian's home. Second, a weak sense of belonging, of isolation and disconnection, is not peculiar to new arrivals, but also affects established Australians. And third, many established Australians want to meet new arrivals but do not know how.

Welcoming initiatives, structures and practices for refugees, asylum seekers and new migrants have a particular history in the policies of Australian governments, and in the approaches taken by NGOs. As Giulia Borri, Brigida Orria and Alex Vailati note of Italian government practices:

> In every social context we can find particular philosophies and expressions of welcoming. Strangers and travelers are part of everyday life even in places that are far from the global flow of symbols and people. Welcoming practices are usually very complex. They have different aims and strategies in every context.
>
> (2014, p. 11)

Globally, the idea of 'welcoming' crops up frequently in policy and civil society discourses about refugees and asylum seekers. Various governments have attempted to establish welcoming infrastructures. Since 2015, for example, European cities have collaborated to improve welcoming initiatives for refugees and other migrants (Bousiou, Bucken-Knapp and Spehar, 2016). Academics critique such welcoming initiatives on a number of fronts. For instance, Borri, Orria and Vailati (2014) assert that welcoming projects are based on essentialist constructions of refugees, and present welcoming as derived from notions of charity and pity, rather than from the empowerment of migrant communities. They argue that welcoming practices can thus intensify stigmatisation and discrimination. Another criticism is that welcoming policies are more informed by geo-political and economic, rather than humanitarian, concerns (Akrap, 2015).

As in Europe, welcoming new arrivals to Australia is also politically complicated. Invaded by the British Empire in 1788, the nation-state of Australia was founded as a settler colony, in which Indigenous people were systematically murdered, dispossessed and disadvantaged—and aspects of such systems persist today. Since Aboriginal people have not ceded sovereignty, this means that non-Aboriginal people are not in a position to welcome new arrivals. The acknowledgement of the country's traditional owners, mentioned above, is a protocol observed at public events, in which local Aboriginal elders welcome non-Aboriginal people to their land. A second reason why welcoming is so complex is that Australia has a long history of racist immigration policies, of not being welcoming- and continues to administer cruel immigration detention practices. This is despite the country's history of large-scale migration, and the fact that multiculturalism is much vaunted in the 'selling' and marketing of Australia (Ho, 2011). While racism towards Indigenous Australians and to other racially minoritised groups persists, prejudiced fears and hatred are now most intensely levelled at Arab and Muslim Australians, both new and established, with particularly notable moral panics occurring after 11 September 2001, and during and after the Cronulla Riots in 2005 (Dreher and Ho, 2009). The Australian government's refugee and asylum seeker policies are now some of the most draconian, and securitised, in the world, with privatised and violent off-shore detention centres, and exclusionary legislation. While there are NGOs (such as the WDP) advocating more support, the Australian government's track record in relation to refugees can best be described as harsh.

In spite of Australia's relatively small per capita intake of refugees, there have been ongoing moral panics about refugees and asylum seekers as a 'deviant population'; the media has frequently presented asylum seekers as invading, racialised, diseased and deviant (Pickering, 2001). Mainstream media, right wing activists and politicians have consistently presented Australia as under siege, with displaced people—refugees and asylum seekers—constructed as 'queue jumpers', and as threats to national security, as well as to supposedly homogenous 'Australian values'. Farida Fozdar and Lisa Hartley write that 'negativity towards refugees in particular is widespread, with up to 75% of the population seeing them as a threat' (2013, p. 130). As a result, visibly different migrants are unlikely to feel welcomed by the majority mainstream population, and may feel ambivalent about whether they belong in Australia.

The WDP draws attention not only to the situation facing refugees, but also to that of international students, who can experience intense loneliness (Sawir et al., 2008), racism from state structures and universities, racialised exploitation as casual workers (Florance and McGhee, 2016), and racist abuse on public transport (Williams, Gailberger and Lim, 2016). Through its food hospitality activism, the WDP seeks to challenge racist and xenophobic views of refugees, and of racialised migrants and international students.

Methodology

Based on our review of the literature, our research question became: How do visual and verbal texts represent the food hospitality activism of the WDP? To answer this, we analysed visual and verbal texts drawn from the WDP's web- and Facebook pages, and from online magazines hyperlinked on the WDP web page's news media section. We selected texts that represented food hospitality activism, particularly photographs of food and commensality and their associated headlines and verbal text. Images selected for analysis were either taken directly by WDP volunteers and re-mediated by mainstream media publications, or they were taken by professional photographers for media stories about the WDP. Our focus was on the semiotic resources and the meaning-making potential of these texts, and not on their conditions of production or their interpretation by audiences (Swan, 2010). But such a focus has it limits. For instance, industry conditions affect how visual and written texts are produced. Photographers cannot control how their digital images are re-purposed by the journalists who compose the written text. Journalists do not write their own headlines, and this can also contribute to shifts in meaning-making potential. Despite the complexities of these production contexts, this chapter works from the view that images and verbal texts work to produce meanings 'beyond' the intentions of their producers.

Theoretical framing, methods and sampling

Our theoretical approach draws on literature from critical race and whiteness studies, feminist studies of digital media, and critical food studies. It is influenced by social semiotics and multimodal discourse analysis (Adami, 2014, 2015a; Nakamura, 2002; van Leeuwen, 2005), with a particular focus on hyperlinking and cross-posting (Adami, 2014, 2015b). Multimodal semiotic approaches are not rigid maps but descriptive frameworks (Jewitt and Oyama, 2001). They are the first step in our analysis, enabling descriptions of analytic categories, followed by explanatory categories, followed by theoretical approaches to enable wider social and political interpretations (Jewitt and Oyama, 2001).

Taking inspiration from Brooke Erin Duffy, Urszula Pruchniewska and Leah Scolere's (2017) argument that media ecologies need analysing, we cut a slice through the WDP's media ecology and, inspired by Ian Cook's (2004) work on following food, we 'followed' the WDP media and their hyperlinks. We followed the hyperlinks to online magazine and newspaper coverage, because hyperlinks indicate the associations that the WDP web pages seek to create as part of their 'virtual neighbourhood' (Martinson, 2006). External links to other sites, along with differences in lexical field and images, influence how users read web sites and can also indicate political effects.

We viewed the WDP web pages and online media coverage hyperlinked from them, took screenshots that we labelled, stored digitally and printed, and noted points of interest in relation to images of food, commensality and people to develop preliminary codes. We then coded all the images on the web pages and online media stories more systematically, adding a sample of 10 images each from the Facebook and Instagram sites. Accessed in January 2015 and in April 2017, our dataset comprised:

- Nine (9) images from the WDP web pages;
- Twenty-one (21) images from 13 online magazine and newspaper stories;
- Ten (10) images from the WDP Facebook site; and
- Ten (10) images from the WDP Instagram account.

We generated codes such as 'ethnic food', 'eating', 'whiteness' and 'commensality' from the literature and the images. Analysis of whiteness is complex because it is both seen and unseen, and it is performed through stylised visual conventions and cultural scripts that normalise whiteness across a range of off- and online media (Flowers and Swan, 2017; Swan, 2010, 2017). Our analysis was informed by our already well-established focus on visual regimes of making race: Lisa Nakamura's work on 'digital racial formation' (2002, 2008), and the 'racialised gaze' and 'coloured semiotic resources' in visual design and digital multi-modality (Fleckenstein, 2014; Hum, 2015).

After collecting our larger sample, we selected three images and their accompanying verbal texts for detailed analysis and interpretation. The images represent each of the three major visual tropes: 'food porn', 'world on a plate' and 'home mode everyday multiculturalism'. The texts were each accessed via the WDP web pages, which hyperlinked to online media publications. Two images were taken by professional photographers on behalf of the media publications, and the verbal texts were written by a journalist. The third image was uploaded to the WDP Facebook page by a WDP volunteer, and was then published in an online newspaper alongside a verbal text prepared by a journalist.

Imaging food hospitality activism

Visually, the most striking feature of the full sample of photographs is the predominance in the online magazine and newspaper publications of close-up and intimate images of dishes of prepared food. When people are featured, the images typically do not show full bodies, but only arms and hands serving food. There were fewer photographs of people interacting over food than one might expect, given that the WDP is about commensality, or as they put it, 'conversations over food'. Indeed, it was typical of the online magazines' reporting on the WDP to focus on dishes of food and not on people. Such images were often in the conventionalised and highly popular genre of 'food porn' (Coward, 1985; Cruz, 2013; Dejmanee, 2016; Ibrahim, 2015; Lavis, 2017). Overall, what is conspicuous across the online newspapers and magazines is the lack of photographs of food preparation, of eating, or of cleaning up after the meal. In contrast, the WDP web pages feature a much higher percentage of images of people eating together. There are also a great number of full shots of people—rather than hands—serving food, or standing near plates of food. The other prominent difference between the images is in their style and aesthetics. The effect of these differences, as we argue below, is that the re-mediated news media images reproduce a pervasive whiteness that preserves offline racist meanings and recirculates them online.

Digital food porn

To turn now to a detailed analysis of the three images, we examine two taken from a national, and one from a regional, online newspaper. We begin with the online version of the *Sydney Morning Herald*'s magazine supplement, *Good Food*. The *Good Food* story about the WDP is dominated by a large photograph of a pavlova. The image sits at the top of the page, and is accompanied by a column of verbal text (see Boys, 2014). The image is brightly lit and shot from above at an oblique angle. It displays a perfectly round pavlova, up close and personal enough to see syrup dripping through the deep folds of whipped cream, and banana and passionfruit slices sliding lusciously down the sides of the white meringue. This image is a classic 'food porn' shot, part of a 'now familiar trend in gastronomic representation' that entails 'spectacularized commensality' (Lavis, 2017, p. 200). Academics and food commentators alike use the term food porn to describe a visual genre of conventionalised images of food, highly stylised such that they appear 'more than real', and that stimulate the senses (van Leeuwen, 2005, p. 170). The stylistic conventions include close-up shots of food, usually desserts, artfully lit with a focus on detail, sharpness, glossiness, colourfulness, depth and 'oozing' (Coward, 1985; Dejmanee, 2016), together producing food porn's 'Rubenesque excesses' (Cruz, 2013, p. 331).

An important point about food porn is its migration and proliferation as a food media genre from offline to online. Tania Dejmanee (2016) describes how the term food porn was used before the Internet to describe images in print media and advertising, but that this style has since been modified for digital media. Ariane Cruz (2013) suggests that 'cyber gastro-porn' has 'perforated' interactive, user-driven digital photograph sharing platforms such as Instagram. Anna Lavis (2017) points to a wide range of platforms on which food porn images are circulated, from Facebook to Pinterest, Tumblr to Instagram. She shows not only how offline images get re-mediated online, but also how online images shape media representations offline:

> Such foodie moments seep beyond the Internet into other forms of popular media, such as UK fashion magazine Marie Claire's 'Insta-grub' section, which comprises seven photographs of food taken by a different celebrity each month.
>
> (Lavis, 2017, p. 200)

Yasmin Ibrahim emphasises that digital food porn elicits 'an invitation to gaze and vicariously consume, and to tag images of food through digital platforms' (2015, p. 2). In this way, she argues, 'our eyes let us "taste" food at a distance by activating the sense memories of taste and smell' (Ibrahim, 2015, p. 4). Food porn works to stimulate our desire and ogling, but remains unattainable. Cruz writes that food porn provides:

> brilliant close-up photographs of splendidly executed dishes created with exotic ingredients—and its chimerical act of transforming a food fantasy (one far out of reach of the quotidian, non-professional American chef) [into] a phantasmagorical yet palatable food reality.
>
> (2013, p. 331)

This fantasy is amplified in that food porn photographs always hide the labour that goes into their production (Lavis, 2017).

It is somewhat surprising that an online food magazine would feature a food porn shot in coverage of the WDP, given that the project is about food hospitality activism. The focus of the WDP is not completely lost on *Good Food*, though, as the headline for the article, 'Welcome Dinner Project connects Australians with refugees' (Boys, 2014), reveals. Underneath the pavlova photograph is the caption: 'Welcome to our world: Welcome Dinners unite people through the simple act of sharing food'. The article acknowledges the aims of the WDP and foregrounds refugees in its verbal text, while the visual text offers an alternative meaning, namely a racialised reading of the WDP that focuses on whiteness.

Very few scholars have commented on the racialisation of food porn, but race can be signified through a number of visual tropes, including food (Flowers and Swan, 2017; Hall, 1997). Amy Bentley (2001), Melissa Click (2009), Perel Gurel (2016), Diana Negra (2002), Lisa Jordan Powell and Elizabeth Engelhardt (2015) all stress how food media can signify whiteness in varying ways, from food's lighting to its marketing and cultural associations. Accordingly, we suggest that the digitalised pavlova, as an image of the national dish of Australia, connotes white Australia in a number of ways. Adapted from a smaller New Zealand dessert in the 1930s, the pavlova with its European colonial meringue, invokes the Russian ballet dancer Anna Pavlova with her femininity, daintiness, lightness and whiteness (Leach, 2010; Leach and Browne, 2008; Symons, 2010). Michael Symons points to its nostalgic appeal in the latter part of the 20th Century as:

> Contrasting markedly with the even earlier, masculine meat pies, damper and billy tea, this feminine food icon harked back to the disappearing full-time home-makers—people's mothers and grandmothers.
>
> (2010, p. 212)

Indeed, many early 20th Century women's community cookbooks called on women to make the perfect pavlova. Thus, the pavlova not only references the feminine whiteness of the ballet dancer, but also white domestic femininity in the days of overwhelmingly white immigration. In this way, the pavlova's connotations of white femininity and nostalgia for an Anglo-centric Australia work to visually counter the message of the WDP and its project of hospitality activism.

Anthropological studies stress that particular foods, meals or cuisines are emblematic of nations (O'Connor, 2008). Most people's day-to-day experience of the nation is not through political rhetoric, but through food, and indeed we can see nationalism invoked in cookbooks, food advertising, ingredients and dishes (Crowther, 2013, p. 139; Palmer, 1998, p. 187). We can think of the *Good Food* image of the pavlova, therefore, as a form of digital 'banal nationalism' (Billig, 1995). Greg Noble (2002) writes how 'banal nationalism', as expressed in Australian homes in the form of trinkets, embeds the nation 'materially in everyday life' (p. 54). In the online food magazine, the image is accompanied by the verbal text, 'welcome to our world'. The verbal text re-inflects the nostalgia for white feminine domesticity connoted by the visual text to position white people as the welcoming hosts of the nation. Groups who are seen to be more 'of the nation' than others are recognised as the arbiters of national culture, and define who can belong and under what conditions (Hage, 2012). Hence, the food hospitality activism of the WDP is visually and digitally re-semioticised as white.

Digital world on a plate

In the second image, taken from another hyperlinked magazine, we can see a different kind of othering at work. Rather than just one image, *Broadsheet*—an online entertainment publication which specialises in events and food reporting—features an incredible seven digital food porn-style photos under the headline and above a block of verbal text (see Kauppi, 2014). The text reads: 'A beautifully simple idea, the Welcome Dinner Project is helping new arrivals and established locals get to know each other over a good feed'.

The dynamic images are at the top of the web page and rotate between a range of beautifully shot images of people helping themselves to an aesthetically appealing buffet table bedecked with well-displayed dishes of food. Some images show disembodied white arms and hands reaching out for the food. One depicts a white male hand and forearm proffering a gleaming stainless-steel pan of 'ethnic'-looking food above a feta cheese salad and a dish of lasagne. Five of the images feature middle class-looking cutlery and bowls, such as wooden salad servers, ramekins, and enamel baking dishes. Two foreground a glistening wok, filled not with brightly coloured, takeaway-style Chinese stir-fried food, but white middle-class fare, signified by the presence of grains and greens.

Overall, these images depict the abundance and diversity of ethnicised dishes available for the taking. Like similar images in the other online publications, they reference the 'world on a plate' trope found in off- and online media, in which a cornucopia of 'foreign' dishes are arranged in buffet style and visualised in an aesthetically appealing way, ready for eating (Cook and Crang, 1996). Ian Cook and Phil Crang argue that the 'world on a plate' trope is a food media motif that depicts and evokes a white middle-class desire to consume a medley of 'foreign' dishes—for what has been called 'food adventuring' (Heldke, 2003). As Sunvendrini Perera and Joseph Pugliese write:

[t]he culinary, with its economy of enrichment and incorporation, signifies the palatable and always aestheticized element of multiculturalism precisely because it still effectively reproduces an assimilationist economy of cultural containment and control.

(1996, p. 110)

Thus, the *Broadsheet* images represent 'edible diversity'—palatable and digestible to the white middle-class palate—but also the eagerness of white people to devour the Other (Ahmed, 2012, p. 204). The racialisation of the images is underscored by the headline, 'Guess Who's Coming to Dinner?', the title of a 1960s film, starring US black actor Sidney Poitier, which tells the story of a man being introduced to his white girlfriend's racist father.

Too often in food media, food is de-contextualised, both visually and textually, in ways that ignore complex histories of colonialism, power, migration, and the unpalatable realities of racism and inequality (Flowers and Swan, 2017; Germann Molz, 2007). While there is extensive criticism directed at the desire of white people to consume ethnic food in offline food media and tourism settings, to date little attention has been given to online representations and, in particular, to the 'world on a plate' trope. What is remarkable is that the *Broadsheet* images of the WDP do not depict ethnicised or racialised bodies. Such visual exclusions are key to the othering of racialised people (van Leeuwen, 2000), and to representing digital food 'multiculturalism without migrants' (Hage, 1997). In film, for example, representations of ethnic food are seen as offering vicarious consumption of culinary adventurism, but 'without ever coming into contact with actual fear-invoking racialised bodies' (Lindenfeld cited in Kelly, 2017, p. 21). As Casey Ryan Kelly insists, 'a strategic rhetoric, whiteness operates [. . .] through the negation of racialized bodies' (2017, p. 25). Again, we can see how digital food images in online food media re-inflect the WDP's food hospitality activism, visually representing the events as a way to 'do' food adventuring. Indeed, a longstanding criticism of Australia's approach to migrants is that they are only welcomed for their food. As Sneja Gunew argues:

In the imagery of official multiculturalism, the host wants only the food and only the mute or stammering bodies cut off from their words and histories. We are asked to produce only food and not fluency.

(1993, p. 41)

Peopling food

In contrast to a comparative lack of images of racialised bodies in most of the hyperlinked newspaper and magazine stories, the WDP's web pages, and its Facebook, Instagram and Twitter accounts, feature hundreds of images of people of different racialised and ethnicised backgrounds interacting during, and at the end, of the group's dinner events. For instance, the web pages present eight professional-looking images of food and commensality, featuring seven with small mixed groups of racially minoritised participants, and one of all white people. On the WDP Facebook, Instagram and Twitter pages, there are hundreds of photographs of food and commensality, with a mix of professional and amateur style close-up and long shots portraying people talking to each other, eating, helping themselves to food, and, standing and seated, in kitchens, dining rooms, lounges and on patios, at intimate and friendly social distances.

While some of the photographs are more professional or stylised (often those cross-posted and repurposed from external sites), most of those on the WDP sites are taken with mobile phones in the genre of photography called 'home mode'. Richard Chalfen (1987) writes about how Kodak film in the 1960s transformed domestic photography, creating a new expressive and aesthetic form, and it is this style that he calls 'home mode'. Seemingly spontaneous, the amateur photographs were stylised and curated by family members according to social norms of family, home and photography. Digital media scholars argue that a digital 'home mode' style of photography is making a comeback on social media as a vernacular antidote to overly stylised, perfect images, albeit with less focus on the family (Ibrahim, 2015; Perlmutter and Silvestri, 2013).

Many of the WDP snapshots of food hospitality activism reflect a 'digital home mode' style, not only in their aesthetic, but also in the focus on the domestic and its ordinariness. We see homely, cluttered, non-aestheticised domestic spaces and objects—aluminium foil, cling film, blinds, straggly garden plants, tables of messy crockery, Tupperware, mismatched furniture, and evidence of food labour. Naturalistic, poorly-lit, with higgledy-piggledy bodies and half-eaten food, these stand in stark contrast to the stylised images of food in the online newspapers and magazines.

One marked type of home mode shot is the photograph taken by the facilitators at the end of the dinner, usually on their mobile phones and conforming to generic conventions: these photos typically show the attendees at the Welcome Dinner all huddling close together with big smiles, looking directly, at a horizontal angle, at the camera, and holding coloured paper speech bubbles. Combined, these conventions signify solidarity and a sense of egalitarian conviviality. These images are then posted and shared on the WDP Facebook, Instagram and Twitter accounts. This type of image contrasts with the 'food porn' and 'world on a plate' photographs on a number of counts.

To illustrate, we describe one such photograph. The image shows a large group of adults and children from diverse racial backgrounds. People are in long shot, with their full figures in frame, and they are waving and holding the WDP cardboard cut-outs of speech bubbles on which they have written their feelings about the event (such as 'happy', 'contented', 'welcome'). People sit or stand closer to each other than in the other, more professional photographs. Although individually dressed, with different body types and hair styles, the image of the group evokes a sense of togetherness or post-meal commensality. The photograph is clearly posed, but the subjects seem relaxed and energetic, if a little self-conscious. They are smiling broadly and looking directly at us, as if inviting us to join in. A table of half-eaten dishes and dirty plates is also included in the image, a rare occurrence in re-mediated food images of the WDP, and in food media more broadly. The featured food and plates do not conform to the middle-class, stylised imagery of food porn. Instead we can see an assortment of plastic containers and plastic picnic plates and cutlery. There are no wine bottles; instead there are large bottles of value-for-money fruit juice, and piles of supermarket, sliced white bread. The image is in quintessential home mode aesthetic: blurry, harshly lit, crowded, and poorly centred.

Such home mode images express an ordinarisation of the Welcome Dinner Project and its food hospitality activism, depicting everyday multiculturalism in the domestic sphere. Helen Grace (2013) argues that the home mode of digital images is more about affective expressivity than aesthetics or content, and many of these WDP images convey warmth, generosity and conviviality, albeit mixed in with some social awkwardness. Given that these photographs are uploaded, posted, shared and circulated across a number of WDP media platforms, they interrupt 'the feed' of 'food porn' and 'world on a plate' photographs, although their circulation is constrained to their platform audiences.

Digital photography is not only a record, but also a form of activity (Pink, 2011). As Sarah Pink (p. 93) notes, amateur photographs of 'real' activities uploaded onto digital platforms by community groups document and communicate 'the experience of being involved in projects and activities'. Thus, the home mode photographs not only show us ethnic food *with* migrants, they constitute in themselves a form of activity—food hospitality activism. They also illustrate a different form of everyday multiculturalism. To date, writers on everyday multiculturalism have focused on public domains, such as shops, malls and schools, and have tended to concentrate on the temporality of the habitual and the mundane in everyday multiculturalism, rather than on planned or engineered multicultural events (Ho, 2011; Noble, 2013, Wise, 2011). In contrast, Welcome Dinners emphasise domestic domains, are highly structured, and require extensive organising. Hosts and homes are checked. Volunteers give up their time to facilitate the dinners and run activities to enable people to talk and share; they arrive early, put up balloons, help prepare the table, and welcome guests. Images of the WDP's everyday multiculturalism depict friendship and commensality in the domestic and intimate sphere. Of course, given that our focus here is on digital images taken, uploaded and shared by the WDP, we do not comment on the effects of its socio-material practices of food hospitality activism, although that is part of our wider project. As Amanda Wise (2011) suggests, there are possibilities for cultural anxiety and the exacerbation of cultural differences in cross-cultural commensality, as well as more positive outcomes. Indeed, the WDP organisers try to anticipate some of these issues in the way they choose their hosts, train volunteers and organise the events. Despite this, some of the digital home mode photos depict bodies that are more ill-at-ease than others—not hostile, but perhaps fearful, less confident or used to the circumstances.

As digital images of food hospitality activism, the WDP home mode photographs evoke an ordinarisation and domestication of racist politics in Australia. Rosalind Krauss (1984) notes that photographs of families and homes are part of the collective fantasy of domesticity and 'family cohesion', and perhaps what we have here are images of a fantasy of the nation. The home is imagined as a place of sociality, hospitality and commensality for strangers, and as a site of politics and hope that counters the wider racism of government policies and mainstream media representations. However, home mode images of hospitality activism and everyday multiculturalism can be re-semioticised once they are re-mediated from WDP sites, as was done, for example, in the online publication *The Perth Voice Interactive* (see Pollock, 2015). The *Perth Voice Interactive* displayed the group photograph discussed above next to the headline 'G'Day mate: Now get stuffed', reproducing the vocabulary and sounds typical of a broad Australian English accent, associated with an 'ocker', Anglo-centric, masculine vernacular, and with connotations of being laid back, informal and conservative (Willoughby, Starks and Taylor-Leech, 2013). Thus, in this process whiteness is re-centred, like the images of the pavlova and 'world on a plate', albeit in differently classed and gendered terms. Its white masculinity stands in strong contrast to the culturally feminised WDP, and to the wider feminine associations of domestic food, the home and hospitality.

Conclusion

In this chapter, we have analysed a sample of digital photographs and verbal texts from the WDP's online media, and from its curated online food and news media coverage. We have shown how the WDP uses social and digital media, especially photographs, to promote its project of food hospitality activism, domestic welcoming and everyday intercultural commensality. In particular, we have demonstrated that while the written text of mainstream media coverage tends to replicate the WDP's core messages, these messages can be undermined by the images that accompany them. While some of these images are drawn from the WDP's digital media, others adopt problematically racist scripts.

In this chapter, we have shown how the WDP's food hospitality activism can be re-semioticised through various genres of digital photograph, including 'food porn', 'world on a plate' and 'home mode everyday multiculturalism'. Like offline food media, online images of food can racialise, other, invoke and normalise whiteness. Because of this, we have illustrated how such images can reinforce offline racism by excluding depictions of migrants. In addition to our discussion of the cross-posting and re-mediation of digital images, we have argued that verbal text often interacts with visual text to produce and reframe meanings. We found that headlines and captions expressed views that undercut the WDP's food hospitality activism, with the effect that they reproduced racialised stereotypes. In contrast, the WDP inserts the racially minoritised into its digital representations of the everyday, tapping into people's desire to connect with the Other, and challenging racist ideas about refugees, asylum seekers and international students. The WDP's visual ordinarisation of food hospitality activism and of everyday multiculturalism organises material and affective hospitality through online tools and images, centring the home in Australian race politics.

The WDP influences how it is represented by providing images and content, much of which is re-used and re-circulated, but, at the same time, it cannot control how its images are re-used and re-semioticised, or how digital images created by other media organisations appear alongside verbal text. Online magazines and newspapers visually translate food hospitality activism into pre-existing, racialised tropes about food and migrants. Not only are re-mediation and re-semioticisation products of digital cultures of sharing, and of digital platforms and their affordances, they are also now part of how journalism is organised, and of how the WDP and other social enterprises have to operate in their public communications.

Our chapter underlines how important it is to think about the separations and the connections between digital and offline food media, and to analyse how the specificities of digital food media produce meaning-making potential. This includes defining and mapping particular digital food genres and artefacts. In particular, we argue that more attention ought to be given to digital racial formation and to multimodal processes of racialisation, including whiteness. This is not simply an academic exercise, but, as we argue elsewhere, it is also about addressing inequalities in visibilities and invisibilities in food media, food politics and food activism (Flowers and Swan, 2017).

References

Adami, E. (2014). Retwitting, Reposting, Repinning; Reshaping Identities Online: Towards a Social Semiotic Multimodal Analysis of Digital Remediation. *LEA-Lingue e Letterature d'Oriente e d'Occidente*, 3 (3), 223–243.

Adami, E. (2015a). Aesthetics in Digital Texts beyond Writing: A Social Semiotic Multimodal Framework. In Archer, A. and Breuer, E. (eds.), *Multimodality in Writing: The State of the Art in Theory, Methodology and Pedagogy*. Leiden & Boston MA: Brill.

Adami, E. (2015b). What's in a Click? A Social Semiotic Framework for the Multimodal Analysis of Website Interactivity. *Visual Communication*, 14 (2), 133–153.

Ahmed, S. (2012). On being included: Racism and diversity in institutional life. Durham: Duke University Press.

Akrap, D. (2015). 'Germany's Response to the Refugee Crisis Is Admirable. But I Fear It Cannot Last'. *The Guardian*. 6 September. Available at: www.theguardian.com/commen tisfree/2015/sep/06/germany-refugee-crisis-syrian. Accessed 1 May 2018.

Attend a Home Dinner. (n.d.). Available at: www.joiningthedots.org/the-welcome-dinner-project/join-a-dinner/attend-a-home-dinner. Accessed October 2017.

Bentley, A. (2001). Martha's Food: Whiteness of a Certain Kind. *American Studies*, 42 (2), 89–100.

Billig, M. (1995). *Banal Nationalism*. Los Angeles: Sage.

Bishara, J. (2015). The Welcome Dinner Project, Melbourne City Institute of Education. Available at: www.mcie.edu.au/the-welcome-dinner-project/. Accessed 24 June 2015.

Borri, G., Orria, B. and Vailati, A. (2014). Ambiguous Welcomings: The Identity Construction of Asylum Seekers in Turin, Italy. *Urbanities*, 4 (1), 11–25.

Bousiou, A., Bucken-Knapp, G. and Spehar, A. (2016). *Local Welcoming Policies for EU Migrants*. Sweden: University of Gothenburg.

Boys, C. (2014). Welcome Dinner Project Connects Australians with Refugees. *Goodfood*, 15 July. Available at: www.goodfood.com.au/eat-out/news/welcome-dinner-project-con nects-australians-with-refugees-20140711-3bt6r. Accessed October 2016.

Chalfen, R. (1987). *Snapshot Versions of Life*. Madison, WI: University of Wisconsin Press.

Click, M. A. (2009). *It's 'A Good Thing': The Commodification of Femininity, Affluence, and Whiteness in the Martha Stewart Phenomenon*. PhD. University of Massachusetts.

Cook, I. (2004). Follow the Thing: Papaya. *Antipode*, 36 (4), 642–664.

Cook, I. and Crang, P. (1996). The World on a Plate: Culinary Culture, Displacement and Geographical Knowledges. *Journal of Material Culture*, 1 (2), 131–153.

Coward, R. (1985). Female Desire and Sexual Identity. In Diaz-Diocaretz, M. (eds.), et al. *Women, Feminist Identity, and Society in the 1980s: Selected Papers* (pp. 25–36). Amsterdam: John Benjamins Publishing.

Crowther, G. (2013). *Eating Culture: An Anthropological Guide to Food*. Toronto: University of Toronto Press.

Cruz, A. (2013). Gettin' Down Home with the Neelys: Gastro-Porn and Televisual Performances of Gender, Race, and Sexuality. *Women & Performance: A Journal of Feminist Theory*, 23 (3), 323–349.

Dejmanee, T. (2016). 'Food Porn' as Postfeminist Play: Digital Femininity and the Female Body on Food Blogs. *Television & New Media*, 17 (5), 429–448.

Dreher, T. and Ho, C. (eds.). (2009). *Beyond the Hijab Debates: New Conversations on Gender, Race and Religion*. Newcastle upon Tyne: Cambridge Scholars Publishing.

Duffy, B. E., Pruchniewska, U. and Scolere, L. (2017). Platform-Specific Self-Branding: Imagined Affordances of the Social Media Ecology. *Proceedings of the 2017 International Conference on Social Media & Society*. Available at: https://dl.acm.org/citation. cfm?id=3097287&preflayout=flat#prox. Accessed 2 August 2017.

Fleckenstein, K. S. (2014). Designing the New Negro: The Color of Late Nineteenth-Century Multimodality. *Computers and Composition*, 33, 13–28.

Florance, L. and McGhee, A. (2016). High Fees, Low Pay: International Students 'Shocked' by Australian Working Conditions. *ABC News*, 13 July. Available at: www.abc.net.au/ news/2016-07-13/international-students-underpaid-australian-working-conditions/ 7586452. Accessed 1 May 2018.

Flowers, R. and Swan, E. (2017). Seeing Benevolently: Representational Politics and Digital Race Formation on Ethnic Food Tour Webpages. *Geoforum*, 84, 206–217.

Flowers, R. and Swan, E. (2018). 'Sauce in the Bowl, Not on Our Shirt': Indochinese Migrants, Taste Education and Aesthetic Knowledge in Ethnic Food Tours to Cabramatta, Sydney. In Leong-Salobir, C. (ed.), *Handbook of Food in Asia*. London: Routledge.

Fozdar, F. and Hartley, L. (2013). Civic and Ethno Belonging among Recent Refugees to Australia. *Journal of Refugee Studies*, 27 (1), 126–144.

Gambarato, R. R. and Medvedev, S. A. (2015). Fish Fight: Transmedia Storytelling Strategies for Food Policy Change. *International Journal of E-Politics (IJEP)*, 6 (3), 43–59.

Germann Molz, J. (2007). Eating Difference: The Cosmopolitan Mobilities of Culinary Tourism. *Space and Culture*, 10 (1), 77–93.

Grace, H. (2013). *Culture, Aesthetics and Affect in Ubiquitous Media: The Prosaic Image*. London: Routledge.

Gunew, S. (1993). Against Multiculturalism: Rhetorical Images in Multiculturalism, Difference and Postmodernism. In Clark, G. L., Forbes, D. and Francis, R. (eds.), *Multiculturalism, Difference and Postmodernism* (pp. 38–53). Melbourne: Longman Cheshire.

Gurel, P. (2016). Live and Active Cultures: Gender, Ethnicity, and 'Greek' Yogurt in America. *Gastronomica*, 16 (4, Winter), 66–77.

Hage, G. (1997). At Home in the Entrails of the West: Multiculturalism, Ethnic Food and Migrant Home-Building. In Grace, H., Hage, G., Johnson, L., Langsworth, J. and Michael, S. (eds.), *Home/World: Space, Community and Marginality in Sydney's West* (pp. 99–153). Annandale: Pluto.

Hage, G. (2012). *White Nation: Fantasies of White Supremacy in a Multicultural Society.* London: Routledge.

Hall, S. (1997). The Spectacle of the 'Other'. In Hall, S. (ed.), *Representation: Cultural Representation and Signifying Practices.* London: Sage.

Heldke, L. (2003). *Exotic Appetites: Ruminations of a Food Adventurer.* London: Routledge.

Ho, C. (2011). Respecting the Presence of Others: School Micropublics and Everyday Multiculturalism. *Journal of Intercultural Studies*, 32 (6), 603–619.

Hum, S. (2015). 'Between the Eyes': The Racialized Gaze as Design. *College English*, 77 (3), 191.

Ibrahim, Y. (2015). Food Porn and the Invitation to Gaze. *International Journal of E-Politics*, 6 (3), 1–12, July–September.

Jewitt, C. and Oyama, R. (2001). Visual Meaning: A Social Semiotic Approach. In van Leeuwen, T. and Jewitt, C. (eds.), *The Handbook of Visual Analysis* (pp. 134–156). London: Sage.

Kauppi, M. (2014). Guess Who's Coming to Dinner? *Broadsheet Online Magazine.* Available at: www.broadsheet.com.au/sydney/food-and-drink/article/guess-whos-coming-dinner. Accessed 23 July 2018.

Kelly, C. R. (2017). *Food Television and Otherness in the Age of Globalization.* New York: Lexington Books.

Koh, G. (2014/2015). Food Porn as Visual Narrative: Food Blogging and Identity Construction. *Southeast Asian Review of English*, 52 (1), 122–142.

Krauss, R. (1984). A Note on Photography and the Simulacral. *October*, 31, 49–68.

Lavis, A. (2017). Food Porn, Pro-Anorexia and the Viscerality of Virtual Affect: Exploring Eating in Cyberspace. *Geoforum*, 84, 198–205.

Leach, H. M. (2010). The Pavlova Wars: How a Creationist Model of Recipe Origins Led to an International Dispute. *Gastronomica*, 10 (2), 24–30.

Leach, H. M. and Browne, M. (2008). *The Pavlova Story: A Slice of New Zealand's Culinary History.* Dunedin: Otago University Press.

Lupton, D. (2018). Cooking, Eating, Uploading: Digital Food Cultures. In LeBesco, K. and Naccarato, P. (eds.), *The Handbook of Food and Popular Culture* (pp. 66–79). London: Bloomsbury.

Martinson, A. M. (2006). Identifying Gender Ideologies in Web Discourse about Abortion. *Draft Paper submitted to the 2nd New Media Research at UMN Conference*, 14–15 September.

Nakamura, L. (2002). *Cybertypes: Race, Ethnicity, and Identity on the Internet.* London: Routledge.

Nakamura, L. (2008). *Digitizing Race: Visual Cultures of the Internet.* Minneapolis, MN: University of Minnesota Press.

Negra, D. (2002). Ethnic Food Fetishism, Whiteness, and Nostalgia in Recent Film and Television. *The Velvet Light Trap-A Critical Journal of Film and Television*, 50, 62–76.

Noble, G. (2002). Comfortable and Relaxed: Furnishing the Home and Nation. *Continuum: Journal of Media & Cultural Studies*, 16 (1), 53–66.

Noble, G. (2013). Cosmopolitan Habits: The Capacities and Habitats of Intercultural Conviviality. *Body & Society*, 19 (2–3), 162–185.

O'Connor, K. (2008). The Hawaiian Luau: Food as Tradition, Transgression, Transformation and Travel. *Food, Culture & Society*, 11 (2), 149–172.

Palmer, C. (1998). From Theory to Practice: Experiencing the Nation in Everyday Life. *Journal of Material Culture*, 3 (2), 175–199.

Perera, S. and Pugliese, J. (1996). The Limits of Multicultural Representation. *Communal/Plural*, 4, 91–113.

Perlmutter, D. P. and Silvestri, L. E. (2013). In the Visual-Digital World, Taking Seriously the Once-Prosaic 'Home Mode' Commentary. *Visual Communication Quarterly*, 20 (3), 126–127.

Pickering, S. (2001). Common Sense and Original Deviancy: News Discourses and Asylum Seekers in Australia. *Journal of Refugee Studies*, 14 (2), 169–186.

Pink, S. (2011). Amateur Photographic Practice, Collective Representation and the Constitution of Place. *Visual Studies*, 26 (2), 92–101.

Pollock, S. (2015). G'Day Mate: Now Get Stuffed, *The Perth Voice Interactive*, Available at: https://perthvoiceinteractive.com/2015/03/09/gday-mate-now-get-stuffed/retrieved. Accessed 9 March 2018.

Powell, L. J. and Engelhardt, E. S. (2015). The Perilous Whiteness of Pumpkins. *GeoHumanities*, 1 (2), 414–432.

Rich, J., Haddadi, H. and Hospedales, T. M. (2016). Towards Bottom-Up Analysis of Social Food. In *Proceedings of the 6th International Conference on Digital Health Conference* (DH 16, pp. 111–120). New York: NY.

Sawir, E., Marginson, S., Deumert, A., Nyland, C. and Ramia, G. (2008). Loneliness and International Students: An Australian Study. *Journal of Studies in International Education*, 12 (2), 148–180.

Swan, E. (2010). Commodity Diversity: Smiling Faces as a Strategy of Containment. *Organization*, 17 (1), 77–100.

Swan, E. (2017). Postfeminist Stylistics, Work Femininities and Coaching: A Multimodal Study of a Website. *Gender, Work & Organization*, 24 (3), 274–296.

Symons, M. (2010). The Confection of a Nation: The Social Invention and Social Construction of the Pavlova. *Social Semiotics*, 20 (2), 197–217.

van Leeuwen, T. (2000). Visual Racism. In Reisigl, M. and Wodak, R. (eds.), *The Semiotics of Racism: Approaches in Critical Discourse Analysis* (pp. 333–350). Vienna: Passagen Verlag.

van Leeuwen, T. (2005). *Introducing Social Semiotics*. London: Routledge.

Vats, A. (2015). Cooking up Hashtag Activism: #Paulasbestdishes and Counternarratives of Southern Food. *Communication and Critical/Cultural Studies*, 12 (2), 209–213.

The Welcome Dinner Project. (n.d.). *Guide for Welcome Dinner Participants*. Internal publication, no place of publication, not available online.

Williams, T., Gailberger, J. and Lim, J. (2016). Adelaide International Students Victims of Racist Abuse, but Most Love Living in Australia. *The Advertiser*, 7 October.

Willoughby, L., Starks, D. and Taylor-Leech, K. (2013). Is the Cultural Cringe Alive and Kicking? Adolescent Mythscapes of Australian English in Queensland and Victoria. *Australian Journal of Linguistics*, 33 (1), 31–50.

Wise, A. (2011). Moving Food: Gustatory Commensality and Disjuncture in Everyday Multiculturalism. *New Formations*, 74 (74), 82–107.

6 Food sovereignty

Deep histories, digital activism and the emergence of a transnational public

Alana Mann

Introduction

Land, energy and water grabs are leading to the dispossession and exclusion of rural publics worldwide, while transnational food and agribusiness companies aggressively expand and promote an industrial food model that urges producers to 'get big or get out'. In response to the catastrophic rural transformations these changes have wrought, 'a new political movement' has emerged (Scoones et al., 2017). This form of emancipatory politics is captured by the concept of food sovereignty, 'the right of local people to control their own food systems, including markets, ecological resources, food cultures, and production models' (Wittman, 2011, p. 87).

A concept mobilised by indigenous, peasant and rural proletarian groups in Latin America and Europe, food sovereignty is presented by its advocates as an alternative model to the increasingly globalised, industrial food system (Meek, 2014). But food sovereignty is not a concern only of the Global South; the movement is gaining prominence and visibility in the Global North as a way to address key issues of food justice. This chapter focuses on food sovereignty campaigns in the Global North in order to investigate how the rise of these campaigns in locales outside of the Global South raises challenges of definition and implementation regarding food sovereignty principles in apparently affluent countries where the basic demands for the right to food and access to land and resources are not so visible. How are food sovereignty principles reflected and translated in discourses regarding concerns about local food environments, and particularly urban ones? Can food sovereignty movements in the Global North achieve structural change in the food system?

Given the informational turn in food politics (Frohlich, 2017), and the increasing reliance of consumers on digital media for information about food (Lupton, 2018), it is logical to focus our attention on digital activism in addressing these questions. Accordingly, this chapter analyses digital platforms and campaigns designed to facilitate solidarity and to create political spaces for resistance against neoliberal control of food systems in Europe, Canada and Australia. Food sovereignty advocates use these digital platforms to create political spaces, to connect, to share strategies, and to engage in 'networked framing', a 'process through which particular problem definitions, causal inter-pretations, moral evaluations, and/or treatment recommendations attain prominence through crowd-sourcing practices' (Papacharissi, 2015, p. 75).

These digital publics focus on specific issues related to the struggle for food sovereignty, including the corporate capture of biodiversity, the incursion of geneti-cally modified organisms (GMOs) into food products, and domestic food insecurity. The scalability of their networks, and their capacity to supplement traditional activist communication and linking practices, enables activists to connect across diverse geographic locations, and to expand the scope of these issue-based campaigns through frame extension and amplification (Snow and Benford, 1988). Their challenges include alerting eaters to the structural injustices embedded in the industrial food system, prescribing viable alternatives, and mobilising publics to engage in praxis that brings about political and social change (Fox and Frye, 2010).

By tracing the discursive framings of campaigns representing principles of food sovereignty in the Global North, this chapter illustrates how digital platforms operate within the wider communication ecology as 'reflexive forms of activism' (Caroll and Hackett, 2006, p. 96). These platforms engage advocacy organisations and ordinary citizens in new forms of political communication, as well as facilitating the co-creation of meaning and contributing to frame building. Empirical analysis of activist-produced web content demonstrates how activists exploit digital media affordances in scaling up their campaigns on local issues. In doing so, they promote food sovereignty as a democratic political project, embracing themes of diversity, inclusivity and social justice. A critical reading, however, requires us to consider whether the food-related digital practices of eaters in the Global North are sufficiently 'political' to address the historic injustices and inequalities of power that persist in food systems, particularly in settler colonies such as Canada and Australia.

Networked food publics

An explosion of food-obsessed communities on social media platforms supports Signe Rousseau's claim that 'social media do what food does best: they bring people together' (2012, p. 5). In these virtual spaces, political activism about food ranges from concerns over food safety to fair wages for food industry workers. Cultural change can be mapped through these examples of 'polyvocal protest' (Ruiz, 2014), which comprise 'a shared set of concepts, vocabulary, terms of reference, evaluations, associations, polarities and standards of argument connected to a coherent perspective on the world' (Rochon, 1998, p. 16).

These perspectives are articulated in concepts such as food citizenship, food sovereignty and food justice - notions that have emerged as a 'perfect storm' of environmental, financial and rural crises affecting communities worldwide, 'from peasants in the Global South to poor families in the decaying urban cores of the post-industrial United States' (Figueroa, 2015, p. 499). They are socially con-structed from networks of ongoing conversations that maintain a particular version of 'reality' for participants. Through discourse, the meanings of these terms are produced, challenged and renegotiated. Demands for greater equity in food systems are situated in broader, dynamic political cultures that influence activist engagement in practices that embrace strategising, organisation, protest and the formation of collective identities (Kavada, 2013).

As this chapter reveals, activists employ digital platforms to present topics, frames and discourses. These create issue-networks: 'assemblage[s] of actors jointly implicated in an issue that no agent, no organisation is effectively taking care of' (Marres and Rogers, 2005, p. 929). These digital media engagements can be interpreted as 'networked publics'. danah boyd (2010) argues that the affordances of networked technologies facilitate the emergence of novel entities that are simultaneously 'spaces constructed through networked technologies' and 'imagined collective[s] that emerge as a result of the intersection of people, technology and practice' (boyd, 2010, p. 39). These publics function in the manner of offline publics in that they enable people to gather and connect for social, cultural and political purposes, but they are also interacting in unique ways determined by networked technologies that reorganise information flows, creating 'emergent socio-political assemblages with shared or interlocking concerns who know themselves as, and act as, publics through media and communication' (Burgess and Matamoros-Fernández, 2016, p. 81). Digital media can facilitate the cross-flow of information between organisations on multiple scales, contextualising the local but also widening the frame through engagement in 'hybrid forums', defined as:

> open spaces where groups can come together to discuss technical options involving the collective, hybrid because the groups involved and the spokes-persons claiming to represent them are heterogeneous, including experts, politi-cians, technicians, and laypersons who consider themselves involved [. . .] where questions and problems taken up are addressed at different levels in a variety of domains.
>
> (Callon, Lascoumes and Barthe, 2001, p. 18)

Through their digital engagement with platforms promoting alternative food-ways and notions of food justice, activists engage in networked framing - revising, rearticulating and redispersing frames that challenge the vertical structure of the corporatised food regime (McMichael, 2009). Their symbiotic, conversational interactions on digital platforms facilitate the performance of identity and participation in processes of frame negotiation. This 'connective action' embodies self-motivated participation through the sharing of personal content that may be co-produced and co-distributed among peers, non-government organisations (NGOs), and other groups with congruent ideas, plans, resources and networks (Bennett and Segerberg, 2012; Benkler, 2006). The primary tension of linking worldviews (that is, actors' thoughts and perceptions) to praxis lies in a composite of ideas and practices 'strategically articulated through language to identify a problem, propose a solution and motivate action' (Fox and Frye, 2010, p. 425).

Framing food sovereignty

Food sovereignty is a radical proposal to correct structural injustices in food systems. It has become synonymous with the international social movement La Vía Campesina ('The Peasant Way'), an international network of over 164 rural peoples' organisations in 79 countries that claims to represent 200 million people (La Vía Campesina, 2017). These diverse associations of farmers, fishers, indigenous and migrant workers stretch across the Americas, Europe, South East Asia and Africa. Their opposition to corporate control of the food system is in effect 'a set of reactions to neoliberal globalisation and the industrial food system [...] an alternative approach predicated on the dispersal of power' (Andrée, Bosia and Massicotte, 2014, p. 11) that draws on human rights frameworks. The dimensions of the right to food, formally recognised by the Food and Agriculture Organisation of the United Nations (FAO, 2004), include non-nutrient values, such as cultural and dietary preferences and protection of the environment. For advocates of food sovereignty, this demands a response to the question 'who will produce food, how, and for whose benefit?', and places the onus on states to 'cooperate internationally to address structural impediments' to the right to food (Ishii-Eiteman, 2009, p. 697).

Food sovereignty has served as a compelling master frame for the mobilisation of La Vía Campesina as an international coalition (Mann, 2014). A 'big tent' (Patel, 2009) accommodating diverse meanings, debates and movements, many rooted in deep local histories, the concept of food sovereignty is open to critique as defensive in standpoint. Opposing the corporate food regime (McMichael, 2009) and the foundations of its development under capitalism, food sovereignty stands against the processes that 'continually seek to subordinate the lives of human beings to the logic of accumulation, competition, wage labour, and the market' (Figueroa, 2015, p. 504). The implications of these processes manifest themselves across the Global North and South in diverse ways—hunger in one place, food swamps in another - 'swelling the ranks of the poor and malnourished on both shores' (ibid.). Here lie the seeds of a common struggle, which is distilled in the 'six pillars' or defining principles of food sovereignty: food production that focuses on food for people, values food providers, localises food systems, puts control locally, builds knowledge and skills, and works with nature (Global Justice Now, n.d.).

The central demands of food sovereignty in the Global South focus on access to productive resources (including land and forests), spaces for peasant production, moral economies, and the preservation of traditional, agroecological farming systems (Figueroa, 2015). In the Global North, the principles of food sovereignty are largely reflected in campaigns and initiatives that aim to bring about change through influencing consumer purchasing and eating practices focused on 'local' food—a form of what Michele Micheletti (2003) calls 'political consumerism'. Underpinned by a strong narrative 'linking the production and consumption of local organic food to positive economic, environmental, and social changes' (Alkon and Agyeman, 2011, p. 2), the 'progressive' food movement in the

Global North is concerned primarily with relations of consumption *vis-à-vis* relations of production by rebuilding rural–urban relationships, and favouring fresh, locally-sourced food that returns value to the producer through alternative food networks (AFNs). Initiatives include Associations for the Maintenance of Smallholder Agriculture (AMAPs) in Europe, community food centres in Canada, and community food hubs in Australia. Their tactics include farmers' markets, fair trade schemes and community-supported agriculture (CSA).

AFNs propose to reconnect with and reconstitute local human, cultural and land ecologies as means to create and connect new spaces and models for engaging publics in debates about environmental sustainability, social justice and economic viability (Gottlieb and Fisher, 1996). As new forms of 'food citizenship' (Renting, Schermer and Rossi, 2012) they seek to reshape the relations between food practices and markets beyond material exchange to a 'moralisation' of food economies. They are lauded as alternative forms of food provisioning, and as spaces of counter-power to the industrial food system that meet consumer preferences. Notions of 'food justice' reflect an overlapping set of concerns. These include: the equitable sharing of the benefits and risks of how food is grown and processed, transported, distributed and consumed; the provision of healthy food for all; ecologically sustainable food systems; fair conditions for food workers; decent profit for producers; and education to create informed eaters. However, the co-optation of discourses such as sustainability, localism and organics (Mann, 2013a) by Big Food raises questions about the extent to which these discourses actually 'reproduce neo-liberal forms, spaces of governance, and mentalities' (Guthman, 2008, p. 1171). These co-opted discourses commonly ignore critical questions of difference, including gender, race and class, and legacies such as colonialism. They therefore close down possibilities for the systemic and structural change that food sovereignty demands, and limit the potential for solidarity between the Global North and South. How digital activists address these endemic inequalities in their framings of food-related issues is vital to the restructuring and transformation of food systems.

Digital activism for food sovereignty

The diverse framings of food sovereignty advocates in the Global North and South are reflected in media objects that circulate globally via digital communication networks. The vision of food sovereignty is explicitly invoked in La Vía Campesina's discussion papers, campaigns and official declarations, such as the *Euskal Herria Declaration* (La Vía Campesina, 2017).[1] A global call to action is promoted annually on the International Day of Peasant Struggle, 17 April, which commemorates the 1996 murder of Brazilian activists. The circulation of these media objects conveys information visibly and invisibly encoded, and promotes unity in diversity. Because members speak and act in the name of food sovereignty, it can be described as a central trope in the constitution of the movement, while power comes from the democratic processes of decision-making that operate within it, underpinned by a resistive epistemology:

We must continue to accelerate political, ideological, organisational, and technical training based on our own concepts, since we know that conventional education suppresses our identity and our ideas. Such training is crucial for our movements to create new and committed actors to forge our own destiny. In our struggle we also need to continue to create our own autonomous communications media, and build our alliances with the alternative media, to build awareness of our culture, our dignity, and our capacity to transform society.

(La Vía Campesina, 2017)

Given this sense of working outside the hegemonic media system, La Vía Campesina bypasses traditional media channels to focus on alternative media platforms and a highly active network of capacity-building partners, such as FIAN International (the Food First Information and Action Network) and Friends of the Earth. The organisation co-authors and posts reports, and publishes empirical research to support the argument that small-scale, agro-ecological farming methods 'produce high yields, environmental and social benefits' (Laughton, 2017). The movement has gained credibility and legitimacy in international civil society and governance arenas, such as the World Committee for Food Security within the Food and Agriculture Organisation (FAO) of the United Nations, where it participates in the Civil Society Mechanism (Mann, 2014). Drawing on the resources of news outlets, including the International Consortium of Investigative Journalists, La Vía Campesina hyperlinks to reports on corporate wrongdoing and failures of global governance (see, for example, Chavkin and Hudson's, 2015 report on the World Bank). Activist members also engage in storytelling via Twitter, Facebook and Instagram, platforms that foster the growing sphere of global social media activism by providing new opportunities for the articulation of concerns and dissent to wider audiences (Cottle and Lester, 2011).

La Vía Campesina has also broadened its capacities for outreach through fluid collaborations with global justice networks such as the World Social Forum, as well as through integrative campaigning and the use of alternative media platforms such as Indymedia.com. It has also developed *La Vía Campesina TV*[2] to share rich multimedia content:

This television is ours; it is a mirror of our daily lives, our dreams and our struggles [...] it brings together audio-visual material and cultural creations from the farmers' organisations themselves, whether they are members of Vía Campesina or not, as well as material produced by friends, allies or sometimes mainstream media.

(La Vía Campesina, 2013)

Described as a 'Babel Tower', La Vía Campesina's web site features expert and non-expert voices in multiple languages, and presents footage of local direct actions, such as tractor convoys in Mexico, land occupations in Brazil, urban protests against genetically modified food in Europe, and against free trade agreements and food dumping in India. It is noted on the site that not all content 'represents the official voice of La Vía Campesina [as the web site] is more of an open hub of sounds and images from the broad food sovereignty movement' (ibid.). Examples include footage of the Landworkers' Alliance launching its post-Brexit policy recommendations outside the Houses of Parliament in London on 21 April 2017. The Landworkers' Alliance and the Community Food Grower's Network focus on the provision of high-quality fresh produce, and highlight the need for small-scale and family farmers to be offered a 'place at the table' in negotiations over the future of UK agriculture policy. They support small-scale producers and diverse mixed holdings as, in their words, 'getting big is a permanent race to the bottom'.

Other examples include *Do Nothing*, an Indian film following the story of a couple who move from chemical farming to the Zero Budget Natural Farming method developed by Subhash Palekar. This film critiques the controversial contribution of the Green Revolution to 'feeding the world', and documents the fight against transnational agribusiness corporations. La Vía Campesina's strong focus on the rights of women, which is also a primary focus of its Women's Assembly,[3] is reflected in its coverage of the International Women's Strike (IWS)/ Paro Internacional de Mujeres that occurred across 40 countries on 8 March 2017 with the accompanying Twitter campaign #Solidarityisourweapon. The ongoing struggle of human rights defenders is represented by *My Father, Baek Nam-gi*, a short, personal video commemorating South Korean activist farmer Baek Nam-gi, #BrotherBaek, killed by police water cannons while protesting against the erosion of the right to assembly under the Park government.

In light-hearted contrast, a four-minute animated film by the Field Liberation Movement, based on a protest in Wetteren on 20 November 2016 at the Flemish Institute of Biotechnology, features two genetically engineered poplar trees discussing the motives of corporations carrying out genetic engineering in the forestry industry. The trees explain that 'the scientists finance themselves by selling patents to biotech companies and then everyone has to pay big companies to plant out our genetically-modified siblings [...] in countries around the world like South America, where the land is cheaper'. These diverse media objects reflect different framings, rhetoric and performative actions on issues ranging from gender equity and basic rights to market concentration and the patenting of biodiversity by corporate actors. As strategies and rhetorical displays, their production is influenced by access to technical resources, local constraints on recognised forms of protest, and enabling (or disabling) political environments, which I will now examine for Europe, Canada and Australia.

Europe: digital mobilisation and direct action

Political, economic and social relationships around food and agricultural production are actively interrogated at local, regional and continental scales in Europe, where resistance to agricultural industrialisation began to foment in the 1960s, in Germany, Austria and Switzerland. This peaked in 1999 with a passionate outcry against *malbouffe* or 'bad food' by José Bové, former leader of farmers' union

Confédération Paysanne, in which he and fellow activists dismantled a McDonald's outlet in Millau, France. Today, Vía Campesina Europe coordinates organisations and farmers' unions from countries including Denmark, Switzerland, France, Italy, the Netherlands, Spain, Greece, Malta and Turkey, and works with other social movements within the European Social Forum. In October 2016, over 500 small-scale food producers, distributors and consumers gathered in Cluj-Napoca, Romania, for the second Nyéléni Europe Forum, which was the biggest-ever European gathering for food sovereignty.[4]

On a community level, principles of food sovereignty are reflected in solidarity contracts between eaters and local farmers. These minimise risk for producers, and provide families with local, fresh produce through box schemes and cooperatives. This is food from *somewhere*, as opposed to 'food from nowhere' (Bové & Dufour, 2001). The first Association for the Maintenance of Smallholder Agriculture (AMAP) was created in 2001 in Provence, France, to be joined later by Geneva's Les Jardins de Cocagne and GASAP (Groupes d'Achat Solidaires de l'Agriculture Paysanne) in Belgium, while in Spain, agroecological cooperatives have existed in Madrid (Bajo el Asfalto está la Huerta—'Under the Asphalt Lies the Garden'), Catalonia (Ecoconsum Catalonia) and Andalucía since the 1990s (Vivas, 2010). Spain is also home to Plataforma Rural, a broad-based coalition that coordinates campaigns against an increasingly concentrated retail sector and two other issues that dominate discussion of food and agriculture policy in Europe: the use of genetic modification in food production, and the Common Agriculture Policy (CAP) governing the farm subsidy system.

A de facto ban on GMO food crops throughout Europe is attributed in part to the highly successful online anti-biotechnology campaign Combat Monsanto,[5] jointly sponsored by La Vía Campesina, Greenpeace, Friends of the Earth, Sherpa, Attac, and Foundation Sciences Citoyennes. This campaign encourages eaters to avoid GMOs on health and cultural grounds, and challenges agribusiness framing of genetically modified foods (GMFs) as safe and crucial to 'feeding the world'. The reframing of GMF as 'Frankenfood', which continues to circulate as a global meme, highlights risk as a mobilising frame in the debate, and exploits the scientific illiteracy of the lay public. As a successful example of digital cam-paigning, Combat Monsanto promotes personalised consumer action, which also underpins the promotion of CSA schemes, local farmers' markets, and Fair Trade products.

Friends of the Earth Europe (FoEE), the largest grassroots environmental network in the region, addresses the GMO issue from a policy standpoint. This organisation unites more than 30 national organisations with thousands of local groups seeking to influence EU policy and to raise public awareness of the environmental threat GMOs pose to biodiversity. FoEE effectively uses political platforms, such as Radio Mundo Real (RWR), a multilingual web-based outlet, and ARC2020, the Agriculture and Rural Convention,[6] to circulate protest rhetoric. Initially created as a multi-NGO platform to influence the reform of the CAP between 2010 and 2013, ARC2020 now focuses on stimulating public debate in Europe on future farming, food and rural policies through alliance building and communication on a variety of platforms. They host debates on Facebook and Twitter (#afterCAP, #milkcrisis, #livestockdebate), and post rich, shareable video content that promotes food sovereignty, such as the FoEE briefing 'Feeding Europe'.[7]

The need to change public policies that favour elites is emphasised by Belgian-based Brigades d'Actions Paysannes,[8] which represents citizens of diverse back-grounds who want to defend peasant agriculture and the right to food, as well as to promote the transition to agro-ecological production methods and the development of an agricultural model based on the principles of food sovereignty. Framing the threat to peasant agriculture as a political rather than technical issue, they support community advocacy and resistance through performative actions against multi-national corporations and blockades organised by farmers. Direct actions are also a favoured tactic of My Agriculture,[9] a network of 50 organisations which brought 50,000 people together for its fifth nationwide 'We are tired of it' demonstration in Berlin in January 2015.[10]

More formal alliances include Hands on the Land for Food Sovereignty,[11] a collective campaign by 16 partners, including FIAN International,[12] the first inter-national organisation to devote its work to the struggle for the realisation of the right to adequate food and nutrition, and now lobbying for a specific Declaration of the 'Rights of Peasants' at the UN (Mann, 2011). Hands on the Land aims to:

> raise awareness on the use and governance of land, water and other natural resources and its effects on the realisation of the right to food and food sovereignty [...] through evidence-based research and material, public events and meetings, trainings [sic], education and advocacy work encouraging citizens, NGOs, policy-makers and journalists to 'take action on food sovereignty'.[13]

Sharing the objective of changing public policies is Farmsubsidy,[14] a network of journalists, researchers, activists and data analysts working together to make CAP more transparent. An example of cross-border, data-driven investigative journalism creating alternative public spheres for the discussion of issues of food and agricul-ture, Farmsubsidy employs freedom of information laws to pressure the govern-ments of EU member states to reveal the 'subsidy millionaires' who are benefiting from a system designed to assist small farmers (Mann, 2013b).

Canada: creating an enabling policy climate

The food sovereignty movement has a long history in Canada, championed by organisations including the National Farmers' Union, the Union Paysanne in Québec, Food Secure Canada and the People's Food Policy Project. Hannah Wittman and Annette Desmarais, co-editors (with Nettie Wiebe) of *Food Sover-eignty in Canada: Creating Just and Sustainable Food Systems* (2011), frame the issue in the following terms:

> [In 2012,] almost 45% of Canada's food production is exported, nearly quadrupling between 1989 and 2009 to meet government food-export targets.

Despite these massive increases in food production, however, Canada's farmers still struggle to make a living; net Canadian farm income since 1985 hovers around zero! Almost half of Canada's farmers are over 55 and the number of farms has declined by 10% since 2006.

(Desmarais and Wittman, 2012)

As in Europe, genetically modified food is a key theme. The Canadian Biotechnology Action Network[15] brings together 16 groups to research, monitor and raise awareness of issues relating to genetic engineering in food and farming. To promote food sovereignty, they work to facilitate collaborative campaigning at the local, regional, national and international levels, enabling individual Canadians to take strategic and effective action through petitions and research to inform policy-making. Food: Locally Embedded, Globally Engaged (FLEdGE)[16] is a more recent platform, hosted by the Laurier Centre for Sustainable Food Systems in Ontario. Featuring an international advisory committee, including experts from the United States, Mexico, Cuba, Germany, France, Wales, the Netherlands, Italy and South Africa, FLEdGE researches issues of agro-ecology, territory, and governance for sustainable food systems. It provides a platform for digital storytelling, featuring short, informative and shareable clips, such as 'Un Mundo Mejor es Posible' ('A Better World is Possible') about agroecology in Cuba, and 'Sometimes the Best Way to Fix a Broken System is to Build a New One' on digital platforms that reconnect producers and consumers.[17] A growing movement of food hubs throughout Canada emphasises social justice, dignity and food literacy. Based on a model developed in the 1970s in Davenport West, Toronto, Community Food Centres 'strive to meet the most basic food needs of their low-income community members while improving physical and mental health, reducing social isolation, supporting local agriculture, and providing ways for participants to get together and make change in their communities'.[18]

Food Secure Canada (FSC)[19] leads a pan-Canadian alliance of food sovereignty-oriented organisations in policy engagement, campaigns, network development, digital engagement through webinars, Facebook and Twitter campaigns, including #FoodPolicyCan, #FoodPolicy4Canada and #EatThinkVote, and, more recently, web engagement sessions for farmers.[20] Importantly, FSC is also approaching food sovereignty from another direction. Its Indigenous Circle[21] introduced a seventh pillar of food sovereignty: 'food as sacred, part of the web of relationships with the natural world that define culture and community' (People's Food Policy Project, 2011). This pillar recognises that local, citizen-driven food systems must prioritise Indigenous access to traditional foods and productive resources, including land and water systems particularly vulnerable to climate change. Food Secure Canada argues that the main principles of Indigenous food sovereignty, and most appropriate protocols for engagement of Indigenous people in democratic decision-making processes, must be understood in order to propose how Indigenous knowledges and eco-philosophies can be better incorporated into governance frameworks. These are articulated in the *First Principles Protocol for Building Cross-Cultural Relationships* (Indigenous Circle, 2010). This protocol recognises that, since the time of contact with non-Indigenous settlers, many traditional

Indigenous harvesters in Canada have experienced declining health directly connected to the lack of culturally important foods in their respective territories. Indigenous conceptions of food sovereignty emphasise food as sacred, reflect deep connections with the environment, and rely on intergenerational transmission of food-related knowledge (Morrison, 2011)-understandings largely ignored in a settler narrative that also exists in Australia.

Australia: fair food, for whom?

Despite being recognised as one of the richest and most politically stable countries in the world, 1.2 million Australians in a population of 23 million are food insecure, that is, have run out of food and been unable to afford to buy more at least once in the previous 12 months (Mann, 2016). Paradoxically, rates of obesity and cardio-vascular disease are increasing. Individuals and families experiencing housing stress, those on low incomes, the elderly and the disabled are most likely to be unable to access fresh, healthy food. Alternative foodways are scarce and unaffordable for many in one of the most concentrated grocery retail sectors in the world.

The food hubs sector is less mature than in Europe and Canada, but strong local examples of digital platforms promoting locavore practices are growing in popularity. These include the online organic delivery service CERES Fair Food in Melbourne,[22] and Food Connect in Brisbane, a social enterprise founded in 2005 by an ex-dairy farmer who aims to 'democratise the food system', paying farmers 'about four times the amount of the big food chains'.[23] The aim of shortening the food chain is also reflected in the work of the now global Open Food Network,[24] a non-profit software platform that 'connects and empowers food producers and hubs in regions or countries', and promotes 'transaction and transformation'.

The Australian Food Sovereignty Alliance (AFSA)[25] aims to break the silo approach to food policy and to bring about much-needed systemic change to Australia's food system (Dixon et al., 2011). AFSA emerged when La Vía Campesina's campaign for food sovereignty drew the attention of civil society groups, farmers and academics. This interest catalysed in 2010 with the announcement of a National Food Plan (NFP), proposed by the Labor Party as an election promise. As a draft of the proposed plan was circulated, it became clear that the process for developing a national food policy would be dominated by large agri-business and retailing interests. A small group of farmers, academics and people from community-based food organisations called for a more transparent, inclusive and participatory process on the basis that:

> The inter-generational ramifications of this policy insist upon the need to set the highest standards in these respects. We believe that it is vital to include stakeholders and participants from across the food and agricultural system, and not only those with the largest economic influence [... This will better

ensure] equitable access to fresh food (particularly for low-income communities), food safety and quality.

(AFSA, 2010)

The result was the groups' crowd-sourced policy document the *People's Food Plan* (AFSA, 2013), based on the *Canadian People's Food Policy Project* (2015). Over 600 people contributed to the draft, which was finalised by the time of the 2013 Federal Election. While the National Food Policy never came into being, the *People's Food Plan* remains a living document that embodies AFSA's four main goals: to create a coherent and inclusive national narrative about 'fair food'; to raise awareness about the serious challenges faced by food and farming systems; to campaign for policy and legislative change at the local, state and federal levels; and to work with members to develop strategies and actions that expand the growth of a fair food system in Australia. Producer concerns include a cost-price squeeze imposed by powerful retailers, barriers to the sale of farm-gate produce (including inappropriate-to-scale regulation), and the need for regenerative agriculture, on which it is aligned with the Regrarians,[26] a producers' network that focuses on holistic land management, permaculture and seed saving.

In Australia, actors concerned with food safety and food insecurity frequently frame their food systems interventions in terms of health. These volunteer-based grassroots organisations include MADGE (Mothers are Demystifying Genetic Engineering,[27] founded in 2007 in response to the Victorian State Government lifting the ban on GM canola), and the Right to Food Coalition (RtFC, formerly the Sydney Food Fairness Alliance).[28] The Right to Food Coalition aims to raise public awareness of domestic food insecurity and of the gaps in social provisioning in order to 'shift the debate from food poverty and charity to one demanding food as a fundamental human right' (Lindberg et al., 2016, p. 5). A key digital strategy in 2016 was a focused Twitter campaign implemented with the assistance of Croakey,[29] a platform providing 'independent social journalism for health', in the lead up to the 2016 Federal Election. This campaign aimed to lend increased visibility to the issue of food insecurity by targeting elected members across a range of portfolios, both Ministers and their Shadows, and to increase the membership of the RtFC. An analysis of the campaign revealed that instances of user-to-user communication were limited and as such represent low levels of political conversation and participation. There is little evidence that the campaign has significantly engaged those experiencing household food insecurity in the conversation (Mann, 2018). What the campaign did reveal, however, is a networked public of pre-existing advocates for the right to food. It initiated a cross-flow of information between aligned movements while supporting activists' goals of developing a sense of collectivity and connectivity between organisations and individuals who share the goal of promoting the right to food within Australia.

One of the issues highlighted by the RtFC is that Aboriginal and Torres Strait Islander people are five times more likely than other Australians to be food insecure on a regular basis. Actions jeopardising the food sovereignty of Aboriginal people include the forced closures of Aboriginal communities, amendments to the

Aboriginal Heritage Act 1972 which reduced the role of traditional owners in decisions about sacred sites in Western Australia, and Pivot North, an intensive agriculture and irrigation project in the Kimberley region. However, there is little active campaigning by the Australian fair food movement on these issues beyond expressions of solidarity.[30]

Digital yet divided

The digital platforms analysed in this study facilitate resource mobilisation, decision-making and information sharing, linking mobilisations and 'what could otherwise be largely independent and disconnected events' (Diani, 2003, p. 12). They serve to increase the connections and coordination between a wide range of anti-neoliberal and anti-corporate movements. However, in contrast to those in the Global South, many platforms that support and promote food sovereignty in highly urbanised communities in Europe, Canada and Australia tend to reflect consumer concerns rather than those of food producers. Specifically, they tend to be less concerned with the rights of small-scale farmers than with 'food from nowhere', and with the right to healthy, affordable food. They aspire to recreate authentic relationships built on trust between growers and eaters, but while there are some campaigning efforts towards policy change, their initiatives often do not offer an explicit critique of the capitalist economy that supports the corporatised food system. In many of these instances, citizens instead express their dissatisfaction with the conventional food retail system by buying directly from producers at farmers' markets, CSAs, food hubs and the like. However, voting with one's fork in this way cannot counter the overpowering influences of liberalised markets and their impacts on rural livelihoods in a global economy. Further, while consumers' local micro-encounters may represent important attempts at communal autonomy, they do not address inequalities within and between communities. As the examples in this chapter show, privileged groups find it easier to participate in both digital campaigns and the AFNs they give rise to. It is not simply that marginalised people lack the financial means to participate in farmers' markets or CSA schemes, or to buy Fair Trade or organic produce; they also have limited input into these initiatives.

The practices of AFNs have been the target of considerable critique, mostly centred on their failure to include socially excluded groups and individuals who experience systemic barriers to food access in their activities and concerns. These are principles central to food sovereignty. However, these messages are sometimes lost when food sovereignty principles are applied to urban constituencies in the Global North. For example, digital applications promoting food hubs or other sites of 'local food' frequently mirror what Prody (2013) refers to as the 'monocultural rhetoric' of the movement, which ignores not only cultural and socio-economic differences, but also ethical issues concerning local and global food production systems. Digital platforms and practices that challenge popular local food framings that reflect middle-class values and proclivities by including more diverse voices, and which engage with wider questions of food access and sustainability, are rare. Instead, many of the examples from Australia, Canada and Europe presented in this chapter rely on the agency of the political consumer, and seek to target policy elites in effecting change. They reflect a 'deficit lens' (Valencia, 1997) that calls for top-down solutions from policy-makers, disregards the useful knowledge gained from the lived experience of minority and low socio-economic communities, and fails to address the digital divides that prevent those most affected by hunger from participating in campaigns.

These findings reveal a need for research into how digital technologies might play a role in more inclusive, participatory food planning that connects cultural, socio-economic and environmental issues and supports resilient and inclusive local food economies. For example, if food hubs are to serve not only as conscious and deliberate interventions to provide fair returns to producers but also to give low income families and individuals access to healthy and affordable food, we may need to rethink 'local' food. This necessitates reaching beyond a geographical concept related to the distance between food producers and consumers. Local food could instead be defined in terms of social and supply chain characteristics, including sustainable production, environmentally friendly distribution practices, and social connections that engage with the more radical, transformative edge of food sovereignty discourses and which include discussions of trade, labour and dispossession.

Further, while food sovereignty has emerged as a compelling catalyst for mobilisation, it is not a universal concept. Indigenous peoples face unique challenges related to food sovereignty in comparison with most small-scale farmers and participants in community-based food organisations. They seek interpretations that respect the rights of individuals and groups to identify the characteristics of their cultures and foodways. Dispossessed, and already engaged in a long struggle for land rights, Indigenous peoples' movements:

> do not demand just any land, but rather their land. And they want control over their land and territories. Thus, closely linked to the concept of territory, are the demands by organisations and movements of Indigenous people for autonomy and self-determination.
>
> (Stevenhagen cited in Grey and Patel, 2014, p. 4)

Food sovereignty prioritises local agricultural production, and upholds the rights of Indigenous peoples to hunt, fish and gather food, as well as the rights of farmers to produce food and the rights of all people to access healthy, affordable and culturally appropriate food. It is opposed to the undermining of traditional agriculture through artificial inputs and food imports engineered through non-democratic processes driven by powerful corporate actors in the food system. Indigenous participation and leadership are essential, as is enabling legislation that recognises Indigenous experiences and understandings of food sovereignty. Accordingly, if the political platforms claiming to represent food sovereignty are to expand beyond the collection of rights attached to food production and consumption and build the broad coalitions necessary to transform societies, they must also embrace the diverse food-generating practices and complex land-management strategies of Indigenous peoples.

Conclusion

In Europe, Canada and Australia, the state now plays a significantly reduced role in regulating the domestic food market. Successive governments have instead privileged corporate influence over food governance, and have promoted large-scale, export-orientated agricultural production that limits the possibilities of realising the right to food or food sovereignty. Resisting this, communities are exercising self-reliance in organising a wide variety of food-related activities that circumvent conventional foodways. Food activists are using digital platforms to politicise issues of food production and consumption. They aim to influence public opinion and inform policy that ensures access to sufficient food for all citizens in a manner consistent with ecological sustainability, public health, economic equality and social justice objectives.

These concerns reflect many dimensions of the pillars of food sovereignty. However, there exist significant barriers to adapting food sovereignty's radical demands for control over food systems (including land, markets, and food cultures) in the Global North, and particularly in urban contexts. Highlighting the connections between global processes through the corporate food regime (McMichael, 2009), and emphasising the shared impacts of economic crises such as that experienced in 2008, can help us see the relationships between rural dispossession in the South and the erosion of social safety nets in the North. Yet these connections are rarely made explicit in the issue-based digital campaigns examined in this chapter. They rely on notions of food as commodity, divorcing it from relationships of power and exploitation that reach back historically to the dispossession of Indigenous peoples.

Digital media can be an important strategic resource for collective identity-building within and between movements. These media facilitate organising, and have the power to create 'large aggregations of de-personalised engagement' (Schneider et al., 2017, p. 16). Individuals, journalists, bloggers, researchers, social enterprises, NGOs and interest groups advocating for food sovereignty in Europe, Canada and Australia are using digital media platforms to connect locally rooted alternatives to a broader struggle for political transformation. Online platforms enable these (typically elite) advocates to connect, and to share perceptions, framings and strategies for food sovereignty in different contexts. However, truly transnational publics are hybrid. They include the vernacular comments and insights of all affected by an issue. The challenge is to connect specific urban and rural places as sites of struggle, and to include the voices of those most profoundly affected by rural transformations. These voices are essential to capturing the subjective experience of a broken food system, and to developing a nuanced understanding of how food scarcity is socially constructed for specific groups and individuals (Mann, 2017).

Connecting the global political economy of food to the lived experience of buying and eating across the Global North and South can only be achieved through intimate understanding of the histories of specific communities. This includes recognising their unique qualities of self-reliance and solidarity against injustice as essential ways to develop sovereignty based in community power and autonomy. Advancing digital methods to study how issue publics emerge and consolidate on digital platforms can teach us how new technologies can contribute to developing and articulating these understandings. The challenge is to take our analysis beyond elite voices to those of marginalised stakeholders, and to enable ourselves to capture the complexity emerging from generative publics engaging with the transformative politics of food sovereignty.

Notes

1 Solidarity statements and actions on issues including seed saving, dignity for migrant workers, climate and environmental justice, and support for human rights defenders, as well as breaking news and coverage of local mobilisations appear on the official web site https://viacampesina.org/, in English, French and Spanish.
2 See https://tv.viacampesina.org/. Accessed 1 February 2018.
3 See https://viacampesina.org/en/vii-international-conference-womens-assembly-declaration/. Accessed 1 February 2018.
4 See http://nyelenieurope.net/. Accessed 1 February 2018.
5 See http://combat-monsanto.org/. Accessed 1 February 2018.
6 See http://www.arc2020.eu/. Accessed 1 February 2018.
7 See http://www.arc2020.eu/feeding-europe-food-sovereignty-and-agro-ecology/. Accessed 1 February 2018.
8 See https://brigadesactionspaysannes.be/. Accessed 1 February 2018.
9 See http://www.meine-landwirtschaft.de. Accessed 1 February 2018.
10 See http://www.wir-haben-es-satt.de/start/home/. Accessed 1 February 2018.
11 See https://handsontheland.net/about/who-are-we/. Accessed 1 February 2018.
12 See http://www.fian.org. Accessed 1 February 2018.
13 See https://handsontheland.net/about/. Accessed 23 October 2018.
14 See http://farmsubsidy.openspending.org/. Accessed 1 February 2018.
15 See https://cban.ca/. Accessed 1 February 2018.
16 See https://fledgeresearch.ca/. Accessed 1 February 2018.
17 See https://fledgeresearch.ca/resources-results/digital-storytelling/. Accessed 1 February 2018.
18 See https://cfccanada.ca/our-story. Accessed 1 February 2018.
19 See https://foodsecurecanada.org. Accessed 1 February 2018.
20 See https://foodsecurecanada.org/resources-news/events/new-farmers-web-consulation-building-food-policy-canada. Accessed 1 February 2018.
21 See https://foodsecurecanada.org/community-networks/indigenous-circle. Accessed 1 February 2018.
22 See www.ceresfairfood.org.au/about-us/. Accessed 1 February 2018.
23 See www.foodconnect.com.au/about-us. Accessed 1 February 2018.
24 See https://openfoodnetwork.org/. Accessed 1 February 2018.
25 See http://afsa.org.au/. Accessed 1 February 2018.
26 See http://www.regrarians.org/. Accessed 1 February 2018.
27 See http://www.madge.org.au/. Accessed 1 February 2018.
28 See https://righttofood.org.au/. Accessed 1 February 2018.
29 See https://croakey.org/. Accessed 1 February 2018.
30 See https://afsa.org.au/blog/category/indigenous/. Accessed 1 February 2018.

References

Alkon, H. and Agyeman, J. (2011). *Cultivating Food Justice: Race, Class, and Sustainability*. Cambridge, MA: MIT Press.

Andrée, P. J., Bosia, A. M. and Massicotte, M. (2014). *Food Sovereignty and Globalization*. Toronto: University of Toronto Press.

Australian Food Sovereignty Alliance (AFSA). (2010). *Letter to Politicians*, Available at: www.australianfoodsovereigntyalliance.org/blog/2010/08/12/letter-to-politicians-august-2010/. Accessed 5 February 2017.

Australian Food Sovereignty Alliance (AFSA). (2013). *The People's Food Plan*. Available at: afsa.org.au/wp-content/uploads/2012/11/AFSA_PFP_WorkingPaper-FINAL-15-Feb-2013.pdf. Accessed 15 April 2017.

Benkler, Y. (2006). *The Wealth of Nations: How Social Production Transforms Markets and Freedom*. New Haven, CT: Yale University Press.

Bennett, W. L. and Segerberg, A. (2012). The Logic of Connective Action. *Information, Communication & Society*, 15 (5), 739–768.

Bové, J. and Dufour, F. (2001). *The World Is Not for Sale: Farmers against Junk Food*. London: Verso.

boyd, d. (2010). Social Network Sites as Networked Publics: Affordances, Dynamics and Implications. In Z. Papacharissi (ed.), *Networked Self: Identity, Community, and Culture on Social Network Sites* (pp. 39–58). New York: Routledge.

Burgess, J. and Matamoros-Fernández, A. (2016). Mapping Sociocultural Controversies across Digital Media Platforms: One Week of #Gamergate on Twitter, YouTube, and Tumblr. *Communication Research and Practice*, 2 (1), 79–96.

Callon, M., Lascoumes, P. and Barthe, Y. (2001). *Acting in an Uncertain World. An Essay on Technical Democracy*. Cambridge, MA: MIT Press.

Caroll, W. and Hackett, R. (2006). Democratic Media Theory through the Lens of Social Movement Theory. *Media, Culture and Society*, 28 (1), 83–104.

Chavkin, S. and Hudson, M. (2015). New Investigation Reveals 3.4m Displaced by World Bank. International Consortium of Investigative Journalists, 16 April. Available at: www.icij.org/blog/2015/04/new-investigation-reveals-34m-displaced-world-bank. Accessed 5 February 2017.

Cottle, S. and Lester, L. (2011). *Transnational Protest and the Media*. New York: Peter Lang.

Desmarais, A. and Wittman, H. (2012). Food Sovereignty in Canada: Movement Growing to Control Our Own Food Systems. *Canadian Centre for Policy Alternatives*. Available at: www.policyalternatives.ca/publications/monitor/food-sovereignty-canada. Accessed 25 September 2017.

Diani, M. (2003). Leaders' or Brokers? Positions and Influence. In M. Diani and D. McAdam (eds.), *Social Movements and Networks: Relational Approaches to Collective Action* (pp. 105–122). Oxford: Oxford University Press.

Dixon, J., Beilin, R., Isaacs, B., Rose, N., Sanathanam-Martin, M. and Young, M. (2011). *Food Security for the Short or Long Term? Australia and New Zealand Agri-Food Research Network*. Available at: http://australian.foodsovereigntyalliance.org/food-security-for-the-short-or-long-term-the-following-is-a-piece-from-the-agri-food-research-network-on-food-security-and-the-governments-new-national-food-policy-working-group. Accessed 5 July 2011.

Figueroa, M. (2015). Food Sovereignty in Everyday Life: Toward a People-Centered Aproach to Food Systems. *Globalizations*, 12 (4), 498–512.

Food and Agriculture Organisation of the United Nations (FAO). (2004). *Voluntary Guidelines to Support the Progressive Realisation of the Right to Adequate Food in the Context of National Food Security*. Available at: www.fao.org/docrep/009/y7937e/y7937e00.htm. Accessed 15 September 2017.

Fox, R. and Frye, J. (2010). Tensions of Praxis: A New Taxonomy for Social Movements. *Environmental Communication*, 4 (4), 422–440.

Frohlich, X. (2017). The Informational Turn in Food Politics: The US FDA's Nutrition Label as Information Infrastructure. *Social Studies of Science*, 47 (2), 145–171.

Global Justice Now. (n.d.) *The Six Pillars of Food Sovereignty.* Available at: www. globaljustice.org.uk/six-pillars-food-sovereignty. Accessed 5 February 2018.

Gottlieb, R. and Fisher, A. (1996). Community Food Security and Environmental Justice: Searching for a Common Discourse. *Agriculture and Human Values*, 3 (3), 23–32.

Grey, S. and Patel, R. (2014). Food Sovereignty as Decolonisation: Some Contributions from Indigenous Movements to Food System and Development Politics. *Agriculture and Human Values*, 32 (3), 431–444. doi: 10.1007/s10460-014-9548-9.

Guthman, J. (2008). Neo-Liberalism and the Making of Food Politics in California. *Geoforum*, 39 (3), 1171–1183.

Indigenous Circle (2010) *First Principles Protocol for Building Cross-Cultural Relationships.* Available at: https://foodsecurecanada.org/sites/foodsecurecanada.org/files/First_Principles_July_2010.pdf. Accessed 1 September 2017.

Ishii-Eiteman, M. (2009). Food Sovereignty and the International Assessment of Agricultural Knowledge, Science and Technology for Development. *Journal of Peasant Studies*, 36 (3), 689–700.

Kavada, A. (2013). Internet Cultures and Protest Movements: The Cultural Links between Strategy, Organizing and Online Communication. In B. Cammaerts, A. Mattoni and P. McCurdy (eds.), *Mediation and Protest Movements* (pp. 75–93). Chicago, IL: University of Chicago Press.

Laughton, R. 2017. A Matter of Scale. Available at: https://landworkersalliance.org.uk/2017/07/small-scale-agroecological-farms-attract-uk-workers-produce-high-yields-of-vegetables-and-deliver-multiple-environmental-and-social-benefits/. Accessed 25 June 2017.

La Vía Campesina. (2013). Available at: https://tv.viacampesina.org/?lang=en. Accessed 28 July 2017.

La Vía Campesina. (2017). *Euskal Herria Declaration*, 26 July. Available at: https://viacampesina.org/en/viith-international-conference-la-via-campesina-euskal-herria-declaration/. Accessed 28 July 2017.

Lindberg, R., Kleven, S., Barbour, L., Booth, S. and Gallegos, D. (2016). Introduction. *In Parity: Beyond Emergency Food: Responding to Food Insecurity and Homelessness*, 29 (2), 4.

Lupton, D. (2018). Cooking, Eating, Uploading: Digital Food Cultures. In K. LeBesco and P. Naccarato (eds.), *The Handbook of Food and Popular Culture*. London: Bloomsbury.

Mann, A. (2011). *Lobbying for Peasant Rights at the UN. Right to Food and Nutrition Watch*. Bread for the World, FIAN International and the Interchurch Organisation for Development Cooperation (ICCO), August.

Mann, A. (2013a). Food Sovereignty in a Post-Organic Era. In B. Mascitelli and A. Lobo (eds.), *Organics in the Global Food Chain* (pp. 201–229). Ballarat: Connor Court Publishing.

Mann, A. (2013b). Bursting the 'Brussels Bubble': The Movement towards Transparency on European Farm Subsidies. *Ethical Space: The International Journal of Communication Ethics*, 10 (2/3), 47–54.

Mann, A. (2014). *Global Activism in Food Politics: Power Shift*. Basingstoke: Palgrave Macmillan.

Mann, A. (2016). The Right to Food and How 1.2 Million Australians Miss Out. *Croakey*, web log post, 10 April. Available at: https://croakey.org/the-right-to-food-and-how-1-2-million-australians-miss-out/. Accessed 15 November 2016.

Mann, A. (2017). Food Sovereignty and the Politics of Food Scarcity. In Dawson, M. C., Rosin, C. and Wald, N. (eds.), *Global Resources Scarcity: Catalyst for Conflict or Cooperation?* (pp. 131–145). London: Routledge.

Mann, A. (2018). Hashtag Activism and the Right to Food in Australia. In T. Schneider, K. Eli, C. Dolan and S. Ulijaszek (eds.), *Digital Food Activism* (pp. 168–184). London: Routledge.

Marres, N. and Rogers, R. (2005). Recipe for Tracing the Fate of Issues and Their Publics on the Web. In B. Latour and P. Wiebel (eds.), *Making Things Public: Atmospheres of Democracy* (pp. 922–935). Cambridge, MA: MIT Press.

McMichael, P. (2009). A Food Regime Genealogy. *Journal of Peasant Studies*, 36 (1), 139–169. doi: 10.1080/03066150902820354.

Meek, D. (2014). Agroecology and Radical Grassroots Movements' Evolving Moral Economies. *Environment and Society: Advances in Research*, 5, 47–65. doi: 10.3167/ares.2014.050104.

Micheletti, M. (2003). *Political Virtue and Shopping: Individuals, Consumerism, and Collective Action*. New York: Palgrave Macmillian.

Morrison, D. (2011). Indigenous Food Sovereignty—A Model for Social Learning. In H. Wittman, A. A. Desmarais and N. Wiebe (eds.), *Food Sovereignty in Canada: Creating Just and Sustainable Food Systems* (pp. 97–113). Halifax: Fernwood Publishing.

Papacharissi, Z. (2015). *Affective Publics: Sentiment, Technology, and Politics*. New York: Oxford University Press.

Patel, R. (2009). Food Sovereignty. *Journal of Peasant Studies*, 36 (3), 663–706.

People's Food Policy Project. (2011). *Resetting the Table: A People's Food Policy for Canada*. Montreal, QC: Food Secure Canada.

Prody, J. (2013). A Call for Polycultural Arguments: Critiquing the Monoculture Rhetoric of the Local Food Movement. *Argumentation and Advocacy*, 50 (2), 140.

Renting, H., Schermer, M. and Rossi, A. (2012). Building Food Democracy: Exploring Civic Food Networks and Newly Emerging Forms of Food Citizenship. *International Journal of Sociology of Agriculture and Food*, 19 (3), 289–307.

Rochon, T. (1998). *Culture Moves: Ideas, Activism and Changing Values*. Princeton, NJ: Princeton University Press.

Rousseau, S. (2012). *Food and Social Media: You Are What You Tweet*. Plymouth: AltaMira Press.

Ruiz, P. (2014). *Articulating Dissent: Protest and the Public Sphere*. London: Pluto Press.

Schneider, T., Eli, K., McLennan, A., Dolan, C., Lezaun, J. J. and Ulijaszek, S. S. (2017). Governance by Campaign: The Co-Constitution of Food Issues, Publics, and Expertise Thorough New Information and Communication Technologies. *Information, Communication & Society*, 14 (6), 770–799. doi: 10.1080/1369118X.2017.1363264.

Scoones, I., Edelman, M., Borras, S. M., Jr., Hall, R., Wolford, W. and White, B. (2017). Emancipatory Rural Politics: Confronting Authoritarian Populism. *The Journal of Peasant Studies*, 1–20. doi: 10.1080/03066150.2017.1339693.

Snow, D. A. and Benford, R. D. (1988). Ideology, Frame Resonance, and Participant Mobilization. In B. Klandermans, H. Kriesi and S. Tarrow (eds.), *From Structure to Action: Social Movement Participation across Cultures* (pp. 197–217). Greenwich, CT: JAI Press.

Valencia, R. R. (1997). *The Evolution of Deficit Thinking: Educational Thought and Practice*. London: Routledge.

Vivas, E. (2010). Food Sovereignty: Something's Moving in Europe. Available at: www.cadtm.org/Food-Sovereignty-something-s. Accessed 25 September 2017.

Wittman, H. (2011). Food Sovereignty: A New Rights Framework for Food and Nature? *Environment and Society: Advances in Research*, 2, 87–105. doi: 10.3167/ares.2011. 020106.

Wittman, H., Desmarais, A. and Wiebe, N. (eds.). (2011). *Food Sovereignty in Canada: Creating Just and Sustainable Food Systems*. Halifax: Fernwood Publishing.

Part 3

Personal food politics and entanglements

7 It's not (just) about the f-ckin' animals

How veganism is changing, and why that matters

Stephen Harrington, Christy Collis and Ozgur Dedehayir

Introduction

For a long time, vegans have been seen in most western cultures as either earnest, boring, 'hippies', or hard-core activists who are constantly on the lookout for opportunities to criticise others' food consumption practices (Cole and Morgan, 2011). Indeed, there is an old joke that runs along the following lines: 'Q: how do you know if there's a vegan in the room? A: Don't worry, they'll fucking tell you!' Keeping that joke alive, the satirical news web site *The Betoota Advocate* (2017) recently reported:

> Australia's peak scientific body, the CSIRO, released the paper earlier this morning at a Canberra press conference where the organisation's spokesman outlined that it takes roughly seven minutes on average for a vegan to tell you that they're vegan.

Some report that 'being a vegan is hard' (Kelly, 2017) because of veganism's long history of being positioned well outside the cultural mainstream, as well as its deep connections with often vocal, sometimes aggressive, animal activism. But (and, as we will outline later on, fortunately) these widely held cultural perceptions are starting to break down rather quickly. In this chapter, we will explore how and why the discourses surrounding vegan foods and vegan diets— in Australia and globally—have shifted so significantly. In doing so, we will argue that entertainment has played a particularly important role in the changing public perceptions of veganism, and has thus helped to catalyse growth of this culinary culture, and to foster a heightened awareness of the broader impacts and implications of dietary choices.

These changes in our culture, intangible and largely climatic, are difficult to quantify. Making our argument by tracing, for instance, the sales growth of some vegan foods, such as nut cheese or soy milk, would be imprecise (because they are not consumed *solely* by vegans, nor are they consumed by *all* vegans), nor would it tell us anything about the politics or culture surrounding the consumption of that food. The same holds true for surveys of people's consumption habits. There has been significant growth in both the production and consumption of products marketed as 'vegan' over the last five years (Nielsen, 2017), but this chapter is particularly interested in the discursive shifts that have in part underpinned this change in the food market. We follow an approach to textual analysis advocated by McKee (2003)—in which a range of texts are gathered and their 'ordinary' meanings analysed for the purpose of answering specific cultural questions—to provide evidence of the changing ways in which veganism is discussed, debated and framed in public discourse. We have collected these texts over a period of approximately 12 months, both as interested consumers and as a team of researchers interested in vegan culture. Of the texts collected, we focus our analysis in this chapter on the ones which are the most significant in terms of how they evidence clear trends, or which have received widespread attention among vegan consumers or in the broader public sphere. For further evidence to support our analysis, we draw upon exploratory interviews with customers at vegetarian restaurants, conducted in Brisbane, Australia, as part of a larger research project into food innovation systems. We conducted these interviews with four customers at each of four restaurants (i.e., 16 in total), approximately half of whom described themselves as currently vegan. The interviews lasted for around 60 minutes on average, and also included questions relating to food and business innovation, responses to which have not been included here. Respondents' names, where provided in this chapter, are pseudonyms to preserve anonymity.

We use the 'food politics' banner as a way of bringing together disarticulated research from across a range of disciplines all of which have had a tangential interest in veganism: cultural studies, marketing and advertising, sociology, philosophy and ethics, environmental science, and, of course, nutrition and public health. In doing so, we expand upon studies, such as those conducted by Arcari (2017, see also Chapter 9 in this collection), Greenebaum (2012), and Cole and Morgan (2011), to anatomise the shifting discursive construction of veganism, and we respond to Greenebaum and Dexter's (2017) call for social sciences analyses of the subject. We do so with the intention of further developing an interdisciplinary approach to the topic, and will conclude this brief analysis by suggesting that these discursive changes have potentially profound consequences for public health, the environment, and government policy.

Plant-based: f-ckin' dope, yo

Veganism is currently one of the fastest growing food trends in the world. In a recent article in *Delicious*, one of Australia's best known food writers (and *MasterChef Australia* judge), Matt Preston, declared that vegan food has gone from a 'culinary joke' to 'the new foodie buzzword', with a substantial presence in the global food scene that it never enjoyed before (Preston, 2017). Businesses are quickly latching on to this trend, too. McDonald's has launched its first vegan burger (only in Finland and Sweden, for now), suggesting, in doing so, that it was simply meeting the demands of a 'strong trend' (Purdy, 2017). In early 2018,

Domino's Pizza launched a vegan range in Australia, and soon thereafter reported that demand was so strong that it was facing a shortage of vegan cheese in its stores across the country, with the company's CEO putting a video message on Facebook urging customers to remain patient while stocks were replenished (Domino's Australia, 2018). Elmhurst Dairy, in New York State, has revived itself as a nut milk producer, after its cow milk operations ceased to be profitable following a downward trend in dairy consumption around the world (Garfield, 2017). In 2017, one of Canada's largest meat companies, Maple Leaf Foods, spent over a quarter of a billion dollars buying out two companies (Lightlife and Field Roast Grain Meat Co.) to expand its reach into the meat-free, 'alternative proteins' market (CTV News, 2017; Watrous, 2017). Meanwhile, food tech startups that are developing meat-substitute food products (e.g., Beyond Meat) are attracting a significant amount of attention from the media and from venture capitalists. Memphis Meats, a company that is developing 'clean meat' that is 'brewed' in steel tanks in laboratories, raised 17 million US dollars in capital in 2016 for further development of its technology, with Bill Gates and Richard Branson among the high-profile investors (Zaleski, 2016).

Although Memphis Meats does not technically produce vegan foods—'clean meat' is developed from cow, pig and chicken cells (taken from live animals), and is essentially indistinguishable from meat produced through animal slaughter—the fact that potential breakthrough alternatives to animal agriculture are attracting so much interest, and are seen as a potentially lucrative business opportunity, is yet further proof that veganism, as motivated by avoiding the suffering of non-human animals, is becoming a more visible part of our culture. There is no shortage of global news outlets reporting that veganism is now part of the mainstream (e.g., CBS News, 2011; Molloy, 2013; Tancock, 2015). In many ways, this shift seems obvious to anyone who is vegan or vegetarian within a cosmopolitan western culture; it seems almost self-evident. Vegan foods are much more readily available, more people seem to be vegan, and vegan eating is easier than it used to be. Podcaster and author Rich Roll—who we discuss later in this chapter—talks often about veganism being firmly established in the *zeitgeist*, and although he is American, the phenomenon he refers to is undoubtedly global. Some of our interviewees expressed similar sentiments:

JANET: *I'm just finding an explosion of vegan products coming into shops and stores now, and the availability of different milks... is a big thing. And, even, you know, different cheeses are just starting to emerge. So, it is amazing. It's lovely to see and it seems like now there's a sudden incline [in popularity]...* (63, Female)

Perhaps the headline change to the vegan food movement in recent years has been the discursive shift away from the use of the term 'vegan' at all. Instead, vegans are increasingly referring to 'plant-based' diets. There are two rather obvious reasons for such a change in approach. The first aspect of this discursive shift is that it allows vegans to move away from both the dowdy associations—

perhaps best distilled in the phrase 'a fringe diet for sandal-wearing health food store workers' (CBS News, 2011)—and extreme activist positions (e.g., 'meat is murder') which, as we noted at the outset of this chapter, have tended to characterise veganism for several decades (see Judge and Wilson, 2015, p. 59), and of which some interviewees were acutely aware:

ANDREW: *'Vegan'... has such a negative connotation socially that people just assume that you're not going to shower and you're going to grow your hair out... You're going to start wearing hemp shoes and stuff, doing drugs and move to West End [a trendy suburb in Brisbane's inner south], and your life's going to plummet.* (24, Male)

In fact, the joke we recounted in the opening lines of this chapter was retold by one interviewee:

SAMANTHA: *There's so many Facebook memes now... 'How do you know someone's a vegan? Because they tell you over and over and over and over.'* (56, Female)

Some of our interviewees believed that one of the reasons veganism has been such a controversial and contested category is because it is a label that inevitably draws attention to the deliberate choices of others who tacitly support a destructive industry:

CAROLINE: *I actually read a really good article on this... about why people get so offended by vegans. It was actually really interesting, it was about our response, we don't want to be bad people, and when someone challenges us saying that we might be, we're like 'no, that's not possible'. I'm not saying meat eaters are bad people, I'm just saying that some meat eaters might take it that we are saying that.* (18, Female)
JENNIFER: *I think it's other people's guilt reflected back on them... It makes sense as a whole and I think they see that and then they realise that their want is stronger than what's right...* (20, Female)

Notably, two interviewees viewed the act of promoting vegan diets as a kind of proselytising:

JAMES: *Maybe [people who reject the vegan label] think that vegans are too outspoken... know-it-alls, try and justify... their lifestyle to people, like pushing a religion.* (29, Male)
CHRISTINE: *I know some people who are vegans that are totally crazy, who were very pushy... It's like religion isn't it? Where you get the crazies...* (27, Female)

These responses mirror previous arguments around the 'quasi-religious' (Hamilton, 2000) characteristics of veganism. Similarly, Cole and Morgan (2011, p. 135) note that a major discursive strand sees veganism as 'a form of dietary asceticism involving exceptional efforts of self-transformation'. So the second reason for the discursive turn away from the word 'vegan' is that rather than being defined by what someone is *prevented* from eating (i.e., veganism equals no animal products), the emphasis becomes much more on what the person *can* and *does* eat. Rather than being framed as abstemiousness, the dietary choices are focused on dedication, which also gives them much stronger health connotations. This is perhaps best summed up by the following two responses. In response to the question 'What does the term "vegan" mean to you?', Larry—a non-vegan himself—expresses this meaning in very simple terms, deploying the word 'strict' along the way:

LARRY: *A vegan has strict eating habits basically.* (60, Male)

Stuart, however, has an entirely different view, and one which emphasises the opportunities that plant-based food brings, seeing it is a way of enhancing and improving upon the options that are already available:

STUART: *When I was less informed... I'd see vegan as tasteless... But, now, like, with a lot of shops opening up and seeing especially the amazing things they can do with, like, vegan desserts... I would rather have a vegan dessert, because I actually like it with a lack of dairy... vegan has now gone for me [from] something that's tasteless, imitation to me as, you know what, it's a filling, more nutritious, lighter version of the foods I used to like.* (44, Male)

Going even further than the 'plant-based' discourse, however, is the fact that veganism has become so much a part of the mainstream, and synonymous with 'good food' to such an extent, that it barely rates being mentioned at all. Just as we might trace the growing acceptance of queer identities in western culture by looking at how homosexual characters in film and television have gone from remarkable and noteworthy (e.g., *Number 96*) to largely unremarkable (e.g., *Modern Family*), we can also see the same occurring to some extent with veganism, where the presence of animal products (or lack thereof) is irrelevant in some cases. The popular Facebook page *Bosh*—which has over 1.5 million likes and is about to launch a cookbook—also uses the term 'plant-based', but strongly downplays this and instead features videos which border on 'food porn': extreme close-ups of sauces being poured on top of dishes, perfect slices of cake being lifted and the like. This imagery then bookends its instructional content, to which a large part of the success of the page can no doubt be attributed. These are, essentially, rapidly sped-up instructions, with many ellipses, devoid of voiceover (just music) or significant human presence, and thus are ideal for quick consumption when scrolling—often with the sound muted—through the Facebook newsfeed. This is a form of what Richard Twine calls 'demonstrative vegan practice' that 'builds bridges' and thus draws 'omnivores or vegetarians into the *sensual* experience of vegan food' (Twine, 2014, p. 636, emphasis added). That the food is vegan goes largely without comment; that it is delicious food is *Bosh's* primary focus.

The *Thug Kitchen* cookbook series, though, is perhaps the ultimate example to draw upon at this point. Starting out as a light-hearted food blog, the series now comprises three top-selling books. The first, *Thug Kitchen: Eat Like You Give a F-ck*—labelled as a '#1 New York Times Bestseller'—opens by explaining the philosophy behind the book. Not until the final paragraph, of eight in total, is there an explicit mention of all the recipes being 'plant-based', and that occurs just once. There is nothing at all on the front or back covers, nor elsewhere in the book, that draws attention to it being a vegan cookbook. Most of the emphasis in the book's introduction is on the importance of 'growing up', eating 'real' foods not 'fucking nonsense' food (like cheap fast food), and eating 'more goddam vegetables' with real nutrition. One of the crucial aspects of the series is, of course, that it is funny and entertaining, thus further rejecting the existing characterisations of veganism by explicitly subverting the artifice and perfection of most cookbooks. The degree of swearing and crude humour (one recipe on their web site suggests that readers should eat a salad: 'your asshole will thank you') evidences the vulgarity that McKee (2012) argues is one of the key aesthetic elements of entertainment. The other aspect is that it emphasises food quality and ease of preparation over and above perfection, precision and animal rights-focused moral virtue. One of our favourite recipes describes how to do 'lazy-ass blanching', which involves adding chopped kale into a boiling pot of noodles towards the end of their cooking time: 'Some people might say do that shit in separate pots, but those are usually the motherfuckers who don't wash their own dishes, so fuck them' (*Thug* Kitchen, 2014, p. 169). *Thug Kitchen* has not been without its critics,[1] but it has shown that, when entering the mainstream, a plant-based diet now does not have to be framed as exceptional, and instead is becoming almost synonymous with simply eating well.

Meat and masculinity

The gendering of veganism is another important discursive domain undergoing significant change. The close association of meat-eating with masculinity in western culture is unmistakable, and has been the subject of numerous scholarly analyses (for example, Buerkle, 2009; Rothgerber, 2013; Sobal, 2005). As Brady and Ventresca (2014, p. 301) note in their study of media representations of a prominent American football player who publicly adopted a vegan diet, '"doing" gender, race, class, sexuality etc. informs and is informed by "doing" food': constructions of identity are performed through food practices at the same time as those practices are shaped by prevailing constructions of identity. When it comes to constructing masculinity through food practices, meat-eating has dominated the semiotic and experiential field. Given the strength of this closed loop of cultural validation—men eat meat, and meat makes men more masculine—the insertion of veganism into the field of masculinity is a charged one. Veganism is not simply a matter of men eating more fruits and vegetables, it is a challenge to one of the central practices and representational apparata through which dominant masculinity is practised and understood. The recent emergence of vegan men and vegan masculinity into popular culture thus represents a significant change in the ways in which veganism is typically presented.

One domain in which vegan men and vegan masculinity have gained substantial traction in popular discourse is through the figure of the vegan athlete. Over the last ten years, numerous prominent and successful athletes have been vocal proponents of veganism, and have asserted the significant contributions of their vegan diets to their athletic successes. Athletes such as Adrian Foster (NFL), Mac Danzig (Mixed Martial Arts), Scott Jurek (ultra running), Tom Brady (NFL), Patrik Babomian (weight lifting), Pat Neshek (Major League Baseball), Salim Stoudamire (NBA), and Carl Lewis (running) have all ruptured conventional associations of meat-eating with masculine physical competitiveness and strength; that many of these athletes perform in sports in which muscular bulk and power are required further disrupts the dominant assumption that meat-eating and powerful masculinity are inseparably tethered. Vegan NFL athlete David Carter directly engages with this uncoupling by branding himself as 'the 300 pound vegan'.

While these athletes are key actors in the recent re-inscription of both masculinity and veganism, perhaps one of the most sustained and impactful figures in this process is Rich Roll. Roll is an ultra-distance triathlete who rose to initial prominence through the publication in 2012 of his memoir, *Finding Ultra: Rejecting Middle Age, Becoming One of the World's Fittest Men, and Rediscovering Myself.* The memoir details Roll's life change from an alcoholic, substance-addicted, overweight lawyer to a fulfilled, recovered, high-performance ultra-distance triathlete; key to this shift, according to Roll, was his change to a plant-based diet. Throughout the book, Roll strongly associates his vegan diet with the conventional attributes of dominant masculinity: he observes that his shift to a vegan diet made him stronger, more muscular, more capable of extreme physical performance, and, tangentially, more successful as a (heterosexual) partner. The use of 'one of the world's fittest men' in the title of his book foregrounds the centrality of the conventionally understood masculine traits of competitive athletic physicality to Roll's vegan narrative and persona. The book's cover image of Roll running shirtless, with his strongly-defined musculature prominently displayed, further cements Roll's association with physical power, and with conformity to conventional 'masculine' physical attributes. Based on the success of his book, in 2013 Roll launched his eponymous podcast, through which he has become an important hub in the vegan celebrity network and the emergent vegan public sphere. The podcast comprises long-form interviews with numerous figures associated with what can loosely be termed the 'wellness' movement; male vegans feature strongly in the selection of interviewees. The male vegans interviewed all possess strong cultural capital. They occupy positions of socio-economic power (Roll interviews numerous doctors and surgeons), physical power (many of Roll's interviewees are athletes), and cultural power (including interviewees such as hip-hop producer Russell Simmons, TV figure Osher Gunsberg, and musicians Moby and John Joseph, the latter an author of a book called *Meat is for Pussies*). The tethering of conventional attributes of masculine power—socio-economic, physical, and cultural—with veganism underpins Roll's interviewee choices, but also the broader cultural impact of his work. With his wife Julie Piatt,[2] Roll has gone on to publish a plant-based cookbook, and to run a plant-based meal planning app, signalling that popular uptake of his podcast and memoir has led directly to his audience members taking up plant-based food consumption.

What is notable about Roll's work is that his discursive articulation of masculinity to veganism (it should be noted that Roll consciously uses 'plant-based' instead of 'vegan') is multivariate. In their analysis of popular media responses to football player Adrian Foster, Brady and Ventresca (2014) conclude that Foster's self-publicised choice to consume a plant-based diet was discursively contained within a rationale of scientific performance enhancement, and that its potential threat to dominant constructions of masculinity was thus somewhat contained. The possibility that Foster may have become vegan due to compassion for animals or care for the environment—both seen as highly feminine positions (Thomas, 2016)—is negated. Greenebaum and Dexter (2017) observe a similar discursive strategy in their interviews with male vegans: many of the men they interviewed did not eschew conventional constructions of masculinity (physically powerful, heroic, unemotional), but rather articulated these to veganism. However, although they are mutually constitutive, the focus of this chapter is on changing representations and understandings of veganism, rather than of masculinity. Roll avoids easy containments of vegan masculinity through discourses such as nutrition: the powerful male vegans he interviews—and he himself—attribute their veganism variously to compassion for animals, environmentalism and spirituality, as well as to scientifically validated physical performance. The cultural association of meat-eating with masculinity remains strong—one of Roll's running jokes/frustrations is the number of times he is asked 'but where do you get your protein?'—but its fortified construction is currently being dismantled. Veganism is increasingly represented and understood as acceptably masculine, and as connected to some of the central attributes of conventional dominant masculinity. Through the public vegan-ness of prominent male athletes, and through the significant popular circulation of Roll's work, a new, vegan masculinity is emerging.

Intersectionality

Another significant shift in popular representations of veganism involves the shift away from veganism being understood as driven solely by an ethic of care for animals, to be seen as connecting multifariously to other lifestyle and social identity choices (Chuck, Fernandes and Hyers, 2016):

AARON: *[It's] a complete lifestyle choice.* (24, Male)

Although there are significant ethical issues associated with industrial farming practices—for example, in 2015, around nine million cows were slaughtered in Australia alone (Long, 2015), and these animals generally don't live in pleasant conditions when they are alive—among our interviewees who followed a vegan diet, it was not, it turns out, all about the animals. At least not primarily. Overwhelmingly, people talked about the health benefits of their chosen diet, but noted that it also could not be separated out from the corollary benefits to animal welfare and the environment.

Judge and Wilson note that 'while environmental advocacy groups have heavily promoted pro-environmental behaviours such as recycling or using public transport; until recently there has been relatively little promotion of plant-based, vegetarian, or vegan diets' (2015, pp. 57–58). This is a surprising fact, given the evidence that exists of the environmental impact of industrial farming of animals for consumption. A UN- and EU-backed report from over ten years ago notes that more CO_2 was emitted by livestock worldwide than by all forms of transport combined (Steinfeld et al., 2006). Animal agriculture is one of the main causes of environmental destruction globally (Vergunst and Savulescu, 2017). And, there is also concern that the significant amount of antibiotics administered to livestock is contributing to elevated risk of antibiotic-resistant bacterial infections (Witte, 1998). One of the crucial pieces of popular culture to pick up on the discrepancy between the environmental impact of animal-based food production and the level of attention given to it by environmental advocacy groups is the documentary *Cowspiracy*. Produced by Kip Andersen and Keegan Kuhn, *Cowspiracy* was released in 2014, and was financed largely through crowd funding.[3] A revised and updated version was executive produced by Leonardo DiCaprio, and released through Netflix over 12 months later, which substantially boosted the film's cultural capital and impact. The documentary itself is roughly divided into two parts: the first draws attention (through 'gotcha' interviews) to the hypocrisy of numerous well known environmental groups for taking dona-tions from meat-producers, and also for not promoting the environmental benefits of going meat- and dairy-free. The second part is focused mostly on arguing that vegan diets are nutritionally complete and optimal for health.

The consumption of animal products—particularly meat—has been linked with higher rates of cancer (Bouvard et al., 2015), type 2 diabetes (Pan et al., 2011), high blood pressure, obesity, dementia (Morris and Tangney, 2014), and osteoporosis (Michaëlsson et al., 2014), among other ailments, with low-income and Indigenous communities hit especially hard by these health problems (O'Dea, Rowley and Brown, 2007). These are among the costliest health problems industrialised western countries face (see Centers for Disease Control and Prevention, 2017). Although most people are unaware of these health risks, the World Health Organization (2015) recently declared processed meat a 'grade 1' carcinogen, and red meat a 'grade 2' probable carcinogen. In 2016, the Netherlands Nutrition Centre—a government-funded programme that creates dietary guidelines—issued a recommendation that people eat no more than two servings of meat per week in light of these emerging findings. Alongside the lesser known *Forks Over Knives, What the Health?* (the semi-sequel to *Cowspiracy*) drew attention to some of these factors, also through 'gotcha' interviews wondering why organisations like the American Diabetes Association were including recipes with processed meat in them on their web sites, or (once again) were taking donations from large meat companies. Like some other prominent vegan texts that have had an impact in the public sphere, *What the Health?* has drawn criticism from those who believe that the directors cherry-picked studies, misreported the data, and overstated their findings by repeatedly drawing comparisons to cigarette smoking (e.g., Belluz, 2017). While being interviewed on the highly mainstream *Dr. Oz Show* in October 2017, the eponymous Mehmet Oz criticised Kip Anderson, saying that 'there will be a lot of people who walk away from this movie scared, more than they should be',[4] but he still generally agreed with the film's overall message, and supported Anderson's mission of raising questions about the health impact of animal products ('Dr. Oz Weighs in. . .', 2017).

The expansion and re-inscription of 'vegan-ness' from being animal-centric to including a broader concern for the impacts of food consumption, through to a concern for individual health, arguably represents a kind of egocentric shift. What was once a selfless pursuit for those who cared for other beings (animals) has now, in many cases, become a concern about impacts that affect all humans (environment), and an interest mostly in the self (individual health or increased athletic performance). To suggest that any one person's rationale is monolithic, let alone selfish is, however, too simplistic, because the plant-based community arguably sits at the intersection of a diversity of concerns. As evidence of this, a word that is often used by the community is 'speciesism', which helps to entangle individual food choices with a suite of power imbalances that includes racism and sexism. This mirrors another ethic at play, which is a kind of atheist or pantheist spirituality that believes 'everything is connected', and thus demands a respect for all other 'earthlings'[5] and for the environment they, and we, live in. Thus, a number of our interviewees used words like 'clean' and 'guilt-free' to describe their feelings about plant-based foods, for example:

CHRISTINE: *I feel like it's a lot cleaner, and I know I felt really good when I was eating like that.* (27, Female)

These responses may be referencing the 'clean' eating movement (to which veganism is undoubtedly related), but could also be reflective of a broader spiritual awareness of what it means to 'feel good' in the first place: that a plant-based diet is not only good for the self, but good for the soul. Perhaps, rather than viewing this as a semiotic gravitational shift away from animal rights, the discursive shifts associated with the plant-based movement should be viewed as a spread and expansion of meaning to view food choices holistically.

Conclusion: to spread the word, or 'nudge the spread'?

In this chapter we have briefly outlined the ways in which veganism—in popular discourse, at least—has gone from an 'alternative' position within western food culture to an increasingly mainstream one. In the process, a number of the existing cultural associations with veganism are being upended. In this analysis, we have opted mostly to bypass a critical cultural approach (e.g., Castricano and Simonsen, 2016), and instead we look optimistically at the phenomenon, given the wider ethical, environmental and health benefits associated with plant-based diets. We acknowledge, though, that there is some danger in suggesting that veganism can magically change the world when it is currently clustered among white, urban elites with time and money to cook vegan food of their own (fresh fruit and vegetables being much more expensive than a fast food meal). Priestley, Lingo and Royal (2016, p. 352) call these 'the material and social conditions that limit access to a vegan diet', and which likely make veganism a near impossibility for a low-income family living in a rural Australian town, for example. Thus there are a range of questions that arise from our analysis which deserve further thought and consideration. Chief among them is how plant-based diets can be promoted and encouraged, and what role governments, policy makers and other actors in the food landscape should play in that mission.

Given the immense challenges and lack of success that governments have already faced in promoting healthy eating (e.g., Hickman, 2010), and the extent to which the regulatory process is captured by the lobbying power of the meat and dairy industries,[6] we suggest that a better policy option might be to avoid expensive, didactic messaging, and instead to use the technique that has come to be known within behavioural economics as 'nudging'. This approach seeks to understand 'choice architecture', and to modify that architecture so as to 'induce behavioural changes and influence the choices of individuals, while leaving the possibility of not following the suggested direction' (Oullier et al., 2010). Noting that human beings are not entirely rational (or have only 'bounded rationality'— see Kahneman, 2003), and are prone to a number of cognitive biases, Thaler and Sunstein (2009, p. 6) explain that a 'nudge' is:

> any aspect of the choice architecture that alters people's behaviour in a predictable way without forbidding any options or significantly changing their economic incentives. To count as a nudge, the intervention must be easy and cheap to avoid. Nudges are not mandates. Putting the fruit at eye level counts as a nudge. Banning junk food does not.

This 'libertarian paternalism' (Thaler and Sunstein, 2003), which is already gaining traction in other areas of public health policy (see Matjasko et al., 2016), would acknowledge that food options for most citizens are bounded by a range of factors, including geographical proximity, price and time, among others (see, for instance, Walker, Keane and Burke, 2010). So government policy might therefore be better off taking small actions to help address some of those constraints, and to 'smooth the path' to a plant-based diet, rather than lecture about its benefits, or shame those who choose alternatives.

There are a number of avenues through which this cultural change can be catalysed. One way is to further explore the use of entertainment that might help build a stronger plant-based dietary and culinary culture (see Doyle, 2016). Rapid change in food culture is possible through the impact of popular culture, as evidenced, for example, by the immense cultural change kick-started in 2009 by the success of *MasterChef Australia* (see Kirkwood and Phillipov, 2015), and it is worth considering how popular media can play a role in nudging. This chapter represents a building block in developing nudges towards plant-based eating: to succeed in gaining cultural traction, nudges need to be informed by popular discursive understandings and sentiments. This chapter has anatomised some of this shifting discursive terrain surrounding plant-based eating. One nudge that our admittedly limited research base might suggest would prove fruitful is to simply bust a few common myths related to veganism: plants have protein; some of the largest land mammals are herbivores; you don't need dairy products for calcium; not all soy milks are created equal; and that meat consumption is not an inherent component of masculinity. One further useful intervention might be to find ways to promote more rapid development of the nascent plant-based food industry that supports this emerging plant-based culture. In the pursuit of more useful 'nudges', however, much more extensive research is required, and should therefore be focused on better understanding the choice architecture around food, and thus the paths that require smoothing. Questions such as: how do people tip from being omnivores, to vegetarians, to vegans? What are the linchpins? What are the meat and dairy 'replacements' that omnivores and vegetarians see as necessary for trying out a plant-based diet—good quality nut cheese? Authentic 'mock meats'? What are the financial challenges associated with veganism? And how can we work to ensure a degree of geographical/regional and economic equity in access to plant-based foods? In the end, some of the 'nudges' may see limited payoffs, but if they are cheap and simple enough, that outcome could still represent a very good return on investment. At the very least, some people might just end up eating more vegetables: an outcome which everyone, even die-hard meat eaters, would agree is pretty f-ckin' sweet.

Notes

1 The two authors behind the series, a white heterosexual couple from California, have been accused (not inconsequentially) by *Jezebel* and *Vice*, among other outlets, of racism and 'cultural appropriation' for using the racially-loaded term 'thug', and 'a tone reminiscent of African American Vernacular English' (Sowunmi, 2014; Ryan, 2014). They are, according to Priestley, Lingo and Royal (2016, p. 365), 'at best offensive and at worst complicit in oppression'.

2 Piatt, a.k.a SriMati, is herself another important node in the vegan public sphere, with her own podcast and cookbooks.

3 Given the limited marketing budget of a crowd funded documentary, Kip Andersen and Keegan Kuhn have relied quite heavily on audiences to help promote and market their films. *What the Health?* was available for paid digital download well before being made available through streaming services, and tapped into the existing energy of the global vegan community by supporting screenings of the documentary organised by individual activists.

4 Oz's criticisms here can't go without a mention of the hypocrisy at play, given that he has been criticised widely for promoting pseudoscience (e.g., homeopathy), and has been found to regularly give misleading medical advice on his show (see Korownyk et al., 2014).

5 *Earthlings* is also the name of a 2005 documentary film on animal cruelty.
6 For example, the dairy industry in Australia is currently engaged in a campaign to stop plant-based products being labelled as 'milk' (see Jasper, 2017), which parallels similar campaigns elsewhere in the world. Similarly, the 'food pyramid' in the US remains a highly contested advisory guideline, the creation of which is subject to a significant amount of lobbying, and is massively constrained by stakeholder influence (see Duhaime-Ross, 2016). As one of our interviewees put it: 'I think the meat lobby's much bigger than the vegetable lobby' (Samantha, 56, Female).

References

Arcari, P. (2017). Normalised, Human-Centric Discourses of Meat and Animals in Climate Change, Sustainability and Food Security Literature. *Agriculture and Human Values*, 34 (1), 69–86.

Belluz, J. (2017). Debunking *What the Health*, the Buzzy New Documentary that Wants You to Be Vegan. *Vox*, 27 December. Available at: www.vox.com/platform/amp/science-and-health/2017/7/25/16018658/what-the-health-documentary-review-vegan-diet. Accessed 29 April 2018.

The Betoota Advocate. (2017). Study Finds the Easiest Way to Tell If Someone Is Vegan Is to Wait until They Inevitably Tell You. *The Betoota Advocate*. Available at: www.betootaadvocate.com/humans-of-betoota/study-finds-easiest-way-tell-someone-vegan-wait-inevitably-tell/. Accessed 12 November 2017.

Bouvard, V., Loomis, D., Guyton, K. Z., Grosse, Y., Ghissassi, F. E., Benbrahim-Tallaa, L., Guha, N., Mattock, H. and Straif, K. (2015). Carcinogenicity of Consumption of Red and Processed Meat. *The Lancet Oncology*, 16 (16), 1599–1600.

Brady, J. and Ventresca, M. (2014). 'Officially a Vegan Now': On Meat and Renaissance Masculinity in Pro Football. *Food and Foodways*, 22 (4), 300–321.

Buerkle, C. W. (2009). Metrosexuality Can Stuff It: Beef Consumption as (Heteromasculine) Fortification. *Text and Performance Quarterly*, 29 (1), 77–93.

Castricano, J. and Simonsen, R. R. (eds.). (2016). *Critical Perspectives on Veganism*. Basingstoke: Palgrave Macmillan.

CBS News. (2011). Vegan Diets Become More Popular, More Mainstream. *CBS News*, 5 January. Available at: www.cbsnews.com/news/vegan-diets-become-more-popular-more-mainstream/. Accessed 4 November 2017.

Centers for Disease Control and Prevention. (2017). Chronic Diseases: The Leading Causes of Death and Disability in the United States, 28 June. Available at: www.cdc.gov/chronicdisease/overview/. Accessed 12 December 2017.

Chuck, C., Fernandes, S. A. and Hyers, L. L. (2016). Awakening to the Politics of Food: Politicized Diet as Social Identity. *Appetite*, 107, 425–436.

Cole, M. and Morgan, K. (2011). Vegaphobia: Derogatory Discourses of Veganism and the Reproduction of Speciesism in UK National Newspapers. *The British Journal of Sociology*, 62 (1), 134–153.

CTV News. (2017). Maple Leaf Further Expands into Alternative Proteins with US$120M Acquisition. *CTV News*, 1 December. Available at: www.ctvnews.ca/business/maple-leaf-further-expands-into-alternative-proteins-with-us-120m-acquisition-1.3702579. Accessed 2 December 2017.

Domino's Australia. (2018). Domino's Australia CEO Nick Knight Is Here with a Message for Our Passionate Vegan Cheese Fans, *Facebook*, 17 January. Available at: www.facebook.com/DominosAustralia/videos/10156404325951412/. Accessed 24 January 2018.

Doyle, J. (2016). Celebrity Vegans and the Lifestyling of Ethical Consumption. *Environmental Communication*, 10 (6), 777–790.

Dr. Oz Weighs in on *What the Health* Film(2017). *The Dr. Oz Show*, 6 October. Available at: www.doctoroz.com/episode/tlc-s-t-boz-opens-about-her-battles-and-overcoming-pain? video_id=5599280433001. Accessed 27 January 2018.

Duhaime-Ross, A. (2016). New US Food Guidelines Show the Power of Lobbying, Not Science. *The Verge*, 7 January. Available at: www.theverge.com/2016/1/7/10726606/2015-us-dietary-guidelines-meat-and-soda-lobbying-power. Accessed 10 December 2017.

Garfield, L. (2017). A Major Dairy Producer Collapsed—Now It's Making Nut Milks and Business Is Booming. *Business Insider Australia*, 23 April. Available at: www.businessin sider.com.au/dairy-farm-nut-milks-elmhurst-2017-4?r=US&IR=T. Accessed 4 November 2017.

Greenebaum, J. and Dexter, B. (2017). Vegan Men and Hybrid Masculinity. *Journal of Gender Studies*, 27 (6), 637–648. doi: 10.1080/09589236.2017.1287064.

Greenebaum, J. B. (2012). Managing Impressions: 'Face-Saving' Strategies of Vegetarians and Vegans. *Humanity & Society*, 36 (4), 309–325.

Hamilton, M. (2000). Eating Ethically: 'Spiritual' and 'Quasi-Religious' Aspects of Vegetarianism. *Journal of Contemporary Religion*, 15 (1), 65–83.

Hickman, M. (2010). Decade of Spending on Health Messages 'Has Had Little Effect'. *Independent*, 10 February. Available at: www.independent.co.uk/life-style/health-and-families/health-news/decade-of-spending-on-health-messages-has-had-little-effect-1894551.html. Accessed 28 December 2017.

Jasper, C. (2017). Dairy Farmers Seek Public Support Over Push to Stop Plant-Based Alternatives Being Called 'Milk'. *ABC News*, 10 August. Available at: www.abc.net.au/news/rural/2017-08-10/dairy-farmers-push-to-tighten-use-of-milk-food-labelling/8790294. Accessed 12 December 2017.

Judge, M. and Wilson, M. S. (2015). Vegetarian Utopias: Visions of Dietary Patterns in Future Societies and Support for Social Change. *Futures*, 71, 57–69.

Kahneman, D. (2003). Maps of Bounded Rationality: Psychology for Behavioral Economics. *The American Economic Review*, 93 (5), 1449–1475.

Kelly, M. (2017). The V Word: What Happens When You Adopt a Vegan Diet for a Month. *news.com.au*, 24 September. Available at: www.news.com.au/lifestyle/health/diet/the-v-word-what-happens-when-you-adopt-a-vegan-diet-for-a-month/news-story/aaaaf96b3 cfb1fd2454f49b841e52a52. Accessed 26 September 2017.

Kirkwood, K. and Phillipov, M. (2015). What MasterChef Teaches Us about Food and the Food Industry. *The Conversation*, 21 May. https://theconversation.com/what-masterchef-teaches-us-about-food-and-the-food-industry-41893. Accessed 4 November 2017.

Kitchen, T. (2014). *Eat like You Give a F-Ck*. New York: Rodale.

Korownyk, C., Kolber, M., McCormack, J., Lam, V. et al. (2014). Televised Medical Talk Shows—What They Recommend and the Evidence to Support Their Recommendations: A Prospective Observational Study. *British Medical Journal*, 17 December. doi: 10.1136/bmj.g7346.

Long, W. (2015). Australia Killing 170,000 Cattle Per Week. *ABC News*, 8 July. Available at: www.abc.net.au/news/rural/2015-07-08/big-beef-kill/6602988. Accessed 12 May 2017.

Matjasko, J. L., Cawley, J. H., Baker-Goering, M. M. and Yokum, D. V. (2016). Applying Behavioral Economics to Public Health Policy: Illustrative Examples and Promising Directions. *American Journal of Preventive Medicine*, 50 (5), S13–S19.

McKee, A. (2003). *Textual Analysis: A Beginner's Guide*. London: Sage Publications.

McKee, A. (2012). The Aesthetic System of Entertainment. In A. McKee, C. Collis and B. Hamley (eds.), *Entertainment Industries: Entertainment as a Cultural System* (pp. 9–19). London: Routledge.

Michaëlsson, K., Wolk, A., Langenskiöld, S., Basu, S., Lemming, E. W., Melhus, H. and Byberg, L. (2014). Milk Intake and Risk of Mortality and Fractures in Women and Men: Cohort Studies. *British Medical Journal*, 27 October. doi: 10.1136/bmj.g6015.

Molloy, A. (2013). No Meat, No Dairy, No Problems: Is 2014 the Year Vegans Become Mainstream? *Independent*, 31 December. Available at: www.independent.co.uk/life-style/food-and-drink/features/no-meat-no-dairy-no-problem-is-2014-the-year-vegans-become-mainstream-9032064.html. Accessed 9 October 2017.

Morris, M. C. and Tangney, C. C. (2014). Dietary Fat Composition and Dementia Risk. *Neurobiology of Aging*, 35 (2), 59–64.

Nielsen. (2017). Plant Based Proteins Are Gaining Dollar Share among North Americans. *Nielsen Insights*, 22 September. Available at: www.nielsen.com/us/en/insights/news/2017/plant-based-proteins-are-gaining-dollar-share-among-north-americans.html. Accessed 12 December 2017.

O'Dea, K., Rowley, K. G. and Brown, A. (2007). Diabetes in Indigenous Australians: Possible Ways Forward. *Medical Journal of Australia*, 186 (10), 494–495.

Oullier, O., Cialdini, R., Thaler, R. H. and Mullainathan, S. (2010). Improving Public Health Prevention with a Nudge. *Economic Perspectives*, 6 (2), 117–136.

Pan, A., Sun, Q., Bernstein, A. M., Schulze, M. B., Manson, J. E., Willett, W. C. and Hu, F. B. (2011). Red Meat Consumption and Risk of Type 2 Diabetes: 3 Cohorts of US Adults and an Updated Meta-Analysis. *American Journal of Clinical Nutrition*, 94 (4), 1088–1096.

Preston, M. (2017). Why Vegan Is the Fastest Growing Food Movement in the World, *Delicious*, 18 May. Available at: www.delicious.com.au/food-files/article/why-vegan-fastest-growing-food-movement-world/pGyK8ZIL. Accessed 19 October 2017.

Priestley, A., Lingo, S. K. and Royal, P. (2016). 'The Worst Offense Here Is the Misrepresentation': Thug Kitchen and Contemporary Vegan Discourse. In J. Castricano and R. R. Simonsen (eds.), *Critical Perspectives on Veganism* (pp. 349–371). Basingstoke: Palgrave Macmillan.

Purdy, C. (2017). McDonald's Is Making the McVegan a Permanent Menu Item in Sweden and Finland. *Quartz*, 18 December. Available at: https://qz.com/1159661/mcdonalds-has-added-a-vegan-burger-to-its-menu-in-europe/. Accessed 20 December 2017.

Rothgerber, H. (2013). Real Men Don't Eat (Vegetable) Quiche: Masculinity and the Justification of Meat Consumption. *Psychology of Men & Masculinity*, 14 (4), 363–375.

Ryan, E. G. (2014). Meet the White People behind 'Thug Kitchen'. *Jezebel*, 29 September. Available at: https://jezebel.com/meet-the-white-people-behind-thug-kitchen-1640479775. Accessed 2 January 2018.

Sobal, J. (2005). Men, Meat, and Marriage: Models of Masculinity. *Food & Foodways*, 13 (1–2), 135–158.

Sowunmi, J. (2014). 'Thug Kitchen' Is the Latest Iteration of Digital Blackface. *Vice*, 4 October. Available at: www.vice.com/en_au/article/ppmvp8/thug-kitchen-is-the-latest-iteration-of-people-profiting-off-digital-blackface-909. Accessed 3 January 2018.

Steinfeld, H., Gerber, P., Wassenaar, T., Castel, V., Rosales, M. and de Haan, C. (2006). *Livestock's Long Shadow: Environmental Issues and Options*. Rome: Food and Agriculture Organization of the United Nations.

Tancock, K. (2015). Vegan Cuisine Moves into the Mainstream—And It's Actually Delicious. *The Globe and Mail*, 13 January. Available at: www.theglobeandmail.com/life/

food-and-wine/food-trends/vegan-cuisine-moves-into-the-mainstream/article22430440/. Accessed 9 October 2017.

Thaler, R. H. and Sunstein, C. R. (2003). Libertarian Paternalism. *American Economic Review*, 93 (2), 175–179.

Thaler, R. H. and Sunstein, C. R. (2009). *Nudge: Improving Decisions about Health, Wealth, and Happiness* (revised ed.). New York: Penguin Books.

Thomas, M. A. (2016). Are Vegans the Same as Vegetarians? The Effect of Diet on Perceptions of Masculinity. *Appetite*, 97 (C (Supplement)), 79–86.

Twine, R. (2014). Vegan Killjoys at the Table: Contesting Happiness and Negotiating Relationships with Food Practices. *Societies*, 4 (4), 623–639.

Vergunst, F. and Savulescu, J. (2017). Five Ways the Meat on Your Plate Is Killing the Planet. *The Conversation*, 26 April. Available at: https://theconversation.com/five-ways-the-meat-on-your-plate-is-killing-the-planet-76128. Accessed 5 May 2017.

Walker, R. E., Keane, C. R. and Burke, J. G. (2010). Disparities and Access to Healthy Food in the United States: A Review of Food Deserts Literature. *Health & Place*, 16 (5), 876–884.

Watrous, M. (2017). Maple Leaf Foods to Acquire Meatless Brand Lightlife. *Food Business News*, 22 February. Available at: www.foodbusinessnews.net/articles/news_home/Business_News/2017/02/Maple_Leaf_Foods_to_acquire_me.aspx?ID=%7BCCFDA57A-270D-40F7-B2B9-9404067BF3F6%7D. Accessed 12 December 2017.

Witte, W. (1998). Medical Consequences of Antibiotic Use in Agriculture. *Science*, 279 (5353), 996–997.

World Health Organization. (2015). Q&A on the Carcinogenicity of the Consumption of Red Meat and Processed Meat. Available at: www.who.int/features/qa/cancer-red-meat/en/. Accessed 28 December 2017.

Zaleski, A. (2016). The Hottest Tech in Silicon Valley Made This Meatball. *Fortune*, 25 April. Available at: http://fortune.com/2016/04/25/memphis-meats-lab-grown-meat/. Accessed 12 December 2017.

8 Vitalities and visceralities

Alternative body/food politics in digital media

Deborah Lupton

Digital media have made activist groups, dissenting voices and food cultures visible to potentially very large audiences in unprecedented ways. Many relate to alternative ways of thinking about and engaging in food practices. Digital media platforms, such as Facebook, Tumblr, Twitter, Instagram and YouTube, provide a multitude of opportunities for people to create their own content concerning their own or others' bodies, as well as food production, preparation and consumption practices, to share this content and to comment on, curate or re-appropriate the material of others.

In this chapter, I adopt a cultural studies perspective, drawing on feminist materialism, to identify some of the influential practices and forms of representation related to the circulation of forces and intensities about embodiment and food cultures as they are expressed in digital media, referring throughout to body/food politics to signify the close relationship between the two. My discussion here is based on the premise that political and power relations are enacted in the quotidian spaces of everyday routines and practices, and are produced through and with performances of embodiment and identity. Therefore, digital media representations of human bodies, or of food production and consumption practices, can be interpreted as political insofar as they privilege some meanings over others, and claim membership or speak to some social groups rather than others.

While people uploading images of their restaurant or home-cooked meals to a social media platform may not seem overtly political, it represents the micro-political level of participatory culture on social media as users attempt to generate meaning and to portray their food practices (and, by extension, themselves) in a certain light. Other content and interactions have a more macro-political intention, directed at challenging or changing dominant structures, organisations or interests. Irrespective of the position taken, much of this online content can be viewed as 'alternative' in the broadest sense, in that it represents bodies and food in ways that promote some meanings and close off others. Advocates of vegan or vegetarian positions, or of 'clean eating', for example, provide an alternative perspective from those promoting other foods or diets on what kinds of foods should be consumed. Fat activists or those advocating body positivism seek to challenge normative assumptions about health, attractiveness, and body weight and size, providing a counter-representation to advocates of weight-loss and thin, or fit, embodiment.

Importantly for my focus here, digital media material about bodies/food often employs images and text that seek to incite intensities and affective forces to persuasively convey meaning and affect audiences.

My discussion begins with an outline of the key theoretical perspectives offered by feminist materialist scholars and the contributions they can make to examining the micro- and macro-politics of body/food cultures in digital media. I take this approach to acknowledge the role played by non-humans, such as digital media and devices, in human embodiment and political practices, and to examine the embodied politics of human–non-human assemblages, focusing on the use of images and hashtags in what is fast becoming a digital culture dominated by these forms of communication. As I show, the features and affordances of digital media engagement are central to the political agential capacities, affects and vitalities that are generated in and with these media.

The chapter is structured around a set of hashtags that are commonly used to invite interest and attention about bodies and food. I examine digital media portrayals of different types of food (particularly those typically coded as 'clean' and 'healthy', compared with those represented as 'indulgent', 'junk' or 'excessive'), human bodies (principally those designated as 'fit', 'thin' or 'fat'), and related concepts of fitness and health, vegetarianism and veganism, meat consumption, fat activism and pro-anorexia ('pro-ana'). In so doing, I seek to demonstrate the very different, but sometimes interrelated, political positions expressed in digital media.

Feminist materialism, digital media and politics

Sociomaterialist positions are useful for highlighting how humans construct and enact meaning with and through things, including digital devices and media. Such perspectives have begun to exert great influence in contemporary social and cultural theory as a result of their capacity to address the entanglements of humans and non-humans in a more-than-human world. This approach not only acknowledges the importance of symbolic ways of conveying meaning (such as language, discourse and image), but also the agency of material objects and how they generate, shape and order human action together with humans.

As articulated in the work of feminist materialist scholars Donna Haraway (2008, 2015, 2016), Karen Barad (2003, 2007), Jane Bennett (2004, 2010) and Rosi Braidotti (2002, 2013) humans are entangled in broader ecologies of other living creatures and non-living objects and spaces. These relationships and assemblages are continually dynamic and emergent, as new actors enter into or leave them, and as humans move through time and space. From this perspective, all actors in these assemblages have agency and vitality, but always with and through other actors. Working together, they create vital forces and agential capacities for feeling, learning or action.

In feminist materialist analyses, questions of ethics and politics are often central. For Bennett, Braidotti, Haraway and Barad, this includes a focus on environmental politics and the politics of embodiment. They contend that recognising non-human actors as agential and affective (in terms of possessing the capacity to affect and be affected), allows greater recognition of the importance of the non-human world to human existence. For Braidotti (2002, 2013), the mutable and distributed nature of human agency offers a politics that is able to challenge current fears and preoccupations. Cartographies of power relations and their associated entitlements, agencies and capacities can provide detailed ways of thinking through and with political practices and subjectivities. They help to think differently about figurations of human action, belief and practice, their implications, boundaries and limitations, and how new modes of being and acting can be configured, and political change effected.

Haraway similarly takes a self-declared feminist socialist stance that is more than human. In her most recent writing, she adopts the term 'Chthulucene' as an alternative to the Anthropocene (a term used to describe the contemporary epoch in world history in which humans are exerting a dominant force over living things and systems) (Haraway, 2015, 2016). For Haraway, the Chthulucene is a vision of the world in which multispecies assemblages of humans and non-humans (both technologies and living creatures) co-exist. She describes the 'tentacular' associations that involve 'myriad temporalities and spatialities and myriad intra-active entities-in-assemblages—including the more-than-human, other-than-human, inhuman, and human-as-humus' (Haraway, 2015, p. 160). When identifying the political dimensions of this world order, Haraway contends that it is important to look at 'which stories tell stories, which concepts think concepts. Mathematically, visually, and narratively, it matters with figures figure figures, which systems systematize systems' (Haraway, 2015, p. 15).

Barad's (2003) insistence on understanding 'how matter comes to matter' also draws attention to the political importance of material things. She proposes a post-human perspective on performativity, which involves recognition of the role of things, as well as of ideas and discourses in configuring the matter of bodies and ecologies of other living creatures. Bennett (2004, p. 348) uses the term 'thing-power' to describe the vital power of human–non-human assemblages, and outlines the 'material recalcitrance' of cultural forms. She contends that a greater awareness of how this thing-power operates can draw attention to the wider political dimensions of human–non-human assemblages. As such, these assemblages can contribute to an ecological project of environmental sustainability by sensitising humans to their complexities, their agential powers and the impact of human interventions.

Applying these philosophical approaches to alternative body/food politics, it can be posited that when humans interact with other humans, non-human living organisms, food and technologies as they move through space and time, assemblages are constantly configured and reconfigured. A micro-politics of relations and capacities operates at the level of the assemblage (Fox and Alldred, 2017), which can accumulate at the macro level to impel political action and change. Agential capacities are central to political motivations and practices. They stimulate and inspire politics, while political action, in turn, can generate further agential capacities.

Feminist materialist perspectives have not yet been commonly employed to examine digital media material. I would argue, however, that they offer great value for thinking through the ways in which digital media contribute to both the micro- and macro-politics of bodies/food. If digital media artefacts are things, as materialist perspectives argue, then analysing the forces, vibrancies and intensities, the 'thing-power', that they generate as humans create or respond to these artefacts is important to understanding their political effects and affects. Throughout the chapter I identify the agential capacities that are generated with and through artefacts such as hashtags, selfies, GIFs and memes, as well as their use of affective forces to convey and animate meaning as part of digital assemblages of bodies/food.

Digital body/food cultures

Digital media offer opportunities for more people than ever before to enact identities and embodiments in public forums, to bring together humans and non-humans to create meaning and action, and to affect and be affected. Digital media's agentive capacities can inspire political action at the personal or collective levels (Kuntsman, 2012; Paasonen, Hillis and Petit, 2015), while their affordances both invite and delimit the actions of human users and other non-human actors. Such affordances are contextual: the design of digital media tends to invite some uses, and the participation of certain actors over others. However, they are also dynamic insofar as users may improvise or turn the capacities of these media to purposes unimagined by the media developers and promoters (Davis and Chouinard, 2017; Nagy and Neff, 2015). Many affordances offered by social media assemblages relate to the memetic nature of these media: the ways in which their meanings can be quickly shared across a large audiences, curated and tagged, as well as reproduced, appropriated, re-mixed and mashed-up in a multitude of, often unexpected or perverse, ways (Beer, 2013; Highfield, 2016; Milner, 2016; Phillips and Milner, 2017; Shifman, 2014).

From photographs or videos uploaded from a smartphone, to GIFs, memes and emojis, visual imagery is employed to create meaning, share affects, perform identities and participate in social networks (Highfield and Leaver, 2016; Rettberg, 2014; Stark and Crawford, 2016; Tiidenberg and Cruz, 2015). 'Selfies' are commonly taken and shared in performances of embodiment. They are also frequently used as part of political action directed at resisting and reframing bodily norms. For example, breastfeeding women have used selfies to challenge normative assumptions about motherhood and the appropriate representation of maternal women's bodies (Boon and Pentney, 2015), rape or sexual abuse survivors and activists have made and displayed selfies to draw attention to their cause (Ferreday, 2017), and members of the LGBTQI community have used these media to render their sexual identities more visible (Duguay, 2016).

GIFs and memes are digital media forms that are predominantly used to convey emotional states. The reaction GIF or image macro meme (displaying an emotional response in a human or other animal) is frequently used to convey and share strong feelings across social media platforms. To achieve impact, they have a blunt approach, tending to rely on less-than-subtle humour, and depicting exaggerated reactive responses that are often derived from television series or films (Shifman, 2014). These forms of media can also be used effectively for social and political critique, as in the case of memes used in China to challenge internet censorship (Mina, 2014), and in the west for feminist consciousness-raising and community-building (Phillips and Milner, 2017; Rentschler and Thrift, 2015).

The opportunity for users to tag and curate media content is one of the most influential affordances offered by new digital media forms (Beer, 2013). Hashtags have become an important way of defining the meaning of images and texts in social media content, and of drawing the attention of others who are interested in the same kinds of content. This includes using hashtags in political campaigns to appeal to interested audiences, to form communities and to organise discussions (Gleason, 2013; Williams, 2015). It is important to note, however, that the often anarchic memetic affordances of social media can also facilitate racism, misogyny, body-shaming, and other forms of attacking, humiliating, insulting, stigmatising, and blaming that contribute to the marginalising of individuals, social groups or organisations, and to the promotion of reactionary political positions (Highfield, 2016; Phillips and Milner, 2017). In other words, the alternative political positions expressed in these forums are not necessarily progressive. This point is important to bear in mind when analysing political engagements in new digital media forums.

In what follows, I conduct a critical analysis of digital media in portraying and enacting human embodiment and food cultures, devoting attention to digital media's relationality, agency and micro-political capacities (Fox and Alldred, 2017). This kind of analysis involves identifying and tracing the relational ontologies that exist between actors in assemblages and how these actors and relations together configure agential capacities at the level of everyday practice. How do these actors and relations affect each other? What new affects, vitalities and capacities do they generate? How do these, in turn, have the potential to effect political change?

This analysis adopts a cultural studies approach to critical interpretation in order to trace some of the key meanings and practices about bodies and food in digital media, and to discuss the ways in which agential capacities are generated in and with these media. My analysis here builds on my previous research on the digitising of bodies (Lupton, 2016, 2017a), the portrayal and monitoring of body weight, shape and size in digital media (Lupton, 2017b), and the datafication of food preparation and consumption in digital cultures (Lupton, 2018). Some of the examples I draw on below were discovered in the course of these studies. Many others were identified in new research I conducted for this chapter.

This approach was not designed to be comprehensive of all media content. Rather, it involved selective cultural analysis that was sensitive to recurring media forms and to the ways in which certain kinds of affects and representations of members of social categories, such as meat-eaters, vegans and vegetarians, fitness and 'clean eating' enthusiasts, and people supporting anorexia, fat activism and body positivism were commonly employed in the media I examined. As I began looking at social media platforms and at how food and bodies were represented, it became apparent that certain hashtags were used to invite attention from relevant audiences and followers (including #cleanfood, #healthy, #foodporn, #thinspo, #proana, #vegan, #vegetarian, #fitspo and #fatspo). I used these hashtags as search terms on Twitter, Pinterest, Facebook and Instagram to review the range of images and messages that appeared, also noting other hashtags that were frequently used with them (for example, #sexy often appeared with #fitspo, as did #cleanfood). I searched the web site Giphy for GIFs, using search terms such as 'vegetarian', 'vegan', 'fat', 'thin', 'food' and 'meat', performed a similar search on YouTube, and a Google search for memes using the same search terms. The material to which I refer below was discovered using these and expanded searches. In the spirit of tagging practices on social media, I have organised my analysis into sections under relevant hashtags denoting their themes.

#vegan #vegetarian #crueltyfree

Social media have become important forums for food activist groups to disseminate their messages (Lupton, 2018; Schneider et al., 2018; Vats, 2015). For example, organisations like PETA (People for the Ethical Treatment of Animals) use social media accounts on Twitter, Facebook and Pinterest to disseminate information about healthy vegan diets and to challenge industries that kill animals or use them in factory farming or the fur industry. This political agenda makes for a very diverse set of images and messages flowing from its Twitter account (which has over one million followers), many of which involve confronting images of animals. Examples include an infographic showing vegan sources of protein, a video of an animal being roughly treated by handlers working in the fur industry (accompanied by the caption 'This is just one life in the fur industry. Show this to anyone who wears fur'), photos and text celebrating the life of an animal rights campaigner, a video of grim-faced, semi-nude animal rights campaigners protesting against bull-fighting (with the words 'stop bull-fighting' written across naked male and female chests), and a video of chicks being drowned ('"The sound of these baby chicks being drowned will haunt you" #Reasons-ToGoVegan'). Somewhat incongruously, interspersed with these confronting images were light-hearted, glossy food images, including a photo of a bowl of fruit and acai berries ('These #vegan recipes will make you OBSESSED with #AcaiBowls'), and another tweet rhapsodising about vegan macaroni and cheese ('As if you need any more reasons—16 reasons why we're really excited for #NationalMacandCheeseDay').

By focusing on the appearance and taste of the food that is displayed, this framing of vegan food represents attempts to render veganism less serious and ethically driven. They are perhaps a deliberate choice to try to lighten the dominant framing of vegans and vegetarians in mainstream culture as moralising killjoys who relinquish pleasure in food for their ethical standpoints (Cole and Morgan, 2011). People who decide to engage in alternative food practices because of ethical or moral convictions are both mocked and supported in digital media. Many memes make fun of the assumed righteousness and earnestness of vegetarians and vegans. One example I found is an image of a hippy-looking woman making a peace sign with the words, 'Saves animals' lives. Slaughters people with insufferable vegan stories'. Another used the popular meme macro-image of actor Gene Wilder in one of his best-known roles as Willy Wonka. Wilder is shown smiling beatifically, accompanied by the sarcastic text: 'Oh, so you don't eat meat? Please tell me exactly how many millions of animal lives you've saved'.

While these negative attitudes are common, a range of memes supporting vegetarian or vegan diets and those who attempt to conform to them also appear online. These include memes such as an owl being drenched with a hose with the words 'Being a vegan in society summed up in one picture', and an angry-looking man accompanied by 'The face you make as you walk by the meat'. Memes and GIFs provide ways of sharing feelings about the everyday joys and frustrations of living as a vegetarian or vegan. In doing so, they attempt to provide light-hearted support for serious ethical eating choices.

This is also evident in a list of GIFs deemed to 'sum up veggie life', available on the VeggieBuzz web site. One example is a clip of Barack Obama making a speech and wiping tears from his eyes, with the subtitle 'Pres. Obama: "Our hearts are broken today"' from the original broadcast. The meme makers have added these words at the top of the image: 'When you find out that some wine and beer isn't vegetarian either'. Arguably in poor taste (as Obama was presumably responding to a national tragedy), like many other GIFs, this one expresses excessive affect relating to what might generally be considered a minor problem faced by vegetarians. This excessive affect, however, works as a symbolic representation of the frustrations and sense of marginalisation vegetarians and vegans encounter in a world in which their dietary practices and ethical precepts are at best considered by others to be non-normative, and at worst are responded to with contempt or even aggression. These digital media artefacts, therefore, contribute to communities of feeling, in which like-minded individuals can express and share their feelings.

#fitspo #cleanfood #healthy

There are abundant examples in digital media of individuals and social groups practising an alternative politics that draws attention to the broader conditions in which people are called on to regulate and manage their food practices, and to the ways in which food is produced and marketed. For example, food selfies in the home kitchen, in the fine dining restaurant, at the street stall in a foreign country, or at the fast-food outlet all convey the performance of selfhood intended by the selfie-taker. Some food selfies involve depictions of people's visits to organic or farmers' markets, or engaged in home gardening or farm fruit-picking excursions, incorporating the wider landscape of food production and consumption. Food selfies, therefore, position humans and food together in spatial contexts, some of which overtly define the political or ethical position of the selfie-taker, as well as the role of food in their everyday lives and relationships.

Selfies can also conform to normative meanings and assumptions about bodies/food that reproduce and support mainstream ideals, including those that privilege a high degree of control over diet, and exercise in the interests of health, physical fitness and sexual attractiveness. Selfies tagged with #fitspo or #fitspiration privilege and celebrate a very specific type of body: young, slim, physically active, toned and usually white (albeit with tanned skin) (Boepple and Thompson, 2016; Tiggemann and Zaccardo, 2016). Notably, many digital body/ food images rely on normative portrayals of gender, sexualities and embodiment. For example, women portrayed around the fitspo theme are represented in overtly sexualised ways: they are typically shown working out in skimpy fitness wear or posing in swimsuits that draw attention to their lean and fit bodies. Indeed, on Instagram the hashtag #fitspo is often used by bikini, fitness or soft-porn models, rather than by average people who are advocates of working out. Men are also sexualised: again, shown in revealing fitness clothes, or shirtless, so that their muscular bodies are highlighted. These fit bodies are invested with and animated by sexual desire, achieved through and with virtuous modes of selfhood that require high levels of control over food intake and the sustained hard physical work of high-level exercising.

Many portrayals and discussions of 'clean eating' on social media also involve a focus on practices of responsibilised selfhood that conform to privileged ideas about self-care and self-management of the body. When people in #fitspo-tagged images refer to food, it is invariably low-calorie, high-protein 'clean' foodstuffs, such as green juices, protein shakes, salads or egg-white omelettes (accompanied by such hashtags as #eatclean, #health or #healthylife). It is suggested that this kind of diet is another contributor (along with exercise) to producing these people's bodies. Food, in the fitspo universe, is an adjunct to the world of leanness, fitness and healthiness, all of which are considered to work together to create the fitspo assemblage. These representations work politically to celebrate, support and reproduce normative ideals of embodiment and food consumption, which are portrayed as morally and ethically defensible.

Social media 'influencers' are another element of the alternative perspectives offered about body/food politics online. Some of the most successful influencers draw on mainstream ideas about the relationship between healthy eating, physical fitness, slim embodiment and sexual attractiveness and combine these with somewhat more challenging political positions on matters such as food quality and additives. They utilise this combination of positions to profit financially from their online popularity. Vani Hari, who calls herself the 'Food Babe', is an example of a micro-celebrity or social media influencer (Marwick, 2015) who has strategically used social and digital media to build her following and to draw attention to her causes, as well as to products she offers for sale. Hari's physical appearance and her story of physical self-transformation are central features of her sales pitch. She maintains a 'Food Babe' web site, and Facebook, Twitter and Instagram profiles (with over 100,000 followers), as well as a YouTube channel, which she uses to promote her ideas about clean eating, nutrition, food safety, good health and weight loss. On her web site Hari recounts her personal story of major weight loss (complete with 'before and after' photos) and of realising how important chemical-free food is to health and well-being. She claims that her actions and those of her 'Food Babe Army' have forced companies like Kraft and Subway to change their practices. Most of Hari's Twitter content focuses on spreading information about such topics as genetically modified food, pesticides and food additives, and promoting healthy eating, while she also uses her social media profile to sell memberships to her healthy eating food plan and weight-loss programmes, in addition to her book, *The Food Babe Way*.

Exponents, like Hari, of 'clean', 'unprocessed' or 'chemical-free' eating focus on food itself, drawing attention to its content, the ways in which it is produced and processed, and the ill-effects food consumption can have on the body if not strictly policed. On Tumblr and Twitter, raw fruit and vegetables dominate the #cleanfood, #cleaneating, #eatclean or #clean hashtags, often accompanied by hashtags such as #health/y, #rawfood, #nutrition, #wellness, #vegetarian or #vegan. Many such images only show the food itself, but hashtags are used to bring in the absent body, referring to healthy bodies, ideal body size or appearance (particularly #fit, #fitspo and #weightloss). Although these types of images often represent the food as attractive and inviting, there are usually few references in text or hashtags to its sensory appeal. Clean food is portrayed as functional—celebrated for contributing to a healthy and fit body, not for indulging the senses and satiating appetites. Most of the focus in these representations is on achieving individual health and well-being, and they conform to dominant ideas about healthy eating and self-responsibility for achieving good health. However, there are sometimes references to broader food production systems, and the inclusion of hashtags such as #sustainability and #organic to make this association directly.

#foodporn #foodgasm #yummy

In addition to these restricted eating practices based on ethical or health-related ideals, digital media also express and acknowledge alternative perspectives that champion food excesses and the struggle for control over appetite and desire for food. In their positive portrayal of indulgent or high-calorie food, and their privileging of the sensory pleasures of these types of food over health-related benefits or the importance of maintaining a slim and fit body, these alternative perspectives are often in direct opposition to #cleanfood, #healthy and #fitspo meanings. However, they can also be used in combination with these other hashtags to generate new forms of meaning and new political perspectives on bodies/food, as I explain below. Moreover, such hashtags can be associated with digital content that reveals deep-seated ambivalence about and struggles over desire for food.

The widespread use of the term 'food porn' makes a direct connection between sexual desire and food. It describes images that represent food in highly aestheticised ways to provoke desire and longing. The term is frequently used as a hashtag on sites like Facebook, Pinterest, Tumblr, Twitter and—especially—Instagram (Mejova, Abbar and Haddadi, 2016). The #foodporn hashtag (and its close relative, #foodgasm) frequently accompanies food selfies on these platforms, and is also a popular genre on the photo-sharing platform Flickr. Attempts to take and post visually appealing images of food are such a common feature of amateur photographs on social media that a range of apps are available that can be used to present the food photographed in the most attractive light (Lupton, 2018).

In her analysis of food photography on women's food blogs, Dejmanee (2016) observes that the term 'food porn' draws attention to the ambivalence—both pleasure and disgust—that physical desire and loss of bodily control evoke in relation to women's consumption of food. She claims that the production of food porn on women's blogs serves as a form of mild subversion of dominant notions of female sexuality, and of the need for discipline of the female body, by diverting attention and desire from the body to food. Bloggers' food porn images allow for excess and desire to be openly articulated and celebrated.

This celebration of excess and desire is not always evident in content that is tagged #foodporn on other digital media platforms, however. For example, in my analysis, I noticed that food porn discourses and images are also used to support restricted and disciplined eating based on thin embodiment and health ideals. A food-related meme that was popular for a time emerged from an Instagram photo blog called *You Did Not Eat That*. This blog was used to collect and display Instagram images showing fashion and fitness models holding a high-calorie item. The blog's founder claimed that the people in the photos only posed with the food for the visual impact, and did not actually eat it. These people were held to account, therefore, for allegedly maintaining the pretence that they were able to maintain the ideal bodies they were displaying and still indulge in junk food.

The #foodporn hashtag is also commonly used with #cleanfood or #healthyliving in Instagram or Tumblr posts in which food is portrayed as both delicious and healthy. In this context, the meaning of food porn is transformed. Rather than referring only to the celebration of indulgent food that is 'unhealthy' or high-calorie, this combination of hashtags represents healthy food as desirable for its sensory as well as its health-giving properties. Other forms of digital media are more ambivalent about the allure of food. When I searched for 'food memes' on the internet, what struck me immediately was the dominance of memes that referred to struggling with greed for the 'wrong' types of food (food culturally coded as fattening, junk or otherwise excessive or unhealthy). These memes often stigmatised fat people as lacking appropriate self-discipline, showing them eating high-calorie food and ridiculing their lack of self-control (Lupton, 2017b), but they also took a universal approach in portraying struggles that everyone faces in limiting their food consumption. Thus, for example, memes showed large platefuls of food with the text 'When you make food for yourself and no-one is around to judge you', a cat with a mouth full of food ('I regret nothing. Nothing') and a fat child ('I'm on a seafood diet. I see food and eat it').

The digital material employed in these portrayals is animated by affects that draw on broader concerns about sexual attractiveness, physical appearance, and the need to discipline bodily urges to achieve idealised embodiment. Fat embodiment is highly stigmatised and punished with ridicule. Struggles over the desire to eat the wrong type or quantity of food (which could lead to fatness) are also acknowledged, but as a common challenge. Underpinning these representations are resonant moral values about the importance of control over appetite, the awareness that others may be watching how much we eat, and the inevitability of becoming fat if self-discipline is relinquished. The 'wrong' food is invested with a vital capacity that invites desire, and that desire requires a high level of self-control to resist.

#thickspiration #fatfetish

Food porn and related visual tropes are also frequently employed in social media portrayals of bodies and food consumption practices that challenge and resist normative ideals of bodily containment and control. Contributors to fat activism and body positivism, for example, use digital media in their efforts to counter fat shaming and stigmatisation. Some activists take and upload selfies on social media as a way to take control over their own image as part of #thickspiration and #fatacceptance initiatives. Images of fat bodies demonstrating their bodily excesses and rolls of flesh, and eating food that is typically culturally coded as 'fattening', 'junk food' or 'unhealthy', carry hashtags like #obeselifestyle and #notyourgoodfatty (Lupton, 2017b; Marcus, 2016; Pausé, 2015).

Body positive and fat activists have also employed the food porn trope (reinvented as #fatfoodporn) to highlight their sexuality and to positively represent their desires and appetites for 'forbidden' foods. Some fat activists go even further, uploading images of themselves not only eating high-fat or junk food, but smearing it over their bodies in an unabashed demonstration of the sensual pleasures of food and the fleshy body, and the refusal to conform to normative standards of body weight, size and 'healthy' food consumption (Lupton, 2017b, 2018).

Lusty eating can be combined with sexualised imagery in digital media to portray fleshy female bodies as sexual objects. For example, a genre of YouTube video portrays BBW ('big beautiful women') in alluring poses, often consuming high-calorie foods to demonstrate their sensuality (Lavis, 2015). The web site 'Fantasy Feeder' similarly makes a direct erotic connection between fat female bodies, excessive food consumption, the sensual pleasures of the flesh, and sexual appeal (Woolley, 2017). These women openly display their appetite and greed, allowing viewers to engage in vicarious excessive food consumption (Lavis, 2015). These acts can be limited to individual modes of resistance, or join in wider community-based efforts to challenge fat-shaming. GIFs and memes can also be used to make transgressive or overtly political points about body shaming. Examples I found included a GIF of a fat woman saying, 'Who are you to have anything to say about my body?', a fat woman pole-dancing and saying, 'I love the way I look', and Khloe Kardashian uttering the words 'My weight doesn't define who I am'.

#meat #epicmealtime

If food porn and body positive messages and images are mostly coded as a celebration of fat female embodiment, my search for meat GIFs on the Giphy web site uncovered videos representing an obsessive and often violent or pornographic celebration of meat, typically coded as masculine. These included GIFs showing angry men shouting 'Salad! Fuck salad!', men rubbing their hands or faces against raw cuts of meat, a male chef urging viewers to 'Give your meat a good ol' rub', and disturbing images of women with their mouths stuffed full to breaking point with sausages, or screaming while sausages are thrown at their faces. These representations are directly opposed to digital content that supports vegetarianism and veganism, often achieving their affective resonances with misogynistic portrayals that reveal the gendered politics of food.

I found similar types of gendered portrayal when I searched for 'meat memes'. Here, again, the images were often bizarre in the extreme ways they presented the visceral desire for meat, and in which they equated meat with male sexuality and violence against women, including anal rape. There were many allusions to 'beating your meat', memes equating meat products such as sausages with penises ('My girlfriend is vegetarian ... but she still eats my meat'), and to women as meat for the consumption of men (including a nude photograph of Kim Kardashian with the words 'expired meat' across her body).

Grotesque feats of cooking and eating are also frequently coded as masculine in digital media. 'Epic Meal Time', a food channel on YouTube with seven million subscribers, features a group of young Canadian men who set themselves challenges to make dishes such as 'the 1 million calorie lasagne', 'the Nutella bomb', 'the slaughterhouse Christmas special' and 'the 100-pound pizza'. The men are shown cooking these dishes, flinging in piles of high-calorie or otherwise 'unhealthy' food: fatty meats (especially bacon), cheeses, alcohol (usually Jack Daniel's whiskey), butter, sugar, chocolate and so on. The images are accompanied by portentous music and satirical voice-overs and captions that frequently seek to sexualise the food, often suggesting bestiality. For example, in the video 'Enough Ribs to Kill a Man', the commentator notes that 'This ribbed sandwich will be ribbed for our pleasure', while a caption for 'Power Pork Patty' invites audiences to 'Like and share this hot pig on pig action. Don't lie, it's your fetish'. In a video about cooking and eating cow 'butts', the men repeatedly draw analogies to women's buttocks. On-screen graphics display the accumulating calories of the meal as ingredients are added, and the team greedily and messily eats their meal at the end, often using their hands. This portrayal of 'dude' masculinity involves the sexualisation of food (particularly meat), the celebration of excess, and grotesque acts of food preparation and consumption. All of these practices evoke a carnivalesque performance of body/food politics, while also reinforcing normative assumptions about and meanings of food and gender.

It is notable that GIFs portraying vegetarians also often feature people stuffing food hungrily into their mouths like animals. In this case, however, the people are usually women, and the food is usually green salad leaves (or, in one case, grass). The implication is that, in their rejection of meat, vegetarians are starving themselves, forced to gorge on green leaves or grass. Vegetarianism is coded as both a feminine and less-than-human food practice, in contradistinction to meat-eating, which is presented as archetypally masculine and human. In both types of GIF—those about avid meat-eaters and those about people who eschew meat—the affects that animate them and give them their power are those alluding to strong, almost desperate appetites for certain types of food. They represent men as desiring red meat in often perverse, sexualised ways, and women as being assaulted by phallic meat products or compensating for their hunger by gorging on vegetable matter like farm animals. In both cases, the animalistic aspects of human corporality—and, specifically, human appetite and eating habits—are emphasised in exaggerated ways to express and generate affect. As such, these representations are further exaggerations of the material I referred to earlier, in which human desire for food is expressed with even greater strength of feeling, and is combined with violence and misogyny. As Carol Adams (2010) has argued of the violent and often pornographic ways in which normative masculinities and virilities are associated with meat-eating in popular culture, these digital media present meat as a 'stand in' for a type of phallocentric and dominant masculinity that seeks to subjugate and mindlessly consume both animals and women. Violence against animals that are killed and eaten is equated with sexual violence and hatred of women.

#proana #bonespo #thighgap

Content creators who upload and share images supporting self-starvation practices represent a contrasting political position on bodily containment. Often organised around hashtags such as #proana, #anorexia, #thinspo, #bonespo or #thighgap (or variants of these terms), these users actively challenge normative ideals concerning bodies deemed to be 'too thin' and subject to too much discipline and control. Rather than championing and celebrating the sensuality of food consumption and the pleasures of fleshly excesses, these portrayals idealise a tightly-contained body in which the carnal appetites are feared and resisted. The typical image circulating in these groups of users is that of an emaciated young woman. The image is often cropped to exclude the woman's face, so as to draw attention to her body, particularly her prominent, bony rib cage and thin legs.

Sexual imagery is prominent here, too. These women often reveal bare flesh and pose in their underwear or tight-fitting clothing to demonstrate their extreme thinness (see also Boepple and Thompson, 2016; Cobb, 2017; Woolley, 2017). People who post and comment on such content often draw attention to what they view as the sexiness and beauty of these extremely thin bodies. In these images, it is food that is the absent referent. Rarely is food shown in these images, but the visual and textual content may refer to the number of calories consumed that day, or to the necessity of resisting the desire for food. User-created content containing these hashtags on Twitter, for example, usually includes such photos, often with aspirational and yearning statements included by the tweeter: for example, 'I aspire to look like you', 'Night-time inspiration. #thinspo always makes me feel better', 'I just want bones', 'Skinny is sexy—big isn't beautiful', 'I only feel beautiful when I'm hungry', and 'Would you love me if I looked like this?' Very similar content is evident on Tumblr, organised around the same hashtags, where the opportunity to use more text also allows self-starvers to discuss their techniques and to provide advice and encouragement to others about how to maintain extreme calorie restriction regimes.

As others have argued (Boero and Pascoe, 2012; Fox, Ward and O'Rourke, 2005; Smith, Wickes and Underwood, 2015), these types of online representation involve an alternative body politics that is 'anti-recovery'. They resist normative assumptions and ideals that portray self-starvation as a problem and a medical condition, and emaciated bodies as repulsive and unhealthy. These texts and images draw on and reproduce agential capacities that urge their creators, and their publics, towards continuing their restrictive food consumption practices. Here, again, affect is a vital element of these capacities. Images and words are employed to articulate the intensity of the desire that self-starving practitioners feel to achieve their ideal of the fleshless body that can contain and discipline hunger, but also to reveal the disgust they feel about their bodies.

Conclusion

In this chapter, I have brought together feminist materialisms and new digital media affordances to examine the role played by social and visual media in enacting alternative body/food politics. My discussion draws attention to the intensities of the entanglements of images, practices and discourses that social and digital media afford. I have claimed that representations and practices related to the use of digital media for portraying human embodiment and food cultures generate potent micro- and macro-political agential capacities. These contribute to the 'thing-power' of the human–non-human assemblages that are formed when humans create, share, comment on, tag, and remix or recombine elements of digital media cultures such as hashtags, selfies, amateur videos, memes and GIFs. These agential capacities do not all work in politically progressive ways, however. Representations of both food and human bodies in social and digital media, as in other forms of popular culture (Lupton, 1996), are characterised by the binary oppositions of control and excess, civility and incivility, masculinities and femininities, and underpinned with moral meanings concerning bodily deportment and appearance and the expression of carnal desires and sensual pleasures.

What is particularly compelling about the agential capacities evident in the digital media I examined in this chapter is the intensely visceral affects that are generated with and through them. These media express and circulate many conflicting and ambivalent affects, noticeable for their sheer intensity and vitality. Very different types of digital media body/food assemblages receive expression. One mode of expression represents idealised bodies as those that are highly contained and controlled, privileging disciplined, 'clean' and healthy eating, ethical food choices, and lean, physically fit bodies. Uncontained, out-of-control bodies and appetites, and choices such as meat-eating, are typically positioned as disgusting, repellent and morally and ethically inferior. Disgust and repulsion for the carnality of fat bodies, animal cruelty, meat-eating, greed, lust, submission to appetite and the desire for 'bad' or 'wrong' food: all are readily found in these digital body/food assemblages. Delight, celebration and pride in performing and displaying the contained, fit, lean body, and in achieving 'clean' and ethical eating complement these darker portrayals.

A range of other digital media artefacts draw on and animate alternative cultural and moral positions on bodies and food that are also often intense and forceful. In these portrayals, the visceral desire for meat and junk foods is presented more positively, as human, and also often as archetypally masculine. Deep-seated ambivalence about human and other animal corporeality, and about the clear relationship between the two, is evident across a range of the portrayals I have here discussed, from pro-ana supporters' desire to conquer their desire for food to achieve an excessively pared-down, fleshless body, to representations of women being prodded with phallic sausages, or of men stuffing large chunks of meat into their mouths with looks of anger or lust. Sexual desire for human bodies and greed for food, and the juxtaposition of human with animal flesh and fleshiness, intertwine and are blurred in images and sentiments that are often profoundly disturbing and confronting.

These assemblages can possess resonant thing-power. These visceralities and vitalities, as expressed in the digital media content I have examined, are central to the agential capacities of these media. They impel the meaning and impact— and, above all, the affective qualities—of digitised body/food politics. Content creators and sharers can express their desires, affects and ambivalences about food in micro-political ways, but the affordances of digital media invite often very large audiences to recognise and respond to these capacities. These are the kinds of affects and vitalities that impel the creation and use of digital media related to alternative body/food politics. They animate these portrayals with intensity that can flow from the content creators and sharers to their audiences. In some cases, these capacities combine to create new assemblages of meaning and practice, and can impel transformation and change in the interests of alternative food politics. In others, they express and facilitate conservative and reactionary responses, serving to reproduce and magnify dominant norms, moral meanings and practices about ideal bodies, sexuality, and gender.

As my analysis suggests, digital media such as selfies, GIFs, memes and amateur videos are important artefacts when considering body/food politics. While this content may appear at first glance to consist largely of anodyne and fun exchanges of information, or of acts of self-representation and social identities, it is often underpinned by darker and more confronting affective currents that reveal broader preoccupations, hostilities and ambivalences about certain kinds of foods and social groups. At the same time as exponents of progressive food politics are able to find outlets for their viewpoints and ideals, digital media also provide a wealth of opportunities for these political positions to be ridiculed and aggressively attacked. These digital media forms provide opportunities for these affects and ideas to be widely distributed and used to support reactionary as well as progressive political standpoints. They can potentially support efforts to effect political change by mobilising and intensifying affect, but can equally provide opportunities for such efforts to be resisted, challenged or undermined.

References

Adams, C. J. (2010). Why Feminist-Vegan Now? *Feminism & Psychology*, 20 (3), 302–317.

Barad, K. (2003). Posthumanist Performativity: Toward an Understanding of How Matter Comes to Matter. *Signs*, 28 (3), 801–831.

Barad, K. (2007). *Meeting the Universe Halfway: Quantum Physics and the Entanglement of Matter and Meaning*. Durham: Duke University Press.

Beer, D. (2013). *Popular Culture and New Media: The Politics of Circulation*. Basingstoke: Palgrave Macmillan.

Bennett, J. (2004). The Force of Things: Steps toward an Ecology of Matter. *Political Theory*, 32 (3), 347–372.

Bennett, J. (2010). A Vitalist Stopover on the Way to A New Materialism. In Coole, D. and Frost, S. (eds.), *New Materialisms: Ontology, Agency and Politics* (pp. 47–69). Durham, NC: Duke University Press.

Boepple, L. and Thompson, J. K. (2016). A Content Analytic Comparison of Fitspiration and Thinspiration Websites. *International Journal of Eating Disorders*, 49 (1), 98–101.

Boero, N. and Pascoe, C. J. (2012). Pro-Anorexia Communities and Online Interaction: Bringing the Pro-Ana Body Online. *Body & Society*, 18 (2), 27–57.

Boon, S. and Pentney, B. (2015). Virtual Lactivism: Breastfeeding Selfies and the Performance of Motherhood. *International Journal of Communication*, 9, 1759–1774. Available at: http://ijoc.org/index.php/ijoc/article/view/3136. Accessed 18 July 2017.

Braidotti, R. (2002). *Metamorphoses: Towards a Materialist Theory of Becoming*. Cambridge: Polity.

Braidotti, R. (2013). *The Posthuman*. Cambridge: Policy Press.

Cobb, G. (2017). 'This Is Not Pro-Ana': Denial and Disguise in Pro-Anorexia Online Spaces. *Fat Studies*, 6 (2), 189–205.

Cole, M. and Morgan, K. (2011). Vegaphobia: Derogatory Discourses of Veganism and the Reproduction of Speciesism in UK National Newspapers. *The British Journal of Sociology*, 62 (1), 134–153.

Davis, J. L. and Chouinard, J. B. (2017). Theorizing Affordances: From Request to Refuse. *Bulletin of Science, Technology & Society*. 36 (4), 241–248.

Dejmanee, T. (2016). 'Food Porn' as Postfeminist Play: Digital Femininity and the Female Body on Food Blogs. *Television & New Media*, 17 (5), 429–448.

Duguay, S. (2016). Lesbian, Gay, Bisexual, Trans, and Queer Visibility through Selfies: Comparing Platform Mediators across Ruby Rose's Instagram and Vine Presence. *Social Media + Society*, 2 (2). doi: 10.1177/2056305116641975.

Ferreday, D. (2017). Like a Stone in Your Stomach: Articulating the Unspeakable in Rape Victim-Survivors' Activist Selfies. In Kuntsman, A. (eds.), *Selfie Citizenship* (pp. 127–136). Basingstoke: Palgrave Macmillan.

Fox, N. J. and Alldred, P. (2017). Mixed Methods, Materialism and the Micropolitics of the Research-Assemblage. *International Journal of Social Research Methodology*. 21 (2), 191–204.

Fox, N. J., Ward, K. and O'Rourke, A. (2005). Pro-Anorexia, Weight-Loss Drugs and the Internet: An 'Anti-Recovery' Explanatory Model of Anorexia. *Sociology of Health & Illness*, 27 (7), 944–971.

Gleason, B. (2013). #Occupy Wall Street: Exploring Informal Learning about a Social Movement on Twitter. *American Behavioral Scientist*, 57 (7), 966–982.

Haraway, D. (2008). *When Species Meet*. Minneapolis: The University of Minnesota Press.

Haraway, D. (2015). Anthropocene, Capitalocene, Plantationocene, Chthulucene: Making Kin. *Environmental Humanities*, 6 (1), 159–165.

Haraway, D. (2016). *Staying with the Trouble: Making Kin in the Chthulucene*. Durham: Duke University Press.

Highfield, T. (2016). *Social Media and Everyday Politics*. Cambridge: Polity.

Highfield, T. and Leaver, T. (2016). Instagrammatics and Digital Methods: Studying Visual Social Media, from Selfies and GIFs to Memes and Emoji. *Communication Research and Practice*, 2 (1), 47–62.

Kuntsman, A. (2012). Introduction: Affective Fabrics of Digital Cultures. In Karatzogianni, A. and Kuntsman, A. (eds.), *Digital Cultures and the Politics of Emotion: Feelings, Affect and Technological Change* (pp. 1–17). Basingstoke: Palgrave Macmillan.

Lavis, A. (2015). Consuming (Through) the Other? Rethinking Fat and Eating in BBW Videos Online. *M/C Journal*, 18 (3). http://journal.media-culture.org.au/index.php/mcjournal/article/view/973.

Lupton, D. (1996). *Food, the Body and the Self*. London: Sage.

Lupton, D. (2016). *The Quantified Self: A Sociology of Self-Tracking*. Cambridge: Polity.

Lupton, D. (2017a). Digital Bodies. In Andrews, D., Silk, M. and Thorpe, H. (eds.), *Routledge Handbook of Physical Cultural Studies* (pp. 200–208). London: Routledge.

Lupton, D. (2017b). Digital Media and Body Weight, Shape, and Size: An Introduction and Review. *Fat Studies*, 6 (2), 119–134.

Lupton, D. (2018). Cooking, Eating, Uploading: Digital Food Cultures. In LeBesco, K. and Naccarato, P. (eds.), *The Handbook of Food and Popular Culture* (pp. 66–79). London: Bloomsbury.

Marcus, S.-R. (2016). Thinspiration Vs. Thickiration: Comparing Pro-Anorexic and Fat Acceptance Image Posts on a Photo-Sharing Site. *Cyberpsychology*, 10 (2). Available at: https://cyberpsychology.eu/article/view/6178/5908. Accessed 5 December 2016.

Marwick, A. E. (2015). Instafame: Luxury Selfies in the Attention Economy. *Public Culture*, 27 (1 75), 137–160.

Mejova, Y., Abbar, S. and Haddadi, H. (2016). Fetishizing Food in Digital Age: #Foodporn around the World. *Tenth International AAAI Conference on Web and Social Media (ICWSM 2016)*, Cologne, pp. 250–258.

Milner, R.M. (2016). *The World Made Meme: Public Conversations and Participatory Media*. Cambridge, MA: MIT Press.

Mina, A. X. (2014). Batman, Pandaman and the Blind Man: A Case Study in Social Change Memes and Internet Censorship in China. *Journal of Visual Culture*, 13 (3), 359–375.

Nagy, P. and Neff, G. (2015). Imagined Affordance: Reconstructing a Keyword for Communication Theory. *Social Media + Society*, 1, 2. Available at: http://sms.sagepub.com/content/1/2/2056305115603385.abstractN2. Accessed 18 July 2017.

Paasonen, S., Hillis, K. and Petit, M. (2015). Introduction: Networks of Transmission: Intensity, Sensation, Value. In Hillis, K., Paasonen, S. and Petit, M. (eds.), *Networked Affect* (pp. 1–24). Cambridge, MA: The MIT Press.

Pausé, C. (2015). Rebel Heart: Performing Fatness Wrong Online. *M/C Journal*, 18, 3. Available at: www.journal.media-culture.org.au/index.php/mcjournal/article/viewArticle/977. Accessed 5 July 2017.

Phillips, W. and Milner, R. M. (2017). *The Ambivalent Internet: Mischief, Oddity, and Antagonism Online*. Cambridge: Polity.

Rentschler, C. A. and Thrift, S. C. (2015). Doing Feminism in the Network: Networked Laughter and the 'Binders Full of Women' Meme. *Feminist Theory*, 16 (3), 329–359.

Rettberg, J. W. (2014). *Seeing Ourselves through Technology: How We Use Selfies, Blogs and Wearable Devices to See and Shape Ourselves*. Basingstoke: Palgrave Macmillan.

Schneider, T., Eli, K., Dolan, C. and Ulijaszek, S. (2018). Introduction –Digital Food Activism: Food Transparency One Bite/Byte at a Time? In Schneider, T., Eli, K., Dolan, C. and Ulijaszek, S. (eds.), *Digital Food Activism*. London: Routledge.

Shifman, L. (2014). *Memes in Digital Culture*. Cambridge, MA: MIT Press.

Smith, N., Wickes, R. and Underwood, M. (2015). Managing a Marginalised Identity in Pro-Anorexia and Fat Acceptance Cybercommunities. *Journal of Sociology*, 51 (4), 950–967.

Stark, L. and Crawford, K. (2016). The Conservatism of Emoji: Work, Affect, and Communication. *Social Media + Society*, 1 (2), 1–11. doi: 10.1177/2056305115604853.

Tiggemann, M. and Zaccardo, M. (2016). 'Strong Is the New Skinny': A Content Analysis of #Fitspiration Images on Instagram. *Journal of Health Psychology*. 23(8), 1003–1011.

Tiidenberg, K. and Cruz, E. G. (2015). Selfies, Image and the Re-Making of the Body. *Body & Society*, 21 (4), 77–102.

Vats, A. (2015). Cooking Up Hashtag Activism: #Paulasbestdishes and Counternarratives of Southern Food. *Communication and Critical/Cultural Studies*, 12 (2), 209–213.

Williams, S. (2015). Digital Defense: Black Feminists Resist Violence with Hashtag Activism. *Feminist Media Studies*, 15 (2), 341–344.

Woolley, D. (2017). Aberrant Consumers: Selfies and Fat Admiration Websites. *Fat Studies*, 6 (2), 206–222.

9 The ethical masquerade

(Un)masking mechanisms of power behind 'ethical' meat

Paula Arcari

Introduction

The notion of ethical food is now part of everyday discourse, representing more socially and environmentally responsible ways of sourcing and producing all kinds of food products, and, most importantly, of labelling these products to communicate their ethical credentials to potential consumers. These ethical credentials extend to the continued, albeit 'better', use of animals for food, and it is this conception of ethical that I critique in this chapter. Most high street supermarkets now offer a range of mass-produced meat products, variously labelled free range, grass-fed, hormone-free, organic, welfare certified, and environmentally friendly—a development illustrative of more mainstream acknowledgment of, and attentiveness to, concerns surrounding the environmental impacts of meat production, as well as for the living animal 'behind the meat'. While some of these market interventions might arguably address ethical issues of corporate dominance, social justice, health, the environment, and animal welfare, I argue they all reproduce a fundamentally dualistic relationship between humans and animals. As such, they signal a doubling down on entrenched power relations in which the use of animals for food is conceived of not only as natural, normal and necessary (Joy, 2009), but also as ethical. Consequently, with respect to the mainstreaming of ethical meat, I highlight that the ways in which 'food' animals are used may be evolving, but that their constitution as food, and the meanings and practices that contribute to that constitution, remain resolutely unchanged. 'Ethical meat' discourses can thus be understood as reinforcing human domination of food animals despite, or indeed because of, their animal-friendly claims. I propose that one of the key mechanisms by which this domination is reinforced is the (re)naturalisation of practices of consumption, commodification, and killing of food animals.

A failure to acknowledge this naturalisation and to problematise human relations to food animals constrains efforts to comprehend the futures and possibilities of food politics, and, more specifically, of wholly plant-based food systems (see also Chapter 7 in this collection). Indeed, across the agri-food, sustainable food, and alternative food network (AFN) literatures, I observe the same human-centric discourse of meat and animals that I observe in climate change, sustainability and food security literature (Arcari, 2017a). I propose, instead, a critically post-human approach to food politics, one that challenges prevailing human-centrism by foregrounding the socially constituted nature of naturalised designations and practices. Essentially, it is about loosening routinised conceptual frames and adopting a critical orientation towards what is accepted and legitimated as normal—a project that also occupied Foucault. Throughout his oeuvre, Foucault's primary concern, as I conceive it, is to conduct an archaeology not only of knowledge, but of every 'thing' this knowledge constitutes and legitimates through the exercise of power (Foucault, 1982, 1989).

Power and states of domination

Power, Foucault (1978, pp. 89, 93) emphasises, 'comes from everywhere', its effects operating through technique, normalisation and control, rather than by right, law and punishment. The exercise of power 'creates and causes to emerge new objects of knowledge' (Foucault, 1980, p. 51). A Foucauldian approach thus appears well-suited to understanding how certain animals are normalised as food objects, while simultaneously challenging that understanding—a sort of preliminary archaeology of 'food' animals.

I conceive of human relations to food animals as constituting 'a state of domination', rather than power relations (Foucault, 1994, p. 283). For Foucault (1982, p. 790), a defining feature of relations of power is the possibility of resistance in which 'several ways of behaving, several reactions and diverse comportments, may be realised'. Without these, there are no power relations, because the subject is 'doomed to perpetual defeat'—frozen within an immobilised, and therefore perpetually asymmetrical, field of blocked power relations (Foucault, 1994, pp. 283, 292). In this state of domination, all possibilities for insubordination have been removed, 'reduc[ing] the other to total impotence' (Foucault, 1982, p. 794).

Non-human animals exist under a shadow of constant expendability. The degree to which any acts of resistance or insubordination are tolerated depends largely on the practices of which they are part, and, more finally, on the whim of those allocated the capacity within these practices to dominate. Such subordinations are, therefore, 'ultimately only stratagems that never succeed in reversing the situation' (Foucault, 1994, p. 292). Under these 'persistent and nonreversible' (Palmer, 2001, p. 351) terms of human/animal relations, the option to dominate is constantly available—a socially acceptable, or at least justifiable, solution to intolerable insubordination. As Palmer observes, 'the trapped wild animal may be shot; the bucking horse can be sent to the knackers' (ibid.), just as the non-breeding sow or recalcitrant cow may be sent for slaughter.[1]

Foucault also observes that 'power is tolerable only on condition that it mask a substantial part of itself. Its success is proportional to its ability to hide its own mechanisms' (1978, p. 86). However, it is not enough to simply conceal negative mechanisms of power. Its positive aspects also need to be foregrounded. Power 'needs to be considered as a productive network which runs through the whole social body, much more than as a negative instance whose function is repression'

(Foucault, 1980, p. 119). I identify naturalisation—whereby the ideological nature of needs and wants is hidden behind a 'naturalized façade' (Belk, Ger and Askegaard, 2003, p. 328)—as a key productive mechanism within ethical meat discourses. The goal of naturalisation is 'to make some practices unthinkable while making others seem "normal"' (Wilk, 2002, p. 11).

Focusing on ethical meat, I aim to foreground and problematise the naturalisation of animals as food within associated discourses, thereby exposing their limitations. More specifically, informed by a Foucauldian conception of power combined with a post-human intent, I show how naturalisation shapes the human-centric discourse of three sets of cultural texts that promote the notion of ethical meat, thereby (re) masking human domination of animals. This ethicalised mask mitigates the negative aspects of animals' domination, which have become increasingly visible under a broader tendency toward commodity defetishisation (Gunderson, 2013) and a heightened concern for animal welfare, while 'productively' enhancing its positive, 'feel-good' aspects.

While the cultural and media mainstreaming of ethical meat has been explored from a critical perspective (Cole, 2011; Pilgrim, 2013; Stănescu, 2010), the way naturalisation functions as a subtle discursive device that reinforces asymmetrical human/animal relations has not been emphasised. Furthermore, cultural texts such as those I explore here reflect, reproduce and reinforce not only problematic human/animal, human/nature dualisms, but also inter-human dualisms. High-lighting and challenging the naturalisation of human's domination of food animals therefore constitutes an important and vital component of efforts to advance a less anthropocentric and more equitable way for all human and non-human animals to co-exist.

My analysis of naturalisation is organised into three parts. First, I address how animals are naturalised as food, second, how their commodification is naturalised, and finally, how killing animals is naturalised. This is similar to Cudworth's (2008, p. 33) account of the 'naturing' of livestock farming, slaughtering and butchery, in which the political economy of meat production is recast as the 'domination of animals-as-nature'. Building on this, I argue that it is not only the constitution of animals-as-nature that shapes their domination, but also meat-as-nature, animal farming-as-nature, and killing-as-nature. Ethical meat, as a site where the discourse of the natural is especially promulgated, is thereby conceived as a reconstituted mask that more robustly conceals human domination of food animals against a new wave of apparent transparency in meat production practices. This analysis complements existing work on the naturalisation of meat-eating in children's films (Stewart and Cole, 2009), the constitution of farming as natural and necessary (Cole and Stewart, 2014; Pilgrim, 2013), and the naturalisation of meat consumption and slaughter (Parry, 2010). Extending these authors' contributions, my argument is that recognising naturalisation as a widely deployed discursive device, and as a key mechanism of domination, can indicate where and how normalised human/animal relations can be confronted, problematised and challenged. To conclude, I argue for a more critical and post-human approach as a necessary way forward for alternative food politics.

The cultural texts

The three sets of cultural texts pertaining to ethical meat that I have chosen to explore are of different genres and were designed for different purposes and audiences. This approach is intended to reveal the ubiquity of the naturalisations related to eating, commodifying and killing animals, and of the ways in which they operate—the language and discourses that shape the constitution of food animals and legitimate their use. Texts comprise the promotional materials of 15 Australian producers of self-described 'ethical' meat, collated between April and November 2014; a three-part Australian documentary-style, investigative TV series titled *For the Love of Meat* (hereafter abbreviated *FLM*), which aired at prime time (7.30pm) on Australian public television network SBS in 2016; and an award-winning US short film titled *The Slaughter*, released in 2013. Producers of ethical meat located in the greater Melbourne region of Victoria, Australia, were recruited as part of a PhD study on the social construction of ethical meat. Their self-identification as producers of ethical and/or sustainable meat was the principle criterion in their recruitment.[2] The stated intention of the TV series *FLM* was to encourage consumers to 'make better choices', and to eat meat 'ethically and sustainably' (SBS Product description). The goal of Jason Kohl, writer and director of *The Slaughter*, was to promote humane slaughter practices, and to show slaughter as 'a humane, respectful and personal process between an animal and its owner' (Kohl, 2014). The promotion of better, more ethical ways to eat meat is the common thread that unites these texts, which I use to foreground the persistence and pervasiveness of naturalisations related to food animals.

My inclusion of multiple genres of text is intended to show how naturalisations associated with using animals as food permeate the social world and its cultural texts, including those not necessarily directed at a food-oriented audience. Their different perspectives mean that each text speaks more directly to one of the three types of naturalisation than the others, although all are implicitly present. Hence, *FLM* foregrounds the naturalisation of eating animals; promotional materials from ethical meat producers foreground the naturalised commodification of animals and their flesh; and finally, *The Slaughter* foregrounds the naturalisation of killing animals.

What is ethical meat and how is it 'alternative'?

My understanding of ethical meat encompasses all meat promoted as being in some way environmentally and/or ethically 'better' than 'conventional' meat. This includes 'organic', 'bio-dynamic', 'free range', 'cage-free', 'hormone-free', 'welfare certified', 'humane', 'happy', 'environmentally friendly', 'local', 'outdoor-bred', 'pasture/grass-fed', 'sustainable', and 'ethical', among others. Conventional or 'mainstream' meat is commonly perceived as the product of industrial production processes and factory farms that are broadly understood to compromise the environment, the welfare of animals, and the quality of the resulting meat. However, organic and free-range systems can be industrial in scale, and factory farm conditions may be welfare certified. Therefore, it can be difficult to perceive exactly what kind of alternative ethical meat actually constitutes, and what practices are being mainstreamed. However, broadly speaking, all the above 'ethical' distinctions evoke the *idea* of meat production practices that are in some way 'better'. In doing so, they often invoke ideas of 'good' meat production as 'traditional' or 'authentic', smaller in scale, set in bucolic surrounds, and overseen by farmers with a deep connection to their land and animals (see Todd, 2009).

Whether concerns relate to the environmental impacts of conventional meat production, to the health impacts of eating particular types or too much meat, or to the welfare of food animals, ethical meat offers an alternative that purports to ameliorate, or even reverse, these concerns. In terms of animal welfare, the comparatively 'better' treatment of some food animals over their still circumscribed and considerably shortened lives is used to cast ethical meat in a more benign light. Relatedly, eating meat is presented as a moral and ethical responsibility, because these animals would otherwise not exist—'how [...] can a few hours of suffering be set in the balance against the enormous benefit of life?' (Salt, 1914, p. 1). Salt terms this the 'Logic of the Larder', and it is a logic that pervades ethical meat discourses.

A common feature of alternative food scholarship is a focus on alternative economies and 'politics of consumer–producer relations' (Goodman, DuPuis and Goodman, 2012, p. 12). Ethical meat is an increasingly widespread and popular expression of these reconfigured arrangements, and is therefore often included in such studies. However, reflecting on Foucault's conception of power, and accepting that 'food politics is suffused with questions of ethics, justice and identity' (Herring, 2015, p. 20), I contend that food politics needs to expand the remit of these questions to include food animals. In the next section, I explain why.

Behind the mask

The 'massive' (Steinfeld et al., 2006) scale of environmental problems attributed to, and the range of health and social issues associated with, meat production and consumption might indicate why these practices need to be reconfigured, but not necessarily why the use of animals as food is inherently problematic. After all, meat is widely regarded as a natural and necessary part of human food systems. It is considered a 'core food' in many cultures, and as an 'important' source of protein, iron and other essential nutrients (Biesalski, 2005); livestock are often posited as playing a vital role in economic and food security, especially for displaced and/or low income communities and households (FAO, 2011); and the importance of integrating livestock and crops to create sustainable, 'holistic', and 'regenerative' systems has gained increasing support.

I refer back to Herring's (2015) claim that food politics is 'suffused with questions of ethics, justice and identity'. Taking this further, Stock, Rosin and Carolan (2016, p. 220) proclaim that, as contributors to agri-food futures, 'we are challenging systems of oppression, alienation and ideology'. If so, then it is human-centric not to extend this challenge across species lines to question the ethics, justice and constructed identities surrounding food animals and the systems that support their domination. More than that, a failure to do so is counter-productive to efforts to address these social injustices, as Wolfe (2003, p. 8) explains:

> as long as it is institutionally taken for granted that it is all right to systematically exploit and kill nonhuman animals simply because of their species, then the humanist discourse of species will always be available to [...] countenance violence against the social other of whatever species or gender, or race, or class, or sexual difference.

A large, well-established body of literature challenges human-centrism and the dualisms it perpetuates, and this provides a different perspective on food systems and human relations with non-human animals that is not currently being reflected in the dominant approaches to agri-food and food politics (see Cole, 2011; Cudworth, 2015; Nibert, 2013; Taylor and Twine, 2014). I would argue that it is precisely the critical thinking this literature provokes that needs to be intensified and mainstreamed in an alternative politics of food, not additional iterations of 'better' meat. Viewed from the perspective of the Anthropocene, the global web of environmental, social, and ethical problems calls for a more radically alternative approach to food that challenges the enduring naturalisation of both food animals and meat. First, however, the form and function of this naturalisation—how it contributes to 'effects of truth' (Foucault, 1980, p. 118)—need to be understood.

Naturalisation

With the emergence of 'ethical' meat, naturalisation has become more pronounced as a mechanism of domination. The reason for this, I suggest, is that 'ethical' discourses help to mask the effects of increased visibility in meat production processes. Over the past two decades, improved surveillance techniques have opened up the largely invisible world of industrial meat production, revealing overt mechanisms of power that were previously hidden—visually and cognitively. New media forms allow this information to be disseminated more widely and rapidly, so that increasing numbers of consumers are becoming conscious of the ethical issues associated with meat consumption, even if they remain unaware of the principle of using animals as food. This new visibility is reflected in popular TV programmes such as *Hugh's Chicken Run, Jamie's Fowl Dinners* and *Kill It, Cook It, Eat It*, investigative exposés such as the Australian ABC's investigation of the live export trade, titled *A Bloody Business*, animal advocacy campaigns by, for example, Animals Australia and People for the Ethical Treatment of Animals (PETA), as well as in countless online media highlighting the (mis)treatment of food animals. Coeval with this increased transparency are new edicts around being responsible consumers. This is evidenced by the rise of regulatory measures and certification schemes, such as 'free range' and RSCPA Approved (see Chapter 10 in this collection), designed to ensure producers are meeting certain standards of animal welfare, and to assure consumers that the meat they buy is somehow 'better'.

In sum, increased transparency has placed meat production and consumption under a spotlight, calling the normalcy of associated practices into question. By re-inscribing the acceptability *in itself* of using animals for food, and by diverting attention rather to the *methods* used, ethical meat discourses emphasise and rearticulate the naturalness of commodifying, killing, and consuming animals. Turning now to the cultural texts, I demonstrate where and how these three forms of naturalisation operate as mechanisms of domination.

'Made for purpose': naturalised as food

'Food' animals are ontologically defined as only ever, and never more than, food for humans (except in exceptional, transgressive circumstances). In this section, I show how this gustatory lens objectifies and reduces individual animals to a collection of sensory attributes. Each of the three sets of cultural texts highlights issues associated with industrial meat production. This concern is explicit in producers' promotional materials and in *FLM*, but is more implicit in the case of *The Slaughter*: 'appaled [sic] by the maltreatment of animals and the low-quality meat their suffering produced' (Kohl, 2014), the director wanted to depict an alternative to industrial meat production, and, more specifically, to industrial slaughter. Each text therefore begins with the unquestioned assumption that animals are food for humans. 'Animals as food' is, of course, a more widespread naturalisation, but these texts reflect and reinforce it in a number of specific ways.

The 'meatification' of chickens, pigs and cows is graphically proclaimed in the introduction to every episode of *FLM*. Panning across a colourful cartoon farm-yard, the screen homes in on each animal. The chicken suddenly 'pops' and turns into a whole roasted carcass, still nestled in the grass, closely followed by the cow and the pig. The transformation from living animal to roasted, steaming meat seems completely natural and 'abracadabra' magical. This treatment trivialises as it naturalises, conceptually 'disappearing' an array of meatifying production pro-cesses and any notion of human involvement in them. Thus distanced from these processes, the viewer is absolved of any responsibility for such a seemingly inevitable, linear and 'natural' sequence of events. Reinforcing the naturalisation of this meatification in these opening credits, TV chef Adam Liaw holds aloft a piece of intestine saying, 'made for purpose, isn't it?'—i.e., making sausages.

Each episode emphasises that eating the flesh of animals is utterly natural. Showcasing production methods that 'are more like nature intended' (chicken plant worker) and allow animals 'to express their natural behaviour' (pork producer), Evans makes every effort to show consumers 'how *pork* is produced', or more simply, 'where their *food* comes from' (emphasis added). These words elide meat's animal origins, allowing the entire cultural text to rest uncritically on the assumption of animals as food by leveraging language that has already identified them as such and carving them up accordingly. Evans refers to a 'breeder farm', and identifies 'breeders, that's the mums', and the calves 'that will become the beef we eat'. A farmer explains to Evans, 'the big story around culled breeders is going into the trim trade, that's headed towards mince'. Extending this objectification, Evans presents a diagram of a cow divided into standardised segments of edible flesh—a popularised cartography of meat that most people are familiar with (see Figure 9.1). Pointing to the 'map', he explains, 'The eye fillet comes from the hind quarter, it sits just under the rib cage and doesn't do much work as a muscle which is why it can be so tender'. Each episode reproduces the normalisation of 'growing' animals in order to kill and eat them, and frames this as a profoundly natural process.

Similarly, the self-described producers of ethical and/or sustainable meat that I interviewed referred to 'their' animals as always already the meat they are destined to become. Assurances that 'our *beef* [is] grown on pastures' (beef producer 1), that '*beef* [. . .] are raised on their mother's milk' (beef producer 2), and they produce 'ethically grown *pork*' (pork producer 1), highlight that it is not the animal that is grown or raised but 'meat'. The living animal seems inconsequential, and they are, figuratively and literally, eliminated. As in Evans' series, ethical producers regard their animals as pork, bacon, beef, meat, and simply '*food* grown with taste in mind' (pork producer 2)—or, with a minimal nod to their alive-ness, as 'stock', 'breeders', 'growers', 'broilers', 'meat birds', and 'weaners'.

Producers also draw on the same normalised cartographies of meat (see Figure 9.1) to reinforce the 'natural' meatification of animals' bodies. Producers enhance this naturalisation with positive sensory associations. Hence, certain breeds are valued for their 'natural fat marbling' (pork producer 2), 'consistency in the carcasses' (beef producer 3), because they are 'slow growing [. . .] prized for its juiciness, flavour and tenderness [. . .] renowned for its "crackle"' (pork producer 3), and for having 'good thigh muscles and ham areas' (pork producer 1). Farmers exert control or 'enhancement' over nature in this regard. They use 'quality study genetics' (beef producer 3), cross-breed for 'perfect marbling and not too much back fat' (pork producer 2), and seek to 'improve the quality of our breeders' to 'improve the quality of our beef' (beef producer 2).

Everything about these animals is conceived through the lens (or map) of consumption. Gustatory qualities constituted as natural are additionally controlled and engineered towards that end. Breeding practices promoted by ethical producers permit an 'expansion of productive forces and the differential allocation of profit' (Foucault, 1978, p. 141), highlighting biopower as another aspect of these animals' domination (Palmer, 2001; Wadiwel, 2002). As Weisberg (2009, p. 30) comments, breeding is 'a practice built directly out of humans' entitlement to the bodies and lives of other animals and to the latter's reduction to the mere stuff of control'.

While promising the sensory pleasure of these animals' flesh, ethical producers assure customers of the naturalness of their edibility. It is, one declares, 'the way pigs should live [. . .] The way pork should taste' (pork producer 3) (see Figure 9.2). Another advises that 'nature takes time, and patience tastes delicious' (pork producer 4). Here, the naturalisation of these animals as simply 'meat' segues into the naturalisation of farming practices as

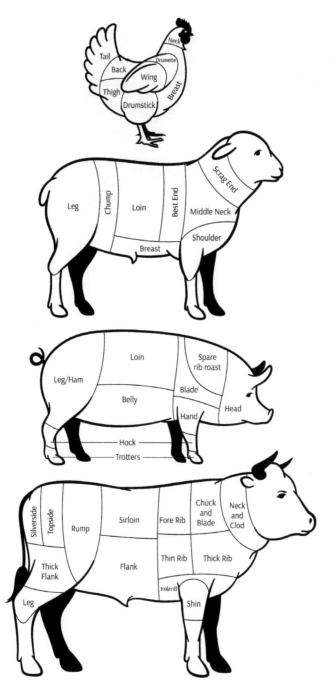

Figure 9.1 Standardised cartographies of meatified chicken, lamb, pig and cow (*Image*: Vlad Klok/Shutterstock.com)

Figure 9.2 Market signage
(*Photograph:* author's own)

the benign pastoral care of food animals. I conceive of raising animals for their meat rather differently, as something illustrative of 'the incessant conversion of the energies of life into dead commodities' associated with humans' separation from nature (Brennan cited in Szerszynski, 2010, p. 16). Meat producers can therefore more accurately be described as custodians of commodified animal flesh. The naturalisation of this commodification is the focus of my next section.

'Can't treat breeders as pets': naturalised pastoral relations (aka commodification)

What is primarily being naturalised in the promotional materials of ethical meat producers is the pastoral role of the farmer in relation to the land and 'their' animals, as excerpts from their web sites illustrate (see Table 9.1). Under so-called 'old-fashioned', 'natural' and 'traditional' farming methods, the paddocks and pastures required for raising food animals, and the practices of grazing and rotation, become 'natural' by association. They come to be understood as part of an ethical, holistic and, above all, natural system. 'Farming' animals, or raising them for meat, is thereby conflated with 'respecting', 'regenerating', 'nurturing', 'enhancing', caring for, and generally supporting key elements of this aspect of nature, including its ecosystems, soils, and biodiversity. As one producer's market signage proclaims, their ecologically safe and sustainable farming practices lead to healthy soils, plants, animals and people.

The discourses of the natural on display in the meat producers' promotional materials, and the conflations that shape them, are illustrative of Pratt's (2008, p. 56) 'pre-set discursive field—that of the natural, the organic, the local, the rooted, the distinctive, the authentic', in which these and other words 'become synonymous, or at least immediately evoke each other'. Hence, meat that is wholesome, clean and healthy, from happy and stress-free animals grazing on green pastures, and using sustainable, old-fashioned, and traditional farming methods that are 'environmentally positive' is constituted and understood as entirely natural. The implicit promise is that by consuming and literally embodying happy animals, raised in lush bucolic environments, the consumer can reconnect with a nature that is mostly lost to them (Todd, 2009, p. 172). Producers of ethical meat similarly allude to their 'old fashioned', 'traditional', 'true', 'natural' and 'happy' animals, which 'make better pork' (pork producer 1) and 'produce the best meat' (beef producer 4). This fusion and naturalisation of various notions about farming, food animals and meat portray consumers' passion for ethical meat as 'a passion for nature' (Todd, 2009, p. 175).

The idea of natural and benevolent pastoral relations is also constituted through the use of images. Food animals are commonly portrayed as relaxed, amiable, and content; their relationships with humans appear affectionate, and their environments evoke pastoral idylls and a romantic 'folksy charm' (Todd, 2009, p. 174). Implying a sense of trust between the farmer and 'their' animals

Table 9.1 Excerpts from the web pages of 'ethical' meat producers

Farm	Animals
'using **sustainable farming techniques**, just **as nature intended**'	'Our animals are **happy** and **stress free**... grow in a **natural** and healthy environment'
'**environmental** farming principles'	'**Free Range** Pigs are **happy** pigs.'
'**traditional** farming methods'	'**live as pigs are meant to**'
'**going back** to the type of farming which was **the norm**'	'lead a **contented low-stress life**'
'care of the **natural** biology and enhancing our **biodiversity—ecologically sustainable**'	'live a **happy life** out in **the open**'
'an **environmentally positive entity**'	'*Beyond* **Free range, pasture-raised**, ethically grown... allowing the behavioral instincts be **real**'
'**regenerating** land... **holistic** farming. **Natural** and ethical farming... farming **naturally**'	'raised the **old fashioned** way'
'a **truly sustainable** way to farm'	'**true free range... happy animals**'
'**clean natural** farming practices'	'Our animals **roam free** across our **paddocks**, eating beautiful **green pasture**'
'**respecting** the land that we farm'	'**Our lovely animals graze** on **native pastures**... live and grow the way **Nature** intended.'
'**environmentally sustainable** and ethical'	'**Natural** Beef'
'health of the **land** and **water** for **future generations**'	'clean, wholesome, **natural** beef and lamb... **genuine** seasonal lamb... **traditionally** aged'
'Regenerative farming to **nurture our land**'	'**real natural pork**'
'what is **best for the soil**'	'helping **to keep the breed alive**'
'we farm **naturally & ethically**'	'getting to be a **TRUE pig**'
'**Natural** farming practices only!'	
'**natural** salt-of-the-earth farming'	
'**natural** grassland environment'	

emphasises the farmers' role as carers for the well-being of food animals, rather than as 'growers' of commodified flesh. Of the 15 producer web sites, three include images of people and animals in close, companionable proximity. A further seven show more intimate scenes, such as piglets snuggling on the farmer's lap, and a child kissing a chick. The assurance that farmers not only love their animals, but that the animals in turn love and trust the farmer, is the implicit message. Family scenes are also common, further conflating this apparently transparent model of farming with all the moral goods associated with family, as well as with nature and the Australian rural tradition. The naturalness of (ethical) meat is thus bolstered by alluding to its wider benevolence—the goodness associated practices bestow not just on animals, but on individuals, families and communities, as I show more clearly below.

However, as Palmer (1997) and Cole (2011) note, these benevolent pastoral relations are ultimately, and often abruptly, upended when it comes to their purpose—producing a marketable product. As the texts affirm, being 'kind to animals [...] results in tender meat' (beef producer 2), and 'happy, stress-free animals produce the best meat' (beef producer 4). Here, the human-centric notion of pastoral care meets its limit, and the state of domination is potentially unmasked.

However, 'growing' meat is naturalised not only as a set of relations but also for its commodity value—a justified and respected way of making a rural living and supporting families. Producers of ethical meat assert that 'you can feel good about directly supporting farmers and their small businesses' (lamb producer 1), and explain that 'food [...] comes from the earth and it comes from hard working families like ours' (pork producer 2). Another promises that 'when you buy from [us] you are supporting a local business that supports other local businesses, employs locals, a family that is raising, educating and supporting two young children' (pork producer 3). To question the commodification of animals, then, is to question the value of family, children and education. Either/or fallacies, or false dichotomies—here presented as either you support meat production or you are against family, small businesses, children, etc.—are a common discursive device, and one that is subtly deployed in these promotional materials. It is also the subtext of *The Slaughter*, in which the death of Marti the pig is justified by financial hardship as well as by the naturalised commodification of her flesh.

The financial bottom line is also evident in *FLM*, appearing as a measure of the quantity of welfare that is profitable, and when more becomes a zero-sum gain. Similar to the ethical producers' texts, productivity is frequently conjoined with welfare, as in 'improving both the lives of pigs and productivity for farmers' (Evans). Welfare becomes a euphemism for productivity. A pig farmer assures Evans that marks on the metal bars of a farrowing crate are from rubbing, not chewing, and besides 'you've got to think of the welfare of the little pigs'. However, the farmer adds, 'pound for pound [...] free range mortality rates are higher than our system', illustrating that this 'welfare' approach is aimed at protecting 'meat', and that what they are 'growing' is commodified, quantifiable flesh. The pig farmer says as much: 'We're feeding them for performance. We're trying to grow meat'.

Commodification, albeit naturalised, could be regarded as one of Foucault's (1980, p. 119) negative aspects of power 'whose function is repression'. In contrast, constitutions of pastoral care and benevolent human/animal relations create a 'productive network' which he considers essential to power's success. Both work together to mask food animals' state of domination, for when the time for pastoral care ends, the naturalised commodification of these animals permits and justifies their deaths. As one producer indicates in a trifecta of objectification (as meat, production unit and commodity), '[we] can't afford to treat our breeders as pets when they're no longer productive' (lamb producer 1).

In *FLM* and across the promotional materials of ethical meat producers, meat is portrayed unquestioningly as a fixture of everyday life, one that comes naturally from 'food' animals. Animal death is normalised as an unfortunate but 'necessary part of the process', and a reminder to consumers to take greater responsibility for animals 'farmed in our name' (Evans). However, I argue that it is not simply the *deaths* of food animals that are naturalised in ethical texts, but, more specifically, their slaughter.

'Are you man enough?' naturalised killing

Across ethical meat discourses, the re-naturalisation (in that it is a re-articulated naturalisation) of killing animals is a significant feature that deserves highlighting. What distinguishes naturalisation from normalisation is an emphasis on killing as part of the natural cycle of life, reflecting humans' position at the top of the food chain, with naturally and/or divinely ordained dominion over all of nature, and drawing on romanticised mythologies surrounding killing animals as both ritual and rite of passage. This naturalisation of killing has become particularly prominent over the past decade, as seen in a swathe of books on eating meat ethically, consciously and mindfully (Cerulli, 2012; Gray, 2016; Leigh, 2015), live TV slaughters by celebrity chefs including Jamie Oliver and Gordon Ramsay, plus a plethora of online texts and videos describing 'humane' and 'ethical' killing (Bell, 2015; McColl, 2015).

Of the 15 ethical producers included in this analysis, three describe the slaughter process on their web sites—one on a blog page (lamb producer 1), and two on their 'frequently asked questions' pages (pork producer 4; beef producer 4). Slaughter is the one part of the production process over which commercial producers typically have no control and, in Australia, must contract to certified third parties. Unable to provide detailed and/or visual evidence of the killing stage, these producers are nevertheless responding as they can to appeals for greater transparency. During visits to farmers' markets I also found several producers who provided photographs of their farms and animals for customers to browse through, and who would readily talk about how their animals were (humanely) slaughtered. *FLM* does provide some strictly managed visual insight into how two of Australia's three 'favourite proteins' (chickens and cows) are slaughtered. The episode on pigs does not broach slaughter, and focuses entirely on welfare issues; stunning techniques for pigs are notably less effective (Cudworth, 2008, p. 38), perhaps making it hard to capture a suitably sanitised scene for general primetime viewing.

Perfunctory, clinical descriptions of slaughter in the promotional materials of ethical producers and in *FLM* certainly normalise killing animals as part of eating meat. However, they stop short of its naturalisation, perhaps because in both sets of texts, *how* these animals die is not problematised, i.e., it does not need to be masked by naturalisation. It is for this reason that I focus on *The*

Slaughter as a text that graphically confronts and naturalises killing (in a fictional context), and also to emphasise that the discourse surrounding ethical meat involves naturalising the ways in which animals are killed (i.e., humanely), along with how they are eaten (i.e., respectfully) and commodified (i.e., kindly). Other authors have recognised this (re)naturalisation of killing animals within the terms of eating ethically as part of a new fetishisation of meat (Miller, 2012; Parry, 2010), often drawing on, and contributing to, poeticised aesthetics of killing (Arcari, 2017b)—aesthetics that are also reflected in *The Slaughter*.

Kohl's film is less about naturalising the edibility of animals and their bodies (although that is part of it), and more about naturalising a fundamental human/animal binary, and, more specifically, an enduring *man*/animal and *man*/nature binary. This binary is used figuratively—a vehicle for the story's narrative, which in turn reveals some of the broader social and cultural meanings associated with this trope. In his attempt to depict slaughter as a 'humane, respectful and personal process', the director perpetuates the human-centric idea of a (divine) natural order in which 'man' has dominion over all animals. By reinforcing this naturalised binary, *The Slaughter* naturalises the already masculinised act of killing, as I will now explain.

The film portrays slaughter as a decidedly male business, imbued with hardship, tough decisions, conflict, violence, and setting feminised emotions aside (see also Cudworth, 2008; Pachirat, 2011). This is emphasised not only by the lack of female presence, but by the visceral and industrial visual and oral texture of the film. On top of this, the director adds the troubled, stereotypically masculinised father/son dynamic with its rich biblical and mythical genealogy. This is a relationship characterised by challenge, conflict, triumph and, of course, violence, and it unfolds using the slaughter of Marti the pig as the conduit.

Killing animals is widely theorised as a masculine, and masculinising, ritual (Cudworth, 2008; Pachirat, 2011; Parry, 2010). In *Killing Tradition*, Bronner (2009) draws on Swan's paean to hunting, and on Ehrenreich's exploration of 'blood rites', to unpack the naturalisation of hunting and killing animals. Swan considers hunting animals and the accompanying blood rituals as natural instincts that 're-enact man's dominion over, and commune with, nature' (Bronner, 2009, p. 55). Appeals to eat only hunted wild animals, widely promoted as the epitome of ethical meat (e.g., Cerulli, 2012; Fearnley-Whittingstall, 2007; Olson, 2014), draw on and reinforce this romanticised naturalisation of the predator/prey, human/animal relationship. Contrastingly, Ehrenreich identifies the taste for meat and the killing this demands as productive of naturalising and naturalised rituals steeped in (masculine) symbolism. For her, such rituals 'positively reinforce the act of killing rather than reflect a positive basic instinct' (Bronner, 2009, p. 56). In other words, rituals, and the symbolic narratives that surround them, cast problematic, and in this case highly gendered, practices in a more positive light. To paraphrase Foucault, they mask a substantial enough part of something disagreeable to make it tolerable and, more ideally, positive.

Efforts to de-masculinise the killing of food animals are a characteristic feature of ethical meat discourses (Mathia, 2014; Pellegrini, 2013) and represent one aspect of this more agreeable mask. Indeed, Parry (2010, p. 85) highlights the role of gender norms in shaping and even perhaps enforcing the rules around ethical meat eating whereby 'women's participation in the slaughter, dismemberment and consumption of animal "others" [is presented] as a way to assert female power' and to mitigate negative masculine associations. *The Slaughter* does not engage with this (problematically) feminist perspective on ethical meat. However, in not doing so, and in drawing on standard masculine tropes, the film further emphasises the naturalisation specifically of *man's* dominion over animals, especially with its allusions to hunting, in which masculine tropes predominate.

For example, the pigs are held in a small fenced area of the farm. The son enters, stalks, corrals and finally entraps the chosen pig, thus completing the first contest between the hunter and his quarry. Shifting to the forecourt of a large tin shed, the father fills two shot glasses with liquor and asks his son if he knows the pig's name. 'Marti', he says. He instructs his son to say with him, 'To Marti' as they chink glasses and down the shot.

In *Killing Tradition*, Bronner quotes the following excerpt from Swan:

> Many hunting rituals involve painting one's body with blood, or drinking the blood of the animals, as it is believed that this conveys the spirit of the animal to the hunter.
>
> (cited in Bronner, 2009, p. 55)

In Kohl's film, liquor can be read as symbolising Marti's blood which, imbued through the toast with her life, soul, or spirit, the father and son then assimilate. Next, father and son are seen standing together in the trailer over Marti. The father indicates to his son where to place the bolt gun and where her throat will be cut afterwards. 'Are you man enough for this?' he says.

Here, the father's challenge to his son's manhood is explicit, and, as in hunting traditions, a direct connection is made to killing an animal as the way to attain it (Bronner, 2009, p. 67). The underlying threat of contempt and ridicule for those who 'fail' to kill on their first hunt is also present. These types of coming-of-age rite, from which women are traditionally excluded, seek to draw out and thereby confirm masculine strength, virility and, ultimately, power over nature and weaker 'others'. Affirming human/nature, human/animal, male/female binaries, Kohl's film reinforces the notion that these divisions are natural, thereby bolstering problematic constructions of masculinity, sexuality, power and the 'other'. Expressions of power and the dualisms that support them are widely recognised (Adams, 1990; Nibert, 2013). Suffice to say here that power is multidimensional (Kim, 2015, p. 11). Human domination over animals does not emerge or exist in a vacuum, and a politics of food needs to recognise how it critically intersects with forms of inter-human domination.

The son does indeed 'man-up', and receives an approving pat on the arm from his father. However, the test of his manhood continues as he graphically struggles to dissect and dismember Marti's suspended carcass. Momentarily, he loses the struggle and vomits. Insults are exchanged: 'I'm amazed we share the same blood', says the father. The son retorts, calling him a 'fucking coward' in reference to his dishonesty regarding their financial situation. Their battle of physical and emotional strength reaches a climax as the father, in his anger, accidentally slices off his son's thumb. Kohl is not questioning normalised constructions of masculinity here. What counts as masculinity is rather expanded to include 'manning up' by being honest—*in addition to*, and not instead of, 'manning up' by killing an animal. The father's violence becomes a transformative experience through which the son finds the fortitude to finish dismembering Marti while his father watches on speechless: his son is a man after all.

The Slaughter depicts killing an animal as a self-actualising experience, in which 'natural' masculine qualities of strength, determination, power over nature, and also a civilising power over one's baser instincts, whether cowardice or dishonesty, can be tested. Using killing as an opportunity for male bonding naturalises animals' disposable status within a reinforced chain of being and makes killing seem essential to being a man. With Ehrenreich, I suggest that the glorification and symbolism surrounding killing animals is not evidence of its rightful place in human cosmologies, but is rather used to make it appear natural and inevitable. The graphic vision and sounds of the slaughter are not intended to shock or disgust, but rather to reflect the current fetish for commodity transparency. As reviewers comment, the film shows 'humane animal slaughter' (Walsh, 2014) and dramatises the 'everyday pain that we try not to see' (Johnson, 2014).

Together with the naturalisations of animals as food and commodity, the naturalisation of killing animals should not be underestimated as another mechanism for masking their domination. Especially surrounding practices and discourses of 'ethical' meat, appeals to a benign cycle of life and death, and poetic notions of animals 'giving' their lives as part of a natural contract, are common. Naturalisations of commodifying, killing, and eating animals therefore serve as a robust mechanism of power that both masks and reinforces animals' state of domination.

These naturalisations are essentially unchanged by efforts to feminise the traditionally male-dominated spheres of slaughter and butchery—efforts that may actually re-inscribe rather than challenge enduring dualisms by making them appear more inclusive and therefore less problematic. Whether masculinised or feminised, using animals for food, however 'ethically', perpetuates a system of domination based on naturalised conceptions of an animal 'other' who is non-human and therefore expendable and/or usable. It is the same dualistic thinking that naturalises and legitimates forms of social domination, including colonialism, patriarchy and capitalism (Cudworth, 2008). These dualisms are co-constitutive and mutually reinforcing. Maintaining one supports the others. As Pilgrim (2013, p. 115) asserts, 'ethical meat eating encourages a practice of masculinity that dominates over animals, women, and nature'.

Conclusion

In this chapter, I have identified naturalisation as a key mechanism by which human domination of animals is masked. I have demonstrated how naturalisations of eating, commodifying and killing animals are especially foregrounded in articulations of ethical or otherwise 'better' meat. An effect of these (re)naturalisations is that the concept of the 'food' animal, and of all the practices it shapes, becomes even more ontologically fixed and (re)legitimised. It is a human-centric concept illustrative of power relations that are 'justified with reference to a "divine" or "natural" order so that these relations appear to be unalterable and unquestionable' (Bujok, 2013, p. 34).

I have also demonstrated how normalised cartographies of meat codify the terms and limits of a human-controlled existence that no stratagems or tricks can change. Hence, I argue that what are commonly understood as relations between humans and food animals instead constitute a state of domination. In addition to the environmental and health impacts of meat production and consumption, the domination of animals that it requires leverages and reinforces broader mechanisms of inter-human domination. With reference, then, to the functions and effects of the naturalisations I have described, uncritical representations of food animals seriously limit thinking about alternative food futures, and uphold food politics that are socially, environmentally and ethically harmful. These representations need to be questioned so that thinking can extend beyond these limitations to consider the next (non-human) social contract (Gabardi, 2017).

A possible way forward is for food studies to acknowledge an enduring human-centrism and to embrace non- and post-human perspectives in the same way as other areas of the humanities and social sciences have done (Cudworth and Hobden, 2017, p. 66). Unified by a shared intent to 'productively trouble habitual ways of thinking and acting on both academia and everyday life' (Castree and Nash, 2004, p. 1342), these approaches are well suited to the aims and intents of a future politics of food as articulated by Herring (2015), Stock, Carolan and Rosin (2015) and Le Heron et al. (2016).

Critical post-humanism highlights that an alternative politics of food must recognise the 'co-constitution and co-evolution of social and natural systems in dynamic configurations' (Cudworth and Hobden, 2017, p. 72)—configurations that are incompatible with human-centric, dualistic thinking. A critical approach is thus prepared to question its social and political framings, and to challenge what is 'impossible to think' (Foucault, 1989, p. xvi). As Sorenson (2014) urges, thinking the unthinkable includes thinking differently about human/animal relations. This is the way to advance towards a true food utopia (Stock, Rosin and Carolan, 2016)—one where neither the margins nor the mainstream contribute to systems that naturalise the domination of non-human and human 'others'.

Notes

1 Both these situations were described to me by producers of (self-identified) ethical and/or sustainable meat during research interviews.
2 To protect the identity of participants, data from the 15 producers of ethical meat are presented according to the type of meat they primarily produce (as most produce more than one), and with a number to indicate different producers: for example, pork producer 1, beef producer 3, etc.

References

Adams, C. J. (1990). *The Sexual Politics of Meat: A Feminist-Vegetarian Critical Theory*. London and New York: Continuum Publishing Corporation.

Arcari, P. (2017a). Normalised, Human-Centric Discourses of Meat and Animals in Climate Change, Sustainability and Food Security Literature. *Agriculture and Human Values*, 34 (1), 69–86.

Arcari, P. (2017b). Perverse Visibilities? Foregrounding Non-Human Animals in 'Ethical' and 'Sustainable' Meat Consumption. *The Brock Review*, 13 (1), 1–30.

Belk, R. W., Ger, G. and Askegaard, S. (2003). The Fire of Desire: A Multisited Inquiry into Consumer Passion. *Journal of Consumer Research*, 30 (3), 326–351.

Bell, R. (2015). Temple Grandin, Killing Them Softly at Slaughterhouses for 30 Years. *National Geographic Magazine*, August 19.

Biesalski, H. K. (2005). Meat as a Component of a Healthy Diet – Are There Any Risks or Benefits If Meat Is Avoided in the Diet? *Meat Science*, 70 (3), 509–524.

Bronner, S. J. (2009). *Killing Tradition: Inside Hunting and Animal Rights Controversies*. Kentucky: University Press of Kentucky.

Bujok, M. (2013). Animals, Women and Social Hierarchies: Reflections on Power Relations. *Deportate, Esuli, Profughe*, 23, 32–48.

Castree, N. and Nash, C. (2004). Mapping Posthumanism: An Exchange. *Environment and Planning A*, 36 (8), 1341–1363.

Cerulli, T. (2012). *The Mindful Carnivore: A Vegetarian's Hunt for Sustenance*. New York: Pegasus Books.

Cole, M. (2011). From 'Animal Machines' to 'Happy Meat'? Foucault's Ideas of Disciplinary and Pastoral Power Applied to 'Animal-Centred' Welfare Discourse. *Animals*, 1 (4), 83–101.

Cole, M. and Stewart, K. (2014). *Our Children and Other Animals*. London: Routledge.

Cudworth, E. (2008). 'Most Farmers Prefer Blondes': The Dynamics of Anthroparchy in Animals Becoming Meat. *Journal for Critical Animal Studies*, 6 (1), 32–45.

Cudworth, E. (2015). Killing Animals: Sociology, Species Relations and Institutionalized Violence. *The Sociological Review*, 63 (1), 1–18.

Cudworth, E. and Hobden, S. (2017). Post-Human Security. In Burke, A. and Parker, R. (eds.), *Global Insecurity* (pp. 65–81). London: Palgrave Macmillan.

FAO. (2011). *World Livestock 2011—Livestock in Food Security*. Rome: FAO.

Fearnley-Whittingstall, H. (2007). *The River Cottage Meat Book*. Berkeley: Ten Speed Press.

Foucault, M. (1978). *The History of Sexuality*. New York: Pantheon Books.

Foucault, M. (1980). *Power/Knowledge: Selected Interviews and Other Writings, 1972-1977*. New York: Pantheon Books.

Foucault, M. (1982). *The Archaeology of Knowledge and the Discourse on Language*. New York: Pantheon Books.

Foucault, M. (1989). *The Order of Things*. London: Routledge.

Foucault, M. (1994). *Ethics, Subjectivity and Truth*. New York: The New Press.

Gabardi, W. (2017). *The Next Social Contract: Animals, the Anthropocene, and Biopolitics*. Philadelphia: Temple University Press.

Goodman, D., DuPuis, E. M. and Goodman, M. K. (2012). *Alternative Food Networks: Knowledge, Practice, and Politics*. Abingdon, Oxon: Routledge.

Gray, L. (2016). *The Ethical Carnivore: My Year Killing to Eat*. London: Bloomsbury Publishing.

Gunderson, R. (2013). Problems with the Defetishization Thesis: Ethical Consumerism, Alternative Food Systems, and Commodity Fetishism. *Agriculture and Human Values*, 31 (1), 109–117.

Herring, R. J. (2015). How Is Food Political? Market, State and Knowledge. In Herring, R. J. (ed.), *The Oxford Handbook of Food, Politics and Society* (pp. 3–40). Oxford: Oxford University Press.

Johnson, N. (2014). If You Don't Kill Your Own Meat, at Least Watch the Slaughter. *Grist*, 29 October. Available at: https://grist.org/food/if-you-dont-kill-your-own-meat-at-least-watch-the-slaughter/. Accessed 20 July 2016.

Joy, M. (2009). *Why We Love Dogs, Eat Pigs, and Wear Cows: An Introduction to Carnism*. San Francisco: Red Wheel/Weiser.

Kim, C. J. (2015). *Dangerous Crossings: Race, Species and Nature in a Multicultural Age*. Cambridge: Cambridge University Press.

Kohl, J. B. (2014). The Slaughter. 2014. *Director's Statement*. Available at: http://bit.ly/1sTPslt. Accessed 7 September 2018.

Le Heron, R. B., Campbell, H., Lewis, N. and Carolan, M. (2016). *Biological Economies: Experimentation and the Politics of Agri-Food Frontiers*. London: Routledge.

Leigh, M. (2015). *The Ethical Meat Handbook*. Gabriola Island, BC: New Society Publishers.

Mathia, R. (2014). Painting the Farm Red: The Chicken-Slaughtering Pinup Girls of Marion Acres. *Modern Farmer*. Available at: https://modernfarmer.com/2014/08/painting-farm-red-chicken-slaughtering-pinup-girls-marion-acres/. Accessed 10 August 2014.

McColl, S. (2015). Meet the Butcher—And Former Vegetarian—Who Now Specializes in Humane Slaughter. *Takepart.com*, 18 March. Available at: www.takepart.com/article/2015/03/18/defining-humane-slaughter/. Accessed 15 December 2017.

Miller, J. (2012). In Vitro Meat: Power, Authenticity and Vegetarianism. *Journal for Critical Animal Studies*, 10 (4), 41–63.

Nibert, D. A. (2013). *Animal Oppression and Human Violence: Domesecration, Capitalism, and Global Conflict*. New York: Columbia University Press.

Olson, M. (2014). *The Compassionate Hunter's Guidebook: Hunting from the Heart*. Gabriola Island, BC: New Society Publishers.

Pachirat, T. (2011). *Every Twelve Seconds: Industrialized Slaughter and the Politics of Sight*. New Haven, CT: Yale Agrarian Studies Series.

Palmer, C. (1997). The Idea of the Domesticated Animal Contract. *Environmental Values*, 6 (4), 411–425.

Palmer, C. (2001). 'Taming the Wild Profusion of Existing Things'? A Study of Foucault, Power, and Human/Animal Relationships. *Environmental Communication: A Journal of Nature and Culture*, 23, 399–358.

Parry, J. (2010). *The New Visibility of Slaughter in Popular Gastronomy*. Master's thesis. Christchurch: University of Canterbury.

Pellegrini, G. (2013). *Girl Hunter: Revolutionizing the Way We Eat, One Hunt at a Time*. Boston: Da Capo Lifelong Books.

Pilgrim, K. (2013). 'Happy Cows', 'Happy Beef': A Critique of the Rationales for Ethical Meat. *Environmental Humanities*, 3, 111–127.

Pratt, J. (2008). Food Values: The Local and the Authentic. In De Neve, G., Luetchford, P., Pratt, J. and Wood, D. C. (eds.), *Research in Economic Anthropology* (pp. 53–70). Bingley: Emerald Group Publishing Limited.

Salt, H. S. (1914). Logic of the Larder. In Salt, H. S. (ed.), *The Humanities of Diet*. Manchester: The Vegetarian Society.

Sorenson, J. (2014). *Critical Animal Studies: Thinking the Unthinkable*. Toronto: Brown Bear Press.

Stănescu, V. (2010). 'Green' Eggs and Ham? the Myth of Sustainable Meat and the Danger of the Local. *Journal for Critical Animal Studies*, VIII (1/2), 8–32.

Steinfeld, H., Gerber, P., Wassenaar, T., Castel, V. et al. (2006). *Livestock's Long Shadow*. Rome: FAO.

Stewart, K. and Cole, M. (2009). The Conceptual Separation of Food and Animals in Childhood. *Food, Culture and Society: An International Journal of Multidisciplinary Research*, 12 (4), 457–476.

Stock, P. V., Carolan, M. and Rosin, C. (2015). Food as Mediator: Opening the Dialogue around Food. In Stock, P. V., Carolan, M. and Rosin, C. (eds.), *Food Utopias: Reimagining Citizenship, Ethics and Community* (pp. 219–225). London: Routledge.

Stock, P. V., Rosin, C. and Carolan, M. (2016). Food Utopias: Performing Emergent Scholarship and Agri-Food Futures. In Le Heron, R., Campbell, H., Nick, L. and Carolan, M. (eds.), *Biological Economies: Experimentation and the Politics of Agri-Food Frontiers* (pp. 212–224). London: Routledge.

Szerszynski, B. (2010). Reading and Writing the Weather. *Theory, Culture and Society*, 27 (2–3), 9–30.

Taylor, N. and Twine, R. (eds.). (2014). *The Rise of Critical Animal Studies: From the Margins to the Centre*. London: Routledge.

Todd, A. M. (2009). Happy Cows and Passionate Beefscapes: Nature as Landscape and Lifestyle in Food Advertisments. In Sandlin, J. A. and McLaren, P. (eds.), *Critical Pedagogies of Consumption: Living and Learning in the Shadow of the 'Shopocalypse'* (pp. 169–179). London: Routledge.

Wadiwel, D. J. (2002). Cows and Sovereignty: Biopower and Animal Life. *Borderlands E-Journal*, 1 (2), 1–8.

Walsh, K. (2014). Watch: Powerful Short Film 'The Slaughter' Brings Light to the Process of Humane Animal Slaughter. *IndieWire*. Available at: www.indiewire.com/2014/10/watch-powerful-short-film-the-slaughter-brings-light-to-the-process-of-humane-animal-slaughter-271074/. Accessed 7 September 2018.

Weisberg, Z. (2009). The Broken Promises of Monsters: Haraway, Animals and the Humanist Legacy. *Journal for Critical Animal Studies*, 7 (2), 22–62.

Wilk, R. (2002). Consumption, Human Needs, and Global Environmental Change. *Global Environmental Change*, 12, 5–13.

Wolfe, C. (2003). *Animal Rites: American Culture, the Discourse of Species, and Posthumanist Theory*. Chicago: University of Chicago Press.

Part 4

Reframing production and consumption

10 The consumer labelling turn in farmed animal welfare politics

From the margins of animal advocacy to mainstream supermarket shelves

Christine Parker, Rachel Carey and Gyorgy Scrinis

Introduction

Throughout the western world there has been a turn towards labelling and certification of animal food products as a means of signalling higher welfare production (Evans and Miele, 2017). In Australia, the terms 'free range', 'sow stall free' and 'RSPCA Approved' have become common on egg, chicken, pork and ham products. These label claims reflect concern about the welfare of those animals that are most confined for the purposes of food production. Layer hens, meat chickens and pigs are typically 'factory farmed' (Harrison, 1964) in precisely controlled sheds with tens of thousands of other animals. The animals themselves are treated largely as components in meat-making machines. This large-scale industrialised production system produces huge amounts of safe, affordable food. It also raises serious animal welfare concerns (D'Silva and Webster, 2010). Indeed, animal advocates have been vocal in protesting the cruelties of industrial, confined animal production, and in arguing for greater government regulation of animal welfare protection, better industry practice and more ethically conscious consumer choices. 'Ethical' labelling has been a key industry response to animal welfare concerns (see also Chapter 9 for a discussion of 'ethical meat').

This chapter argues that higher welfare and free range label claims are an outcome of regulatory politics. They reflect political contests within a network of public and private actors—government agencies, supermarkets, industry associations, civil society organisations and consumers—over how production should be governed and presented to the public. The chapter critically examines the degree to which free range and higher welfare label claims on Australian animal food products have shifted concerns about farmed animals' lives from the 'margins' of the animal advocacy movement to the 'mainstream' of everyday consumer choice. It also asks what has been lost and gained as dominant industry and retailers have adopted these label claims.

This case study of the regulatory and market politics of ethical labelling and consumption in relation to farmed food animals in Australia reveals trends and challenges that have a wider relevance. International institutions and national governments all over the world favour market-based action, such as labelling, for consumer choice and industry self-regulation as modes of response to the many pressing ecological, health, and worker, farmer and animal justice issues facing the food system. The fact that Australia has seen such a high degree of market penetration of, and public debate about, voluntarily labelled free range and higher welfare animal foods makes it a rich case study for critically examining the potential and limitations of labelling for consumer choice as a strategy for increasing public enagagement in food system governance.

This chapter is structured in three parts. The first argues that the widespread adoption and use of higher welfare label claims on animal food can be seen as a response to civil society campaigns to politically activate mainstream consumers and involve them in the governance of the food system (Holzer, 2006). At the same time, label claims also exhibit the creativity of industry and retailers in appropriating and accommodating civil society critiques of dominant production and distribution systems (Richards, Lawrence and Burch, 2011). We suggest that in order to evaluate the impact of these label claims it is critical to 'backwards map' the regulatory politics behind them (Parker, 2014). In the second part, we analyse the politics of 'free range' and higher welfare claims on egg, chicken and pork and ham products in Australia using empirical data. Our analysis reveals a shift of animal welfare from the 'margins' of specialist animal advocacy movements to the 'mainstreams' of supermarket shelves, consumer and food advocacy organisations, and consumer protection regulatory enforcement. The third part critically examines the impact of this shift from the margins to the mainstream on the market, the governance of the market, and the lives of the animals themselves. Although animal welfare concerns may have reached the mainstream through labelling, we argue, the improvements for the lives of animals are at best marginal and incremental, and higher welfare labelling is often misleading. This indicates a governance gap—a chasm between what can be achieved via voluntary certification and labelling (even with ongoing supermarket support and civil society activism) and the need for a more inclusive and sustainable official regulatory governance system for animal welfare practice.

Food labelling as regulatory politics

Ethical consumption and food labelling

The debate over how animal welfare should be regulated in food production is just one skirmish in what have been labelled the 'food wars'—a series of contests over how best to address the environmental, health and social challenges of food production, distribution and consumption into the future (Lang and Heasman, 2015). The marketing and information claims on retail food packaging have become one of the arenas of conflict and contestation in the food wars. These have included: successful campaigns to mandate the labelling of genetically modified foods in Australia and the United States (Roff, 2007); trademarks of denominations of origin and markers of locally distinctive small-scale production throughout Europe and, increasingly, in other jurisdictions; the advancement of ecological sustainability through a range of organic and agro-ecological certification schemes and voluntary claims that are in turn critiqued or championed by different interests (see Guthman, 2007, and Chapter 1 in this volume); and contests over the mandating of certain health and nutrition information on food labels (nutrition information panels, traffic light warnings) to encourage healthy diets and the voluntary placement of health claims on packaging by industry, which are themselves often contested by public health groups (see Scrinis and Parker, 2016). As these examples suggest, label and marketing claims are often political in the sense that they are both constituted and contested by a polycentric network of actors all seeking to influence the governance of food production and consumption. These include various government agencies, supermarkets, producers, social movement advocates, and citizens (Parker et al., 2017).

Social movements sometimes seek to exert political influence over markets by advocating for consumers to 'buycott' (support by buying) some goods and boycott (refuse to buy) others on the basis of the qualities of the goods and the way they were produced (Holzer, 2006). Label claims are often the mechanism by which these qualities or production practices are made apparent. This may create an opportunity for citizen engagement in the governance of supply chains that is not available by other means—neither through government regulatory processes nor industry practice and governance. Thus 'voting with your fork' is proposed as a powerful way to change the food system (cf. Guthman, 2007). It is intended to allow citizens to contest both industry practice and government regulation, and to advocate for alternative mechanisms to govern industry practices, such as different business-to-business requirements (supermarket supply standards) or labelling and certification standards (production and process standards)—all of which may be represented on the label. Indeed, in contemporary neoliberal western societies, labelling and information disclosure to support consumer choice are often lauded as important market-based alternatives to onerous mandatory regulation (Shaw and Black, 2010).

Evaluating the regulatory politics of food labelling

Label claims put forward to resolve the tension between current production practices and competing public interest goals (such as animal welfare) may help to improve production practices and to incorporate a broader range of concerns and voices in their governance. It is, however, a question for empirical investigation whether labelling for consumer choice does or does not affect markets, networks of governance, and, ultimately, production practices and animals' lives.

This chapter summarises key findings from a larger research project that seeks to 'backwards map' (Parker, 2014) the regulatory politics behind 'free range' and higher welfare labelling practices in Australia. Our focus is not on empirically investigating what impact label claims might have on consumer behaviour (cf. Hodgkins et al., 2012), nor on how consumers understand these labels (cf. Bray and Ankeny, 2017). Instead our focus is on how the marketplace is framed and constructed in the first place, and on how that framing and construction can change through regulatory politics. Therefore we inquire into how the label claims seen in the marketplace have been constituted by political and regulatory contests between producers, retailers, social movement advocacy and government, as well as the consequences of these for production practices and for animals' lives.

This chapter therefore asks two questions: to what degree has free range and higher animal welfare labelling in Australia opened up public discourse over animal food production beyond industry and animal advocacy groups to include more voices and more players with an influence over everyday production practices and consumption choices? And to what degree has the penetration of different label claims into the market created different production systems with different impacts on the lives of animals, as well as different regulatory networks that might drive further change?

Methodology

We rely on three key data sources for our analysis. The first is a comprehensive analysis of all publicly available official policy documents and reports, and all newspaper articles from major Australian newspapers, relating to the ethical governance of animal welfare in egg, chicken meat, pork and ham production from 1990 to 2016.[1] Second, we examined the higher welfare claims in the Australian market place via a product survey of egg, chicken meat, and pork and ham products available for retail sale in a selection of retail outlets in Melbourne in 2015.[2] Third we compared the various animal welfare claims identified on these products with information about the accreditation schemes and production practices behind them. This was achieved through a desktop review of accreditation organisations' and producers' web sites, and through interviews with representatives of the organisations responsible for the accreditation systems, Australia's two major supermarkets, producers, and animal welfare and consumer NGOs. In this paper, we focus on reporting data from the first two sources and summarise high-level findings from the third source.

Animal welfare from the margins to the mainstream

Our review of policy documents and newspaper articles shows that since about the year 2000, concern about the welfare of animals confined in large-scale intensive systems has been a topic of public discussion, civil society contestation, and industry action. The key issues in this debate all relate to how animals are housed within intensive production systems: the farming of layer hens in bare 'battery' cages; the confinement of sows in stalls for the purposes of mating, gestation and suckling of their offspring; and the overcrowding of meat chickens inside large barns.

The absence of government commitment to enacting and enforcing higher standards of animal welfare to address these issues has prompted industry and retailer innovation in free range and higher animal welfare labelling to address public concern and civil society contestation of that labelling. Figure 10.1

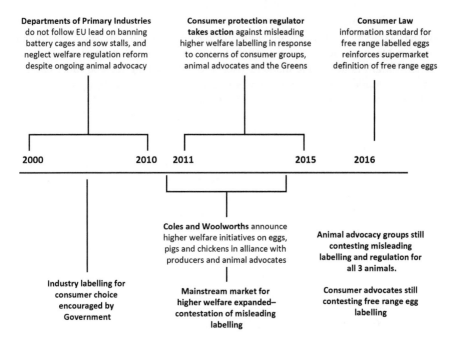

Figure 10.1 Timeline of welfare regulation and labelling in Australia: eggs, pigs and chickens, 2000–2016

summarises key policy and market developments within that time frame. The top half of the diagram shows official government policy decisions and regulatory actions. The bottom half shows the development of private labelling initiatives. The timeline shows the shift of regulatory politics from civil society activism aimed at government reform of animal welfare regulation towards supermarket-led higher welfare labelling initiatives to respond to public concern. The final phase is consumer-oriented contestation of misleading higher welfare labelling leading to consumer protection regulatory action. These developments, and the interaction between government, civil society, and industry and retailers, are briefly outlined in the following sections.

A government animal welfare policy of labelling for consumer choice

The official regulatory standards affecting farmed animal welfare in Australia are the *Model Codes of Practice*. These are decided via a cooperative process between federal and state primary industries ministers who share responsibility for regulating animal welfare in Australia's federal system. These standards are designed to allow large-scale, intensive, shed-based farming, and have scant regard for animals' affective suffering or desire to engage in natural behaviors

(Sharman, 2009). In the case of layer hens and meat chickens, for instance, the standards allow high stocking densities, and do not restrict flock size, nor mandate outdoor access or enrichment opportunities inside or outside the shed. Australian governments have adopted an explicit policy of leaving the most contentious animal welfare issues to the market to sort out via labelling for consumer choice, and have deprioritised ongoing government funding and staffing support for evidence-based animal welfare standard-setting, monitoring and enforcement.

Layer hens and egg production provides the clearest example of this approach. In 1999, the European Union introduced a new directive that would ban conventional bare 'battery' cages and require 'enriched' or 'colony' cages by 2012 (see Parker et al., 2017, p. 2). This prompted Australian government animal welfare authorities to commission a review to consider whether to follow suit. But this review recommended, instead, to empower industry to label eggs as 'cage', 'barn', or 'free range', a market-based option that was adopted by government (Standing Committee on Agriculture and Resource Management, 2000, pp. 10–11). Similarly, in relation to pigs and meat chickens, Australian animal welfare authorities declined to follow UK and EU leadership on phasing out sow stalls,[3] and lifting animal welfare standards for poultry production (see Robins and Phillips, 2011). This was despite very active ongoing campaigning by leading Australian animal advocacy groups—including Animals Australia, the RSPCA, and Voiceless—on both issues (see Animals Australia, 2005; Sharman and Kossew, 2008; Sherman, Sherman and Sharman, 2005).

Australian agricultural animal welfare regulation has been severely criticised by animal welfare advocates (as noted above), by academic commentators (Goodfellow, 2016, pp. 218–219; Phillips and Petherick, 2015) and, most recently, by the Productivity Commission (a federal government body that evaluates regulation) (Productivity Commission, 2016, pp. 199–259) for weak standards, lack of independence, and inadequate resourcing in standard-setting, monitoring and enforcement. Yet attempts to introduce more independent and professional standard-setting have, to date, been stymied and delayed. For example, the national Australian Animal Welfare Strategy was introduced to revise and renew animal welfare standards in 2004, but its coordinating office was de-funded by the Commonwealth government in 2014 (Productivity Commission, 2016, pp. 185–186). Alternative attempts at reform have included a number of bills introduced by the Greens (the third most significant political party in Australia) into federal and state parliaments to ban battery cages and sow stalls, and to introduce an independent regulator of animal welfare at state or commonwealth level (see Productivity Commission, 2016, p. 230). However, these initiatives have been largely unsuccessful.

Supermarkets expand mainstream market for higher welfare labelled products

After 2011, when it became clear that government welfare authorities intended to leave it to the market to improve the animal welfare of layer hens, pigs and meat chickens, Australia's two major supermarkets, Coles and Woolworths, filled the animal welfare governance vacuum. The two Australian supermarkets followed the example of UK supermarkets in making the creation and advertising of higher animal welfare labelled products a prominent part of their brand identity (Parker and Scrinis, 2014).

By 2014, both of Australia's two dominant supermarket chains had loudly announced plans to improve animal welfare standards for a range of products, with a particular focus on phasing out the sale of caged eggs. Woolworths had already announced it would phase out cage eggs in 2009. In 2010, Coles announced that it would phase out own-brand caged eggs and drop the price of free range eggs. In 2012, in response to public conflict over the meaning of 'free range' (see below), Coles announced it would set its own standards for free range egg production and heavily advertised its commitment to cage-free own-brand eggs (see Figure 10.2). In 2013, Woolworths followed suit on the free range standard and upped the ante by announcing it would phase out the sale of both own-brand and branded cage eggs and would cease using cage eggs as an ingredient in its own-brand products (see Parker et al., 2017, p. 14). By 2015, the vast majority of carton eggs in Coles and Woolworths stores were free range (although free range eggs still represent only 40% of the total retail market once all retail outlets are counted, see Parker et al., 2017).

In 2010, Coles announced that it would no longer source own-brand pork products from production systems in which sows (breeder pigs) were kept in sow stalls (The Age, 2010). As of 2013, all Coles brand pork is 'sow-stall free' (Long, 2013). By 2014, Coles and Woolworths had also both implemented 'RSPCA Approved' certification labelling for all own-brand chicken meat sold in store (Parker, 2017). A growing proportion of retail pork and ham products in Australia is now 'sow stall free',[4] and around 60% of chicken meat is labelled 'RSPCA Approved' (RSPCA, 2016). Additionally, Coles and Woolworths also sell accredited free range chicken meat (representing 20% of the total retail market, see Australian Chicken Meat Federation, 2011), and free range pork and ham products (up to 5% of the total retail market).[5] They also offer pork and ham labelled 'outdoor bred, raised indoors on straw', and accredited organic chicken meat (each a tiny proportion of the market).

The result is that, by 2015, the vast majority of egg and chicken products in the two dominant supermarkets, as well as an increasing proportion of pork and ham products, had some form of higher welfare label claim. The mainstreaming of higher animal welfare onto the supermarket shelves has been achieved through alliances between the supermarkets and animal welfare, and industry—or civil society-based certification groups. The dominance of 'RSPCA Approved' chicken meat in the supermarkets is dependent on an alliance between the supermarkets (which adopted it as the baseline animal welfare standard for own-brand chicken), the RSPCA (a fairly mainstream, but highly respected, animal welfare organisation, see Chen, 2016, p. 167), and chicken producers (notably mid-tier producer Hazeldenes, which worked with Coles in the first instance to trial and adopt the 'RSPCA Approved' standard, with the two largest producers coming on board soon after).

The prominence of 'sow stall free' is due to a convergence of the interests of Coles, which announced a phase out of sow stalls for own-brand products in

2010 (The Age, 2010), and industry association Australian Pork Limited, which decided to implement a voluntary phase out of sow stalls a few months later (Sydney Morning Herald, 2010). This was a clear response both to very active animal advocacy campaigning in relation to industry practices, and to disappointment in government failure to completely ban sow stalls. Animals Australia conducted a long-running campaign based on the movie *Babe*, and Voiceless and the RSPCA were also very active in campaigning against sow stalls. Coles' ability to introduce 'sow stall free' also depended on the fact it could source sow stall free pork and ham from Europe where the law had already changed. However, as we show below, 'sow stall free' is not completely free of the use of sow stalls (for pregnant sows at least). Moreover, farrowing crates for sows to suckle the piglets before weaning are still used.

Coles and Woolworths took advantage of the lack of a government ban on battery cages, and lack of trust in the industry accreditation standard for 'free range' eggs (see below), to create their own campaigns encouraging the purchase of cage free, as well as to establish their own standards for free range. Although the supermarket free range standard is based on an industry association accreditation (from the Australian Egg Corporation), this is not emphasised on the label (see Parker and De Costa, 2015, p. 933). Rather, the supermarkets' strategy of eliminating cage eggs from their shelves and setting extra standards for industry is emphasised in their advertising.

The supermarkets have appropriated an animal welfare 'halo effect' by adopting welfare standards that are higher than official government standards and by being seen to respond proactively to the animal welfare concerns that have been brought to the attention of the public by animal advocacy groups. Figure 10.2, for example, shows a banner featuring Curtis Stone in store, pointing out that all Coles ownbrand eggs are cage free. Coles has similar advertisements, also featuring Stone in its own advertising magazines, online, and in feature articles in the wider media (see also Figure 10.3). Woolworths features Jamie Oliver on various value-added ready-to-cook products that use free range eggs and chicken, as well as in recipes in its instore magazine and in media articles. In an 'RSPCA Approved' blog post (RSPCA, 2015), Oliver is quoted as saying that 'me and Woolworths put our heads together on loads of issues, from health and well-being to animal welfare, and decided to set ourselves some ambitious goals to raise the bar'. This resulted in the adoption of 'RSPCA Approved' standards for meat chickens by Woolworths, and, according to the blog, it is still improving free range egg standards. This gives consumers the impression that public concern about animal welfare is receiving a tangible and personal hearing by the supermarkets via celebrity chefs (see Lewis and Huber, 2015).

The clear messaging of even the more radical animal advocacy organisations has significantly supported the supermarkets' welfare-friendly ethical branding strategy by encouraging supporters to buy as 'kindly' as possible (see Rodan and

Figure 10.2 Coles in-store advertising of cage free eggs using celebrity chef Curtis Stone
(*Photograph*: author's own)

Figure 10.3 Coles magazine advertisement for 'RSPCA Approved' chicken 'at no added
cost to you'

(*Photograph*: author's own)

Mummery, 2014). For example, Animals Australia's long-running 'make it possible' campaign recommends that 'Step 1' for supporters is to 'vote with your trolley': '[M]ake kind choices. Avoid factory farmed, buy fewer animal products, or even go meat-free [. . .] The choices you make at the supermarket can ensure a kinder world for these animals'.[6] Indeed the RSPCA, in particular, has actively facilitated and supported the supermarkets' ethical branding strategy with its 'RSPCA Approved' certification scheme for various animal products.

A shift to consumer advocacy and consumer protection regulation

As free range and higher welfare labels gained prominence on supermarket shelves, so did public debate about the meaning of these terms and the certification standards behind them. Figure 10.4 demonstrates this by showing the extraordinary rise in discussion of 'free range' labels in relation to egg, chicken, and pork and ham products in newspaper articles since 2000. It shows how discussion of animal welfare was expanding well beyond the traditional animal advocacy groups and Primary Industries departments to include consumer advocacy organisations and consumer protection regulators. The latter ultimately took legal action against industry players in all three industries (chicken meat, eggs, and pork and ham) for misleading labelling.

The chicken meat industry was the first to attract consumer protection regulatory attention. In 2011, Australia's powerful national consumer protection

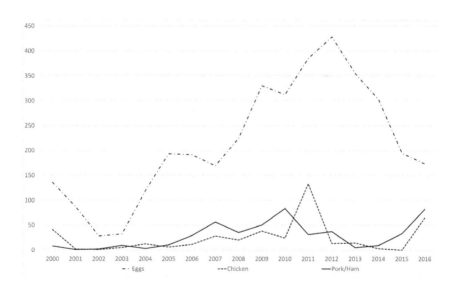

Figure 10.4 Mentions of 'free range', 'bred free range' and 'sow stalls' in articles about animal welfare and eggs, chicken meat and pork/ham in major Australian newspapers, 2000–2016

regulator, the Australian Competition and Consumer Commission (ACCC), commenced enforcement action for misleading conduct against industry body Australian Meat Chicken Federation (ACMF), and three major chicken meat producers for claiming that meat chickens grown conventionally inside barns with tens of thousands of birds and no outdoors access were 'free to roam'. The consumer action was prompted by a complaint and lobbying from the Barristers Animal Welfare Panel working with Animals Australia, one of Australia's most prominent animal advocacy organisations. The commencement of that action in 2011 garnered much media attention, and by 2013 the ACCC had succeeded in court against all of the defendants (see Parker, 2017).

At the same time, public concern about the definition of 'free range' eggs had erupted, as Figure 10.4 clearly shows. Conflict centred on whether 'free range' birds were or were not kept in a system in which most hens actually went outside on most days. Critics argued that most so-called 'free range' eggs were produced in conditions where hens were largely confined in crowded conditions in barns and given only theoretical access to outdoor ranges (see Parker and De Costa, 2015). The outcry over misleading free range egg labelling was led by a combination of animal welfare, consumer and small-scale free range advocacy groups, together with Greens MPs (see Carey, Parker and Scrinis, 2017, pp. 267–268). The ACCC responded by taking a series of successful enforcement actions against producers who had misleadingly labelled their eggs 'free range' (see ACCC, 2015b). In 2012, both the egg and chicken meat industry associations withdrew proposals they had previously made to introduce industry accredited 'free range' certification standards in their respective industries. Due to the public interest in, and outcry over, misleading free range egg labelling, government consumer protection ministers stepped into the debate in 2014 and announced that they would produce a consumer law information standard defining free range eggs for the purposes of labelling. The result was a standard that defined free range largely in line with the standard that had been developed by the two dominant supermarkets (see Carey, Parker and Scrinis, 2017).

From 2007, small-scale alternative free range pig farmers groups had also contested 'bred free range' labelling promoted by the mainstream pig industry (McCosker, 2016; see also Sherman, Sherman and Sharman, 2005). They argued that the term 'bred free range' was misleading, because it gave the mistaken impression that the grower pigs (or piglets) who become pork and ham were raised outdoors. The 'bred free range' system, in fact, keeps the sows (mother pigs) outdoors, with huts for giving birth and suckling the grower pigs (piglets). The grower pigs are, however, put into barns once they are weaned to grow out ready for slaughter. Between 2012 and 2015, the ACCC investigated misleading 'free range' and 'bred free range' label claims in the pork industry, and obtained court-enforceable undertakings from three major producers, and an agreement with industry body, Australian Pork Limited, to change the labelling and address what the ACCC considered to be misleading practices (ACCC, 2015a).

From the margins to the mainstream

Our analysis of newspaper articles shows clearly and quantitatively the way that participation in policy discussion about animal welfare regulation for pigs and chickens expanded beyond animal advocacy groups, the animal industry and Primary Industries departments between 2000 and 2015. Figures 10.5a–c shows two years in which the most newspaper articles were published about animal welfare in relation to eggs, meat chickens and pigs respectively. These show that the number of different voices has expanded in a context in which (as shown in Figure 10.4) the amount of public attention and discussion has also expanded (see also Parker et al., 2017).

Animal welfare labelling is a political movement in which animal advocacy groups have successfully mobilised people in their everyday lives (i.e., as consumers) through alliances with supermarkets, and with a broader range of political and consumer advocacy groups. But in order to do so, a degree of 'frame bridging' has been required (Holzer, 2006, p. 411). The following section discusses the effects of this broadening of animal welfare from the margins to the mainstream in terms of the impacts on production practices and animals' lives, as well as the impacts for future governance of animal welfare.

Impact of shift from margins to mainstream

Our analysis above shows that animal welfare concerns have indeed moved from the margins to the mainstream through supermarkets' adoption of higher welfare labels and consumer advocacy destabilisation of existing industry welfare labelling practices. As Peter Chen (2016, p. 129) has suggested, the Australian animal protection policy field 'is a network with a contested centre'. The state does not act as the central authoritative actor, and there is an ongoing and dynamic contest of power between 'key network participants', including the major animal advocacy organisations and key industry groups. Chen suggests that 'the emphasis away from state regulation in Australia means that entrepreneurialism dominates over hierarchical power, leading the network to be more dynamic and changeable than other areas of policy-making', and handing greater opportunities for influence to both activists and private service providers, including supermarkets (Chen, 2016, p. 129). However, as Chen (2016, p. 128) also suggests, the uptake of private, supermarket-led animal welfare standards for labelling means that policy networks often mirror power in supply chains.

Impact on production practices and animals' lives: 'better welfare at no extra cost'!

Chen (2016, p. 200) describes the relationship between the supermarkets and the RSPCA as a 'resource exchange', one 'that creates a degree of mutual capture'. Both sides of this mutual capture can be identified in free range and higher welfare labelling in Australia. On the one hand, as we have seen, animal

2000 — Departments of Primary Industries decide not to ban cage eggs (n=144)

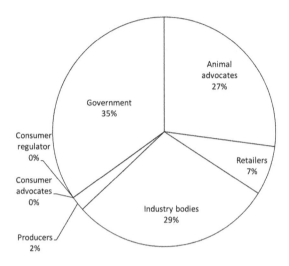

2013 — Industry standards discredited, consumer regulators taking action and supermarkets make own standards (n=114)

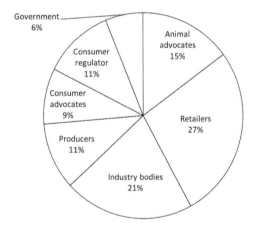

Figure 10.5a Proportion of newspaper articles mentioning different stakeholders: eggs, 2000 and 2013

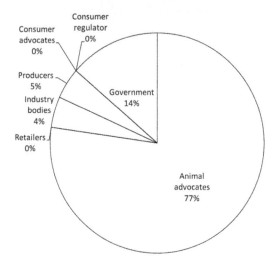

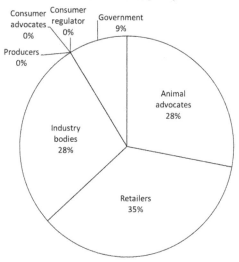

Figure 10.5b Proportion of newspaper articles mentioning different stakeholders: pigs, 2006 and 2010

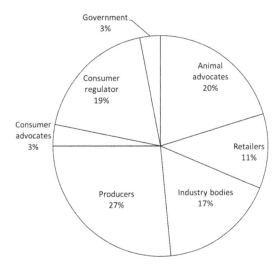

2011 — Coles announces RSPCA Approved; ACCC actions "free to roam" claims (n=77)

Government 3%
Animal advocates 20%
Consumer regulator 19%
Retailers 11%
Consumer advocates 3%
Producers 27%
Industry bodies 17%

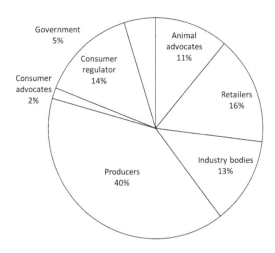

2013 — ACCC succeeds in "free to roam" case (n=70)

Government 5%
Animal advocates 11%
Consumer regulator 14%
Consumer advocates 2%
Retailers 16%
Producers 40%
Industry bodies 13%

Figure 10.5c Proportion of newspaper articles mentioning different stakeholders: meat chickens, 2011 and 2013

advocacy concerns 'captured' the attention and action of the mainstream super-markets and the wider public. Free range and higher welfare labelled products are now both prominent on supermarket shelves, and in a substantial, if not dominant, proportion of the grocery market for these foods. On the other hand, the consequence of the mainstreaming of animal welfare concerns through labelling is that the supermarkets have assumed power over the issue. This comes with its own set of consequences. The transfer of animal welfare from an animal advocacy concern to a matter of general consumer concern has shifted the frame from absolute standards of animal welfare to a balanced consideration of ethics, price and taste. The supermarkets have positioned themselves as the authoritative judges of how to balance these qualities. Their overarching approach is exemplified in the claim, shown clearly in Figure 10.3, in which celebrity chef Curtis Stone for Coles advertises 'RSPCA Approved' chicken as 'better welfare at no extra cost to you'. Intervening in the 'free range' egg debate, Coles similarly placed itself as authoritative mediator between conflicting industry and animal advocacy groups in the consumer interest:

> We have issued a standard that sets out a maximum stocking density of 10,000 birds a hectare. [...] We came to this figure after consulting with industry and welfare groups, and we believe it strikes the appropriate balance between animal welfare and keeping free-range egg prices within reach of most Australians.
>
> (Coles, 2012)

As Jane Dixon (2002, p. 113) puts it, supermarkets' adoption of ethical brand identities that promote concern for animal welfare while maintaining low prices sells the idea that both are possible at the same time.

The implications for production practices and animals' lives are that these higher welfare products represent at best a small incremental improvement for the vast majority of animals raised according to these schemes, and perhaps a substantial improvement in a very small minority of niche products from animals who are raised in genuinely different systems. These labels represent misleading 'welfare washing' of the reality that most animals, even those in higher welfare systems, still live confined, brutal lives in large-scale industrial factory farms. Moreover, an ever greater number of pigs, chickens and hens are living lives of confinement and suffering as more and more eggs, chicken meat, and pork and ham is produced and eaten (see D'Silva and Webster, 2010). With regard to eggs, 40% of retail carton eggs are now free range, but the vast majority of these are produced in large industrial facilities with outdoor stocking densities of 10,000 per hectare, where hens have no meaningful life in an enriched environment in which they can engage in natural behaviours and social arrangements. Moreover, the 40% free range figure does not include the vast amount of eggs produced for catering, hospitality and processed foods that represent about half of egg produc-tion in Australia (Parker et al., 2017)—the vast majority of hens in Australia are still in bare battery cages.

As for meat chickens, the 'RSPCA Approved' system now dominates production. It may represent a minor improvement for the birds, since it requires slightly lower stocking densities and slightly better indoor conditions for the birds. This includes minor enrichments in the barn to allow some opportunities for exercise, and better management of the environment to avoid harming the animals' health. But it does not introduce a substantially different system. Only a small minority of birds are free range or organic: that is, given an opportunity to go outside. Given their short lives, and their being bred for maximum meat production, free ranging is largely meaningless for these birds. They are only able to access the outdoors about half way through their short lives, are too young and timid to do so, and may already lack the physical strength to manage outdoor forays (see Parker, 2017).

The majority of breeder pigs in Australia are 'sow stall free', but even the Coles sow stall free standard includes up to 24 hours in a sow stall at the beginning of pregnancy, and the Woolworths sow stall free standard allows up to five days in a sow stall. Moreover, the sow stall free standards of both major retailers allow sows to spend three to four weeks in a 'farrowing crate' during suckling of piglets. Both mother pigs and piglets are kept indoors in confined and crowded spaces for their entire lives. Only a small fraction of Australia's pig herd is kept in free range systems, and free range production is very challenging for environmental reasons (Australian Pork Limited, 2017).

Impact on possibilities for future reform

Animal advocacy concerns also 'captured' the attention and action of government and non-government consumer advocacy organisations to achieve a regulatory response. Consumer protection action occurred when animal welfare was reframed as addressing the misleading of (ethical) consumers, and thus obtained the support of consumer groups, MPs and, importantly, consumer protection regulators, to delegitimate industry labels. Switching the framing from poor animal welfare to misleading labelling also switched the government regulatory arena from the ineffective animal welfare regulation authorities to the more effective consumer protection regulator. This was essential to obtaining effective government action, as consumer law action can only take place on the basis of misleading and deceptive conduct, not on grounds of inadequate animal welfare.

However, making consumer protection-based attacks on the misleading nature of industry labelling is essentially a negative strategy. It does not provide a positive action for consumers, given that animal advocacy organisations do not create their own animal food production systems (with the important exception of 'RSPCA Approved' certification). Supermarkets filled the power gap, claiming to be legitimate 'food authorities' (Dixon, 2007), or intermediaries between animal advocacy organisations, consumers and producers. This was most evident in relation to the debate over free range egg labelling, during which the supermarkets set an outdoor stocking density of 10,000 hens per hectare, neatly occupying the middle ground between the egg industry (which had proposed

20,000 hens per hectare) and animal and consumer rights groups (which advocated for 1,500 hens per hectare, as reflected in alternative small-scale free range certification standards in the UK). This approach was then reflected in a new consumer law standard defining free range eggs for the purposes of labelling, which took on the supermarkets' 10,000 hens per hectare stocking density and defined free range as 'meaningful access' to an outdoor range, rather than most hens ranging most days (see Carey, Parker and Scrinis, 2017). The standard was described by the Australian Government as purporting 'to increase consumer certainty, not to prescribe a particular set of production practices or to regulate animal welfare' (Treasury, 2015). Thus the regulatory politics had shifted from a concern with animal welfare regulation to a concern with the consumer protection regulation of labelling.

This approach—now institutionalised in the consumer law standard for free range egg labelling—may lock in the cheap, incremental animal welfare improvement discussed in the previous subsection. The combination of supermarket baseline higher welfare standards plus premium products gives consumers and civil society advocates the illusion of a range of choice, and of the possibility of voting with their shopping trolleys. Yet at the same time it conceals or deflects attention from three other, potentially more important, ways of addressing animal welfare concerns.

First, it diverts attention from the need to create and innovate with alternative production practices, such as small-scale agro-ecological farming, and technologies like new designs for sheds, ranges, and the genes of the animals themselves. Watered down, inexpensive supermarket welfare labelling fills the market space instead. Second, it focuses attention on the need for consumer certainty and transparency, while obscuring the possibility that official government standards for animal welfare could be improved. Labelling may help create better options in the marketplace, but market-led labelling alone does not prohibit or remove poor practices from the marketplace (see Chapter 1 for a similar point about organic labelling). Instead, it may placate many of those members of the public who do care about animal welfare, and remove some of the pressure for regulatory reform to improve the baseline for all animals. Third, market-led labelling may encourage and legitimate increased production and consumption, with very small patches of significantly improved welfare and larger patches of incremental improvement. Even larger swathes of very poor welfare remain. Supermarket appropriation of higher welfare brand identities deflects attention from the need for radically reduced animal food production and consumption, including via advocacy for both cruelty-free consumption (minimising and abstaining from use of animals at all, and the development of tasty, viable alternatives), and high quality, low quantity meat production and consumption (e.g., reducetarian, locavore, 'slow meat' and nose to tail consumption).

Conclusion

Ethical consumption is one strategy for expanding the range of voices and concerns in public policy discourse. Our case study shows how Australian animal advocacy organisations mobilised consumers, retailers and brands to seek improvements for animals that government had not provided via baseline regulation. In this context, higher welfare labelling must be understood, at least partly, as a contest of regulatory politics: who will gain power over production practices and the lives of animals via what is on the label, and what consequences will this have?

Our analysis has shown that higher welfare labelled egg, chicken and pork products now dominate the supermarket shelves, but this represents, at best, a very small incremental improvement in the lives of those animals. Some label claims are simply deceptive: for example, cage or barn eggs are sometimes labelled free range, and many 'free range' eggs offer hens only a theoretical opportunity to access a bare and unappealing outdoor range from a large, crowded shed. Australia's two dominant supermarkets, Coles and Woolworths, have gained power over animal welfare governance via ethical consumption, but most higher welfare labels in the supermarkets are misleading 'welfare washing'. That is, they deliver a small incremental improvement from a very low baseline while implying to consumers that an absolute standard of good welfare has been reached; 'RSPCA Approved' chicken and sow stall free pork arguably fall into this category. Taking into account the great expansion in animal production and consumption facilitated by supermarkets, and the large range of processed and packaged foods in which animal products are used, higher welfare labelling represents a marginal improvement at best.

Our analysis has also shown that the rise of higher welfare labelling has helped to mainstream animal welfare concerns about factory farming with the wider public, and has broadened the range of actors with a voice in the animal welfare policy debate. This creates possibilities for ongoing dynamism and change in both animal food production practices and in official governance of animal welfare. To date, however, the result is 'more diffuse than specific' (Miele and Lever, 2013)—not wholesale changes in animal supply, but contestation, problematisation and expansion of stakeholders and discourses in governance systems. Alliances between supermarkets and animal advocates to produce higher welfare labelling seemed promising, but so far they have blurred animal welfare concerns, even as they have created a bridge for animal advocacy into the mainstream (Holzer, 2006). The danger is that supermarket ethical branding will simply present consumers with a predigested set of higher welfare choices that do not, in fact, give much voice to animal welfare concerns. There is also still a dangerous lack of official government and public policy attention to improving and enforcing minimum animal welfare regulation standards, as well as a lack of attention to encouraging innovation and experimentation in true alternatives.

Further and ongoing contestation of both higher welfare labelling and underlying animal welfare policy and practice is necessary to prompt greater change in the future. Contestation of what these labelling terms actually mean, and whether they mean what they say, will provide an opportunity to draw greater attention to the lives of the animals in a way that may drive ongoing change in practice and policy. The hope is that ongoing debate will ultimately lead to more than just 'welfare washing' and enhanced marketing strategies, but in fact to better animal welfare regulation.

Notes

1 The official policy documents were used to create timelines of policy debates and decisions for each of the three animal food product categories, which were in turn used as the basis for defining search terms to collect all relevant newspaper articles in major Australian newspaper articles digitally archived in Factiva (a total of 1,483 articles). We chose 1990 as the start year because before that many fewer articles were digitally archived. For further discussion of this methodology and its limitations, and for more detailed analyses of certain issues, see Parker et al. (2017), Parker (2017) and Carey (2017).
2 For more detail of these data see Parker and De Costa (2015).
3 The UK implemented a total ban in 1999, and the EU announced, in 2001, a so-called 'partial ban' on sow stalls after the first four weeks of pregnancy from 2013.
4 Around 70% of the Australian sow herd is sow stall free (Australian Pork Limited, 2017). All Coles own-brand imported product is sow stall free. Woolworths has only made that commitment for fresh own-brand product, not for processed, and it does not label pork and ham as sow stall free.
5 5% of the Australian sow herd is in free range production systems, and another 5% in the 'outdoor bred, raised indoors on straw' system. See http://aussiepigfarmers.com.au/pigs/our-farming-systems/outdoor-bred-system/. Figures are also based on our own product survey in 2015.
6 See http://www.makeitpossible.com/take_action/.

References

The Age. 2010. Coles Broadens Sow Stall Free Pork. *The Age*, 8 November, p. 8.
Australian Competition and Consumer Commission (ACCC). (2015a). ACCC Concludes Review of 'Free Range' and Other Similar Claims in the Pork Industry. Available at: www.accc.gov.au/media-release/accc-concludes-review-of-free-range-and-other-similar-claims-in-the-pork-industry-0. Accessed 19 November 2017.
Australian Competition and Consumer Commission (ACCC). (2015b). *ACCC Enforcement Guide–Free Range Hen Claims*. Canberra: Commonwealth of Australia.
Australian Pork Limited. (2015). *Standards Manual, Australian Pork Industry Quality Assurance Program, Version 4.0*. Canberra: Australian Pork Limited.
Australian Pork Limited. (2017). Our Farming Systems: Free Range System. Available at: https://aussiepigfarmers.com.au/pigs/our-farming-systems/free-range-system/. Accessed 19 November 2017.
Animals Australia. (2005). Press Release: New SaveBabe.com Billboards Up!, Available at: www.animalsaustralia.org/media/press_releases.php?release=41. Accessed 19 November 2017.
Australian Chicken Meat Federation. (2011). *The Australian Chicken Meat Industry: An Industry in Profile*. Sydney: Australian Chicken Meat Federation.
Bray, H. J. and Ankeny, R. A. (2017). Happy Chickens Lay Tastier Eggs: Motivations for Buying Free-Range Eggs in Australia. *Anthrozoös*, 30 (2), 213–226.
Carey, R. (2017). 'Pigs and Higher Welfare Labelling in Australia', (paper available from Christine Parker as first/corresponding author upon request).
Carey, R., Parker, C. and Scrinis, G. (2017). Capturing the Meaning of 'Free Range': The Contest between Producers, Supermarkets and Consumers for the Higher Welfare Egg Label in Australia. *Journal of Rural Studies*, 54, 266–275.
Chen, P. (2016). *Animal Welfare in Australia: Politics and Policy*. Sydney: Sydney University Press.

Coles Supermarket Australia (2012). Coles Helping Australians with Better Animal Welfare at No Added Cost to Consumers. Media release October 2012.

Dixon, J. (2002). *The Changing Chicken: Chooks, Cooks and Culinary Culture*. Sydney: University of New South Wales Press.

Dixon, J. (2007). Supermarkets as new food authorities. In Burch, D. and Lawrence, G. (eds.), *Supermarkets and Agri-Food Supply Chains*. Cheltenham: Edward Elgar.

D'Silva, J. and Webster, J. (eds.) (2010). *The Meat Crisis: Developing More Sustainable Production and Consumption*. London: Earthscan.

Evans, A. and Miele, M. (2017). Food labelling as a response to political consumption. In Keller, M., Halkier, B., Wilska, T.-A. and Truninger, M. (eds.), *Routledge Handbook on Consumption*. London: Taylor & Francis.

Goodfellow, J. (2016). Regulatory capture and the welfare of farm animals in Australia. In Cao, D. and White, S. (eds.), *Animal Law and Welfare—International Perspectives*. Switzerland: Springer International Publishing.

Guthman, J. (2007). The Polanyian Way? Voluntary Food Labels as Neoliberal Governance. *Antipode*, 39, 456–478.

Harrison, R. (1964). *Animal Machines: The New Factory Farming Industry*. London: Vincent Stuart Publishers.

Hodgkins, C., Barnett, J., Wasowicz-Kirylo, G., Stysko-Kunkowska, M., Gulcan, Y., Kustepeli, Y., Akgungor, S., Chryssochoidis, G., Fernández-Celemin, L., Bonsmann, S. S. G., Gibbs, M. and Raats, M. (2012). Understanding How Consumers Categorise Nutritional Labels: A Consumer Derived Typology for Front-of-Pack Nutrition Labelling. *Appetite*, 59, 806–817.

Holzer, B. (2006). Political Consumerism between Individual Choice and Collective Action: Social Movements, Role Mobilization and Signalling. *International Journal of Consumer Studies*, 30 (5), 405–415.

Lang, T. and Heasman, M. (2015). *Food Wars: The Global Battle for Mouths, Minds and Markets*. Abingdon: Earthscan.

Lewis, T. and Huber, A. (2015). A Revolution in an Eggcup? Supermarket Wars, Celebrity Chefs and Ethical Consumption. *Food, Culture & Society*, 18 (2), 289–307.

Long, W. (2013). Coles Defends Sow Stall Record. *ABC Rural*, 10 January. Available at: www.abc.net.au/news/rural/2013-01-10/coles-defends-sow-stall-record/6298428. Accessed 19 November 2017.

McCosker, L. (2016). *Pigs, Pasture and Profit*. Morrisville, NC: Lulu Publishing Services.

Miele, M. and Lever, J. (2013). Civilizing the Market for Welfare Friendly Products in Europe? The Techno-Ethics of the Welfare Quality® Assessment. *Geoforum*, 48, 63–72.

Parker, C. (2014). The Food Label as Governance Space: Free-Range Eggs and the Fallacy of Consumer Choice. *Recht Der Werkelijkheid*, 35, 101.

Parker, C. (2018). The Meat in the Sandwich: Welfare Labelling and the Governance of Meat Chicken Production in Australia. *Journal of Law and Society*, 45, 341–369.

Parker, C., Carey, R., De Costa, J. and Scrinis, G. (2017). The Hidden Hand of the Market: Who Regulates Animal Welfare Under a Labelling for Consumer Choice Approach? *Regulation and Governance*, 11, 368–387.

Parker, C. and De Costa, J. (2015). Misleading the Ethical Consumer: The Regulation of Free-Range Egg Labelling. *Melbourne University Law Review*, 39, 895–949.

Parker, C. and Scrinis, G. (2014). Out of the Cage and into the Barn: Supermarket Power Food System Governance and the Regulation of Free Range Eggs. *Griffith Law Review*, 23 (2), 318–347.

Phillips, C. J. C. and Petherick, J. C. (2015). The Ethics of a Co-Regulatory Model for Farm Animal Welfare Research. *Journal of Agricultural and Environmental Ethics*, 28, 127–142.

Productivity Commission. (2016). *Regulation of Australian Agriculture*. Canberra: Government Printer.

Richards, C., Lawrence, G. and Burch, D. (2011). Supermarkets and Agro-Industrial Foods: The Strategic Manufacture of Consumer Trust. *Food, Culture and Society*, 14, 29–47.

Robins, A. and Phillips, C. J. C. (2011). International Approaches to the Welfare of Meat Chickens. *World's Poultry Science Journal*, 67, 351–369.

Rodan, D. and Mummery, J. (2014). The 'Make It Possible' Multimedia Campaign: Generating a New 'Everyday' in Animal Welfare. *Media International Australia*, 153, 78–87.

Roff, R. J. (2007). Shopping for Change? Neoliberalizing Activism and the Limits to Eating Non-GMO. *Agriculture and Human Values*, 24, 511–522.

RSPCA. (2015). Why is Jamie Oliver so excited? *RSPCA*. Available at: https://rspcaapproved.org.au/blog/?p=1628. Accessed 22 August 2017.

RSPCA. (2016). *Approved Farming Scheme: Impact Report 2016*. Canberra: RSPCA.

Scrinis, G. and Parker, C. (2016). Front-of-Pack Food Labeling and the Politics of Nutritional Nudges. *Law & Policy*, 38, 234–249.

Sharman, K. (2009). Farm animals and welfare law: An unhappy union. In Sankoff, P. and White, S. (eds.), *Animal Law in Australasia: A New Dialogue*. Annandale: Federation Press.

Sharman, K. and Kossew, S. (2008). 'From Nest to Nugget — An Exposé of Australia's Chicken Factories', *Voiceless: The Fund for Animals*. Available at: http://www.voiceless.org.au/sites/default/files/from_nest_to_nugget_report_online_final.pdf. Accessed 19 November 2017.

Shaw, D. and Black, I. (2010). Market based Political Action: A Path to Sustainable Development? *Sustainable Development*, 18, 385–397.

Sherman, B., Sherman, O. and Sharman, K. (2005). *From Paddocks to Prisons: Pigs in New South Wales: Current Practices, Future Directions*. Paddington: Voiceless.

Standing Committee on Agriculture and Resource Management. (2000). *Synopsis Report on the Review of Hen Housing and Labelling of Eggs in Australia*. Canberra: Commonwealth of Australia.

Sydney Morning Herald. (2010). No more sow stalls says pork industry. *Sydney Morning Herald*, 18 November. Available at: www.smh.com.au/environment/animals/no-more-sow-stalls-says-pork-industry-20101118-17yon.html. Accessed 19 November 2017.

Treasury. (2015). *Free Range Egg Labelling: Consultation Paper*. Canberra: Commonwealth of Australia.

11 Confronting food waste in *MasterChef Australia*

Media production and recalcitrant matter

Luke van Ryn

Introduction

Perhaps the most readily made critique of *MasterChef Australia* is of its excessive production aesthetic: a constantly changing cornucopia of abundant produce for contestants to choose from (Tumarkin, 2012, pp. 10–11). Several questions arise when confronted with *MasterChef Australia*'s images of excess: where does all of this food go? How much of the produce we see on TV is actually used? How does all this food come to be there in the first place? By taking these questions seriously, this chapter relates the representation of food and wastage on *MasterChef Australia* to larger questions of sustainable production, ethical consumption and food security. Food television programmes make an immense contribution to the mainstreaming of food sustainability discourses around the world, and this chapter analyses how media production workers construct, understand and justify their representation and performance of food politics. Through attention to the design of challenges, the networks assembled to produce the programme, and the justificatory repertoires of informants, the chapter positions food waste as a key matter of concern for contemporary food politics.

Food waste is a pressing issue that has long been politicised in wealthy nations like the US, UK and Australia (Patel, 2007). In Australia, for example, between 5 and 10 billion Australian dollars of food is thrown out annually, a gross wastage not only of money but also of the water, energy, labour and—in the case of animal products—suffering that went into making that food (Edwards and Mercer, 2012, p. 188; Reynolds et al., 2014, p. 1254). Historically, food waste has been most prominent as a political issue during wartime. During the First World War, British government advertisements encouraged thriftiness in the home with slogans such as 'Food is ammunition. Don't waste it' (Evans, Campbell and Murcott, 2012, p. 13). During the Cold War, the US government emphasised maximising domestic food production, regardless of demand, through legislation such as the 1973 'Farm Bill', passed as the Agriculture and Consumer Protection Act (Nestle, 2007). Since then, waste activism has tended to focus on household and municipal waste production, rarely on waste further up the value chain (Evans, Campbell and Murcott, 2012, p. 19). That is, blame for food wastage frequently falls upon households (and the women who are overwhelmingly charged with food provisioning in those households), rather than, for example, on supermarkets' visual standards for fresh produce that cause a 'large-scale rejection of edible food on cosmetic grounds' (Devin and Richards, 2018, p. 1). The problem of food waste is an increasing focus for mainstream food politics, and it has been the subject of primetime television documentary programmes *Hugh's War on Waste* (BBC, 2016) and *War on Waste* (ABC, 2017), as well as promotional collaborations between major supermarkets and celebrity chefs including Jamie Oliver (Woolworths Group, 2017).

Beyond producer, retailer and consumer practices, media institutions play a powerful role in both the construction of discourses of food waste and the circulation of 'waste matter' (Hawkins and Potter, 2006) through their production routines. The case study of *MasterChef Australia* was selected for its prominence on the Australian and international food media landscape, its powerfully norma-tive attitude to what constitutes 'good food', and the strange infrequency with which it discusses food sustainability. The absence of such issues is notable because the programme emerged alongside a growing interest in food sustain-ability elsewhere in popular media, with media texts connecting 'good food' to a minimal environmental impact.[1] The scope of this chapter includes the on-screen representation of food waste in *MasterChef Australia*, media workers' justifica-tions of production practices in relation to food waste, and the structural impact of the design of on-screen challenges.

MasterChef Australia is a reality competition television programme in which contestants are eliminated over the course of each series until one person is named the winner. In the 2017 series, the prize was 250,000 Australian dollars in cash, and a regular column in *Delicious*, a glossy monthly cooking and lifestyle magazine. The *MasterChef* format began in 1990 in the UK. It was then licensed by FremantleMedia Australia from its creators Shine UK for a period of three years (2009–2011), after which the licence reverted to Shine Australia (now Endemol Shine Australia), which has produced the programme since 2012. Much of *MasterChef Australia*'s content remained consistent across the two production companies: Matt Preston, George Calombaris and Gary Mehigan have remained as judges, and the formal tropes of the programme have remained consistent across this shift in production.

MasterChef Australia has been a remarkable success for its producers, and for broadcaster Channel 10. Series finales regularly break ratings records, and the appearance of ingredients on the programme has caused supermarket sales spikes (Hargreaves, 2011; Hunter, 2010). Local versions of *MasterChef* have been produced in more than 50 countries, including Argentina, Brazil, Croatia, Finland, Germany, India, Malaysia, New Zealand, Poland, Russia, Saudi Arabia, Thailand, Ukraine and Vietnam. Many international broadcasters have also imported *Master-Chef Australia* for their audiences, with the programme airing in more than 30 countries, including Afghanistan, Belgium, Canada, Denmark, Greece, India, Pakistan, South Africa, and the UK. In addition, episodes of *MasterChef Australia* circulate through informal and 'pirate' distribution channels such as BitTorrent. Its participation in food discourses therefore extends beyond Australia to a global and active audience.

Through a series of interviews with media professionals who have worked on *MasterChef Australia*, I investigated the networks by which food travels into, through, and out of the production, and the means by which media workers justify their choices. Informants worked in a variety of roles, from a runner tasked with completing odd jobs, to senior producers in charge of designing challenges and presenting storylines. Through semi-structured interviews, I analysed the enrolment of sponsors and partners into the production, the values at work in the context of media production, and the ways that media workers justify their actions in 'critical moments' (Boltanski and Thévenot, 1999, p. 359)—occasions when the smooth workplace routines were ruptured and producers were called on to reflexively engage with their practices.

The analysis revealed that the producers of *MasterChef Australia* saw food waste as a significant political issue, and sought to mitigate waste in the programme's production. Unsurprisingly, however, concern for food sustainability was often subordinated to the expediencies of television production. Through interviews, waste (and efficiency) emerged as a critical issue not only for food sustainability but also for media production. The need to make use of limited ingredients is relevant to actors across the design, competition and reception of *MasterChef Australia*. It is therefore not the case, as we might imagine from the programme's silence on issues of sustainability, that the production workers behind *MasterChef Australia* are either ignorant of or opposed to those concerns. Rather they feel a strong tension in their professional lives to tell meaningful stories about food without compromising on making 'quality television'. Food waste provides a matter of concern to bring together the critical reflections of media workers and scholars.

While food waste may appear to be an inevitable outcome of the opulent aesthetic of the programme, it is in fact a product of programme design. It is in this area of design that critical media scholars might best address themselves to contemporary media production. Equally, while mainstream media programmes could do more to represent sustainability on-screen, it is important to note the many ways in which sustainability is enacted in the context of production. Therefore, the task of critical media research is to be attuned to how these representations come to be, so as to highlight the ways they might be different. Such an analysis extends beyond a diagnosis of a programme's (dis)engagement with issues of food sustainability to consider how sustainability might be presented and understood differently. This research offers to media scholars an understanding of the production of food discourses; to scholars of food sustainability it offers an analysis of the practices, routines and organisations by which global issues of food sustainability are constructed, exacerbated, and mitigated in an institutional context.

This chapter begins with a review of research related to food waste, sustainability and media before unpacking the conceptual and methodological tools deployed in the present study. It then explores food waste in the production of *MasterChef Australia*, through both representational (on-screen) and non-representational (off-screen) dimensions, and concludes by arguing for the relevance of production research for critical studies of contemporary food media.

The meanings of food sustainability

Food sustainability is part of a nexus of political approaches to the problem of nations' and individuals' ability to feed themselves. 'Food security' is a major paradigm of agricultural research and policy design, often with the goal of increasing food production as a solution to hunger and malnutrition in the developing world (Singer, 2011). We have also seen 'food control' in the form of government rationing, and 'food sovereignty' as a focus on farmers' self-determination through organisations such as La Vía Campesina (Lang and Barling, 2012, p. 322). Food sustainability as an approach to the politics of food emphasises the design of food systems as part of broader debates concerning sustainable development (Lang and Barling, 2012, p. 322). Often 'invisible', food waste is a growing domain for food sustainability research, policy and activism (Evans, Welch and Swaffield, 2017, p. 6). Research in the US, Australia and Europe suggests that most developed nations produce food far in excess of their domestic consumption requirements, and that a great deal of this food is wasted along the production, distribution and consumption chain (Patel, 2007). The energy, water and labour put into this wasted food would greatly serve both the populations of developing countries, as well as under-fed people in developed countries. Food waste therefore threatens food sustainability at the level of the household, the nation and the planet.

There have been ongoing critiques of the consumer-centric politics of ethical consumption (see Chapters 1, 3 and 10 in this collection), as well as questions of the wider affordability of ethical food products. free-range animal products, Fair Trade coffee and chocolate, and local produce all attract higher prices than their conventional counterparts (Littler, 2011, pp. 34–35). Yet it is possible to argue that this type of consumption becomes a lot more affordable when waste is reduced. Given that the average Australian family discards 14% of their weekly fresh produce, with a national value of between 5 and 10 billion Australian dollars (RaboDirect, 2017), one solution could be to buy more expensive, sustainable produce in smaller quantities. From this perspective, food wastage can potentially be seen as an impediment to more 'ethical' and sustainable food consumption choices in the home.

It is in relation to minimising suffering that the 'ethics' of ethical consumption often become most explicit. Fair Trade certification protects workers from exploitation, and thereby minimises the human suffering involved in consuming goods like coffee (Utting, 2009). The rise of free-range labelling for animal products acknowledges consumer concerns about animal welfare, even if the standards of that welfare can be opaque (Parker and de Costa, 2016, and Chapter 10 in this collection). Dietary restrictions like vegetarianism or veganism are aimed at reducing the suffering of animals (Singer and Morris, 2006, see also Chapters 7 and 9). Importantly, some of these consequentialist ethical approaches can also speak to waste as a larger political concern. In particular, the breeding of animals for human consumption involves a tremendously wasteful use of water and nutrients. The shift to a plant-based diet, then, whether for religious, health or ethical reasons, incorporates a strong argument for its efficacy as a means of addressing food sustainability. Waste sits in tension with these ethics, as refusing food (such as that which contains animal products) can be seen as wasteful, yet is necessary to signal a political standpoint in relation to the ethics of such products (Foer, 2009). Refusal, however, needs to be matched with the creation of alternatives (Fordyce and van Ryn, 2014). Whatever the definition of food sustainability, reducing food waste can be seen as one tool for developing more sustainable food systems.

Sustainability in food television

The majority of media studies research on food media has concerned itself with the textual representation of food. It has often been argued that the contemporary visibility of food media is both evidence and cause of an alienation from the matter of food itself (Adema, 2000; Hansen, 2008; Ketchum, 2005). Other studies have addressed the use of new media for the communication of food risks, as well as for building alternative food networks (Stevens et al., 2016). These analyses often present a clear picture of the rhetorics and logics that guide the construction of sustainability messages, but they are less able to describe how the contexts of media production inform those representations, and how those representations might be otherwise. The approach taken in this chapter therefore broadly follows a 'critical media industry studies' approach, based on 'a "helicopter" level view of industry operations, a focus on agency within industry operations, a Gramscian theory of power that does not lead to complete domination, and a view of society and culture grounded in saturation and articulation' (Havens, Lotz and Tinic, 2009, p. 246).

Historical analyses of food television—that is, a generic grouping of television programmes that take the production and consumption of food as a central theme—have noted a shift from cooking as labour to cooking as leisure (de Solier, 2005, p. 469). The first wave of cooking programmes coincided with the middle class relocation from cities to suburbs (Spigel, 1992). Cooking was seen as a responsibility, a core task, and a source of stress, which television programmes sought to mitigate by teaching viewers techniques for food preparation. New labour-saving devices like pressure-cookers and refrigerators were rallied to maximise the efficiency of the modern kitchen (Cromley, 2010), although these threatened the traditional knowledge valued by many home cooks (de Certeau, Giard and Mayol, 1998). Television in this 'cookery-educative' mode (Strange, 1998) is concerned with teaching the viewer how to cook. This lost mode of food television is mourned by many commentators, including Toby Miller (2007, p. 143):

> In the era of 'open' TV, food television's address of the consumer has displaced any meaningful address of the citizen, thanks to deregulatory policies that facilitate media businesses targeting specific cultures. The dominant interpellation is about learning to govern the self through orderly preparation, style, and pleasure—the transformation of potential drudgery into a special event, and the incorporation of difference into a treat rather than a threat.

Food sustainability issues are sometimes taken up in the 'lifestyle television' genre, especially in combination with celebrations of local and seasonal food. Such programmes tend to be produced by smaller companies, distributed through less mainstream channels, and addressed to smaller audiences. Programmes such as the *River Cottage* series (Channel 4, 1999–2012) encourage viewers to take pleasure in eating seasonally, locally, and sustainably, blending hedonism with ethical consumption (see Thomas, 2008). Other programmes, such as the campaigning culinary documentaries *Jamie's School Dinners* (Channel 4, 2005) and *Hugh's Chicken Run* (Channel 4, 2008), seek to engage citizens with food politics—taking issue with food provision in public schools and the conditions of intensive chicken production respectively—to improve the sustainability of British foodways through consumer choice and pressure on governments. While often criticised for contributing to a neoliberal 'responsibilization' of consumers (rather than of policy-makers or food producers), television programmes like these have had a demonstrated impact on purchasing habits, production techniques and policy settings (Bell, Hollows and Jones, 2017; Hickman, 2008). However, the contribution of non-activist food programmes to discourses of food sustainability has rarely been studied. As with campaigning documentaries like *Hugh's Chicken Run*, the representation of ingredients on *MasterChef Australia* has had a notable effect on purchasing patterns in Australian supermarkets (Hargreaves, 2011; Hendy, 2010; Hunter, 2010) with compounded effects on the problem of food waste when those purchased ingredients go unused. Additionally, the practices of food media production also have environmental impacts through the type and volume of food procured for the production, the design of competitions, and the ways in which surplus food is managed.

This interest in the representation of sustainability (and the sustainability of representation) has only rarely been triangulated through research into the contexts of media reception or production. Studies of television as a medium for food sustainability have found that viewers may cook and eat better by watching explicitly educational food programmes (Clifford et al., 2009; De Backer and Hudders, 2016, p. 500). From a health communication perspective, Phillipov (2012) argues pragmatically that the social benefits of people cooking from scratch may outweigh the problematic quantities of butter and salt included in the recipes of *MasterChef Australia*.

The study of media production (Caldwell, 2008; Havens and Lotz, 2012; Hesmondhalgh and Baker, 2008; Mayer, 2011) has only infrequently addressed food media. For example, a study of lifestyle media in Asia found production workers using food television to cultivate appreciation for regional differences among Indians, and, in China, to link Buddhist dietary practices to environmental sustainability (Lewis, Martin and Sun, 2016, pp. 100, 186). Phillipov (2016) interviewed artisanal food and beverage producers who had been featured on the Australian television documentary programme *Gourmet Farmer* (SBS, 2014–present). Her study highlighted a frequent disjuncture between food producers' expectations and the demands of media production, concluding that: 'the needs of the television industry [...] will always be prioritised in television production practices' (Phillipov, 2016, p. 599). In a similar fashion, this chapter draws out tensions between the demands of television production and food sustainability—especially food waste, to which we now turn.

Conceptualising waste and assembling critique

This chapter conceptualises the intersection between food sustainability and media production in a framework developed from the 'pragmatic sociology of critique' (Boltanski, 2011). Briefly, this sociological approach concerns itself with the production of normative discourses and critical reflection in everyday life. The best-known product of this research is an exhaustive analysis of the changing 'spirit of capitalism': the ethical discourse that underpins contemporary capitalist enterprise (Boltanski and Chiapello, 2005). Capitalism needs an ethical component because it is theoretically insatiable, in contrast with people, who are satiable and therefore require some sort of justification for working and consuming more than is strictly necessary (Boltanski and Chiapello, 2005, pp. 7–8). Examples of these ethical drives include the ideas that work is a good in itself (cf. Weber, 2001, p. 26) and 'ethical consumerism' (Devinney, Auger and Eckhardt, 2010). Researchers associated with this approach have also used it to compare environmentalist discourses in Europe and the US, finding an emphasis on 'patrimony' in the former and 'wilderness' in the latter (Thévenot, Moody and Lafaye, 2000, p. 265). This approach was chosen here for its ability to treat the concerns of environmental sustainability and media production 'symmetrically' (Callon, 1986)—that is, in the same register, whether discussing the technical or the social. It is hoped that this will allow the chapter's reflections to be understood by the subjects of that critique—in this case, media production workers—who are best placed to bring about changes.

At the heart of the pragmatic sociology of critique is an attempt to grasp the rhetorical tools we draw on in everyday life to justify our actions (Boltanski and Thévenot, 2006). Luc Boltanski and Laurent Thévenot point to six common principles by which actors justify themselves. These are the *inspired, domestic, civic, fame, market* and *industrial* 'polities', or 'orders of worth' (Boltanski and Thévenot, 2006, pp. 83–123). The *inspired polity* is the world of saints, artists, and the insane, who are great when they are 'odd, wonderful and emotional'. The important techniques in this polity are 'to dream, to imagine, to rebel' (Boltanski and Thévenot, 1999, p. 370). The *domestic* polity emphasises kinship and tradition. Relevant actors are 'chiefs, bosses, or even relatives', who are valued when they are 'distinguished, straightforward, faithful' (Boltanski and Thévenot, 1999, p. 370). The polity of *renown* (or *fame*) contains a model of justice based on reputation. The chief actors in this polity are 'stars, opinion leaders, journalists', who are worthy when 'famous, recognised, successful, convincing'. The *market* polity is a model of justice based on competition between actors, who are deemed worthy when they have become wealthy. The *industrial* polity, in turn, values 'experts', and its actors are valued when they are 'efficient, productive, operational' (Boltanski and Thévenot, 1999, p. 373). To this model Boltanski and Chiapello (2005, p. 109) added the 'projective' or 'network' polity, which celebrates activity, mobility and connection.

The different polities or 'worlds' of value are all drawn on in different ways in the production and construction of *MasterChef Australia*: contestants' emotional performances in confessional segments are valued in terms of 'inspiration'; 'domestic' values are drawn on when contestants cook food that celebrates their family or cultural heritage; the inclusion of celebrities in the programme associates the production with the values of 'fame'. The values of the 'market' polity are found in the very structure of the reality competition, as contestants vie for success at others' expense; 'industrial' values drive the programme's emulation of standardisation and apprenticeship; and it is a kind of 'network' morality that charges contestants to make the most of the opportunity for exposure and contacts that the programme represents. 'Civic' values are mostly seen when producers argue for the programme's educational merit, but these are rarely celebrated on-screen. In the larger project of which this chapter forms a part, these values are used as an interpretative guide for understanding the kinds of ethical principles that media production workers deploy when making *MasterChef Australia*, the broader production ecology's shaping of the programme's sustainability outcomes, and the avenues by which the programme's production may be reformed in the direction of sustainability.

The 'pragmatic sociology of critique' framework is useful for answering three inter-related questions pertinent to the subject of food waste: how do media production workers justify the decisions they make in their work? How do the various 'worlds' vary in strength from moment to moment? And how can the relatively weak forms of justification (such as environmental sustainability) be made stronger? (cf. Giulianotti and Langseth, 2016, p. 134).

Researching media production

This chapter is based on semi-structured interviews with media production workers who worked on *MasterChef Australia*. Many production workers followed the production to Melbourne from Sydney when the production licence reverted from FremantleMedia Australia to Shine Australia (now Endemol Shine Australia) in Series 4, highlighting the flexibility and mobility often required of media production workers (Paterson, 2012). Semi-structured 'expert' interviews (Meuser and Nagel, 2009; Pfadenhauer, 2009; Plesner, 2009) were chosen to allow the respondents to highlight the areas of investigation that were the most relevant to their own working situation. Recruitment proceeded via the snowball method, mimicking the common media industry practice of hiring through informal networks rather than through institutional hierarchies (Paterson, 2012). This 'word of mouth' recruitment method was a necessary way of circumventing the production companies' lack of interest in the research, as well as its control of production discourses through non-disclosure agreements. All interviews here are cited pseudonymously according to the production role of the respondent for two reasons: firstly, these titles give readers some sense of the position that each respondent occupies in the production; secondly, the use of pseudonyms protects the anonymity of respondents.

Interpretation in the expert interview paradigm initially sticks closely to the terms used by respondents. In this regard, the present study follows the example of previous studies of media professionals (Deuze, 2008; Paterson, 2012). Important to the 'pragmatic sociology of critique' paradigm is an understanding of actors' 'critical capacity': their ability to reflect upon their experience and produce critiques of situations that they encounter (Boltanski and Thévenot, 1999). Initial analysis of the interview responses sought to understand the phenomena or 'matters of concern' (Latour, 2004) most relevant to the respondents. These interviews were then coded cumulatively and integratively in order to identify themes that were present within and between interviews. The analysis shuttled back and forth between the interview transcripts and the thematic codings, repeatedly testing each against the other in the manner of a hermeneutic circle.

Waste on screen: in search of surplus

A rare example of the on-screen depiction of food waste in *MasterChef Australia* occurred in Episode 22 of Series 4 (which aired on 30 May 2012). It featured a challenge that specifically focused on food waste. While it is usual practice for major production sponsors to be featured in their own 'big event' challenge throughout the course of a series—such as a challenge in which contestants pitch airline meals to Qantas CEO Alan Joyce—this was the first time in the series' history that a food rescue organisation was featured. Moreover, it was the first time that issues of food waste were editorialised on the programme. With production partner OzHarvest, the producers devised a challenge for contestants to 'rescue' surplus food from commercial kitchens, and produce a meal for 25 of 'Sydney's food elites'. The episode emulated the practices of OzHarvest, which deploys vans around major Australian cities to retrieve surplus produce from restaurants and deliver it to charities and other organisations that feed those in need. The episode drew attention to food waste in restaurants, and celebrated contestants' ingenuity in working with ingredients that are on hand. Yet this challenge also demonstrates a tension between food ethics and the demands of television production, and so is a critical moment in the production of *MasterChef Australia* when issues of sustainability could be treated differently.

Matt Preston laid out the challenge's aim for the contestants (and viewers) in this way:

> Every year, 7.5 million tonnes of usable food ends up in landfill. 1.5 million Australians are believed to not have enough food to eat to end up with a proper diet. Your job is to knock up an entrée, main and dessert that will get our guests to open up their wallets and donate to OzHarvest, so that they can continue their important work. The team that raises the most, wins.

The contestants were divided into two teams and provided with cars and a list of restaurants with surplus produce to donate. Like many of the time-bound challenges seen in the series, the challenge was presented as a race, with frequent cross-cutting between footage of the teams, and emphasis on the contestants hurrying to gather the most and best produce. This is a test of 'making do' (de Certeau, Giard and Mayol, 1998)—of invention and efficiency, but also of navigation, running, negotiating with restaurant staff and so on.

Preston's claim to the guest judges that 'everything that you are going to eat today would have ended up in landfill if it wasn't for OzHarvest' is contradicted by the donation of several ingredients which were unlikely to be wasted: Red Team was given a side of salmon ('Don't tell anyone!', joked the chef at Sydney's Four Seasons), while the Blue Team received a whole barramundi from the Intercontinental. Although the chefs, programme sponsors and guests laudably embraced the spirit of *noblesse oblige*, the challenge's focus on converting surplus food into monetary value distorts its ethical frame. The 25 guest judges together donated 9,000 Australian dollars to the Blue Team, and 3,000 Australian dollars to the Red Team, suggesting a clear preference for the dishes the Blue Team produced. This collection of 12,000 Australian dollars for OzHarvest was later dwarfed by the Commonwealth Bank's 'Women in Focus Giving Community' donating 20,000 Australian dollars in appreciation of the Blue Team's fish pie. While the challenge takes seriously the virtue of working hard to mitigate food waste, the victory was decided not according to food recovery (and thrifty conservation of ingredients) but by the affective power of food origins (even as waste) to inspire the whimsical generosity of the elite. The collective expertise of the critics, chefs and restaurateurs was outweighed by a single donor with a large budget. In the end, the construction of food recovery as an important practice in contemporary hospitality industries (including the production context of *MasterChef Australia*) is weakened by a sense of food appearing spectacularly for contestants without any material history, labour, or responsibility for its use.

The on-screen representation of uncertainty and scarcity is further undercut by production workers' accounts of the design of the challenge. In order to ensure that the teams would actually be able to feed the guests with the produce they collected, the producers called ahead to restaurants to find out what surplus they would have available, and rescheduled the filming of the episode to a date when there would be more 'leftovers'. This 'planned wastage' exists throughout the mainstream food system, and is a prime target for action on sustainability. Examples of this wastage include preferences for overstocking rather than understocking in retail operations, the rejection of produce on the basis of its appearance, and the growth in portion sizes over the past 20 years (Thyberg and Tonjes, 2016, p. 118).

This episode takes waste as its key concern, yet does not relate waste to the everyday production routines of the programme. While many elements of the programme concern efficiency, this test introduces the metric of waste, a criterion that the rest of the programme does not acknowledge. The episode addresses a 'blind spot' of waste, yet its treatment of that blind spot is very narrow, because the *representation* of the show's waste minimisation would not be an efficient use of screen time and would run contrary to the show's 'sexy, aspirational' design brief (interview with Art Director, 24 February 2014). As has been noted in a different context (Phillipov, 2016), the demands of television production all too often take precedence over the values specific to the production and consumption of food.

Waste off-screen: from abundance to recovery

While food waste is very infrequently represented on-screen, surplus produce has been a target of off-screen production practices from the programme's outset. In the first series of *MasterChef Australia*, the surplus produce that was not consumed in a day's or week's filming was distributed among production staff, who relished the opportunity to emulate at home the achievements of the contestants. From the beginning of the second series, the production partnered with OzHarvest to collect and distribute surplus produce to food charities. At that point, most informants saw the problem of food waste as solved. Yet their frequent recourse in interviews to the creation of food waste as 'the nature of the beast' (interview with Production Coordinator, 5 March 2014) suggests that there is work still to be done in helping media production workers imagine more sustainable alternatives.

Initially, food waste appeared to the production staff to be a surplus or bonus, and was treated accordingly. Informants spoke fondly of 'Market Days' on set, when they were able to take home leftover produce to cook for themselves. Waste is thus treated as a kind of seasonal abundance—not unlike harvest festivals—and production staff looked forward to such bonuses:

> All the stuff that was going out of date, they'd just lay it all out in bread trays... you almost had to sweet-talk the food people: 'When's the market day coming up?'
>
> (Interview with Runner, 6 February 2014)

> You've just finished a challenge where they've all been cooking with rhubarb and there's rhubarb left over, so you'd go home and cook the favourite rhubarb dish that you'd tasted... That was the lovely thing about it: the cameraman, everybody, the next day we'd say, 'Wow, I cooked this and it really worked!' It's part of that team-building thing. But that sort of stopped a little while in. I don't know why, I think someone had an objection to it.
>
> (Interview with Senior Producer, 27 March 2014)

> ... all the food that wasn't used in the challenges was then put out, and the crew just came and got it. You'd go home with a whole duck, or these swimmer crabs, or whatever, but after the first series it started going to OzHarvest instead, which is obviously a much, much better and more worthy destination than people who are getting paid quite well to work (laughing) and to feed themselves just fine.
>
> (Interview with Story Producer, 17 February 2014)

For the Senior Producer, the surplus produce was an occasion to challenge themselves to use new ingredients, learn new techniques, and develop their skills alongside the contestants. They argued that this opportunity brought the team together and raised morale among the workers, a common compromise between 'industrial' and 'inspirational' values (Boltanski and Chiapello, 2005, p. 459). Yet as the Story Producer noted, there are better uses for this surplus food than as perks for the crew. To this end, OzHarvest was brought on board as a partner in the production. The Chef Coordinator described the motivation for this transition:

> To look good, we needed a vast amount of produce, and obviously more than enough for the contestants to cook, make mistakes, cook, make mistakes, that sort of thing. Anything that was left over that wasn't touched, so anything that was in the pantry, for example, that the contestants didn't take, is 100% given to OzHarvest. I think we had a pantry twice a week, so they would come and collect twice a week. Occasionally, staff might be able to take something home if they really wanted to, but really it was all about giving it back to the community that needed it the most. And that was a huge part of it. Everybody that worked on that show really supported that, if that makes sense, so it was a great thing for us. Not that we take credit for it, it was something the producers decided to do. And it's something that Gary and George and Matt [the show's judges] were particularly passionate about.
> (Interview with Chef Coordinator, 18 February 2014)

This passion is described by the Production Coordinator in terms of a business-like sense of efficiency on the part of the judges, who own and operate restaurants, which contestants may in turn carry with them in future food business ventures:

> And I think that for the boys [judges George Calombaris and Gary Mehigan], that comes down to a sense of money. They own restaurants, they know how expensive it is to do it; you don't make profits running high-end restaurants [wastefully]. So it was good for the talent [the contestants on the show] to have that drilled into them. Hopefully.
> (Interview with Production Coordinator, 5 March 2014)

This transition from an informal method of dealing with waste—by distributing it among the production staff—to a centralised solution dictated by the executive producers, frustrated some staff. In the main, though, all of my informants spoke very highly of OzHarvest's involvement in the production:

> [Then] we had OzHarvest come in and take all of the fresh produce that wouldn't be used, that couldn't be used. Some of it was used for testing the contestants' recipes for the website, some of it was used to go to the house, so that the contestants could use it on weekends and at night, to practise. And the remainder went to OzHarvest. Then that relationship just developed

and they would come and pick up the food after every pantry challenge, or when we had a lot left over.

(Interview with Senior Food Producer, 5 May 2014)

In this way, production workers drew on civic justifications—such as putting the needs of the many over the needs of the few (Boltanski and Thévenot, 2006, p. 185)—for the partnership with OzHarvest. Informants often spoke of OzHarvest taking 'everything', so that 'very little' food was discarded each day:

They came up with quite good systems to move the food on. I'd say there wasn't a lot of food wasted; there wasn't a lot of stuff that was actually physically chucked out.

(Interview with Runner, 6 February 2014)

Yet this more or less seamless collection of surplus produce might prevent media production workers from seeing just how much food is left over, and how procurement might be arranged differently.

When discussing the topic of food waste, production workers focused on surplus ingredients: 'untouched' fruit, vegetables, meat and dry goods that remained unused after the day's filming. As respondents noted, OzHarvest and other food rescue groups are very capable of preventing the wasting of these ingredients. More difficult to recuperate, however, is the broader kind of wastage that has been 'touched': ingredients that are consumed by producers and contestants in the practising and testing of recipes—the repeated 'making mistakes' mentioned by the Guest Chef Coordinator above. Such food waste may be composted, a proven method of improving food sustainability (Priefer, Jörissen and Bräutigam, 2016; Thyberg and Tonjes, 2016), but is very frequently sent to landfill. There is also the food waste that is created in the design of the programme and its challenges: the selection of particular parts of animals or vegetables for recipes, the constant displays of abundance, and the volumes of food sacrificed in the name of making 'good food' and 'good television'.

A rare reflection on the design of challenges reinforced the production workers' responsibility for determining the rules within which food is wasted:

There was a lot of wastage, and accusations of wastage, like that whole idea that to make the perfect chip[2] you'd have to cut this oblong thing out of a whole potato, where does the rest of it go? So I'd love to say that accusations of wastage were unfounded, but especially in the early parts of the show, absolutely there was [wastage]. Yeah, and once we all got our heads around it, and thought 'Hang on a minute, it doesn't actually have to be like this'. And then, yeah, it went to OzHarvest every day, pretty much when we were done.

(Interview with Story Producer, 17 February 2014)

While the Story Producer here acknowledges that food waste is something that the producers created in the design of challenges, they return to OzHarvest as the solution to this problem, which is then presented as requiring no further thought. Frequently, though, it is the very *accumulation* of waste that leads to changes being made in the direction of sustainability (Hawkins and Potter, 2006). In Haraway's terms, food wastage behind the scenes may cause a 'nourishing indigestion' (2008, p. 300) that might prompt better ways of living together. Focusing on OzHarvest as the 'solution' to the problem of food waste as 'output' had the effect of inoculating the production from considering the ways that waste might be created as 'intake'.

Ultimately, informants insisted, food waste was an inevitable 'casualty' of the production (interview with Production Coordinator, 5 March 2014). Despite the production changing its methods of dealing with surplus food across the series, production staff retained a conception of food waste as a necessary by-product of the television they were making, rather than something that was created as part of the design of challenges (and hence contingent upon decisions made by producers). In interviews, respondents recounted their creation *de novo* of challenge formats for a programme that was 'new to everyone' (interview with Senior Food Producer, 5 May 2014). Yet food waste was repeatedly characterised as inherent to the production format and largely outside production workers' control. Therefore, while both the broadcast text and the production context were occasionally capable of tackling food waste as a problem, treating food waste as an *occasion* (for bonuses to staff or a collection opportunity for OzHarvest off-screen, or as a special episode on-screen) prevented a broader consideration of the waste that was created in the design of the programme itself.

Conclusion: food waste as an occasional concern

This chapter has viewed critical moments in the representation and production of food waste on *MasterChef Australia*. This analysis presents not only an understanding of one of the key political problems of the programme, but also a sense of where changes might be made to produce more sustainable outcomes. As we have seen, production staff are sensitive to issues of food waste, even if their conception of the problems and solutions associated with it differ from those of scholars, viewers and activists. Treating the on-screen representation of food waste only on rare occasions (such as a special episode focused on OzHarvest), rather than as a more consistent theme throughout the programme risks those concerns being forgotten the moments the credits roll. Additionally, the mitigation of food waste through a partnership with OzHarvest, while laudable, may prevent production staff from questioning the range of ways in which waste is created—and therefore might be avoided—'upstream' in the design of the show's challenges.

MasterChef Australia is often criticised for its emphasis on spectacle, drama and conspicuous consumption (Niell, 2016; Seale, 2012). These elements have been seen as detracting from a focus on food and cooking. Yet the programme does make a substantial contribution to Australia's food discourse, and to the meanings associated with 'good' food. It therefore has the potential to play a role in how the problem of food waste is understood and, perhaps, mitigated. By taking seriously the ethical values of the programme's production staff, I have critiqued the programme in a way that might be recognisable to the professionals who make it, and who are therefore in a position to change it. At a more abstract and reflexive level, this chapter might also demonstrate a way forward for media research that concerns itself with sustainability. While the representation of sustainability has been the topic for a great deal of important work in the discipline, we have a great deal more to learn about the way that these representations come to be. Conducting research among media production workers is a difficult but nonetheless valuable way of understanding the values that drive the creation of the media that we study, as well as the 'critical moments' when we might apply pressure for positive change.

Notes

1 Examples include the *River Cottage* series in its British (Channel 4, 1999–2012) and Australian versions (Keo Films, 2013–16). See Lewis (2012) for a discussion of the 'greening' of lifestyle television.
2 In episode 2 of Series 3 (broadcast 2 May 2011), contestants were challenged to produce a batch of potato chips from a sack of potatoes. They were ranked by speed and on the degree to which their chips were of a similar size and shape. As the Story Producer alludes to, efficiency and waste mitigation were not considered relevant for this challenge.

References

Adema, P. (2000). Vicarious Consumption: Food, Television and the Ambiguity of Modernity. *Journal of American and Comparative Cultures*, 23 (3), 113–123. doi: 10.1111/ j.1537-4726.2000.2303_113.x.
Bell, D., Hollows, J. and Jones, S. (2017). Campaigning Culinary Documentaries and the Responsibilization of Food Crises. *Geoforum*, 84, 179–187. doi: 10.1016/j. geoforum.2015.03.014.
Boltanski, L. (2011). *On Critique: A Sociology of Emancipation*. Translated by G. Elliott. Cambridge: Polity.
Boltanski, L. and Chiapello, E. (2005). *The New Spirit of Capitalism*. Translated by G. Elliott. London: Verso.
Boltanski, L. and Thévenot, L. (1999). The Sociology of Critical Capacity. *European Journal of Social Theory*, 2 (3), 359–377. doi: 10.1177/136843199002003010.
Boltanski, L. and Thévenot, L. (2006). *On Justification: Economies of Worth*. Translated by C. Porter. Princeton: Princeton University Press.
Caldwell, J. T. (2008). *Production Culture: Industrial Reflexivity and Critical Practice in Film and Television*. Durham, NC: Duke University Press.
Callon, M. (1986). Some Elements of a Sociology of Translation: Domestication of the Scallops and the Fisherman of St Brieuc Bay. In Law, J. (eds.), *Power, Action and Belief: A New Sociology of Knowledge?* (pp. 196–223). London: Routledge.
Clifford, D., Anderson, J., Auld, G. and Champ, J. (2009). Good Grubbin': Impact of a TV Cooking Show for College Students Living off Campus. *Journal of Nutrition Education and Behaviour*, 41 (3), 194–200. doi: 10.1016/j.jneb.2008.01.006.
Cromley, E. C. (2010). *The Food Axis: Cooking, Eating, and the Architecture of American Houses*. Charlottesville: University of Virginia Press.
De Backer, C. J. S. and Hudders, L. (2016). Look Who's Cooking. Investigating the Relationship between Watching Educational and Edutainment TV Cooking Shows, Eating Habits and

Everyday Cooking Practices among Men and Women in Belgium. *Appetite*, 96: 494–501. doi: 10.1016/j.appet.2015.10.016.

de Certeau, M., Giard, L. and Mayol, P. (1998). The Practice of Everyday Life. Translated by T. J. Tomasik, *Vol. 2*: *Living and Cooking*. Minneapolis: University of Minnesota Press.

de Solier, I. (2005). TV Dinners: Culinary Television, Education and Distinction. *Continuum Journal of Media and Cultural Studies*, 19 (4), 465–481. doi: 10.1080/10304310500322727.

Deuze, M. (2008). *Media Work*. London: Polity.

Devin, B. and Richards, C. (2018). Food Waste, Power, and Corporate Social Responsibility in the Australian Food Supply Chain. *Journal of Business Ethics*, 150, 199–210. doi: 10.1007/s10551-016-3181-z.

Devinney, T. M., Auger, P. and Eckhardt, G. M. (eds.). (2010). *The Myth of the Ethical Consumer*. Cambridge: Cambridge University Press.

Edwards, F. and Mercer, D. (2012). Food Waste in Australia: The Freegan Response. *The Sociological Review*, 60 (2), 174–191. doi: 10.1111/1467-954X.12044.

Evans, D., Campbell, H. and Murcott, A. (2012). A Brief Pre-History of Food Waste and the Social Sciences. *The Sociological Review*, 60 (2_suppl), 5–26. doi: 10.1111/1467-954X.12035.

Evans, D., Welch, D. and Swaffield, J. (2017). Constructing and Mobilizing 'The Consumer': Responsibility, Consumption and the Politics of Sustainability. *Environment and Planning A*, 49 (6), 1396–1412. doi: 10.1177/0308518X17694030.

Foer, J. S. (2009). *Eating Animals*. New York: Little, Brown.

Fordyce, R. and van Ryn, L. (2014). Ethical Commodities as Exodus and Refusal. *Ephemera*, 14 (1), 35–55.

Giulianotti, R. and Langseth, T. (2016). Justifying the Civic Interest in Sport: Boltanski and Thévenot, the Six Worlds of Justification, and Hosting the Olympic Games. *European Journal for Sport and Society*, 13 (2), 133–153. doi: 10.1080/16138171.2016.1183930.

Hansen, S. (2008). Society of the Appetite: Celebrity Chefs Deliver Consumers. *Food, Culture and Society*, 11 (1), 49–67. doi: 10.2752/155280108X276050.

Haraway, D. J. (2008). *When Species Meet*. Minneapolis: University of Minnesota Press.

Hargreaves, W. (2011). MasterChef Linked to Food Sales Rise. *Sunday Herald Sun*, July 16. Available at: www.heraldsun.com.au/entertainment/masterchef-linked-to-food-sales-rise/news-story/5f761aa15cf8b55c4d8c76497a8036c4. Accessed 25 November 2017.

Havens, T. and Lotz, A. D. (2012). *Understanding Media Industries*. Oxford: Oxford University Press.

Havens, T., Lotz, A. D. and Tinic, S. (2009). Critical Media Industry Studies: A Research Approach. *Communication, Culture & Critique*, 2 (2), 234–253. doi: 10.1111/j.1753-9137.2009.01037.x.

Hawkins, G. and Potter, E. (2006). Waste Matter: Potatoes, Thing-Power and Bio-Sociality. *Cultural Studies Review*, 12 (1), 104–115. doi: 10.5130/csr.v12i1.3417.

Hendy, N. (2010). MasterChef Helps Coles' Sales Sizzle. *The Australian*, July 23. Available at: www.theaustralian.com.au/business/business-spectator/masterchef-helps-coles-sales-sizzle/news-story/4a4d72d77008941aaec668a1f2aab650. Accessed 25 November 2017.

Hesmondhalgh, D. and Baker, S. (2008). Creative Work and Emotional Labour in the Television Industry. *Theory, Culture & Society*, 25 (7–8), 97–118. doi: 10.1177/0263276408097798.

Hickman, M. (2008). The Campaign that Changed the Eating Habits of a Nation. *The Independent*, 28 February. Available at: www.independent.co.uk/life-style/food-and-drink/news/the-campaign-that-changed-the-eating-habits-of-a-nation-788557.html. Accessed 7 September 2018.

Hunter, T. (2010). The MasterChef Effect. *The Sydney Morning Herald.* Available at: www. smh.com.au/entertainment/tv-and-radio/the-masterchef-effect-20100722-10lsg.html. Accessed 26 November 2017.

Ketchum, C. (2005). The Essence of Cooking Shows: How the Food Network Constructs Consumer Fantasies. *Journal of Communication Inquiry,* 29 (3), 217–234. doi: 10.1177/ 0196859905275972.

Lang, T. and Barling, D. (2012). Food Security and Food Sustainability: Reformulating the Debate. *The Geographical Journal,* 178 (4), 313–326. doi: 10.1111/j.1475-4959.2012.00480.x.

Latour, B. (2004). Why Has Critique Run Out of Steam? From Matters of Fact to Matters of Concern. *Critical Inquiry,* 30 (2), 225–248. doi: 10.1086/421123.

Lewis, T. (2012). 'There Grows the Neighbourhood': Green Citizenship, Creativity and Life Politics on TV. *International Journal of Cultural Studies,* 15 (3), 315–326. doi: 10.1177/ 1367877911433753.

Lewis, T., Martin, F. and Sun, W. (2016). *Telemodernities: Television and Transforming Lives in Asia.* Durham, NC: Duke University Press.

Littler, J. (2011). What's Wrong with Ethical Consumption? In Lewis, T. and Potter, E. (eds.), *Ethical Consumption: A Critical Introduction* (pp. 27–39). New York: Routledge.

Mayer, V. (2011). *Below the Line: Producers and Production Studies in the New Television Economy.* Durham, NC: Duke University Press.

Meuser, M. and Nagel, U. (2009). The Expert Interview and Changes in Knowledge Production. In Bogner, A., Littig, B. and Menz, W. (eds.), *Interviewing Experts* (pp. 17–42). New York: Palgrave Macmillan.

Miller, T. (2007). *Cultural Citizenship: Cosmopolitanism, Consumerism and Television in a Neoliberal Age.* Philadelphia: Temple University Press.

Nestle, M. (2007). *Food Politics: How the Food Industry Influences Nutrition and Health.* Berkeley: University of California Press.

Niell, A. (2016). Serving Suggestion: *MasterChef*'s Narrow View of Food Culture. *Kill Your Darlings,* July 13.

Parker, C. and de Costa, J. (2016). Misleading the Ethical Consumer: The Regulation of Free-Range Egg Labelling. *Melbourne University Law Review,* 39, 895–949.

Patel, R. (2007). *Stuffed and Starved: Markets, Power and the Hidden Battle for the World's Food System.* London: Portobello.

Paterson, R. (2012). Working as a Freelancer in UK Television. In Dawson, A. and Holmes, S. P. (eds.), *Working in the Global Film and Television Industries* (pp. 91–108). London: Bloomsbury.

Pfadenhauer, M. (2009). At Eye Level: The Expert Interview—A Talk between Expert and Quasi-Expert. In Bogner, A., Littig, B. and Menz, W. (eds.), *Interviewing Experts* (pp. 81–97). New York: Palgrave Macmillan.

Phillipov, M. (2012). Communicating Health Risks via the Media: What Can We Learn from *MasterChef Australia? Australasian Medical Journal,* 5 (11), 593–597. Available at: http://dx.doi.org/10.4066%2FAMJ.2012.1460. Accessed 1 September 2017. doi: 10.4066/AMJ.2012.1460.

Phillipov, M. (2016). Using Media to Promote Artisan Food and Beverages: Insights from the Television Industry. *British Food Journal,* 118 (3), 588–602. doi: 10.1108/BFJ-06-2015-0219.

Plesner, U. (2009). *Disassembling the Mass Mediation of Research*. PhD. Department of Communication, Business and Information Technologies, University of Roskilde, Denmark.

Priefer, C., Jörissen, J. and Bräutigam, K-R. (2016). Food Waste Prevention in Europe—A Cause-Driven Approach to Identify the Most Relevant Leverage Points for Action. *Resources, Conservation and Recycling*, 109 (Supplement C), 155–165. doi: 10.1016/j. resconrec.2016.03.004.

RaboDirect. (2017). Food and Farming Report. *RaboDirect*. Available at: www.rabodirect. com.au/blog/2017/10/16/11/50/financial-health-barometer-food-farming-report/. Accessed 17 October 2018.

Reynolds, C. J., Mavrakis, V., Sandra Davison, S. B., Høj, E. V., Sharp, A., Thompson, K., Ward, P., Coveney, J., Piantadosi, J., Boland, J. and Dawson, D. (2014). Estimating Informal Household Food Waste in Developed Countries: The Case of Australia. *Waste Management & Research*, 32 (12), 1254–1258. doi: 10.1177/0734242X14549797.

Seale, K. (2012). *MasterChef*'s Amateur Makeovers. *Media International Australia*, 1 (143), 28–35. doi: 10.1177/1329878X1214300105.

Singer, P. and Morris, J. (2006). *The Ethics of What We Eat*. Melbourne: Text Publishing.

Singer, R. (2011). The Corporate Colonization of Communication about Global Hunger: Development, Biotechnology and Discursive Closure in the Monsanto Pledge. In Cramer, J. M., Greene, C. P. and Walters, L. M. (eds.), *Food as Communication, Communication as Food*. New York: Peter Lang.

Spigel, L. (1992). *Make Room for TV: Television and the Family Ideal in Postwar America*. Chicago: University of Chicago Press.

Stevens, T. M., Aarts, N., Termeer, C. J. A. M., and Dewulf, A. (2016). Social Media as a New Playing Field for the Governance of Agro-Food Sustainability. *Current Opinion in Environmental Sustainability*, 18, 99–106. doi: 10.1016/j.cosust.2015.11.010.

Strange, N. (1998). Perform, Educate, Entertain: Ingredients of the Cookery Programme Genre. In Geraghty, C. and Lusted, D. (eds.), *The Television Studies Book* (pp. 301–312). London: Arnold.

Thévenot, L., Moody, M. and Lafaye, C. (2000). Forms of Valuing Nature: Arguments and Modes of Justification in French and American Environmental Disputes. In Lamont, M. and Thévenot, L. (eds.), *Rethinking Comparative Cultural Sociology: Repertoires of Evaluation in France and the United Space* (pp. 229–272). Cambridge: Cambridge University Press.

Thomas, L. (2008). 'Ecoreality': The Politics and Aesthetics of 'Green' Television. In Palmer, G. (eds.), *Exposing Lifestyle Television: The Big Reveal* (pp. 177–188). London: Routledge.

Thyberg, K. L. and Tonjes, D. J. (2016). Drivers of Food Waste and Their Implications for Sustainable Policy Development. *Resources, Conservation and Recycling*, 106 (Supplement C), 110–123. doi: 10.1016/j.resconrec.2015.11.016.

Tumarkin, M. (2012). Sublime and Profane: Our Contemporary Obsession with Food. *Kill Your Darlings*, 8.

Utting, K. (2009). Assessing the Impact of Fair Trade Coffee: Towards an Integrative Framework. *Journal of Business Ethics*, 86 (1), 127–149. doi: 10.1007/s10551-008-9761-9.

Weber, M. (2001). *The Protestant Ethic and the Spirit of Capitalism*. Translated by T. Parsons. London: Routledge. Original edition, 1930.

Woolworths Group. (2017). Woolworths and Jamie Oliver Help Customers to Reduce Food Waste. Last modified 10 May. Available at: http://crs.woolworthsgroup.com.au/page/news/ planet/woolworths-and-jamie-oliver-help-customers-to-reduce-food-waste/. Accessed 20 November 2017.

12 Supermarkets, celebrity chefs and private labels

The 'alternative' reframing of processed foods

Michelle Phillipov and Katherine Kirkwood

As chapters throughout this collection have shown, an intensified media interest in food and food politics has provided alternative food movements with a range of new political resources through which to imagine and enact a progressive food politics. At the same time, it has also granted large food businesses and retailers additional resources to pursue market opportunities that have quite different outcomes in mind. This final chapter considers retailers' and manufacturers' adoption of the language of the 'alternative' as an example of a potential 'end point' in the mainstreaming of alternative food politics. It will do this by focusing on the relationships between supermarkets, celebrity chefs and private label products as key sites through which major retailers are now responding both to alternative food discourses and to growing media and public criticism of mainstream food systems.

Supermarkets' increasing domination of food retail has become a key locus of concern about the impacts of industrialised foodways in the US, the UK, Australia and elsewhere. Academic critics have described supermarkets as 'non-places' disconnected from social and community life (Augé, 1995), and as exemplifying 'Food from Nowhere' that seeks to elide the industrial, technical, geographic and social processes associated with its production (Campbell, 2009). Popular journalistic exposés have highlighted negative effects of supermarkets' large-scale, corporatised forms of food provisioning on food consumers and producers. In such accounts, supermarkets are presented as both a lynchpin in the ascendency of industrial food systems, and as entities that use their market power to reshape diets, food production practices and food economies in their own interests (see Blythman, 2007; Knox, 2015; Pollan, 2008).

Popular accounts have described supermarkets as cornucopias of highly processed 'edible food-like substances' rather than places selling 'real' food (Pollan, 2008, p. 1), as places governed by an ethic of 'permanent global summertime' in which fresh produce is available all year regardless of seasonality (Blythman, 2007, p. 76), and as corporations prepared to bully anyone—food producer, manufacturer or consumer—who poses an obstacle to their market power (Knox, 2015). Like earlier critiques of the fast food industry (see Nestle, 2013; Schlosser, 2002), the concerns are not just about supermarket practices, but also about supermarket food itself. As supermarkets have increased their market power, they have also emerged as what Jane Dixon (2007) calls 'new food authorities', an identity through which they have sought to transform themselves from faceless corporations to 'family-friendly' food and lifestyle authorities, advising consumers on matters of health and domesticity, and offering them products to help manage their busy lives (see also Dixon, 2008, p. 111).

Paralleling supermarkets' expanding influence has been the increasing mainstream visibility of 'alternative' food practices that has been described throughout this collection. For proponents of alternative food, supermarkets are frequently constructed as an Other against which 'good' food can be defined (Phillipov, 2017). For example, the rise of food sovereignty and local food movements (see Chapter 6) are often framed as reflecting a desire to connect with food producers and to reject the 'unjust', flavourless, anonymous foods of the industrial food system. For most consumers in the Anglophone west, this is a food system that is typically and primarily accessed via the supermarket (Pollan, 2008; Symons, 2007). The rise of popular food media has also seen an increasing number of celebrity chefs, television cooking shows, cookbooks, and other media encouraging consumers to source their food from people they know, rather than rely on the anonymous products that come, in the words of one celebrity chef, 'wrapped in plastic from the supermarket' (Hugh Fearnley-Whittingstall cited in Phillipov, 2017, p. 56). As the emerging genre of the food documentary has made clear, the ascendency of the supermarket is understood as a growing assault on 'real food' (Lindenfeld, 2010a, 2011).

Ongoing critiques of supermarket practices and processed supermarket food have contributed to an expansion in how alternative food politics are expressed and mobilised. They have also posed sustained image-management problems for supermarkets, which have in turn adopted a number of strategies to restore consumer trust and to re-engage consumers with supermarket food (Richards, Lawrence and Burch, 2011). As Richards, Lawrence and Burch (2011) argue, unlike the more direct producer-consumer relationships associated with 'alternative' food practices, the essence of supermarket trading involves anonymous relationships between retailer and consumer, and so is not well suited to building and maintaining relationships of trust. With growth in the alternative food sector driven, at least in part, by the perception of more open and transparent trust relationships between producers and consumers (Goodman, DuPuis and Goodman, 2012, p. 242), and with this rise of alternative food practices contributing to the growing critique of both supermarkets and supermarket food, large retailers have increasingly recognised the importance of engaging with 'alternative' food practices and discourses.

This has involved adopting a range of strategies, including: an increased emphasis on 'freshness' and 'fresh food' provisioning, featuring in-store redesigns aimed at creating an artisan 'market place' atmosphere (Keith, 2012); new advertising and marketing campaigns, such as sponsorship of popular food television programmes (Lewis and Phillipov, 2016; Phillipov, 2016); reputational enhancement and direct quality claims through private label offerings and private standards labelling (Richards, Lawrence and Burch, 2011); expanded lines of 'free range' and 'ethical' produce (see Chapter 10 in this collection); and alliances with media and cultural intermediaries, such as celebrity chefs (Lewis and Huber, 2015; Phillipov, 2017). While many of these responses may be seen as (somewhat cynical) attempts to minimise reputational damage in the face of negative media coverage or unfavourable public opinion, they also form part of a suite of methods through which supermarket identities and food politics are currently being refashioned and reframed (see Lewis and Phillipov, 2016).

This chapter focuses on one of these strategies: supermarket 'brand partnerships' with celebrity chefs. As lifestyle experts and knowledge intermediaries that connect audiences with food in multiple ways (Barnes, 2017; Hollows and Jones, 2010a), celebrity chefs have become 'key sites through which the ethics of "good" shopping and eating in an increasingly industrialized and globalised food market are interrogated and mobilized within contemporary media culture' (Lewis and Huber, 2015, p. 290). Their significant cultural influence has made celebrity chefs attractive as supermarket brand partners. Such brand partnerships now reach beyond traditional celebrity-fronted advertising and marketing campaigns to also include celebrity-branded supermarket product lines. This latter strategy combines the cultural and political cachet associated with celebrity chefs with supermarkets' increasing focus on private labels. Private labels are supermarket 'own brands', the often lower-priced products in competition with those from brand manufacturers (Burch and Lawrence, 2007). While traditionally seen as a 'cut price' or 'budget' option, over the past 15 years or so, supermarkets have been working to change the negative perception of private labels through more gourmet, 'higher end' offerings, and, increasingly, through partnerships with celebrity chefs. The rise of celebrity-branded private labels, then, forms part of a broader strategy to redefine private labels not as cheap imitations of branded products, but as spaces of innovation and novelty, as means by which to reshape supermarket brand identities, and as sites of progressive food politics (see Burch and Lawrence, 2007; Lewis and Phillipov, 2016; Phillipov, 2017).

Celebrity-branded private labels have so far garnered relatively little scholarly attention, but they are a powerful example of how criticisms of supermarkets—criticisms that frequently draw upon the tenets and values of the 'alternative'—can be positively incorporated and repurposed by mainstream retailers to (re)shape the meanings associated with supermarkets and supermarket food. This, we argue, is one of the significant, and perhaps inevitable, consequences as alternative food politics moves from the 'margins' to the 'mainstream'. To reveal these processes at work, we will focus on two examples of supermarket product lines that highlight the extent to which 'alternative' critiques of supermarkets and supermarket food have now become central to supermarket brand management: the 'Created with Jamie' and 'Heston for Coles' product lines. These were produced as part of partnerships between British celebrity chefs Jamie Oliver and Heston Blumenthal and Australian supermarkets Woolworths and Coles, respectively.

Oliver and Blumenthal offer ideal case studies not only because of their international renown, but also because their forays into the Australian supermarket space are examples of the type of brand partnership that is now a stock in trade strategy of supermarkets around the world. In partnering with Woolworths, for example, Oliver brought with him an established record of supermarket sponsorship, most notably with Britain's Sainsbury's supermarket, for which he had been a brand ambassador between 2000 and 2011—a relationship that similarly involved the introduction of lines of branded products, and which was credited with increasing Sainsbury's sales by 1 billion US dollars (Strategic Direction, 2011, p. 16). Blumenthal is also a veteran of the supermarket brand partnership, having periodically released products with UK supermarket chain Waitrose since 2010 (see Chandler, 2011; Wallop, 2010). As a site for examining the politics of celebrity chef brand partnerships and the changing reputations and promotional strategies of supermarkets, the Australian supermarket sector offers a similarly ideal locale for analysis. This is because Australian grocery retail is among the most concentrated in the world, with Coles and Woolworths control-ling around 70% of Australia's grocery market, which is worth 89.8 billion Australian dollars (Roy Morgan Research, 2016). This effective duopoly has been the subject of significant public and media debate about its impacts on farmers, suppliers and consumers, as well as several investigations by the national consumer watchdog, the ACCC (Australian Competition and Consumer Commission) (see Knox, 2015; Phillipov, 2017). This makes questions of food politics especially urgent in the Australian context, while its more compact operational scale also makes it an effective barometer of international trends.

On the surface, 'Created with Jamie' and 'Heston for Coles' appear to offer contrasting case studies, in part because Oliver's reputation for family-friendly, healthy meals meant that his brand partnership with Woolworths was widely hailed as a success, while Blumenthal's associations with molecular gastronomy and 'high end' cooking meant that his partnership with Coles was widely seen as a poor fit for a mainstream supermarket chain. However, we argue that both partnerships capitalised on the fluidity and flexibility inherent in the categories of 'processed' or 'supermarket' food, and, in doing so, formed part of a suite of strategies designed to intervene in criticisms of supermarket practices. In the case of Oliver, this involved negotiating his associations with healthy home cooking while spruiking a range of processed products; in the case of Blumenthal, his expertise in sense-bending molecular gastronomy was invoked to lend a different kind of legitimacy to processed supermarket foods. In both cases, we argue, concerns about supermarkets and supermarket food are not only difficulties that supermarkets now need to overcome, but are also opportunities to discursively reconstruct and redefine 'supermarket food' in new, and more positive, ways.

We begin this chapter by locating current criticisms of supermarkets within the context of changing discourses associated with supermarkets and supermarket food products in the late 20th Century. We do this by considering the role of food media, and of celebrity chefs in particular, in shaping contemporary food discourses, practices and politics as they relate to supermarket food. We then outline some of the supermarket responses to changing media and consumer attitudes before introducing the two case studies. Through textual 'readings' (Phillipov, 2013) of the discursive and visual conventions associated with the media commentary and marketing strategies of the 'Created with Jamie' and 'Heston for Coles' product lines, as well as those linked to each chef's media and professional identities, we will show how the apparent tensions between the celebrity chefs' gourmet credentials, espoused public positions on food politics issues and their production of supermarket private label products are, paradoxically, key to the symbolic work these products perform. This is significant, we argue, because by capitalising on the ambiguities associated with 'processed foods', supermarkets can incorporate criticisms into the development of new product lines and promotional platforms. In other words, criticisms are now not only 'problems' to be managed, but are also a desirable and profitable boon to supermarket product marketing and innovation, and this has implications for how contemporary food politics may be mobilised, enacted and understood.

Supermarkets, celebrity chefs and the politics of processed foods

Our arrival at this current point in food politics—where supermarket food has come to be conceived as (industrial) 'Food from Nowhere', against which (alternative) 'Food from Somewhere' can be positively defined—is the result of historical changes associated with food systems discourses, food-related values and identities, and the meanings associated with particular kinds of food products. The notion of supermarkets as alternative food's Other would be largely familiar to readers of this collection. Criticisms of the supermarket as a lynchpin in a globalised food system and its attendant power to shape food cost, availability and the production practices of various food industries has been discussed at length in both academic and popular commentaries. Along with broader concerns about supermarket practices (such as the consequences of their market dominance and their treatment of farmers and suppliers), a key theme of these criticisms has been concern about the nature of supermarket food, and, in particular, about super-market food as *processed food*—a type of food now increasingly synonymous both with corporate power over the food system and with deleterious effects on the health and well-being of consumers.

It is a concern perhaps most famously encapsulated by Michael Pollan (2008, p. 148) when he advised readers to avoid the 'hundreds of [processed] foodish products in the supermarket that your ancestors simply wouldn't recognise as food'. It is a concern also expressed by Joanna Blythman (2007) when she described the sophisticated mechanisms through which supermarkets encourage consumers to choose higher-profit-margin processed foods, such as ready meals, rather than unprocessed fresh produce, as strategies to transfer wealth from food production to retail. In many of these accounts, food processing is a problem not just for its food systems impacts, but also because it diminishes food's health and nutritional value (see Nestle, 2013), and changes the very nature of food itself. Supermarkets' 'edible food-like substances' are understood to be both the opposite of 'real' food and the epitome of consumers' alienation from the food they eat and how it is produced (Pollan, 2008, p. 1).

That supermarkets could be described as cornucopias of processed foods is hardly surprising given their relatively recent histories as fresh food retailers (see Symons, 2007). However, the current negative associations reflect significant changes to the meanings and values associated with food processing. Until around the mid to late 20th Century, processed foods were perceived not as problematic, but as desirable luxuries and convenience foods. Canned and packaged foods were presented as a housewife's liberation from domestic drudgery (Levenstein, 2003), as reflecting an abundance and variety of choice across the seasons (Tunc, 2015), as a gourmet novelty (Symons, 2007), and as pure, healthy and hygienic (Petrick, 2009). Advertising frequently presented the uniformity and scientific precision of processed food as preferable to the 'laborious and supposedly hit-and-miss practices of the "traditional" housewife' (Humphery, 1998, p. 28), while the glamour of celebrity also shaped these perceptions. For example, Lovegren (2005, p. 217) notes the elevated credentials of processed foods during the 1960s, given that 'even the Kennedys' chic White House French chef used canned mushroom soup in his beef stroganoff'. Australian readers would similarly remember advice from publications such as *The Australian Women's Weekly* well into the 1980s and 1990s on how to prepare glamorous, gourmet dinner parties using canned and frozen produce. Supermarket foods have also long been a staple of daytime television cooking shows, with programmes like the long-running *Huey's Cooking Adventures* (1997–2010) sponsored by cut-price supermarket BI-LO, and *Ready Steady Cook* (2005–2013) sponsored by a range of major food manufacturers.

More recently, however, popular food discourses have been characterised by what Lewis and Phillipov (2016, p. 106) call an 'artisanal turn', and this has significantly altered the status of both supermarkets and processed foods. This artisanal turn has not been complete: the recipes of daytime and cable food programming still rely on the convenience of packaged and prepared foods (consider, for example, Rachael Ray's use of pie shells, ice cream and pizza dough, among other ingredients, see Lindenfeld, 2010b), while primetime cooking shows, such as Jamie Oliver's, frequently use prepared curry mixes, frozen and canned goods. Nonetheless, there has been an increasing critical focus on the industrialisation of food in mainstream media (Lewis and Phillipov, 2016, p. 106), driven, in part, by a growing sense of consumer alienation from conventional food systems (Versteegen, 2010), and by the rise of celebrity chefs advocating 'cooking from scratch' for reasons of taste, health, and the performance of desirable lifestyles (Hollows, 2003; Rousseau, 2012).

These celebrity-driven media texts deploy the chefs' food-related expertise in ways that construct specific notions of what constitutes 'good' food. From *River Cottage* (1999–) to *Gourmet Farmer* (2010–), 'good' food is presented as 'Food from Somewhere': small-scale, artisan, local, 'connected'—the antithesis of the food of the industrial food system. This 'artisanal turn' has occurred alongside an increasing number of public scandals associated with mainstream retailers. In Australia, these have led to ACCC investigations and legal action, and have put supermarkets' business activities squarely in the media spotlight. For example, in 2011, when Coles supermarkets lowered the price of its own-brand milk to a considerably discounted 1 Australian dollar per litre (a move immediately matched by Woolworths), it not only prompted considerable backlash from media, farmers and the public, but also resulted in a Senate Inquiry into milk pricing, the reputational fall out from which is arguably still ongoing. Australian supermarkets have also been at the centre of accusations of bullying suppliers in order to increase the market share of private labels—accusations which have led to successful legal action against both major supermarkets and to substantial negative publicity about both retail chains (see Knox, 2015; Phillipov, 2017).

This combination of changing food discourses and growing disquiet about supermarket food has necessitated that supermarkets reposition themselves in a number of ways. In particular, supermarkets have sought to 'strategically manufacture consumer trust' (Richards, Lawrence and Burch, 2011), and to capitalise on contemporary discourses of ethical consumption (Lewis and Huber, 2015, p. 295) in ways designed to address negative perceptions of supermarket foods. Some of these strategies involve celebrity endorsement. In the Australian context, celebrity chefs who possess recognisable 'ethical capital', such as Jamie Oliver and Curtis Stone, have been used to front supermarket campaigns designed to push back against mounting critique of supermarket practices, and to actively claim and shape the emerging spaces of political and ethical consumerism through, for example, celebrity-fronted campaigns spruiking the supermarkets' transition to 'RSPCA (Royal Society for the Prevention of Cruelty to Animals) Approved' egg and chicken meat products (Lewis and Huber, 2015, p. 295, see also Chapter 10).

In addition to celebrity brand partnerships, supermarkets have also sought to reframe private label products as sites of innovation and as expressions of new ethical commitments. For example, the Australian television show *Recipe to Riches* featured contestants pitching new products to be sold on the 'Woolworths Select' private label. Although *Recipe to Riches*' purported aim was to 'lift [...] the lid on the food we buy', with the exception of some brief factory footage in the final episode of Series 2, the show revealed very little about the processes of food manufacture. Instead, it showed contestants preparing food much like they would at home: chopping chillies and dates by hand; individually zesting and juicing lemons; and preparing apple purée in a regular home blender. As Lewis and Phillipov (2016) have argued, the principle effect of these representational techniques has been to reframe the meanings of supermarket food—and of supermarket private labels—from anonymous corporate products to 'batched up' versions of home-cooked recipes as methods to 'authenticate supermarkets and gloss over the realities of global agribusiness' (Lewis and Phillipov, 2016, p. 121). It is in this context of changing food discourses and new supermarket responses that brand partnerships with celebrity chefs have been put into the service of crucial cultural and symbolic work.

Created with Jamie

Of the two partnerships, the 'Created with Jamie' products were introduced with the most media fanfare. Brought to market in 2015, and with names like

'Created With Jamie Chicken Fillet Smashin' Chilli Garlic Rosemary', 'Created with Jamie' pestos, pasta sauces, oils, vinegars, spices and seasonings, pastas, frozen fish, soups and meat dishes referenced many of the culinary 'signatures' that would be familiar to audiences of Oliver's television series and cookbooks, such as his emphasis on 'big' Mediterranean flavours and his 'Essex-boy patter in which food is "pukka" and "wicked"' (Ashley et al., 2004, p. 175). As well as the launch of 'Created with Jamie' products, announcements of the partnership between Oliver and Woolworths emphasised Oliver's role in boosting the super-market's ethical credentials, with Oliver's initial video media release stating his intention to 'work [...] across the whole of [Woolworths'] business, front and back end', and to work with the supermarket chain to ensure its transition to free range eggs by 2018.[1] More recent campaigns have focused on issues such as healthy eating, especially in relation to fruit and vegetable consumption, and food waste. In each case, and across all of its communication channels, Woolworths draws upon the combined connotations of Oliver's reputation for lifestyle cookery, as established through his 'Naked Chef' persona (see Moseley, 2001), and his ethical commitments, as established through his globally prominent campaigns on food issues (see Hollows and Jones, 2010a). Both dimensions of Oliver's brand have been key features of the marketing campaigns linked to the Woolworths–Oliver partnership, and, in particular, of the media coverage of 'Created with Jamie' products.

This media coverage has consistently emphasised the partnership between Oliver and Woolworths as both a coup and a 'natural fit' for the supermarket chain. This link was made explicitly in the Woolworths media release announcing the partnership. As then-Managing Director Tjeerd Jegen was quoted as saying: 'Jamie is world famous for his passion for fresh food, and Woolworths is Australia's fresh food people' (JamieOliver.com, 2013). It was a point frequently emphasised across Woolworths' communications. For instance, in a media release about Oliver's appearance at the Sydney Royal Easter Show, then-Director of Woolworths Supermarkets Dave Chambers is quoted as saying that 'Jamie is all about fresh food and we are the fresh food people so it makes perfect sense for him to meet the farmers who grow our fruit and vegetables' (Woolworths, 2015). The release concludes with a reference to the 'Created with Jamie' range as one made with the 'freshest locally sourced ingredients' (Woolworths, 2015), emphasising the semiotic link between 'Created with Jamie' products and 'fresh' food. A similar link between 'Created with Jamie' products and 'from scratch' cooking frequently appeared in food blogs and product reviews. For example, one review specifically distinguished the products from ready meals and other 'bad' types of processed food by describing them as a better alternative to 'cutting corners and being lazy' for a 'tired mother'.[2]

Industry news also made much of the seemingly 'natural' fit between the shared brand values of Woolworths and Oliver. *Food & Drink Business* described 'Created with Jamie' products as 'good and honest food' that reflect Oliver's values.[3] Such sentiments appeared to be largely accepted across mainstream media commentaries on the topic (e.g., Marriner and Whyte, 2013). Overall, the media response to the Woolworths–Oliver partnership would seem to confirm Lewis and Huber's (2015, p. 294) observation that:

> Oliver—a 'living brand' whose ethical credibility is embodied in his trust-worthy persona, wholesome family-oriented lifestyle, familiar warmth and bonhomie, and performed in his widely mediated food and health activism— [did indeed] help [. . .] to 'ethicalize' Woolworths' [brand identity] while requiring relatively little labor from the company's marketers.

However, while appearing to require little marketing spin, the 'naturalness' of the Woolworths–Oliver partnership nonetheless depended on complex symbolic work by both Woolworths and Brand Oliver. Aligning Oliver's brand identity with a line of supermarket products was anything but 'natural'. Despite using processed foods in many of his recipes, Oliver has been an explicit advocate for cooking from scratch, particularly in the campaigning culinary documentaries that have contributed to his transition from celebrity chef to global megastar (Bell, Hollows and Jones, 2017). In these documentaries—*Jamie's School Dinners* (2005), *Jamie's Food Revolution* (2010–2011) and *Jamie's Ministry of Food* (2008), in particular—obesity and diet-related disease are attributed not only to takeaways and fast food, but also to a reliance on a diet of processed foods. Indeed, across all three programmes, Oliver repeatedly advocates 'cooking from scratch instead of opening boxes' of processed foods as the solution to a range of diet-related public health crises. Given the global reach and political impact of these programmes—for example, the campaign associated with *Jamie's School Dinners* was so successful that it prompted then-Prime Minister Tony Blair to commit an additional 280 million British pounds in funding to school meals (BBC News, 2005)—for Oliver to encourage consumers to 'open a box' or packet of 'Created with Jamie' products potentially poses a significant reputational problem.

Phillipov (2017) has previously argued that the apparent contradiction between political messages encouraging audiences to cook from scratch and commercial messages to buy Jamie Oliver-branded packaged food products is something that is carefully managed within the celebrity chef's media texts. Most powerfully, Oliver's campaigning culinary documentaries play with the ambiguities of what 'counts' as processed foods in ways that draw upon the complex and shifting meanings associated with 'cooking' versus 'reheating' and 'acceptable' versus 'unacceptable' food processing. We can see this most clearly in *Jamie's Food Revolution* when Oliver is shocked to learn that American school children, whose daily lunches always include milk, overwhelmingly choose the flavoured milks, rather than what Oliver calls the 'natural' milk varieties (the 1% or skim milks). Flavoured milk may contain sugar and other additives, but to describe a product like 1% or skim milk as 'natural' is a powerful rhetorical move that simulta-neously elides the significant amount of processing required to produce all of the milk products on offer and makes an important distinction between 'good' and 'bad' processing. As Slocum et al. (2011, p. 185) argue, this results in 'some forms of processing [. . .] becom[ing] naturalized, and thus invisible, while other processing [. . .] is denaturalized'. Similar rhetorical moves also occur across other food categories in the series, most notably in relation to poultry in *Jamie's School Dinners* (see Phillipov, 2017).

While one of the primary effects of these strategies is to smooth over the contradictions between the campaigning and the commercial arms of the Jamie Oliver brand identity, they also have flow-on benefits for Woolworths. Just as Oliver is able to profit from the ambiguities associated with the types or levels of food processing deemed acceptable or unacceptable, the shifting meanings inherent in the categories of 'cooking' and 'processed food' similarly allow Woolworths to combine Oliver's reputation for fresh and healthy cooking, a range of co-branded processed foods, and the supermarket chain's own brand identity as the 'Fresh Food People'.

Central to this is the redefinition of 'Created with Jamie' products not as convenience foods or pre-prepared 'ready' meals, but as an *'easy-to-cook fresh food range'* (emphasis added).[4] Unlike the passive 'opening boxes' that characterises the consumption of 'bad' processed foods, the 'Created with Jamie' range typically requires some effort from the consumer. In the case of most products in the range, the food is sold pre-prepared and pre-portioned, but with the actual cooking to be done at home. For example, the 'Created With Jamie Spiced Lamb Rump Skewers' come pre-seasoned and pre-skewered, ready to be cooked at home, while the 'Created With Jamie Crispy Parmesan and Tomato Smashin' Chicken Fillets' come with premade breadcrumb mix to be applied before cooking. The television commercials for the 'Created with Jamie' range encourage viewers to use these products to 'cook' and 'be creative',[5] while other promotional quotes, cited across a number of media outlets, indicate that a goal of the 'Created with Jamie' range is 'inspiring people [. . .] to cook'.[6]

Indeed, even the name 'Created with Jamie', while ostensibly meant to signify Oliver's partnership with Woolworths, also has the additional implication that the home cook is actively 'creating' these meals 'with' Oliver. This works to further reframe the meaning of his products to include active 'cooking' and not just passive reheating or 'opening boxes', and through the products' characterisation as an 'easy-to-cook fresh food range', to build in additional connotations of these products as 'fresh' rather than processed foods. While, for Oliver, it may mean that his brand identity becomes 'ironically embedded in the very marketized and corporatized foodways that [his] own food practices and ethics would seem to eschew' (Lewis and Huber, 2015, p. 290), for supermarkets desperate to respond to mounting critique, the capacity of products like the 'Created with Jamie' range to play with the ambiguities associated with 'supermarket' and 'processed' foods can be deployed to lend a positive halo to both. At a time when supermarkets are experiencing increasing pressure to adapt to changing consumer preferences and politics, reframing processed supermarket products in this way allows them to become vehicles through which to access both the Jamie Oliver 'lifestyle' and his ethical and political capital. However, while this melding of the celebrity chef's brand identity with that of the supermarket was widely hailed as a success in this case, Heston Blumenthal's with Coles was somewhat more complex.

Heston for Coles

In fact, the partnership between Coles and Blumenthal left many shaking their heads. Coles' ongoing relationship with Australian celebrity chef Curtis Stone had been effective in helping the supermarket to 'ethicalise' its brand through initiatives such as hormone free beef, sow stall free pork, cage free eggs and 'RSCPA Approved' chicken (see Lewis and Huber, 2015). But not to be outdone by its supermarket rival, Coles announced its own partnership with a British celebrity chef just days after Woolworths' Oliver announcement. Like Woolworths and Oliver, the Coles–Blumenthal partnership also involved a range of co-branded supermarket products. The 'Heston for Coles' range included 15 products, many of them incorporating Australian native ingredients, such as slow-cooked Asian pork roast with lemon myrtle, and slow-cooked beef ribs with pepperberries. Others lent 'Heston magic' to more familiar products, such as his 'Remarkable Beef Burgers' and potato-topped lamb and rosemary pie. The range was to be updated twice yearly to eventually span all supermarket categories, including meat, deli, bakery and grocery items (Stock, 2014). Unlike Oliver's 'Created with Jamie' range, however, a search of the Coles web site at the time of writing revealed that the 'Heston for Coles' range was no longer listed for sale. It appears that the Blumenthal–Coles partnership has become one more in a line of haphazard celebrity partnerships for the supermarket chain, which have also included One Direction, Status Quo, Dawn French, and Casey Donovan.

In contrast to the 'Created with Jamie' announcement, media commentary struggled to make sense of the Coles–Blumenthal relationship. Blumenthal's 'boffin' persona, complete with scientist safety goggle-styled spectacles and lab coat-style chef's whites (see Hollows and Jones, 2010b, p. 527), along with his reputation for molecular gastronomy established through his Michelin-starred restaurant The Fat Duck, made him appear a far less natural fit for a mainstream Australian supermarket than Oliver's culinary 'man of the people' or 'new lad' celebrity identities (see Hollows, 2003). For example, Marriner and Whyte's (2013, p. 28) report on the apparent misalignment claimed that:

> The Coles partnership with Blumenthal—announced a few days after the Woolworths/Oliver signing—is harder to understand than the Oliver partnership, given the chef's high-end Michelin star pedigree and Coles' 'down, down, prices are down' mantra.

They quote consumer psychologist Adam Ferrier as saying, 'Heston doesn't represent the values Coles has, Coles isn't about molecular gastronomy' (cited in Marriner and Whyte, 2013, p. 28).

Coles maintained that the partnership with Blumenthal was indeed a natural fit, and its promotional discourses emphasised 'Heston for Coles' products' capacity for both innovation and democratisation. In media releases announcing the partnership, for instance, Coles' then-Marketing and Store Development Director Simon McDowell stated that the relationship with Blumenthal 'signals an amazing new opportunity for Coles and one that reinforces our commitment to continually push the boundaries of food innovation'.[7] When promoting the launch of the 'Heston for Coles' range, general manager of Coles brand and customer insights Kendra Banks emphasised its democratising potential:

> We have created some new products and some fantastic Aussie flavours with a bit of the Heston magic and we are really proud of this range because that Heston magic will now be on tables across Australia... Not everyone can get a booking at the Fat Duck I'm reliably assured, but everyone will be able to find the Heston for Coles range, which will be available nationwide.[8]

The language of 'Heston magic' also dutifully appeared throughout the reviews of food bloggers who had received the products, although mainstream press reviews were far less effusive and—as illustrated in John Lethlean's (2014) review for national newspaper, *The Australian*—less likely to quote promotional discourses so directly.

At a time of mounting concern about supermarket practices and products, Coles has been the hardest hit of the two major Australian supermarket chains, having been at the centre of both the 2011 'milk wars' and of several very public legal actions brought by the ACCC. While this can perhaps make partnering with a figure like Blumenthal even more incongruous, it need not be seen as simply a marketing misstep, but rather as a different sort of attempt to reframe the meanings of supermarket food. In contrast to Oliver's products, where the emphasis on 'freshness' and 'cooking' and 'creating' served as a semiotic sleight of hand to elide the processing involved in the production of packaged supermarket products, Blumenthal's brand persona is one in which practices of industrial food processing are not only positively refigured but also wholeheartedly embraced.

Blumenthal's celebrity identity has been shaped by his scientific approach to cooking, and this is a common feature across his media appearances, television programmes, cookbooks, and his work at The Fat Duck. Dishes at The Fat Duck, for example, are designed to:

> challenge diners to reflect on seemingly obvious categories—for example, the distinction between sweet and savory, hot and cold, raw and cooked— that organize our normal culinary and cultural experience.
>
> (Hollows and Jones, 2010b, p. 527)

His recipes are frequently created using ingredients and techniques gleaned from the food manufacturing industry, including modern thickeners, sugar substitutes, enzymes, liquid nitrogen, sous-vide, dehydration, among 'other nontraditional [sic] means' (Adrià et al., 2006).

In his cookbooks, while Blumenthal admits that the food manufacturing industry does not always put its technical resources to the 'most worthwhile of culinary objectives', the fact that commercial food companies are often at the forefront of scientific developments in food means that they serve as a source of inspiration for his own recipes: for example, when he was 'working with an ice-cream company that marketed a choc ice wrapped in plastic packaging which somehow boosted the delightful brittleness of the chocolate in the mouth', he took a roll of this plastic from them to use in his own restaurant's dishes (Blumenthal, 2011, p. 25). Moreover, Blumenthal's television appearances, such as his BBC2 show *In Search of Perfection* (2006–2007), offer a decisive shift away from the lifestyle preoccupations of other television cooking shows (including Jamie Oliver's) to feature scientists as on-screen experts (Hollows and Jones, 2010b, p. 528). So sustained has been his focus on food science that Blumenthal has received honorary degrees at the Universities of Reading, Bristol and London for promoting the scientific understanding of cooking, and has been made a Fellow of the Royal Society of Chemistry (Brien, 2017, p. 205).

Such a focus on the chemical properties of ingredients and on experimental cooking techniques inspired by the food manufacturing industry is the almost total opposite of the nostalgia valorisation of the 'natural' and the 'traditional' that has proliferated in popular food media and ethical food discourses (see Versteegen, 2010). Indeed, if much popular food media now seeks out 'authentic' traditions 'as a kind of antidote to contemporary food culture marked by a scientization and rationalization of food production and consumption' (Lewis, 2008, p. 59), the techniques and ingredients of molecular gastronomy are the very definition of what Pollan (2008, p. 148) has described as things that your 'great grandmother wouldn't recognize as food'—that is, the scientised and rationalised products of the industrial food system.

Blumenthal's particular approach to food science, however, works to reframe his processed foods not only as of higher status than those churned out by food factories, but also as sites of novelty, whimsy and wonder. For example, in his television programme *Heston's Fantastical Foods* (2012), Blumenthal uses a scientific approach to remake giant versions of the nostalgic foods he associates with his 1970s childhood. Each of the foods he makes—from a five-metre high 99 Flake ice cream, to an oversized packet of 'dunkgestive' biscuits—share a similar history as being the highly processed products of the industrial food industry. They are also designed to invoke childhood pleasures associated with those foods, and, as he says in a slightly different context, 'to capture that nostalgia, to bring to each dish the kind of trigger that would transport people back to their cherished memories of that food' (Blumenthal, 2006). Indeed, a (regular-sized) version of the 'dunkgestives' were slated to be added to the 'Heston for Coles' range as part of a sweets selection (Boothroyd, 2014), but the 'Heston for Coles' range was discontinued before this occurred.

Like 'Created with Jamie', the promotional discourses surrounding the 'Heston for Coles' range did incorporate some of the tropes of 'fresh produce' and 'local suppliers' that one might expect of a supermarket chain attempting to diminish the negative connotations associated with processed supermarket foods. For example, in *Food & Beverage News*, Blumenthal framed the 'Heston for Coles' range as an expression of his love for Australian produce: 'I've been coming to

Australia now for 12–14 years and the produce here is amazing. From the seafood obviously to the best beef in the world, and the truffles, but also the native produce' (cited in Boothroyd, 2014). Nonetheless, while aspects of Coles' promotional discourses drew upon the 'artisan turn' in contemporary food politics, they did not attempt to obscure or diminish the products' industrial methods of manufacture. In promoting the 'Heston for Coles Remarkable Beef Burger', for instance, industrial production methods were foregrounded as evidence of the product's innovation. As Blumenthal told Boothroyd (2014):

> We've developed a technique during the mincing process... As the mince comes out of the machine you basically catch it and then roll it into a big sausage... then when you cut the patties, all of the fibres are running one way, so when you bite down onto the burger, it's really quite delicate.

Merging Blumenthal's celebrity status and credibility in using otherwise derided food processing techniques can thus be seen as part of an attempt to reinvent processed foods and supermarket private labels, not as the unglamorous and lowbrow products manufactured for corporate profits, but as sites of novelty and innovation that challenge negative perceptions of supermarket foods. In this case, the goal was perhaps less to attempt to reinvent processed supermarket foods as a cypher for 'home cooking' than it was to bring some 'Heston magic' to beleaguered supermarket brands.

Conclusion

A major consequence of the increasing 'mainstream' visibility of 'alternative' food politics has been the mounting global criticism of supermarket products and practices. Central to this is the problematic place now occupied by the processed food products that have proliferated in supermarkets since the mid-20th Century. Intensified media and consumer interest in the 'artisanal' and the 'authentic' have positioned processed food as 'good' food's Other, and have necessitated a range of brand management responses from major supermarkets—the effects of which can be clearly seen in the highly contested Australian context, but which are also symptomatic responses exhibited by supermarkets elsewhere in the world. As we have shown through the case studies of the 'Created with Jamie' and 'Heston for Coles' product ranges, changing media and consumer attitudes to supermarket food have prompted alliances between supermarkets, private label brands and celebrity chefs as ways of seeking an 'alternative' framing of supermarket foods. In doing so, we have argued that ongoing criticisms of supermarkets provide major retailers with a range of opportunities to reshape the meanings associated with supermarkets and supermarket food.

In the case of 'Created with Jamie', Woolworths was able to capitalise on Oliver's 'everyman' persona and on his brand identity focused on home cooking and fresh food, and to link it to its own identity as the 'Fresh Food People'. As a brand management strategy, the success of the product range rested on its capacity to play with the ambiguities inherent in the categories of both 'cooking' and 'processed' foods. Though pre-portioned and pre-packaged, 'Created with Jamie' products typically require some assembly and cooking on the part of the shopper, inviting them to feel as if the dishes are indeed 'Created *with* Jamie', and not simply a product of passive engagements with the processed food industry. In the case of 'Heston for Coles', the supermarket adopted a different—and less well received—strategy to engage consumers with processed supermarket foods. It involved more wholeheartedly embracing the scientific techniques of industrial manufacturing, reframing them both as sites of innovation and as means of accessing an elusive 'Heston magic'.

Both 'Created with Jamie' and 'Heston for Coles' product lines can be seen as different responses to characterisations of supermarket foods as Food from Nowhere—either by appropriating artisanal discourses of home cooking on the one hand, or by positively revaluing industrial manufacturing processes on the other. Their differing degrees of success—as illustrated by both the ongoing viability and positive media reception of 'Created with Jamie' products, compared to the quite different outcomes for the 'Heston for Coles' product lines—perhaps reflect the increasing dominance of the 'artisanal turn' on the terms in which 'good' food is valued and understood. 'Good' food as Food from Somewhere is frequently framed in quite specific terms in media and popular discourse—as 'fresh' food, as food produced on a smaller scale, as food that offers consumers a source of 'connection'. Given the increasing hegemony of this 'artisan turn' in contemporary food politics, it became perhaps impossible for 'Heston for Coles' products to return to processed foods the mid-Century's positive sheen, or to successfully invoke the nostalgia that the products' marketing attempted.

'Created with Jamie' and 'Heston for Coles' products are each examples of the increasingly sophisticated brand management strategies that are being adopted by conventional food retailers and manufacturers—in this case, by utilising the cultural and political capital of international celebrity chefs to reframe the activist discourses designed to challenge supermarkets' control of the food system. That the most successful example of this, 'Created with Jamie', was the one that sought to blur the meanings associated with the 'mainstream' and the 'alternative', rather than the one that sought to positively revalue the 'mainstream', has significant implications for how progressive food politics is now both mobilised and appropriated in a context of intensified mediation. In particular, the blurring of 'alternative' and 'mainstream' discourses necessitates careful attention to the relationships between media's potentialities and possibilities, its progressive and reactionary outcomes, and to the forms that these may take. As the examples in this chapter (and elsewhere in this collection) illustrate, media is now a central vehicle for the enactment of alternative food politics and the mitigation of critiques of conventional food systems—though we do not always know in advance the conditions under which this does or does not occur. Attention to media as thoroughly imbricated in political questions and concerns is now essential to the project of alternative food politics, especially as it moves further from the 'margins' into the 'mainstream'.

Notes

1 Released 3 October 2013. Available at: www.youtube.com/watch?v=ZYbLowjhdro. Accessed February 2017.
2 See www.baby-mac.com/2014/11/created-jamie-range-woolies/. Accessed 5 April 2018.
3 See www.foodanddrinkbusiness.com.au/news/jamie-oliver-scopes-out-the-space. Accessed 5 April 2018.
4 See https://au.news.yahoo.com/sunday-night/a/23399952/jamie-olivers-best-roast-chicken/. Accessed 5 April 2018.
5 See, for example, https://vimeo.com/156220183. Accessed 5 April 2018.
6 See, for example, https://au.news.yahoo.com/sunday-night/a/23399952/jamie-olivers-best-roast-chicken/. Accessed 5 April 2018.
7 See https://web.archive.org/web/20150929201121/http://www.coles.com.au:80/about-coles/news/2013/10/02/heston-blumnethal-to-partner-exclusively-with-coles. Accessed 18 February 2018.
8 See www.foodanddrinkbusiness.com.au/news/coles-rolls-out-new-heston-blumenthal-range. Accessed 5 April 2018.

References

Adrià, F., Blumenthal, H., Keller, T. and Harold, M. (2006). Statement on 'New Cookery'. *The Guardian*, 10 December. Available at: www.theguardian.com/uk/2006/dec/10/foo danddrink.obsfoodmonthly. Accessed 5 April 2018.

Ashley, B., Hollows, J., Jones, S. and Taylor, B. (2004). *Food and Cultural Studies*. London: Routledge.

Augé, M. (1995). *Non-Places: Introduction to an Anthropology of Supermodernity*. Translated by J. Howe. London: Verso.

Barnes, C. (2017). Mediating Good Food and Moments of Possibility with Jamie Oliver: Problematising Celebrity Chefs as Talking Labels. *Geoforum*, 84, 169–178.

BBC News. (2005). TV Chef Welcomes £280 M Meals Plan. *BBC News*, 30 March. Available at: http://news.bbc.co.uk/2/hi/uk_news/education/4391695.stm. Accessed 1 March 2015.

Bell, D., Hollows, J. and Jones, S. (2017). Campaigning Culinary Documentaries and the Responsibilization of Food Crises. *Geoforum*, 84, 179–187.

Blumenthal, H. (2006). *In Search of Perfection: Reinventing Kitchen Classics*. London: Bloomsbury.

Blumenthal, H. (2011). *Heston Blumenthal at Home*. London: Bloomsbury.

Blythman, J. (2007). *Shopped: The Shocking Power of Britain's Supermarkets*. London: Harper Perennial.

Boothroyd, A. (2014). Blumenthal Goes Native with New Coles Range. *Food & Beverage Industry News*, 22 May. Available at: https://foodmag.com.au/heston-blumenthal-goes-native-with-new-coles-range/. Accessed 5 April 2018.

Brien, D. L. (2017). Something Diabolical but Delicious: Heston Blumenthal's 'Gothic Horror Feast.' *Australasian Journal of Popular Culture*, 6 (2), 203–217.

Burch, D. and Lawrence, G. (2007). Supermarket Own Brands, New Foods and the Reconfiguration of Agri-Food Supply Chains. In Burch, D. and Lawrence, G. (eds.), *Supermarkets and Agri-Food Supply Chains: Transformations in the Production and Consumption of Foods* (pp. 100–128). Cheltenham: Edward Elgar.

Campbell, H. (2009). Breaking New Ground in Food Regime Theory: Corporate Environmentalism, Ecological Feedbacks and the 'Food from Somewhere' Regime? *Agriculture and Human Values*, 26, 309–319.

Chandler, V. (2011). Heston Reveals His Desserts for Waitrose This Year – Including a Brand New Retro Twist. *Good Housekeeping*, 17 November. Available at: www.good housekeeping.co.uk/food/food-news/heston-waitrose-panettone-black-forest. Accessed 5 April 2018.

Dixon, J. (2007). Supermarkets as New Food Authorities. In Burch, D. and Lawrence, G. (eds.), *Supermarkets and Agri-Food Supply Chains* (pp. 29–50). Cheltenham: Edward Elgar.

Dixon, J. (2008). Operating Upstream and Downstream: How Supermarkets Exercise Power in the Food System. In Germov, J. and Williams, L. (eds.), *A Sociology of Food and Nutrition: The Social Appetite* (pp. 100–123). Oxford: Oxford University Press.

Goodman, D., DuPuis, M. and Goodman, M. K. (2012). *Alternative Food Networks: Knowledge, Practice, Politics*. London: Routledge.

Hollows, J. (2003). Oliver's Twist: Leisure, Labour and Domestic Masculinity in *the Naked Chef*. *International Journal of Cultural Studies*, 6 (2), 229–248.

Hollows, J. and Jones, S. (2010a). 'At Least He's Doing Something': Moral Entrepreneurship and Individual Responsibility in *Jamie's Ministry of Food*. *European Journal of Cultural Studies*, 13, 307–322.

Hollows, J. and Jones, S. (2010b). Please Don't Try This at Home: Heston Blumenthal, Cookery TV and the Culinary Field. *Food, Culture & Society*, 13 (4), 521–537.

Humphery, K. (1998). *Shelf Life: Supermarkets and the Changing Cultures of Consumption*. Cambridge: Cambridge University Press.

JamieOliver.com (2013). Woolworths and Jamie Oliver to Inspire a Healthier Australia, *JamieOliver*, 4 October. Available at: www.jamieoliver.com/news-and-features/news/woolworths-jamie-oliver/. Accessed 7 September 2018.

Keith, S. (2012). Coles, Woolworths and the Local. *Locale: The Australasian-Pacific Journal of Regional Food Studies*, 2, 47–81.

Knox, M. (2015). *Supermarket Monsters: The Price of Coles and Woolworths' Dominance*. Collingwood: Redback.

Lethlean, J. (2014). Heston's Spruiking for Coles Is Just a Step Too Far. *The Australian*, 27 September. Available at: www.theaustralian.com.au/archive/executive-living/hestons-spruiking-for-coles-is-just-a-step-too-far/news-story/5e217f0a9406b07b6c58c8f6db9b 74bc. Accessed 5 April 2018.

Levenstein, H. (2003). *Paradox of Plenty: A Social History of Eating in Modern America*. Berkeley: University of California Press.

Lewis, T. (2008). *Smart Living: Lifestyle Media and Popular Expertise*. New York: Peter Lang.

Lewis, T. and Huber, A. (2015). A Revolution in an Eggcup? Supermarket Wars, Celebrity Chefs and Ethical Consumption. *Food, Culture & Society*, 18, 289–307.

Lewis, T. and Phillipov, M. (2016). A Pinch of Ethics and A Soupçon of Home Cooking: Soft-Selling Supermarkets on Food Television. In Bradley, P. (ed.), *Food, Media and Contemporary Culture: The Edible Image* (pp. 105–124). Hampshire: Palgrave Macmillan.

Lindenfeld, L. (2010a). Can Documentary Food Films like *Food Inc.* Achieve Their Promise? *Environmental Communication*, 4 (3), 378–386.

Lindenfeld, L. (2010b). The Ethics of Food Television: Does Rachel Ray Really Promote Healthy Eating? In Vandamme, S., van de Vathorst, S. and de Beaufort, I. (eds.), *Whose Weight Is It Anyway: Essays on Ethics and Eating* (pp. 167–173). Leuven: ACCO Academic.

Lindenfeld, L. (2011). Digging Down to the Roots: On the Radical Potential of Documentary Food Films. *Radical History Review*, 110, 155–160.

Lovegren, S. (2005). *Fashionable Food: Seven Decades of Food Fads*. Chicago: University of Chicago Press.

Marriner, C. and Whyte, S. (2013). Whose Kitchen Rules? Coles and Woolies Look to Celebrities to Win Shopper Dollars. *The Sun-Herald*, 22 December, p. 28.

Moseley, R. (2001). 'Real Lads Do cook… But Some Things are Still Hard to Talk About': The Gendering of 8–9. *European Journal of Cultural Studies*, 4, 32–39.

Nestle, M. (2013). *Food Politics: How the Food Industry Influences Nutrition and Health*. Berkeley: University of California Press.

Petrick, G. M. (2009). Feeding the Masses: H.J. Heinz and the Creation of Industrial Food. *Endeavour*, 33 (1), 29–34.

Phillipov, M. (2013). In Defense of Textual Analysis: Resisting Methodological Hegemony in Media and Cultural Studies. *Critical Studies in Media Communication*, 30, 209–223.

Phillipov, M. (2016). 'Helping Australia Grow': Supermarkets, Television Cooking Shows and the Strategic Manufacture of Consumer Trust. *Agriculture and Human Values*, 33, 587–596.

Phillipov, M. (2017). *Media and Food Industries: The New Politics of Food*. London: Palgrave Macmillan.

Pollan, M. (2008). *In Defense of Food*. London: Penguin Books.

Richards, C., Lawrence, G. and Burch, D. (2011). Supermarkets and Agro-Industrial Foods: The Strategic Manufacture of Consumer Trust. *Food, Culture & Society*, 14, 29–47.

Rousseau, S. (2012). *Food Media: Celebrity Chefs and the Politics of Everyday Interference*. London: Berg.

Roy Morgan Research. (2016). Supermarket Weep: Woolies' Share Continues to Fall and Coles and Aldi Split the Proceeds (Media Release). 24 October. Available at: www.roymorgan.com/findings/7021-woolworths-coles-aldi-iga-supermarket-market-shares-australia-september-2016–201610241542. Accessed 14 April 2017.

Schlosser, E. (2002). *Fast Food Nation: What the all-American Meal Is Doing to the World*. London: Penguin.

Slocum, R., Shannon, J., Cadieux, K. V. and Beckman, M. (2011). 'Properly, with Love, from Scratch': Jamie Oliver's Food Revolution. *Radical History Review*, 110, 178–191.

Stock, D. (2014). Pies, Snags and Burgers on the Menu at Coles as Heston Blumenthal Launches New Range. *news.com.au*, 20 May. Available at: www.news.com.au/lifestyle/food/pies-snags-and-burgers-on-the-menu-at-coles-as-heston-blumenthal-launches-new-range/news-story/96643d8e45cc591ea056d8c6b248cb9d. Accessed 5 April 2018.

Strategic Direction. (2011). Jamie Oliver at Sainsbury's: Analysis of a Brand Alliance. *Strategic Direction*, 27, 16–17.

Symons, M. (2007). *One Continuous Picnic: A Gastronomic History of Australia*. Carlton: Melbourne University Press.

Tunc, T. E. (2015). Eating in Survival Town: Food in 1950s Atomic America. *Cold War History*, 15 (2), 179–200.

Versteegen, H. (2010). Armchair Epicures: The Proliferation of Food Programmes on British TV. In Gymnich, M. and Lennartz, N. (eds.), *The Pleasures and Horrors of Eating: The Cultural History of Eating in Anglophone Literature* (pp. 447–464). Goettingen: VandR Unipress.

Wallop, H. (2010). Heston Blumenthal Launches Range of Food at Waitrose. *The Telegraph*, 6 July. Available at: www.telegraph.co.uk/foodanddrink/foodanddrinknews/

7873046/Heston-Blumenthal-launches-range-of-food-at-Waitrose.html.   Accessed   5 April 2018.

Woolworths. (2015). Jamie Oliver Opens the Sydney Royal Easter Show in the Woolworths Fresh Food Dome (Media release). *Woolworths Limited*, 26 March. Available at: www. woolworthsgroup.com.au/page/media/Latest_News/It%E2%80%99s_great_to_have_Ja mie_Oliver_headline_the_Sydney_Royal_Easter_Show_in_our_Woolworths_Fresh_ Food_Dome_He_provides_cooking_inspiration_to_millions_around_the_world_while_ Woolworths_provides_the_grwww.woolworthsgroup.com.a. Accessed 7 September 2018.

Index

3D-printed foods: online news depiction 88–9; promissory themes, association 80–1

aeroponics technology 85
affordances 3, 6–9; concept, application 7–8; media 12
agricultural innovations, development 79
Agriculture and Consumer Protection Act, passage 216–17
agri-food production, scale (bending) 46
agtech: innovation 86; startups 75–7; sustainable, term (definition) 88–9
alternative body/food politics 151
alternative consumption, value 66–7
alternative food: expensive statement purchases 64–5; middle class usage 56; movements 78–9; scholarship 173
alternative food networks (AFNs) 1, 86, 117, 125; concerns 11; consumption choices 4; nomenclature 4; scholarship 169–70; visibility, increase 5
alternative food politics 37
alternative hedonism 5
Andersen, Kip 143, 144
Anglophone West 10
animal flesh: eating 175–6; sensory pleasure 176, 179
animal food, welfare label claims 194
animals: advocacy 193; animals-as-nature 171; considerations 135; ethical meat producer 176; farmed animal welfare politics, consumer labelling 193; food animals 175, 183–4; husbandry 87; killing, glorification/symbolism 185; killing, naturalisation 185; lives, improvement 205, 209–10; naturalisation 185; products, consumption (problems) 143–4; reform, impact 210–11

Animals Australia 174
animal welfare 196–205; consumer labelling 193; improvement, cost increase (absence) 205, 209–10; regulation, policy discussion (expansion) 205; shift, impact 205–11; supermarket impact 198–203
Anthropocene 153
aquaculture 81–2
aquaponics (AP) 84; technology, basis 81
ARC 2020, 120–1
Arcari, Paula 9, 11, 169
Ark of Taste (Slow Food Movement) 64
Associations for the Maintenance of Smallholder Agriculture (AMAPs) 117
asylum seekers, welcoming initiatives 98
athletes, veganism 141
Australia: animal welfare regulation/ labelling, timelines 197f; arrivals, welcoming 99; breeder pigs, sow stall free status 210; fair food, analysis 123–5; food hospitality activism 97; food safety/ insecurity, concern 124; *Model Codes of Practice* 197
Australian Competition and Consumer Commission (ACCC) 204, 237; investigations 239–40; legal actions 245
Australian Food Sovereignty Alliance (AFSA) 123–4
Australian Meat Chicken Federation (ACMF) conduct, problems 204
Australian Pork Limited 200
Australian Women's Weekly, The 239

Babe (film) 200
Bajo el Asfalto está la Huerta (Under the Asphalt Lies the Garden) 120
Banks, Kendra 245
Barad, Karen 152–3
Barling, David 77, 79

battery cages 196, 198; government ban, absence 200
Bennett, Jane 152
Betoota Advocate, The 135
Beyond Meat 137
bifurcation 24; dualistic thinking, rejection 26–7; significance 26–8
Big Allotment Challenge 55
Big Food: co-optation 4; questions 117
biotechnology, studies 79–80
blood rites, exploration 183
Bloody Business, A (investigation) 174
Blumenthal, Heston 10, 236–7; celebrity identity 245; "Heston magic," language 245; supermarket brand partnership 244–7
bodies/food, normative meanings/assumptions (selfie conformance) 158
Boltanski, Luc 222
#bonespo 163–4
BØRSEN 41–2
Bosh 139
bounded rationality 145
Bové, José 119
boyd, danah 115
Braidotti, Rosi 152
brand partnerships, supermarket 236
Branson, Richard 137
"bred free range": labelling, problems 204; mentions 203f
breeder pigs, sow stall free status 210
breeders, treatment of 179–82
Brigades d'Actions Paysannes 121
Broadsheet (images) 105
Buck, Daniel 26
Butz, Earl 23

cage free eggs, Coles in-store advertising 201f
Calombaris, George 227
Canada, policy climate (creation) 121–3
Canadian Biotechnology Action Network 122
Canadian People's Food Policy Project 124
Carey, Rachel 8, 193
celebrity-branded private labels 236
celebrity chefs 9, 238–40; impact 234; supermarket brand partnerships 236; Woolworths brand partnerships 236–42
CERES Fair Food 123
certification costs, impact 32–3
Chalfen, Richard 106
chemical farming, reduction 119

chicken meat industry, consumer protection regulatory attention 203–4
"Chthulucene" 153
class differentiation 67
#clean 159
clean eating: advocacy 151–2; movement 144; social media portrayals/discussions 158
#cleaneating 159
#cleanfood 157–9, 160
Cold War 216–17
Coles-Blumenthal partnership 244–7
Collis, Christy 8, 14, 135
colony cages, chickens 198
CombaGroup 81, 85–6; aeroponics technology 85; self-presentation 85
commodification 179–82; power, negative aspect 181–2
Common Agriculture Policy (CAP) 120
Commonwealth Bank, Women in Focus Giving Community 225
community-based food organisations 123
Community Food Centres, impact 122
community supported agriculture (CSA) 27–8, 117; impact 3; schemes, promotion 120
Confédération Paysanne 120
consumer advocacy, shift 203–4
consumer precarity, threat 24
consumer protection regulation, shift 203–4
consumption: collective strategies 65; politics 13
cookery-educative mode 220
COOP supermarket 48
Copenhagen University, OPUS project 47
corporate environmental greenwashing 65
corporate food regime: opposition 116; vertical structure 115
Cowspiracy (Andersen/Kuhn) 143
'Created with Jamie' 237, 240–3; products, redefinition 243
Crimson Giant 67
Cronulla Riots 99
#crueltyfree 156–7
Cultivating a Movement (Reti/Rabkin/Farmer) 29
cultural capital, usage 66–7
cultural heritage 223
cultural intermediaries 9
cultural texts (ethical meat) 172
cultured meat 80

Dedehayir, Ozgur 8, 14, 135
desire, celebration 160
Desmarais, Annette 121
digital activism 113
digital body/food cultures 154–6
digital food: concept 6; media 95–6; porn
    102–4
digital media 95, 152–4; alternative body/
    food politics 151; artefacts, things
    (relationship) 154; impact 115;
    participation 112
digital mobilisation 119–21
digital photography 107
digital platforms, analysis 125–6
digital race formation 101
direct action 119–20
diversified production, evidence 45
Dixon, Jane 209, 234
domestic polity 222
domestic spaces of production, heritage
    foods (assocation) 67
domination 170–1
Do Nothing (film) 119
"dunkgestives" 246

Earthbound Farms, initiation 27
#eatclean 159
eco-efficiency: corporate logic 11;
    definition 84
eco-habitus 66
ecological agriculture 34
ecological sustainability, advancement 195
egg production 198
eggs, newspaper mentions 20f
elite lifestyle 60–1
Elmhurst Dairy 137
Elsley, Penny 98
enriched cages (chickens) 198
entrepreneurial activism 89–90
entrepreneurial urban farming 83
#epicmealtime 162–3
Essento 81, 86–8; sustainability 87–8
ethical consumers 85
ethical consumption: ethics 219; food
    labelling, relationship 194–5
ethical labelling 193
ethical masquerade 169
ethical meat 193; alternative 172–3; cultural
    texts 172; defining 172–3; mainstreaming
    171; power, (un)masking mechanisms
    169; producers 180t
European Social Forum 120
European Union, certification schemes 58

Euskal Herria Declaration 117
Evans, Matthew 9
excess, celebration 160
export markets, agri-food production 44

Fairfax media 96
fair food, narrative 124
Fair Trade products, promotion 120
fair trade schemes, usage 117
Fantasy Feeder 161
Farm Bill, passage 216–17
farmers' markets: promotion 120; usage 117
Farmsubsidy 121
farm-to-restaurant market, wholesalers 30–1
fat activism 161
Fat Duck, The 245
#fatfetish 161
#fatfoodporn 161
Fat Lazy Blondes 63
feminist materialism 152–4; analyses
    152–3; usage 151
Ferrier, Adam 244
Field Liberation Movement 119
Field Roast Grain Meat Co., expansion 137
Finding Ultra (Roll) 141
*First Principles Protocol for Building
    Cross-Cultural Relationships* 122–3
fish farming 81
#fitspo 157–9
flesh. *see* animal flesh: eating 175–6;
    sensory pleasure 176, 179
Flowers, Rick 7, 95
food: analysis 6–15; anonymous food 235;
    appearance/taste, focus 156–7; artisanal
    turn 239; control, appearance 219;
    discourses, change 240; food-related
    NGOs/associations 75; futures, vision 90;
    justice, articulation 114–15; labeling 7;
    media interest, increase 5; media politics
    1; media texts, proliferation 6;
    naturalisation 175–9; "new food
    authorities" 234–5; peopling 105–8;
    photography, analysis 160; real food,
    assault 235; right, dimensions
    (recognition) 116; security 78; studies 5;
    unsustainable food 77–9; wars 194–5
food animals: killing, de-masculinisation
    efforts 183–4; ontological definition 175
Food Babe Way, The (Hari) 159
Food & Beverage News 246
food citizenship 117; articulation 114–15
Food First Information and Action Network
    (FIAN) 118, 121

"Food from Nowhere" 234; opposition 120
"Food from Somewhere" 238
#foodgasm 159–61
food hospitality activism 95; imaging
  101–2; visual/verbal text, representation
  (methodology) 100–1
food innovation: development 79;
  systems 136
food labelling: analysis, methodology 196;
  ethical consumption, relationship 194–5;
  regulatory politics, evaluation 195–6;
  regulatory politics, role 194–6
Food: Locally Embeded, Globally
  Engaged 122
food politics: ethics/justice/identity,
  questions 173–4; informational turn
  113–14; media, relationship 3–6;
  networked food politics 114–15;
  touchstone concerns 15–16; usage 136
food porn 139; racialisation 103; term,
  usage 159–60; trope, usage 161
#foodporn 159–61
food production: mainstream success 37;
  processes, development 81
Food Programme, The 64, 66
Food Secure Canada (FSC) 121
food sovereignty organisations,
  alliance 122–3
food sovereignty 113; action 121;
  articulation 114–15; demands 116–17;
  digital activism 117–19
framing 116–17; mobilisation 126;
  principles 114; principles, application
  125–6; priorities 126
Food Sovereignty in Canada 121
food sustainability 11; meanings 219–20;
  television coverage 220–2
foodtech: innovation, sustainable
  (definition) 88–9; startups 75–7
food television
food sustainability 220–2; historical
  analyses 220–1
food waste: confrontation 216; off-screen
  waste 226–9; on-screen waste 224;
  politics 218; problem 216–17; production
  casualty 229; reduction 88; surplus
  ingredients 228
Forks Over Knives 143–4
For the Love of Meat (FLM) 9–10, 172, 175
financial bottom line 181; meat, portrayal
  182; visual insight 182
fossil fuel-based fertilisers, usage
  (reduction) 84

Free Farmers, political program 46
"free range": labels, discussion 203; media
  mentions 203f; regulatory politics 195–6;
  "free range" eggs ; debate, intervention
  209; definition, public concern 204;
  labelling, consumer law standard 211;
  free range, term (usage) 193
"fresh food" provisioning, empasis 235–6
"freshness," emphasis 235–6
Friedmann, Harriet 4
Friends of the Earth Europe (FoEE) 120–1

gastro-porn 102
Gates, Bill 137
gendered portrayal, types 162
genetically modified foods (GMFs), safety/
  importance (perspective) 120
genetically modified organisms (GMOs):
  Europe ban 120; incursion 114
Getz, Christy 26
GIFs, usage 154–5, 157, 161
Global Food Innovation Summit 75
Global North: food sovereignty 114;
  political food movement 116–17; urban
  constituencies, food sovereignty
  principles (application) 125–6
Global South/Global North, food justice
  concerns (unification) 7
Good Food (Sydney Morning Herald
  supplement) 102
good food, veganism (comparison) 139
"good" shopping, ethics 236
"gotcha" interview 143–4
Gourmet Farmer 221–2
green capitalism, rise 4
"green mainstream" 29
Green Revolution 119
greenwashing 65
Groupes d'Achat Solidaires de l'Agriculture
  Paysanne (GASAP) 120
Guide for Welcome Dinner Participants 97
Günsberg, Osher 141
Guthman, Julie 8, 23

habitus, term (usage) 66
halo effect 200
Hands on the Land for Food
  Sovereignty 121
Haraway, Donna 152–3
Hari, Vani ("The Food Babe") 12, 159
Harrington, Stephen 8, 14, 135
Hartman Group 29
#healthy 157–9

#healthyliving 160
heirloom (consumer discourses) 59
heirloom tomatoes, status symbols 60–1
herbicides, avoidance 84
heritage: discourse, elite power
  (relationship) 57; political aspirations 68;
  price 63–5; term, elites (relationship)
  61–3
heritage apple, varieties 61
heritage consumers 67
heritage foods: discourses 57–61, 67;
  discourse, sites 60; posh, defining 57;
  production, domestic spaces (association)
  67; reinvention 58; social distinction 55
heritage 'jewels' 63–4
heritage Marmande tomatoes 63
heritage Natoora carrots 63
Heritage Seed Library 59
heritage seeds, exchange 59
heritage taste 65–8; access 13
heritage vegetables: definition, problem
  55–6; mainstream 59; nostalgia 62–3
'Heston for Coles' 237, 244–7; framing
  246–7
Heston's Fantastical Foods 246
higher welfare labelled products,
  mainstream market (supermarket
  expansion) 198–203
Holm, Lotte 48
home consumption 47–51
home cooking 47–51; scale, political
  dynamics 49
home mode: images 107; shot, types 106
Huey's Cooking Adventures 239
Hugh's Chicken Run 174, 221
Hugh's War on Waste 217
human/animal binaries 184
human/nature binaries 184
human–non-human assemblages, political
  dimensions 153
hydroponics 81–2

Ibrahim, Yasmin 102–3
Indigenous Australians, racism
  (persistence) 99
Indigenous Circle 122
Indigenous people, food insecurity 124–5
Indigenous peoples' movements, land
  demands 126
industrial food: production, impact 13;
  system, anonymous food 235
industrialised agri-food system, critique 46
industrial polity 222

innovation, technologically deterministic
  visions 76
In Search of Perfection 246
inspired polity 222
intermediaries 3, 9–12
intermediation, complexities 12
International Day of Peasant Struggle 117
intersectionality 142–4
in vitro meat (IVM) 80

Jamie's Food Revolution 242
Jamie's Fowl Dinners 174
Jamie's Ministry of Food 242
Jamie's School Dinners 221, 242–3
Jegen, Tjeerd 241
Joseph, John 141
Joyce, Alan 224

Kardashian, Khloe 161
Killing Tradition (Bronner) 183–4
Kill It, Cook It, Eat It 174
Kirkwood, Katherine 10, 234
Kuhn, Keegan 143

labelling, government animal welfare policy
  197–8
Lakeside Organic Gardens, conversion 27
Landworkers' Alliance 119
Lang, Tim 77, 79
large-scale industrial agriculture, benefit 46
Larkey, Jeff 29
late modernity, instrumental
  culture 5–6
La Vía Campesina 78, 116–18, 219;
  web site 118–19; women,
  rights (focus) 119
La Vía Campesina, food sovereignty
  campaign 123
La Vía Campesina TV 118
Lavis, Anna 6
layer hens 198
Leer, Jonatan 9, 11, 37
Les Jardins de Cocagne 120
Lewis, Tania 6
libertarian paternalism 145
life politics, focus 13
Lightlife, expansion 137
livestock operations, growth 26
local food, meaning/evaluation 86
Lupton, Deborah 12, 88, 151

macro-political capacities 3, 6
mainstream discourses 14

mainstreaming: strategies 38; US
  trajectories 23
mainstream market, supermarket expansion
  198–203
malbouffe (bad food) 119–20
male/female binaries 184
Manchester Turnip 63
Mann, Alana 7, 113
marketing strategies, impact 27–8
market signage, example 178f
market solutions, mainstreaming 11
masculine symbolism 183
masculinity: articulation 142; meat,
  relationship 140–2; veganism,
  relationship 142
MasterChef Australia: case study 217;
  example, usage 8; excess, images 216;
  expert interview paradigm, interpretation
  224; media worker choices 218;
  OzHarvest production involvement
  227–8; purchasing pattern impact 221;
  success 217
MasterChef Australia food waste:
  confrontation 216; on-screen depiction
  224; politics 218; program design 218
McDowell, Simon 244–5
meat: cartographies, usage 176; ethical
  meat, power (un)masking mechanisms
  169; GIFs, usage 162; masculinity,
  relationship 140–2; meat-as-nature 171;
  memes, imagery 162; portrayal 182
#meat 162–3
meat chickens, newspaper mentions 208f
meat consumption: ethical issues 174–5;
  problems 143–4
meatification 175, 177f
Meat is for Pussies (Joseph) 141
meat production: environmental impacts/
  problems 173–4; health/social issues
  173–4
media: affordances 12; analysis 6–15;
  construction/circulation, analysis 8–9;
  content, tagging/curating 155; cultural/
  political work 2; food politics,
  relationship 3–6; forms, recurrence
  155–6; images, analysis 80;
  micro-political/macro-political
  capacities 14–15
media/food landscape, complexity 2–3
media production 216; contexts 220;
  research 223–4; study 221–2
Mehigan, Gary 227
memes, usage 154–5, 161

Memphis Meats 137
men: "are you man enough" 182–5;
  representation 163
Meyer, Claus 38, 39, 47
Meyer's House of Food 48
Micheletti, Michele 116
micro-political capacities 3, 6
micro-political/macro-political,
  tension 13
migrants, welcoming initiatives 98
Model Codes of Practice (Australia) 197
Mothers are Demystifying Genetic
  Engineering (MADGE) 124
Müller, Anders Riel 9, 11, 37
My Agriculture 121
My Father, Baek Nam-gi 119

Nakamura, Lisa 101
National Farmers' Union 121
National Food Plan (NFP) 123
National Organic Standards Board
  (NOSB) 24
naturalisation 174–5, 182–3; analysis 171;
  identification 171; killing 182–5; pastoral
  relations 179–82
Negus, Keith 10
networked food politics 114–15
networked publics 115
"new food authorities" 234–5
New Nordic Cuisine (NNC) 9, 37–9; aim
  39; discount NNC restaurants 42–3;
  distancing 42; launch 41–2;
  mainstreaming 40, 42, 50; phases 38–9;
  politics of scale, relationship 39–41;
  principles, adoption 45; social
  entrepreneur reliance 11; values-based
  approach, entrepreneurial approach
  (comparison) 46; values, food producer
  perception 44
New Nordic Diet (NND) 41; development
  38, 47; ingredients/flavours, accessibility
  47–8
New Nordic Everyday Food 48
New Nordic Food initiative (Nordic Council
  of Ministers) 50
New Nordic Food Project (NNF) 38, 40;
  values/principles, qualities 44
New Nordic Manifesto 40, 43; values/
  principles 43–4
New Nordic restaurants, success 39
News Corp 96
niche food producers, significance 11
noblesse oblige spirit, embracing 225

NOMA (restaurant) 38–9; effect 42; NNC, distancing 42; NNC launch 41–2; NNC mainstreaming 40–1
non-heritage food production/retail, portrayal 60
non-human animals, expendability 170
Nordic Council of Ministers, New Nordic Food initiative 50
#notyourgoodfatty 161
nut milk production 137
#nutrition 159
Nyéléni Europe Forum 120

Obama, Barack 75
Oliver, Jamie 10, 236–7, 246; 'Created with Jamie' 237, 240–3; media coverage 241
Oliver, Tom 64
OPUS: project 48–9, 50–1; research results 41; scale, bending 47
organic agriculture, farm area growth 45–6
organic certification, price premium 24
organic contracts, usage 27
organic crops, supply (increase) 33
organic farming, growth 25–6
organic farmland, reduction 30
organic growth/change 25–6
organic label, paradox 23
organic mainstreaming, growth 23–4
organic market: stability 31; volatility 33; vulnerability 29–30
organic practices, adoption 32–3
organic production, curtailing/ceasing 30
organic regulation 32
organics, mainstreaming 23
OzHarvest 224–7; production involvement, food television 227–8
Oz, Mehmet 144

Palekar, Subhash 119
Parker, Christine 8, 193
Pavlova, Anna 103
People for the Ethical Treatment of Animals (PETA) 156, 174
People's Food Plan 124
People's Food Policy Project 121
personal content, co-production/ co-distribution 115
Perth Voice Interactive 108
pesticides, avoidance 84
Phillipov, Michelle 1, 10, 234
photography: digital home mode style 106; home mode genre, adoption 7
Piatt, Julie 142

pigs, newspaper mentions 207f
plant-based diets: choice, media responses 142; discourse 139; language 8–9; popularity, increase 136–40; promotion, absence 143; reference, increase 137–8
Plataforma Rural 120
platform vernacular 7
political consumerism 116–17
political consumers (ethical consumers) 85
politics, impact 152–4
politics of scale 27–8; New Nordic Cuisine, relationship 39–41
polities 222–3
polity: domestic polity 222; industrial polity 222; inspired polity 222; renown/fame polity 222
Pollan, Michael 238
poshness, unease 62
power: Gramscian theory 220; mechanisms, (un)masking 169; negative aspect 181–2; tolerance 170–1
power, relations: cartographies/entitlements 153; doubling down 169
Preston, Matt 136, 224–5, 227
price premiums, competition (impact) 33
private labels: celebrity-branded private labels 236; impact 234
#proana 163–4
processed foods: alternative reframing 234; ambiguities 238; meaning 10; perception 239; politics 238–40
production: issues 77; maintstreaming 43–6; principles, setting (promotion) 44; processes, retooling 45
production practices: animal welfare impact 205, 209–10; implications 209
pro-environmental behaviours, environmental advocacy 143
promissory enterprises 11
promissory organisations, role 80
promissory themes, importance 80–1
Protected Designation of Origin and Protected Geographical Indication (EU) 58
Publisi, Christian 42
Purple Flowered Russian 67

racialised bodies, images (absence) 105–6
racialised gaze 101
Radio Mundo Real (RWR) 120–1
Ragged Jack 67
#rawfood 159
Ready Steady Cook 239

real food: assault 235; opposite 238
#ReasonsToGoVegan 156
Recipe to Riches 240
Reclaim the Fields 56
Redzepi, René 38, 41
refugees, welcoming initiatives 98
regenerative agriculture 34
regulation, market control 11
RELÆ: A Book of Ideas (Puglisi) 42
RELÆ, creation 42
renown/fame polity 222
resources, mobilisation 80
return on investment (ROI), increase 86
"Rights of Peasants" 121
Right to Food Coalition (RtFC) 124
River Cottage series 221, 239–40
Roll, Rich 137, 141–2
Royal Society for the Prevention of Cruelty
    to Animals (RSPCA) Approved, label
    193, 200, 209; certification 210–11; Coles
    magazine advertisement 202f; system,
    domination 210
RSCPA Approved, label 174, 199, 244
chicken 244
RSPCA. *see* Royal Society for the
    Prevention of Cruelty to Animals

Salford Black runner beans 63
scalar strategies 40
scale bending 40; problems 37
scale jumping 40; problems 37
Schneider, Tanja 11, 75
science and technology studies (STS):
    criticism 79; perspectives 76
Scrinis, Gyorgy 8, 193
Seeds&Chips 75–6
seed swapping 67
self-discipline, absence 160
selfies, usage 158
self-transformation, efforts 139
sexual imagery, prominence 163–4
sexualised imagery, lusty eating
    (combination) 161
slaughter process, description 182
Slaughter, The (film) 172, 175, 182–3;
    animal, killing 185; subtext 181
Slow Food: centering 59; self-description 65
Slow Food Movement 75; Ark of Taste 64
Smith, Rob 60
social class, performance 57
social distinction, heritage foods
    (relationship) 55
social entrepreneurs 43–4

social injustices, addressing 174
social justice 34
social media, clean eating portrayals 158
social networks, imagery (usage) 154
social structures, impact 34
sociotechnical dimensions 79–80
sociotechnical expectations/futures 79–81
sociotechnical imaginaries 80–1;
    presence 81
South Korea 40
"sow-stall free" brand 199; prominence
    199–200
sow stall free, term (usage) 193
"sow stalls," mentions 203f
speciesism 144
status symbols 60–1
Stone, Curtis 201f, 202f209, 244
super-bitter craft beers, phenomenon 66
supermarket foods: disquiet 240;
    meanings 10
supermarkets 238–40; accounts 234–5;
    celebrity chefs, brand partnerships 236;
    celebrity chefs/private labels, impact 234;
    impact(*see* animal welfare); influence,
    expansion 235; welfare-friendly ethical
    branding strategy 200, 203
sustainabilty: addressing 77; ecological
    sustainability, advancement 195; Essento
    definition 87–8; food sustainability 11,
    219–20; presentation 84;
    representation 221
sustainable foods: futures, entrepreneurial
    visions 75, 81–8; promises 75;
    redefinition 89–90
sustainable, term (definition) 88–9
Sutton Seeds 59
Swan, Elaine 7, 95
Sydney Food Fairness Alliance 124

technologies, conditions 79
Terre de Semences Association
    Kokopelli 59
terror, French idea 58
Thévenot, Laurent 222
#thickspiration 161
#thighgap 163–4
thing-power, term (usage)
    153–4
Thug Kitchen cookbooks 14, 140
Torres Strait Islander people, food
    insecurity 124–5
transnational public, emergence 113
Twine, Richard 139

Union Paysanne 121
United Nations Food and Agriculture
   Organisation (FAO) report 87
"Un Mundo Mejor es Posible" 122
unsustainable food 77–9
UrbanFarmers 83–4
UrbanFarmers (UF) 81–4; sustainable
   features 84
user-generated content 163–4
US organic movement, increase
   31–2

values-oriented business practices 87
van Ryn, Luke 8, 216
#vegan 156–7
veganism: change, importance 135; dietary
   restrictions 219; establishment 137; good
   food, comparison 139; intersectionality
   142–4; masculinity, relationship 140–2;
   popularity, increase 136–40; promotion,
   absence 143; quasi-religious
   characteristics 138–9; textual
   analysis 136
veganism, language 8–9
vegan men/masculinity 141
vegan-ness, expansion/re-inscription 144
vegan, term (meaning) 139
#vegetarian 156–7
vegetarianism, dietary restrictions 219
vegetarians, GIF portrayal 162–3
VeggieBuzz 157
Vía Campesina Europe 120
Vilsack, Tom 23
violent masculinity, endorsement 14
visual exclusions, importance 105
visual imagery, usage 154
vitalities/visceralities 151
voluntary labels, usage 31–3
"voting with your fork" 195

waste: conceptualising 222–3; concern
   225–6; food waste 88, 216–18; off-screen
   waste 226–9; on-screen waste 224; screen
   display 224–6

#weightloss 159
Welcome Dinner Project (WDP) 95;
   Australian food hospitality activism
   97; digital food porn 102–4; events
   97–8; impact 104; media coverage 103;
   ordinarisation, home mode image
   expression 107; photographs,
   usage 96; re-mediation/
   re-contextualisation 96–7;
   web pages/platforms, usage 96
Welcome Dinner Project (WDP),
   food hospitality activism: digital
   images 107–8; imaging 101–2;
   snapshots 106; theoretical framing/
   methods/sampling 100–1; visual/verbal
   text, representation (methodology)
   100–1
welcoming: initiatives 98;
   politics 98–9
welfare label claims 194
#wellness 159
What the Health? 144
Whole Foods 27
Wiebe, Nettie 121
Wilder, Gene 157
Wincott, Abigail 13, 55
Wittman, Hannah 121
Wodehouse, P.G. 62
women: food blogs, food photography
   (analysis) 160; rights (La Vía
   Campesina focus) 119
Women in Focus Giving Community
   (Commonwealth Bank) 225
Woolworths supermarkets: brand
   partnerships (*see* celebrity chefs);
   "easy-to-cook fresh food range" 243;
   "Fresh Food People" 243

You Did Not Eat That (blog) 160
#yummy 159–61

Zero Budget Natural Farming,
   method 119

For Product Safety Concerns and Information please contact our EU
representative GPSR@taylorandfrancis.com
Taylor & Francis Verlag GmbH, Kaufingerstraße 24, 80331 München, Germany

www.ingramcontent.com/pod-product-compliance
Ingram Content Group UK Ltd.
Pitfield, Milton Keynes, MK11 3LW, UK
UKHW021618240425
457818UK00018B/623